# IMPORTANT!

## What Makes Windows 98 Special?

The most exciting feature of Windows 98 is its seamless integration of Internet Explorer 4, Microsoft's Web browser. **This integration makes possible several exciting new features through its Active Desktop.**

As this book was going to press, there was a legal injunction pending to prevent Microsoft from integrating Internet Explorer 4 with Windows 98. If this injunction prevails, the copy of Windows 98 you purchase may not have Internet Explorer 4 built in.

**Without Internet Explorer 4, you will miss out on many of the exciting features described in this book,** so we recommend that you get and install Internet Explorer 4 right away. It's easy–*and free!* Just visit Microsoft's Web site (http://www.microsoft.com) and download your free copy of Internet Explorer 4. Run the installation program, and you're ready to go.

Even if you choose not to use Internet Explorer 4, Windows 98 still has many great new features to offer, including more powerful utilities and easier-to-use file management, all of which are covered in this book.

Congratulations on choosing Windows 98! It can be a great tool for making your computer work harder and smarter. Now, sit back and relax, and let this book teach you how to harness the power of Windows 98 for your own PC productivity.

# WINDOWS 98 FREQUENTLY ASKED QUESTIONS

Here are the answers to some of the common questions or problems you might have when working with Windows 98. Also included is the chapter number in the book where you can go for more information about the subject.

**Q.** How can I play my favorite music CD on my computer?

**A.** The easiest way is to just put the CD in the CD-ROM drive and let the AutoPlay feature do the work for you. If you don't have AutoPlay you can launch the CD Player from the Entertainment menu. *See Chapter 11.*

**Q.** How can I control the type of material my children see on the Internet?

**A.** Internet Explorer allows you to set Parental Controls to limit the type of material that can be accessed. *See Chapter 17.*

**Q.** How can I troubleshoot a problem I'm having?

**A.** Windows 98 comes with a troubleshooting utility that will walk you through the same steps that a technical support representative usually uses. *See Chapter 13.*

**Q.** How can I add a shortcut to my Desktop?

**A.** Use the Find dialog box to find the program for which you want to create a shortcut. Right-click and choose Create Shortcut. *See Chapter 5.*

**Q.** How do I install a new program?

**A.** Open the Control Panel and choose Add/Remove Programs. If you want to install a Windows accessory, use the Windows Setup tab. *See Chapter 8.*

**Q.** Why can't one computer on my network see another computer on my network?

**A.** You need to make sure that all computers in the network have the same workgroup name. *See Chapter 14.*

**Q.** What do I need to surf the Internet?

**A.** You'll need a modem, a service provider, and a Web browser. *See Chapter 17.*

**Q.** Why wasn't disk space freed up when I deleted a bunch of files through the Windows Explorer?

**A.** Deleted files are temporarily stored in the Recycle Bin. When the Recycle Bin is emptied, the disk space will be freed up. *See Chapter 2.*

**Q.** What is the difference between Cut and Copy?

**A.** When an item is Cut, the item is removed from the original location to the Windows Clipboard. When text is Copied, the item remains in the original location and is duplicated to the Windows Clipboard. *See Chapter 3.*

**Q.** Do I have to pay to access the Internet?

**A.** Usually yes. Most Internet service providers do charge for their services. The fee varies with the plan you subscribe to, but the average is between 10 and 20 dollars per month. *See Chapter 15.*

**Q.** Can I add graphics to my e-mail?

**A.** Outlook Express includes some graphics from which you can choose, or you can use any GIF or JPEG graphic you have access to. It is possible, however, that some of your recipients may not be able to display the graphics. *See Chapter 16.*

**Q.** How can I back up files on my computer?

**A.** Use Microsoft Backup. You can back up to a variety of media, including floppy disks, Zip disks, and tapes. *See Chapter 13.*

**Q.** How can I change the amount of time before my screen saver comes on?

**A.** Right-click on the Desktop and choose Properties from the menu that appears. Then, click on the Screen Saver tab. Change the Wait time. *See Chapter 5.*

**Q.** How can I use one printer from all computers on my network?

**A.** You need to share a printer. *See Chapter 14.*

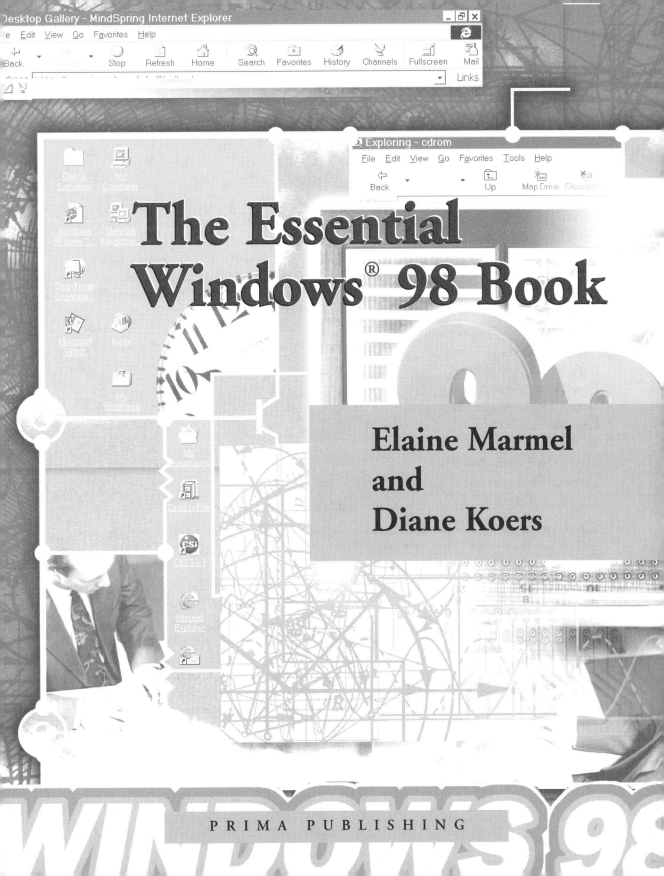

# The Essential Windows® 98 Book

**Elaine Marmel**
**and**
**Diane Koers**

PRIMA PUBLISHING

Prima Publishing and colophon are registered trademarks of Prima Communications, Inc., Rocklin, California 95677.

**Publisher:** Matthew H. Carleson

**Managing Editor:** Dan J. Foster

**Acquisitions Editor:** Deborah F. Abshier

**Project Editor:** Kevin Harreld

**Technical Reviewer:** Paul Marchesseault

**Copy Editor:** June Waldman

**Interior Layout:** Marian Hartsough

**Cover Design:** Prima Design Team

**Indexer:** Katherine Stimson

Microsoft and Windows are registered trademarks of Microsoft Corporation.

**Important:** If you have problems installing or running Microsoft Windows 98, notify Microsoft at (425) 635-7056 or on the Web at **www.microsoft.com**. Prima Publishing cannot provide software support.

Prima Publishing and the authors have attempted throughout this book to distinguish proprietary trademarks from descriptive terms by following the capitalization style used by the manufacturer.

Information contained in this book has been obtained by Prima Publishing from sources believed to be reliable. However, because of the possibility of human or mechanical error by our sources, Prima Publishing, or others, the Publisher does not guarantee the accuracy, adequacy, or completeness of any information and is not responsible for any errors or omissions or the results obtained from the use of such information. Readers should be particularly aware of the fact that the Internet is an ever-changing entity. Some facts may have changed since this book went to press.

ISBN: 0-7615-0967-4

Library of Congress Catalog Card Number: 96-72129

Printed in the United States of America

98 99 00 01 02 DD 10 9 8 7 6 5 4 3 2 1

*To my mom.*

*Thank you for loving me and sharing with me. Words seem so inadequate…*

*—Elaine Marmel*


*To Mom, who always said "Can't never could do anything."*
*Thanks.*

*—Diane Koers*

# Contents at a Glance

# Contents

**Chapter 3**    **Common Features in Windows Programs . . . . . . . . 39**

# Acknowledgments

I'd like to thank everyone who worked on this book, but a few bear special mention. Thank you, Debbie Abshier, for the opportunity to write this book. Thank you, Diane Koers, for making the project more interesting and enjoyable than usual by co-authoring this book with me; I enjoyed sharing the experience with you. Thank you, Paul Marchesseault, for an outstanding job editing this book technically—and for making sure we "told no lies." Thank you, Jan Snyder, for your usual top-notch job overseeing the development of this book; you spoil me, Jan. And thank you, Kevin Harreld, for an outstanding job of putting the project together and keeping me on track. Do you know that you're a very tactful fellow?

—Elaine Marmel

I am deeply thankful to the many people at Prima Publishing who worked on this book. Thank you for all the time you gave and for your assistance.

To Debbie Abshier, for the opportunity to write this book and her confidence in me. To Jan Snyder, Kevin Harreld, Paul Marchesseault, and June Waldman for all their assistance in the development of this book, and for assuring that it is technically and grammatically correct. I certainly kept all of you busy on this one! Special thanks goes to Elaine Marmel for being a wonderful friend and for always being there to coach me through the difficult areas.

Lastly, to my husband. Thank you again Vern, for all your support and never-ending faith in me. For thirty years, you've believed in me. I love you.

—Diane Koers

# About the Authors

**E**laine Marmel is President of Marmel Enterprises, Inc., an organization that specializes in technical writing and software training. Elaine spends most of her time writing and has authored and co-authored over 25 books about software products, including Prima's *Office 97 Fast & Easy* and *The Essential Word 97 Book*. Elaine is also a contributing editor to *Inside Peachtree for Windows* and *Inside QuickBooks for Windows*, both monthly magazines.

Elaine left her native Chicago for the warmer climes of Florida (by way of Cincinnati, OH; Jerusalem, Israel; Ithaca, NY; and Washington, D.C.), where she basks in the sun with her PC and her cats, Cato, Watson, and Buddy, and sings barbershop harmony.

**D**iane Koers owns and operates All Business Service, a software training and consulting business formed in 1988 that services the central Indiana area. Her area of expertise is in the word processing, spreadsheet, and graphics area of computing as well as providing training and support for Peachtree Accounting Software. Diane's authoring experience includes Prima's *Lotus 1-2-3 97 Fast & Easy, WordPerfect 8 Fast & Easy,* and *Windows 98 Fast & Easy.* She has also developed and written software training manuals for her clients' use.

Active in her church and civic activities, Diane enjoys spending her free time traveling and playing with her grandson and her three Yorkshire Terriers.

# Introduction

Essential things are things that you really need. Air and water fall into this category. Some people believe that chocolate and true love also fit the definition of essential. This book on Windows 98 also qualifies as an essential. It is structured to give you exactly what you need if you want to be successful with Windows 98: clear, concise explanations of features grounded in examples.

Early versions of Windows introduced DOS-based computer users to the world of the graphics interface. Windows 95 took that graphics world, provided a 32-bit operating environment, and made getting your job done easier. Windows 98 expands that foundation; you should find working in Windows 98 to be even faster, easier, and more efficient than you experienced in any prior version of Windows. This book gives you the information that you need to take advantage of Windows 98's features.

## Who Should Read This Book?

This book is for you if you want to learn the ins and outs of working in Windows 98. If you recently upgraded to Windows 98 from an earlier version of Windows, you might want to see what's new in this version of the software. Maybe you want to learn more about Windows than you already know. Or maybe you have never used Windows before and need to learn all the basics. This book is for you.

*The Essential Windows 98 Book* isn't a typical reference book, because it's organized around the work you do, not the software features of the product. So whether

**Note**

> If you consider yourself a novice at computers, you might want to try reading *Windows 98 Fast & Easy*, also from Prima.

you're new to Windows or consider yourself pretty handy with it, this book will help you work with the operating system even better than you already do.

# Overview of Contents

This book is divided into logical parts to help you easily find the information you need.

Part I, "Getting Started with Windows 98," gives you your first look at the Windows 98 environment, including valuable Help features. You'll learn about the features that are new to Windows 98, get a basic understanding of the Windows Desktop, and explore the common features in all Windows programs. The last chapter in this part gives details about using the Windows Explorer to help you manage files, folders, and drives in the Windows 98 environment.

Part II, "Setting Up and Customizing Windows," explores your options for customizing the Windows environment so that it suits the way you work. You'll learn to manage the Desktop, install and configure printers, and customize the Start menu and the Taskbar. In the last chapter in this part, you'll explore the Windows Control Panel and learn how the icons you find in the Control Panel can help you install new software or hardware and customize your working environment.

Part III, "Windows Accessories and Tools," shows you how to take advantage of the accessories and tools that come with Windows 98. You'll learn about Word-Pad and Notepad, the two text editors that ship with Windows 98. You'll have fun exploring the multimedia features of Windows 98, including games and Paint, the graphics program supplied by Microsoft. On a more serious note, you'll learn about the tools in Windows 98 that help you safeguard your system and enhance its performance.

Finally, Part IV, "Your Window to the World," focuses on connectivity. In this section, you'll learn how to network with Windows 98, use the other connectivity tools provided with Windows 98, and work with the Internet Explorer and its new integration with your Windows Desktop. You'll also learn how to set up and use Microsoft Fax and Microsoft Mail so that you can send faxes and e-mail from your computer. In the last chapter in this section, you'll explore your options for using Windows 98 while you're on the road.

*Caution*

For those of you who like to skip stuff, *don't* skip the appendixes in this book. They contain important information about installing Windows 98 that you really need to read *before* you install.

# Conventions Used in This Book

Whenever a feature is mentioned that's covered more thoroughly in another chapter, you'll see a gray box in the margin that indicates where the information can be found.

To keep instructions clear and concise, some standard conventions are used in this book.

For starters, you can do almost everything in Windows using either your mouse or keyboard commands—your choice. We've tried to give you the easiest way to get things done, but your preferences might differ from ours, so we occasionally provide alternative ways of performing commands. Table I.1 contains examples of instructions that you'll encounter throughout the book.

If you are asked to type any text, that text will appear in bold. Whenever a new term or phrase is introduced, it is italicized so that you can be alert to the definition that follows. Also, clicking on the mouse refers to the left mouse button unless it is specified to use the right one.

*Note*

**Your mouse functions differently in Windows 98 than it did in previous versions of Windows, and you'll find that you don't need to double-click as much as you used to. For more information on mouse behavior, check Chapter 2, "Understanding the Desktop and Starting Programs," and Chapter 12, "Learning to Control the Mouse—Using Games."**

## Table I.1  Instruction Conventions

| Instruction | Meaning |
| --- | --- |
| Choose File, Open | Either press the Alt key and type the underlined hot keys (F, O) or use your mouse pointer and click on the File menu to open it and select the Open command. |
| Press Ctrl+F | Hold down the Ctrl key on your keyboard and then press the F key. |
| Press End, Home | Press the End key on your keyboard, release it, and then press the Home key. |
| Click on the Save button | Tools are represented by buttons on a toolbar. Clicking on a button with your mouse pointer invokes the tool's function. The button name used in this book matches the name that appears when you point to a toolbar button. |

# Special Elements

You'll find several special elements throughout the book that will call attention to specialized information. Here's how they look:

*Note*

A Note provides a format for easy learning. Notes provide a bit more technical information about a feature or procedure.

## Hands On: Accomplishing a Specific Task

Whenever you are asked to follow a series of steps, a Hands On section is included. This element will help you quickly identify specific step-by-step procedures.

*Tip*

Tips suggest alternate ways to do certain things, as well as clever shortcuts or tricks for using Windows.

## Single- versus Double-Click

The instructions and figures throughout this book assume that you are using a Web Style Desktop. When you use the Web Style Desktop, you click instead of double-click to open files, folders, and programs. If you are using the Classic Desktop, I've included the Double-Click icon you see in the margin next to this paragraph for your convenience.

*Caution*

If you're in danger of making a mistake or losing information while performing a step, you are warned with a caution. You are also told how to get out of trouble if you stumble.

We hope you'll find that *The Essential Windows 98 Book* is an essential part of your day-to-day productivity. Now it's time to get to work!

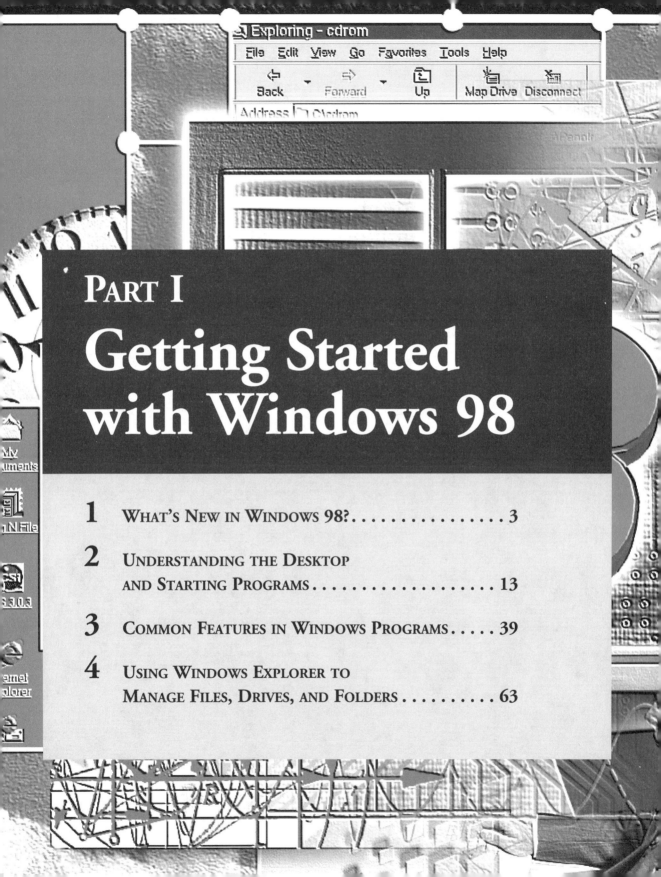

# PART I

# Getting Started with Windows 98

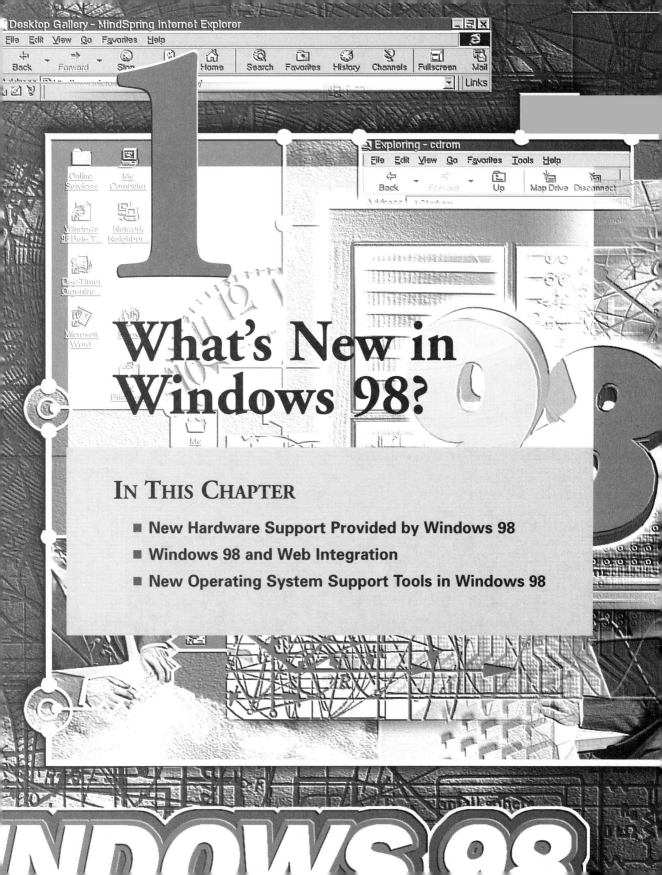

# What's New in Windows 98?

## IN THIS CHAPTER

- New Hardware Support Provided by Windows 98
- Windows 98 and Web Integration
- New Operating System Support Tools in Windows 98

So, what is new in Windows 98? That's the big question. Windows 98 uses Windows 95 as its foundation and provides enhancements and improvements to that platform. Many of the "visible" changes in Windows 98 were actually provided by Internet Explorer 4.0, which Microsoft released in October 1997. If you previously updated your Web browser to Internet Explorer 4.0, you are familiar with visual enhancements such as the Channel Guide and the Quick Launch toolbar. As you can see in Figure 1.1, the Windows Desktop remains a familiar place.

Many of the improvements in Windows 98 focus on adding hardware support for more advanced technologies. Other changes include improvements that help you manage your computer more effectively and speed up your processing.

Some of the "new stuff" will not impact the average beginning or intermediate user; therefore, you'll find a brief synopsis of these new features in this chapter. We do, however, cover other new features that affect the average beginner or intermediate user—briefly in this chapter and in more detail in other chapters in the book.

For Windows 95 users who are upgrading to Windows 98, the setup process will seem streamlined, because Windows 98 seems to have a better idea how to configure your hardware. The Windows 98 setup procedure also updates utilities that you have already installed.

> For more information on installing Windows 98, see Appendix A.

**Figure 1.1**
The Windows 98 Desktop closely resembles the Windows 95 Desktop.

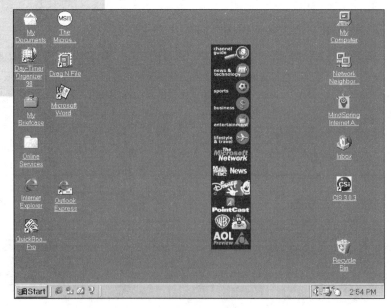

# New Hardware Support

Many of the new features in Windows 98 involve providing operating system support for new hardware technologies. As you know, hardware and software work together to provide you with a functioning computer. Developing new hardware technologies is only half of the picture. Developing an operating system that can support those new technologies is the other half. Windows 98 can provide support for the following new technologies and techniques:

- Universal Serial Bus and IEEE 1394
- Win32 Driver Model
- ACPI Power Management
- Broadcast reception
- Simultaneous use of multiple monitors on one PC
- Effective management of space on large hard disks

## Connecting Devices to Your Computer

Warning: it's about to get a little bit technical here—just enough to help you understand the impact of Windows 98 support for Universal Serial Bus and IEEE 1394 serial bus connections.

Both Universal Serial Bus (USB) and IEEE 1394 serial bus are types of connections built into computers that PC and electronics equipment manufacturers can use to hook *peripheral devices* to computers. Traditional peripheral devices include keyboards, mice, joysticks, telephones (for modems), printers, and scanners, but as technology and its users become more sophisticated, digital cameras, camcorders, and video disks have begun to fall into the category of peripheral devices attached to computers. The focus behind both USB and IEEE 1394 technology is to eliminate the need to install cards into dedicated computer slots and reconfigure the computer system each time a user attaches a new peripheral device to the computer. Instead, PCs using USB and/or IEEE 1394 allow computer peripherals to be automatically configured as soon as they are physically attached. Down the road, adding a peripheral device to a computer should be as easy as plugging in a new lamp.

So, you ask, what's the difference between USB and IEEE 1394? USB is a standard that was developed by PC and telecommunication industry leaders, including Compaq, DEC, IBM, Intel, Microsoft, NEC, and Northern Telecom. USB devices became available as early as October 1996—and you may have heard them referred to as "plug and play" devices. USB handles the more traditional PC connections, like keyboards, mice, joysticks, and handheld scanners, as well as some of the more advanced computer game devices, high-fidelity audio, and highly compressed video.

The Institute of Electrical and Electronics Engineers (IEEE) developed the IEEE 1394 standard. Also called FireWire, IEEE 1394 will target a different set of peripherals that consumers may want to attach to PCs—high-bandwidth devices such as digital camcorders, cameras, and digital video disk players.

Because of the differences in the two technologies, they probably will not compete with each other; instead, they will complement each other. My crystal ball indicates that PCs of the future will contain both connection types. And Windows 98 supports both technologies.

## Sharing Drivers between Windows 98 and Windows NT

The Win32 Driver Model, known as WDM, is the new unified driver model for Windows 98 and Windows NT. WDM will enable you to use a single driver for certain devices and buses on either operating system. Existing drivers, known as *legacy* drivers, will continue to work, but WDM will support new classes of devices and buses, such as Universal Serial Bus (USB), Human Interface Devices (HID), IEEE 1394, digital audio and digital video players, still image, and video capture. For corporate shops where some computers use Windows NT and some use Windows 98, WDM will make installing peripherals independent of the operating system—and therefore, a whole lot easier.

## Starting Your Computer

Advanced Configuration and Power Interface (ACPI) is a new power management specification that intends to save power by placing full control of the computer's power management in the operating system; previously, the computer's BIOS managed the computer's power.

So, how does ACPI affect the average desktop computer user? ACPI contains the *OnNow* feature, which is similar to a notebook computer's *resume* feature. ACPI monitors the devices on your computer and shuts down any device not being used—including drives, monitors, and even the power supply's fan—to minimize power consumption and extend battery life. If your computer supports ACPI and OnNow and uses Windows 98 as the operating system, you won't need to power off your machine. The OnNow feature enables you to immediately resume your work without rebooting your computer. In the near future, turning on your computer will seem a lot like turning on a TV, radio, and or stereo.

## Watching TV on Your Computer

You always knew, from the first moment you saw a computer monitor, that some-day, you'd watch TV on a computer. Yes, that day is arriving quickly. You can insert TV tuner cards into your computer. Along with a TV tuner card, though, you need an operating system that can support broadcast reception. Windows 98 includes software that "broadcast enables" your computer. With a broadcast-enabled computer, the distinction between a computer and a TV becomes a bit fuzzy, since you'll be able to use your computer both to inform and to entertain. In addition to receiving television programming from cable, airwaves, and satel-lites, you can receive live data from Web pages, stock quotes, news feeds, and streaming audio and video.

Again, my crystal ball suggests that the demand for this new technology will grow; as the demand grows, you'll also find more providers of broadcast infor-mation. That is, you'll find more networks providing information that you can receive on your broadcast-enabled computer. Remember, this technology is new; you may not want to race right out and buy a TV tuner card for your PC. But when you're ready, your operating system will support TV broadcasts.

## Using Multiple Monitors on One Computer

Windows 98 supports the use of multiple monitors on one computer. Of course, you can use multiple-display support for the standard uses—desktop publishing, presentations with notes, or just an expanded desktop. In addition, using two PCI monitors, you also can read e-mail on one computer and click an HTTP link; your Web browser starts on the second monitor. Or, with multiple monitors, your game can have left, right, and center displays.

The new Windows also supports the Accelerated Graphics Port, a connector that lets high-end 3-D video boards use a PC's cheaper main memory for 3-D acceleration.

## Managing Hard Disk Space

The File Allocation Table (FAT) stores information about the location of files on your hard disk. The original FAT file system was invented in 1977 and was designed to work on floppy disks. Over the years, the FAT file system has been modified to successfully manage data on both floppy and hard disks.

The current FAT file system (also called FAT16) can manage hard disks as large as 2 gigabytes (GB); with the development of very large disks, FAT16 has basically reached its limitations. For disk drives up to 2GB, you can use FAT16 and retain only one logical drive (Drive C). But if you own a computer with a hard disk that is larger than 2GB , you must *partition* the disk; that is, you must divide the physical disk into multiple logical partitions. Therefore, a 6GB drive using FAT16 would contain three logical drives—C, D, and E.

FAT16 stores and manages information about the location of your files. As part of the management and storage, FAT16 allocates space on the drive in segments called clusters, and each file you save is placed in a cluster. If the file is larger than the cluster, then the file receives additional space in the cluster. However, if the file is smaller than the cluster, the unused portion of the cluster remains "empty" unless you use a disk utility to optimize the usage of space on your hard disk. If the cluster size on your hard disk is large, you can assume you are wasting a lot of disk space. And, as a fact of life with FAT16, the larger the disk, the larger the cluster size.

Enter FAT32. FAT32 arrived originally with the release of Windows 95 OSR-2. FAT32 is an enhanced and expanded file management system that can recognize physical drives up to 2 terabytes in size, so you don't need to partition the drive and can use one large C drive. In addition, the cluster size under FAT32 is smaller than the cluster size under FAT16, resulting in less wasted space on the FAT32 drive. Although FAT32 was introduced in Windows 95 OSR-2, that release did not contain any easy means to convert existing FAT16 drives to FAT32 drives—Windows 98 does.

> For more information on FAT32 conversion, see Chapter 13.

However, FAT32 also has some down sides; for example, you cannot use disk compression on a FAT32 drive. Also, some older DOS programs will not run on a FAT32 drive because of the original method used to code them. For the most part, however, FAT32 is an improvement in today's world. And, Windows 98 contains a conversion utility that will change your existing FAT16 drive into a FAT32 drive.

# Windows 98 and the Web

You'll find a strong focus on the Internet in Windows 98. For example, Windows Explorer integrates local, intranet, and Internet resources into a single, logical view; in fact, you can use Windows Explorer to access URLs. In addition, if you haven't yet gone online, the new Internet Connection Wizard makes setting up a new Internet connection very easy because it obtains correct configuration information directly from your Internet service provider. The Dial-Up Networking feature now includes the capability to link and synchronize multiple modems; if you're lucky enough to have a speedy ISDN telephone connection, the ISDN Connection Wizard makes it easier to configure hardware.

Much of the Web integration was introduced when Microsoft released Internet Explorer 4.0. As well as being a Web browser, Internet Explorer 4.0 contains:

> **For more information on Internet Explorer 4.0, see Chapter 17.**

- Outlook Express, a new e-mail client
- NetMeeting, software that supports Internet conferencing and whiteboarding
- NetShow, networked multimedia software for on-demand audio and video capabilities
- FrontPage Express, a Web page editing tool based on Microsoft's award-winning FrontPage Web page creation software
- Personal Web Server, software that makes any Windows 98–based system into a personal Web server

Internet Explorer 4.0 also provided some visual and functional changes to the Desktop:

- Select a style for the Desktop and control the appearance of your Desktop icons
- Use channels to receive Web content on your computer
- Change the way your mouse operates

## Choosing Your Desktop Style

You can now control the style of your Desktop and the appearance of the icons on your Desktop. If you want to make your Desktop look and act like the World Wide Web, you can. When you make your Desktop look and act like the World Wide Web, windows that you open will contain a toolbar across the top as well as an area down the side that describes each item in the window as you select the item (see Figure 1.2).

> **For more information on Active Desktops and customizing your Desktop, see Chapter 5.**

Or, if you prefer, you can retain the Desktop appearance provided in Windows 95 (see Figure 1.3).

When you let your Desktop look and act like the World Wide Web, your Desktop can be an *active desktop*; that is, you can customize your Desktop to display information that you can update from the Internet. For example, in Figure 1.4 you see a weather map from the MSNBC active desktop.

**Figure 1.2**
When you set up your Desktop to look and act like the World Wide Web, the appearance of traditional windows changes.

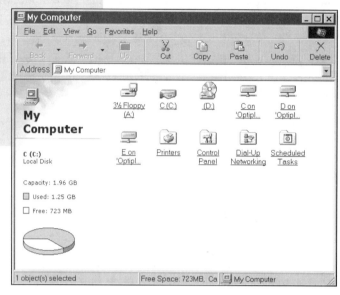

**Figure 1.3**
This figure and Figure 1.2 show the same window—but here the Desktop is set up to emulate Windows 95.

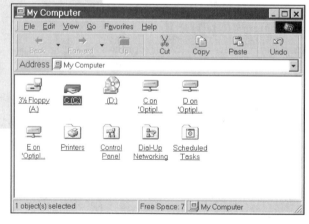

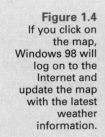

**Figure 1.4**
If you click on the map, Windows 98 will log on to the Internet and update the map with the latest weather information.

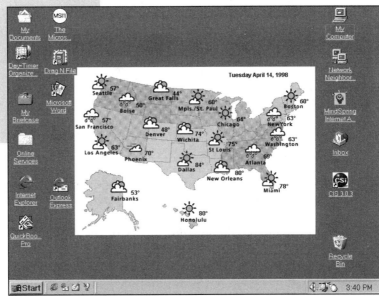

## Receiving Internet Information from Channels

> For more information on channels, see Chapter 17.

Internet Explorer 4.0 introduced channels. *Channels* are Web sites that deliver information from the Internet to your computer. When you *subscribe* to a channel, you receive updated information from the channel on a regular basis. Some channels also provide screen savers that you can use on your computer.

## Using New Mouse Functions

> For more information on mouse functioning, see Chapter 2.

Internet Explorer 4.0 introduced a new mouse clicking style, which you can choose to use if you want. The new style eliminates, in most cases, the need to double-click.

In addition, Windows 98 introduces some new functionality for Microsoft's IntelliMouse—also called the "wheel mouse." The wheel on this mouse provides additional "pointing" functions if your software takes advantage of the wheel. Previously, only Office 97 and Internet Explorer 3.0 supported the wheel mouse. Windows 98 provides some additional ways for more applications to take advantage of the wheel, so you may find the wheel functioning in more applications.

# New Operating System Support Tools

New and improved support tools help you manage Windows 98 more efficiently and effectively. New tools help you update the operating system as needed, manage the space on your hard drives and back them up more easily, and track and verify your critical system files.

## Updating Windows 98

> For more information on using the Windows Update Web site resource, see Chapter 13.

Using a new Microsoft Web site, registered users of Windows 98 can keep their computers up-to-date. The new Web site, called Windows Update, continually provides access to the latest drivers and operating system files. The product information at this site is constantly updated, so you should find your computing experience with Windows 98 easier than it was with Windows 95 or Windows 3.1.

## More Ways to Back Up and Restore

> For more information on using Windows 98 Backup, see Chapter 13.

In Windows 95, the Backup applet supported a limited number of parallel and IDE backup devices. Windows 98 supports a larger number of parallel and IDE devices, as well as SCSI devices.

## Monitoring Critical System Files

> For more information on using the System File Checker, see Chapter 13.

The System File Checker is a utility that keeps track of the operating system's critical files and verifies their integrity. If System File Checker finds a problem with your system files, it offers to restore missing, corrupted, or replaced files.

## Making Windows Run More Efficiently

> For more information on using the Windows Tune-Up Wizard, see Chapter 13.

The Windows Tune-Up Wizard helps you get the best performance from your computer by checking your hard disk for problems and freeing hard disk space. The Tune-Up Wizard automatically schedules regular tune-up jobs at a time you specify.

# Understanding the Desktop and Starting Programs

## IN THIS CHAPTER

- **Understanding the Parts of Your Desktop**
- **Getting Help Offline and Online**
- **Changing the Way the Mouse Works**

Early versions of Windows introduced DOS-based computer users to the world of the graphic interface. Windows 95 took that graphic world, provided a 32-bit operating environment, and made getting your job done easier. In Windows 98, the operating system continues to evolve.

# Understanding the Desktop

The Desktop (see Figure 2.1) is the first screen you see after you turn on your computer and it finishes loading Windows. Think of the Desktop as the central place from which you work. The Desktop is always in the background even after you start a program and begin working.

## About Those Icons . . .

On the Desktop, you'll see icons that perform two basic functions: the icon either opens a window or starts a program. For example, when you either click or double-click on the My Computer icon, a window opens (see Figure 2.2).

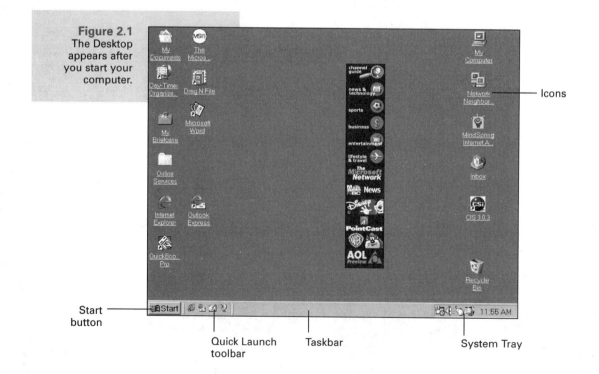

**Figure 2.1**
The Desktop appears after you start your computer.

Icons

Start button

Quick Launch toolbar

Taskbar

System Tray

**Figure 2.2**
When you click on the My Computer icon, you see a window like this one.

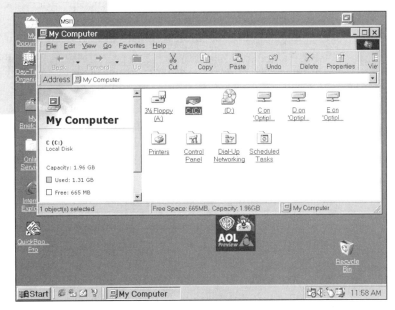

*Note*

Windows 98 sports two different Desktop interfaces: the Standard Desktop introduced in Windows 95, and the Active Desktop, introduced with Internet Explorer 4.0. The Active Desktop enables you to view and use your Desktop as a Web page. Because Internet Explorer 4.0 and Windows 98 are basically integrated, you'll see screens using the Active Desktop throughout this book. In Chapter 5, you'll learn how to switch between the Standard Desktop and the Active Desktop.

*Tip*

If you're using the Active Desktop and you point at an icon in the window, you'll see an explanation of the icon on the left side of the window.

*Note*

When you use the Standard Desktop, you double-click Desktop icons to take an action. When you use the Active Desktop, you can change your settings so that you click on Desktop icons only once to take an action. You'll learn more about mouse behavior later in this chapter.

Shortcut icons and program icons both launch programs. So, what's the difference between a shortcut icon and a program icon? Well, the shortcut icon points to the program, in its folder on your hard disk, and launches it. The program icon actually represents the program. If you've been using computers for a while and you're somewhat familiar with DOS, think of shortcut icons on the Desktop as the DOS equivalent of a batch file that points to the correct directory and file to launch the program. Program icons, on the other hand, point directly at programs that are *not* stored in a special directory. In fact, for program icons the only place you'll find the actual program file is on your Desktop.

> For more information on creating shortcuts on your Desktop, see Chapter 5.

You're probably wondering how you can tell the difference between a shortcut icon and a program icon. Shortcut icons always contain a small arrow in the lower-left corner that points up and to the right (see Figure 2.3).

You're also probably wondering how to distinguish between a program icon and an icon that opens a window. Unfortunately, there's no good way. The My Computer icon, the Recycle Bin icon, and the Network Neighborhood icon (if it appears) are icons installed by Windows 98, and they all open windows. As for other icons on your Desktop . . . well, if the icon looks like a folder, the chances are excellent that clicking it will open a window. But there are no hard and fast rules for distinguishing between program icons and icons that open windows.

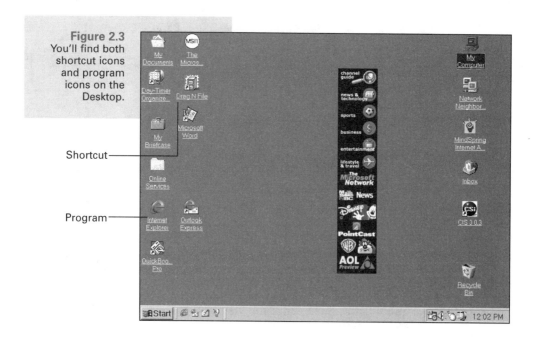

**Figure 2.3**
You'll find both shortcut icons and program icons on the Desktop.

Shortcut—

Program—

The Recycle Bin helps you avoid accidentally deleting files. You'll learn more about the Recycle Bin and how to use it later in this chapter.

## System Tray

In the lower-right corner of your screen, you see the System Tray. The System Tray contains icons that represent programs that were loaded when you started Windows. Again, if you've been using computers for a while, you may be familiar with TSRs—an acronym that stands for *terminate and stay resident* and specifically refers to programs that run "in the background" while you do other things on your computer.

If you move your mouse pointer into the System Tray and point at any of the icons in it, a screen tip will tell you what that icon represents (see Figure 2.4).

## Quick Launch Toolbar

To the right of the Start Button, you see the Quick Launch toolbar. This toolbar, like the System Tray, contains icons, but the icons in the Quick Launch toolbar

**Figure 2.4**
When you point at the time that appears in the System Tray, you can find out today's date, according to your computer's system clock.

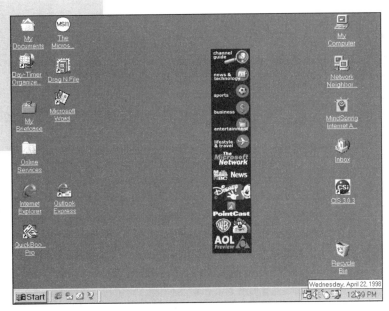

**Figure 2.5**
The icons in the Quick Launch toolbar enable you to quickly switch between Internet Explorer 4.0 features. Using the icons in the Quick Launch toolbar, you can quickly switch between features you often use.

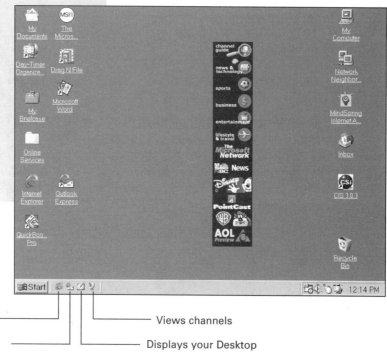

Launches Internet
Explorer Browser ──────────────── Views channels

Launches default
e-mail program ──────────────── Displays your Desktop

**See Appendix B for more information on viewing TV from your computer.**

allow you to switch rapidly between the Desktop and the Channel Viewer, e-mail, or the Internet (see Figure 2.5).

Some of these icons are self-explanatory. For example, the left-most icon will switch you to the Internet if you are already connected, or it will launch the Internet Explorer and offer to connect you to your Internet service provider. Similarly, the second icon from the left will open your default e-mail program.

*Note*

**On the Quick Launch toolbar, you may see an icon to launch TV Viewer if you installed the TV Viewer applet. When you click on the Launch TV Viewer icon, a wizard guides you through setting up your computer to watch TV. It switches to the TV Viewer applet, which displays the Program Guide listing, from which you can select a program to watch. You download program listings either from your local PBS station or from the Internet.**

**See Chapter 17 for more information on channels.**

The right-most icon on the Quick Launch toolbar switches you to the Channel Viewer, where you can view channels and receive information from the Internet on your computer.

• • • • • • • • • • • • • • • • • • • • • • • • • • • • • • • • • • • • • • • • • • • • • • • •

The Show Desktop icon in the Quick Launch toolbar is particularly useful if you run multiple programs simultaneously and want to return to your Desktop. Instead of minimizing each program individually, simply click on the Show Desktop icon.

• • • • • • • • • • • • • • • • • • • • • • • • • • • • • • • • • • • • • • • • • • • • • • • •

**For more information on Windows 98 and toolbars, see Chapter 5.**

Windows 98 contains other toolbars you can use; in addition, you can create toolbars.

## Start Menu

The Start button appears in the lower-left corner of the screen. When you click this button (or press the Windows key on your keyboard), the Start menu appears (see Figure 2.6).

**Figure 2.6**
The Start menu is aptly named; from it, you can start programs, open documents, get help, and more.

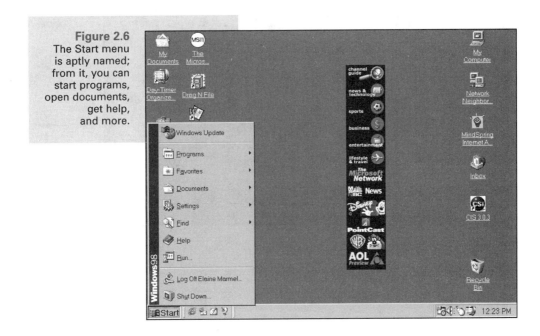

If you point at any option on the Start menu that displays a right-pointing arrow, a menu of additional choices will fold out (see Figure 2.7).

See Table 2.1 for an explanation of the choices on the Start menu. You'll learn more about using these options throughout this book.

# Taskbar

The Taskbar appears, by default, at the bottom of your screen—but you can move it by dragging it. You'll learn how to drag in the next section.

The icons on the Taskbar represent programs that are currently open (see Figure 2.8).

You can use the Taskbar to switch between open programs. Slide the mouse pointer into the Taskbar, point at the program that you want to use, and click the left mouse button. Windows will display the program.

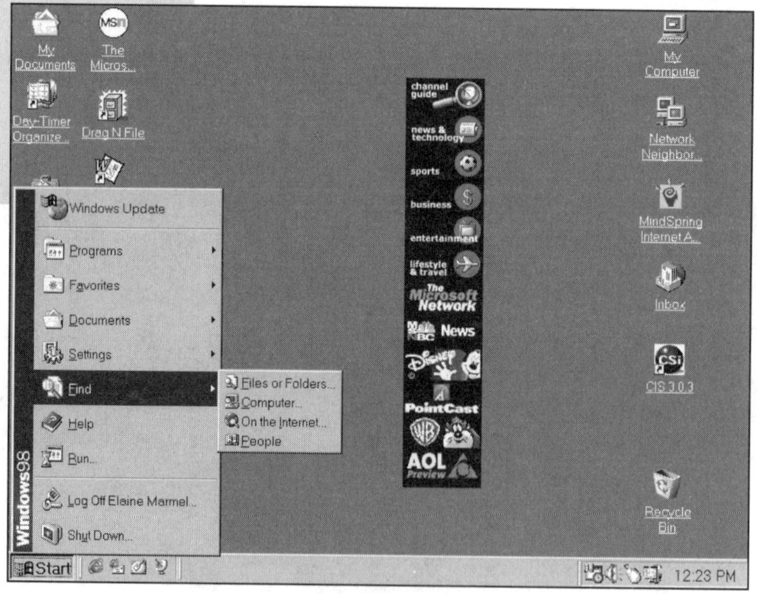

**Figure 2.7**
Pointing at the Find command on the Start menu displays an additional menu of choices.

## Table 2.1 The Start Menu

| Menu Choice | Function |
| --- | --- |
| Windows Update | Checks the Internet for updates to the operating system. |
| Programs | Lists programs you have installed on your computer. |
| Favorites | Lists Web pages you have designated as favorites while surfing the Internet. |
| Documents | Lists documents you've recently opened. |
| Settings | Lists options you can use to change the settings of the operating system. |
| Find | Lists items you can find for which search, such as files or folders on a computer or computers on a network. |
| Help | Provides help on the operating system. |
| Run | Enables you to run programs for which you know the executable file name. |
| Log Off | Enables users who share a computer to log off but leave the computer running so that someone else can log on. |
| Shut Down | Enables you to shut down the computer correctly, restart the computer, or restart the computer in MS-DOS mode. |

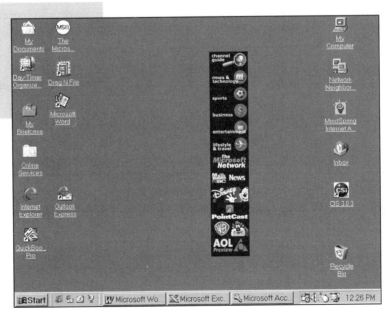

**Figure 2.8**
From the Taskbar, you can see that Excel, Word, and Access are all open.

# Using the Mouse

For more information on how to use the mouse effectively, see Chapter 12.

Using the mouse is a major part of navigation in Windows. So using the mouse effectively is an important part of working efficiently in Windows.

Using the Standard Desktop provided originally in Windows 95, you could take four possible mouse actions on the Desktop and in folders: clicking, double-clicking, dragging, and right-clicking. If you set up Windows 98 to use the Standard Desktop, these four actions still exist and work just as they did in Windows 95:

- **Clicking**—Selects an icon. To select an icon, you click it.

To select multiple contiguous items in a list, click the first item in the list, hold down the Shift key, and click the last item in the list. To select multiple noncontiguous items in a list, hold down the Ctrl key and click each item.

- **Double-clicking**—Sets in motion the action associated with the icon. If you double-click a program or shortcut icon, you start the associated program. If you double-click a folder or an icon that opens a window, the window opens.

- **Right-clicking**—Displays a shortcut menu of commands appropriate for the item on which you right-clicked.

- **Dragging**—Moves whatever you drag. To drag, point at the object you want to move—an icon or the Taskbar—and press and hold the left mouse button. Before releasing the mouse button, slide the mouse until the object appears where you want it. When you release the mouse button, the object will appear in its new location. You can drag icons on the Desktop to new locations that suit your taste.

If you use the Active Desktop in Windows 98, the behavior of the mouse *can* change:

By default, using the Active Desktop changes the mouse behavior. However, you can use the Active Desktop and retain the mouse behavior from Windows 95. See the next section.

- **Pointing**—Selects an icon. To select an icon on the Desktop, just point at it.

*Tip*

To select multiple contiguous items in a list, *point at* the first item in the list, hold down the Shift key, and *point at* the last item in the list. To select multiple noncontiguous items in a list, hold down the Ctrl key and *point at* each item.

- **Clicking**—Performs the function that double-clicking performed under Windows 95—it sets in motion the action associated with the icon.

Dragging and right-clicking perform the same functions they performed under Windows 95 or Windows 3.1, and you use the same techniques you used in Windows 95 and Windows 3.1 to perform these functions. Double-clicking is virtually eliminated in Windows 98 *on the Desktop*. You may still find double-clicking in applications.

## Hands On: Changing the Way the Mouse Behaves

You can choose the type of mouse behavior you want to use.

1. Click on the Start button, and the Start menu appears.
2. Highlight Settings, and a menu folds out (see Figure 2.9).

**Figure 2.9**
Choose Folder Options from the Settings menu.

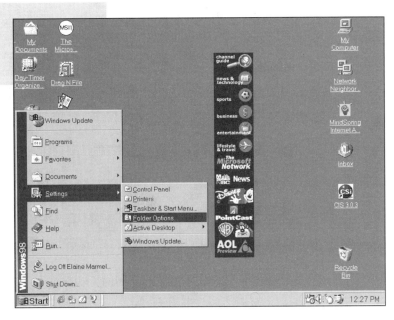

**3.** Click on <u>F</u>older Options. The Folder Options dialog box opens.

**4.** Click on the C<u>u</u>stom option buttons.

**5.** Click on the <u>S</u>ettings button to display the Custom Setting dialog box (see Figure 2.10).

**Figure 2.10**
Use the Custom Settings dialog box to select a behavior pattern for the mouse.

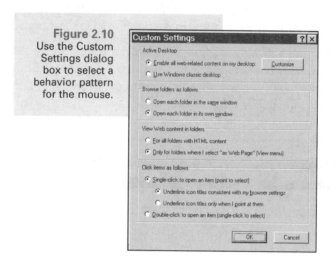

**6.** Use the bottom section of the dialog box to select the mouse behavior pattern you want:

- Choose <u>S</u>ingle-click to open an item to use the Active Desktop mouse functionality provided in Windows 98. If you choose this option, you can also choose to underscore icons using your browser settings (which, typically, means at all times) or only when you point at them.

*Tip*

You might want to choose to underline icons using your browser settings so that icons are always underscored on your Desktop as a reminder of the type of mouse functioning you selected.

- Choose <u>D</u>ouble-click to open an item to use the Standard Desktop mouse functionality provided in Windows 95.

**7.** Click on OK to save your settings and redisplay the Folder Options dialog box.

**8.** Click on OK again to close the Folder Options dialog box.

# Starting and Closing Programs

You can start programs by choosing from the Programs menu or by choosing from the Documents menu. The Programs menu, shown in Figure 2.11, lists all the programs you have installed on your computer. To start a program, click on the Start button and highlight the Programs menu. If necessary, highlight the folder containing the program; otherwise, click on the program. Windows will start the program.

As an alternative, you can start a program by opening a document associated with the program—and the Documents menu, shown in Figure 2.12, lists the documents you most recently opened. If the document you want to update appears on the Documents menu, choose it from the menu. Windows will start the program that created the document *and* load the document.

# Using the Recycle Bin

The Recycle Bin is a special icon on the Desktop that stores anything you delete. But, you ask, why *store* something that has been deleted? By storing deleted items

**Figure 2.11**
The Programs menu lists all the programs installed on your computer.

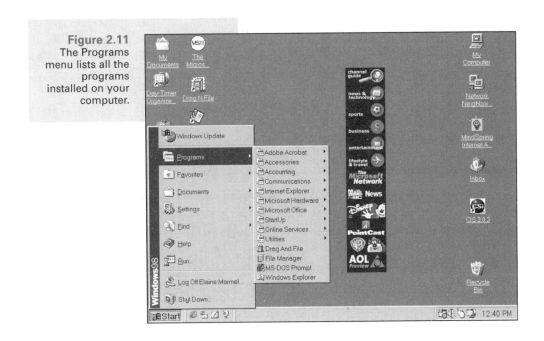

**Figure 2.12**
The Documents menu lists the documents you opened most recently.

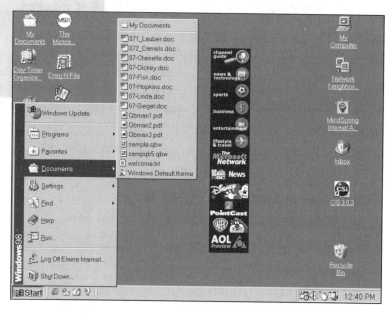

in the Recycle Bin, you can "undelete" items that you *accidentally* delete. Next logical question: How do you *really* delete something? You know—you *meant* to delete it. Easy: You empty the Recycle Bin. And the last logical question: How do you undelete something you deleted? You restore it from the Recycle Bin. In Chapter 4, you'll learn how to place a file in the Recycle Bin. For now, here's a look at using the Recycle Bin.

*Note*

If you really hate the idea of taking an extra step to get rid of files, you can disable the Recycle Bin. If you do disable the Recycle Bin, whenever you delete a file, the file will be gone immediately and *you will NOT be able to restore it*. Beginning computer users, I strongly urge you to use the Recycle Bin; in fact, I strongly urge *everyone* to use the Recycle Bin because we all make mistakes and accidentally delete files occasionally. However, I also believe that you are grownups, and I respect your right to make your own choices. Therefore, the steps to disable the Recycle Bin are included.

## Hands On: Disabling the Recycle Bin

To disable the Recycle Bin and *directly delete files and folders with no opportunity to restore them*, follow these steps:

1. Right-click while pointing at the Recycle Bin.

2. From the shortcut menu that appears, choose Properties. The Recycle Bin Properties box appears (see Figure 2.13).

**Figure 2.13**
The Recycle Bin Properties box controls whether you use the Recycle Bin.

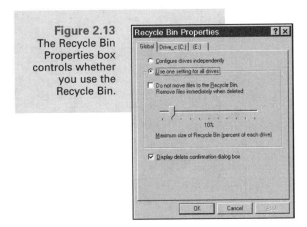

3. Place a check in the Do Not Move Files to the Recycle Bin check box immediately above the slide bar.

*Note*

If you want to use the Recycle Bin for some but not all hard drives, choose the Configure Drives Independently option button. You'll then be able to click the tab for each drive and place a check in the Do Not Move Files to the Recycle Bin check box as desired. Note that the Recycle Bin is not available for floppy drives or for removable hard disk drives such as Zip drives or SyQuest drives.

## Hands On:  Working with the Recycle Bin

You use the Recycle Bin to delete one or more files permanently from your system or to restore a file you accidentally deleted.

1. Right-click on the Recycle Bin to display a shortcut menu (see Figure 2.14).

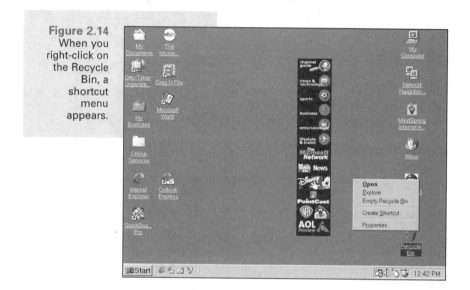

**Figure 2.14**
When you right-click on the Recycle Bin, a shortcut menu appears.

2. To view the contents of the Recycle Bin, choose <u>O</u>pen (see Figure 2.15).

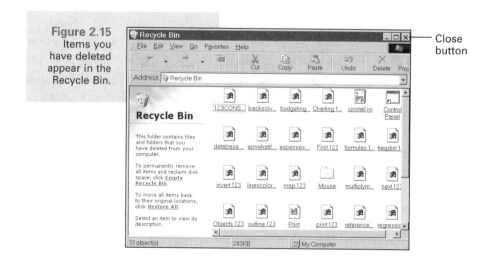

**Figure 2.15**
Items you have deleted appear in the Recycle Bin.

Close button

You can click on the Recycle Bin to open it and skip steps 1 and 2.

3. To restore an item, first select the item you want to restore.

   ■ To select an item using Standard Desktop mouse movement, click on the item.

   ■ To select an item using Active Desktop mouse movement, point at the item until its name appears selected.

4. Click on File to open the File menu and then choose Restore. Windows places the deleted item back in the location from which you deleted it.

5. To delete a single file, select that file, open the File menu, and choose Delete. To delete all files in the Recycle Bin, open the File menu and choose Empty Recycle Bin.

6. To close the Recycle Bin, click on the Close button in the upper-right corner of the Recycle Bin window.

If you want to empty the Recycle Bin without viewing the contents, perform step 1 and choose Empty Recycle Bin from the shortcut menu.

# Getting Help

Help in Windows 98 has a new look and feel. And in addition to using the Help feature that comes with Windows 98, you have other support options:

■ You can use a troubleshooting wizard.

■ You can get help from the Web.

■ You can contact Microsoft.

## Using Help

To open Windows Help, click on the Start button. From the Start menu, click on Help. The Help window appears (see Figure 2.16).

The buttons at the top of the Help window help you navigate through Help topics. The Hide button makes the left portion of the Help window disappear (see Figure 2.17).

The Back and Forward buttons help you navigate through Help topics you have already viewed. Click on the Back button once to display the Help topic you just

**Figure 2.16**
The opening
Help window in
Windows 98.

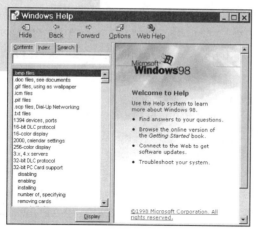

**Figure 2.17**
You'll see a
Show button
that you can use
to redisplay the
left side of the
window.

viewed; click on the Back button twice to display the second to the last topic you viewed. Click on the Forward button to move forward through topics you have previously viewed. Alternatively, you can move backward and forward through topics by clicking the Options button, which displays a menu containing commands to move you backward and forward through Help topics. You also can print the topic currently displayed by choosing Print from the Options menu.

The Web Help button is discussed later in this chapter.

To find a specific Help topic, you can use one of three methods—the Contents tab, the Index tab, or the Search tab.

# Using the Contents Tab to Search for Help

Use the Contents tab in Help the same way that you would use the table of contents of a book. The topics on the left side of the Help window are preceded by either a book icon or an icon that looks like a sheet of paper that contains a question mark (see Figure 2.18). Think of each topic preceded by a book icon as a chapter in a book. Chapters organize information related to the main topic. The topics preceded by the other icon are actual Help topics. Opening a book icon either leads to you related subjects or displays actual Help topics.

When you finally choose a Help topic, the help appears in the right side of the window (see Figure 2.19).

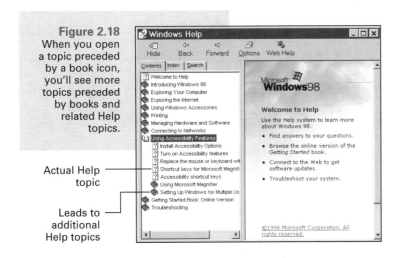

**Figure 2.18**
When you open a topic preceded by a book icon, you'll see more topics preceded by books and related Help topics.

Actual Help topic

Leads to additional Help topics

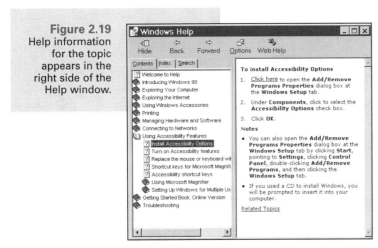

**Figure 2.19**
Help information for the topic appears in the right side of the Help window.

## Using the Index Tab to Search for Help

The Index tab was designed to let you search for help using the same techniques that you would use while searching the index of a book for information. When you display the Index tab (see Figure 2.20), you see an alphabetical list of Help topics on the left side of the Help window.

To find Help topics for a particular subject, move to the text box at the top of the Index tab and type a word or phrase that describes the subject (see Figure 2.21). In the list, Windows highlights the first topic containing the word or phrase you supply.

**Figure 2.20**
As you would expect, Help topics appear in alphabetical order on the left side of the Index tab.

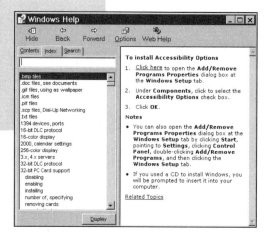

**Figure 2.21**
Type some letters, a word, or a phrase to search for Help topics in the Index.

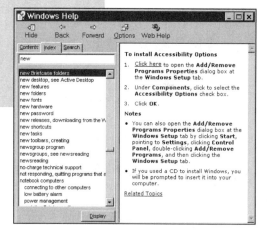

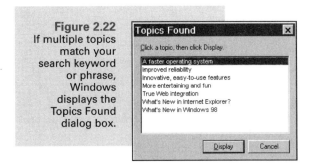

**Figure 2.22**
If multiple topics match your search keyword or phrase, Windows displays the Topics Found dialog box.

If necessary, use the arrow keys on the keyboard to move up or down in the list. When Windows has highlighted the topic most closely matching the subject for which you were searching, click on <u>D</u>isplay. If Help contains more than one topic related to your subject, you'll see the Topics Found dialog box shown in Figure 2.22.

Highlight the topic that most closely matches the subject on which you want information and click on <u>D</u>isplay. The topic appears in the right side of the Help window.

## Using the Search Tab

When you search Help using the Search tab, you perform a search that closely resembles the search a word processor performs when you choose the Find command. This technique is particularly useful when you have no clue what topic Windows has assigned to the subject on which you want help—or the subject may be covered under several different topics.

On the Search tab (see Figure 2.23), you type a keyword or phrase for which you want Windows to search. When you click on <u>L</u>ist Topics, Windows displays all Help topics that contain the keyword or phrase you typed.

You can view each topic Windows suggests by highlighting the topic in the lower-left portion of the Help window and then clicking on <u>D</u>isplay. The contents of the topic will appear on the right side of the Help window.

*Tip*

Longer keyword phrases limit the topics Windows will find because Windows displays only the topics that contain the *exact phrase* that you typed in the keyword box. To view fewer topics, type a longer keyword phrase.

**Figure 2.23**
Supply a keyword or phrase that Windows should use to search for Help topics.

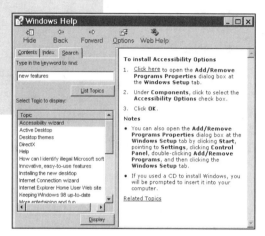

# Getting Help from the Internet

## Hands On: Getting Help for Windows from the Web

Help for Windows is also available on the World Wide Web, and you can access that help directly from inside the Windows Help window.

1. Open Windows Help by clicking on the Start button and choosing Help from the Start menu.

2. Click on the Web Help button on the toolbar at the top of the Help window. The Support Online from Microsoft Technical Support Help topic appears on the right side of the Help window (see Figure 2.24).

3. Click on the Support Online link. If you don't connect to the Internet directly, you'll see the dialog box that helps you connect to the Internet using your Internet service provider. If you connect directly to the Internet (or after you have signed on to the Internet), you'll see Microsoft's Web site that provides support for Windows (see Figure 2.25).

> For help getting connected to the Internet using your Internet service provider, see Chapter 15.

*Note*

Your copy of Windows 98 must be registered before you can access this site. Windows 98 will check for your registration, and, if your copy is not registered, a wizard will walk you through registration.

**Figure 2.24**
When you request Help from the Internet, this Help topic walks you through finding the correct location on the Web.

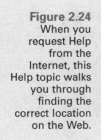

Web Help button

**Figure 2.25**
At this Web site, you can get help with Windows problems.

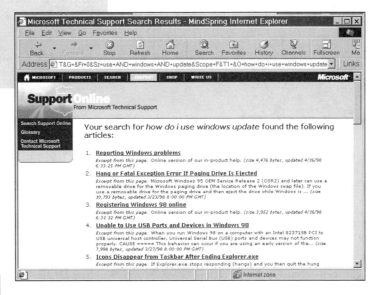

**For more information on using hyperlinks and a Web browser on the Internet, see Chapter 17.**

**4.** Open the first list box and select the appropriate subject.

**5.** Type your question in the text box.

**6.** Click on the Find button. Microsoft's Knowledge Base will be searched and a Web page displaying a list of articles that contain information about the question you typed will appear (see Figure 2.26).

**Figure 2.26**
When you pose a question on the Web, you'll see articles in Microsoft's Knowledge Base that relate to your question.

7. Scroll through the article titles and use hyperlinks to jump to the details of an article that interests you.

# Troubleshooting Wizards

Troubleshooting wizards are another way Windows 98 offers you help. Troubleshooting wizards help you determine the cause of a problem, which, in turn, can help you resolve the problem. Often, a troubleshooting wizard will appear automatically as you're trying to do something, but sometimes, when you encounter problems, Windows will display a message telling you to run a particular troubleshooting wizard. Windows 98 contains the following troubleshooting wizards:

- Dial-Up Networking
- Direct Cable Connection
- DirectX
- Display
- DriveSpace
- Hardware Conflict
- Memory
- Modem

- MS-DOS Programs
- Networking
- PC Card
- Print
- Sound
- Startup and Shutdown
- The Microsoft Network

Figure 2.27
Open the
Windows 98
Troubleshooters
book to see and
use a trouble-
shooting wizard.

To run any of these wizards, click on the Start button and choose <u>H</u>elp. From the Help menu, on the Contents tab, open the Troubleshooting book. Inside the Troubleshooting book, you'll see the Windows 98 Troubleshooters (see Figure 2.27).

When you use a troubleshooter, you'll be using Windows Help simultaneously. For that reason, you must be able to see the Help window while you run the troubleshooter so that you can follow the troubleshooter's steps exactly. Use the Hide button in the Help window to display just the troubleshooter's text and reduce the amount of space the Help window requires on the Desktop. To quickly minimize all open windows, switch to the Desktop using the Show Desktop icon in the Quick Launch toolbar. If necessary, resize the Help window.

**For more information on resizing and moving windows, see Chapter 3.**

## Hands On: Running a Troubleshooter

When you run a troubleshooting wizard, Windows helps you determine what is "going wrong" on your computer—and helps you try to fix the problem. This Hands On exercise walks through using a troubleshooting wizard—in this case, the Startup and Shutdown troubleshooter.

1. Click on Start and choose <u>H</u>elp.

2. On the <u>C</u>ontents tab, open the Troubleshooting book.

3. Open the Windows 98 Troubleshooters book.

4. Choose the Startup and Shutdown troubleshooter. On the right side of the Help window, the troubleshooter poses its first set of questions (see Figure 2.28).

5. Choose the option that best describes the problem you're experiencing and click on Next. Depending on the option you choose, you'll see either a set of steps that you can use to try to resolve your problem or more questions to further narrow the problem. The first option is selected in Figure 2.28; the troubleshooter responded with a proposed action to try in Figure 2.29.

6. Try steps proposed by the troubleshooter until you resolve your problem.

**Figure 2.28**
A trouble-shooting wizard poses a set of questions to narrow down your problem.

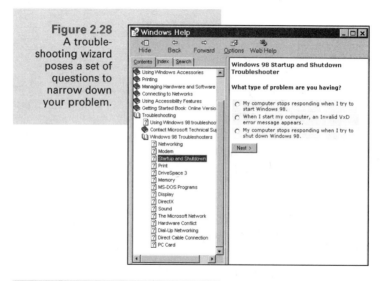

**Figure 2.29**
The trouble-shooter proposes actions to resolve your problem.

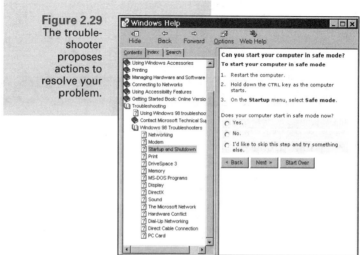

# 3

# Common Features in Windows Programs

## IN THIS CHAPTER

- **Common Windows Components**
- **Common File Operations**
- **Common Editing Commands**

In the days before Windows became the industry standard, each computer program you used had a different method of doing things. For example, to save a file in your word processing program you might have pressed the F7 key at the top of your keyboard, but to save a file in your spreadsheet you might have pressed the / (slash) key, then the letter F, and then the letter S. There was no consistency between applications or software manufacturers.

The advent of Windows changed that situation, and now with Windows 98 the consistency between software programs has grown even more. You will find that all Windows programs share many common operating features and have a similar onscreen appearance.

This chapter shows you some of the features and commands that will be the same no matter which Windows application you are using. Even when you start to use a new program, you'll find that you will already know a lot about using it. This global interface reduces your learning time substantially because you will be able to concentrate on the features specific to your software and not the mechanics of operating it.

# Working with Windows Components

A window is still a window; however, if you are upgrading from Windows 3.1, you will see a change in the location and design of the Minimize, Maximize, and Close buttons. One item that is new to Windows 98 is an address bar to show you the path and location of the folder or icon you are currently viewing. As you move your mouse pointer over an item, a description of the item appears on the left side of the window. Information such as the type, the file size, and the last modified date are shown. See Figure 3.1 for an example.

The logo for Internet Explorer is visible in the upper-right corner of the window, just under the Minimize, Maximize, and Close buttons. If you are connected online, clicking on the Internet Explorer logo launches Microsoft Internet Explorer and takes you to the Microsoft home page within the confines of the current window. If you are not already connected, clicking on the logo will launch your Internet connection.

## Identifying the Title Bar

All windows have a title bar. It's the long narrow box across the very top of a window. The title bar displays the name of the window as well as several small buttons described in the following paragraphs.

**Figure 3.1**
Windows
describes any
item in the
current window.

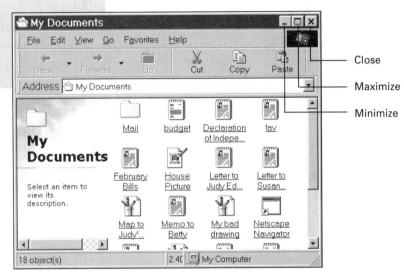

— Close
— Maximize
— Minimize

*Note*

**When a window is *active,* or currently being used, the title bar is *highlighted*, meaning that its color is different from the color of other open windows. The identifying color helps you distinguish the window you are working on.**

## Using the Close Box

Every window has a Close box in the upper-right corner that you can click. A Close box is just what it sounds like — a box to close a window. One single click is all it takes to put the window away.

Your screen may have two Close boxes — they serve almost the same purpose. If you are in an application such as Microsoft Word or Lotus 1-2-3, you will see a Close box for the document window and one for the application window. The Close box for the document puts away just the current document while leaving the application open and ready to use. Clicking the application Close box closes both the document and the application. Figure 3.2 illustrates a program with two Close boxes.

## Using the Maximize Button

Frequently, you will want a window or program to fill the entire screen. Having several screens displayed can be distracting. To enlarge a window, you use the *maximize* feature. A maximized window is much easier to read than a smaller one.

The Maximize button is the next to last icon located in the upper-right corner of a window. If the window can be maximized, the button looks like a single square. See figure 3.2.

**Note**

**Occasionally, you will encounter a window that cannot be maximized.**

**Tip**

Another way to quickly maximize a window is to double-click its title bar. Double-clicking toggles between maximized and restored window sizes.

## Using the Restore Button

After a window has been maximized, you can restore it to its original size and location by clicking on the Restore button. The Restore button is in the same

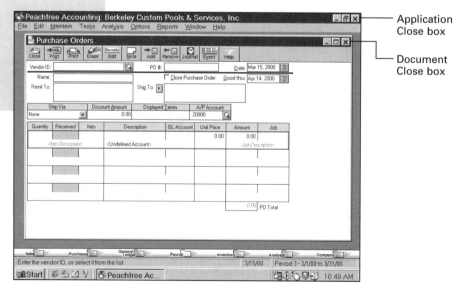

**Figure 3.2**
The document window and the application window have independent Close boxes.

Application Close box

Document Close box

location as the Maximize button and looks like two small windows. (The button represents the larger [maximized] window and the smaller [restored] window.) See Figure 3.2.

## Using the Minimize Button

Sometimes a window is hiding another window or your Desktop. You could close the interfering window, but that really isn't necessary. You can *minimize* the window—set it aside for a while—out of the way. See Figure 3.2.

Minimized windows aren't really windows. In reality, they are a button displayed on the Taskbar.

To minimize all open windows at once, position the mouse pointer anywhere over a blank spot on the Taskbar and then click the right mouse button to bring up the shortcut menu. From the shortcut menu select Minimize All Windows.

## Using the Control Menu

The Program Control menu is another button on the title bar of a window, but this one is located in the upper-left corner of a window. This button looks like a miniature icon of the window or program you are using. The Program Control menu is an alternate way to maximize, minimize, restore, move, resize, or close a window. All your choices are wrapped up together in one menu as you can see in Figure 3.3.

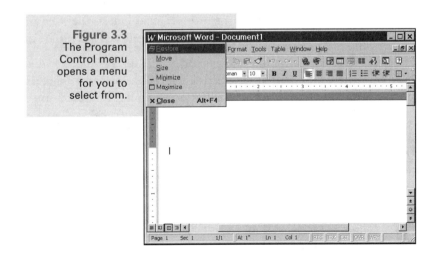

**Figure 3.3**
The Program Control menu opens a menu for you to select from.

As you will discover later in this chapter, moving and resizing a window with the mouse is usually much easier than moving or resizing using the keyboard, and you've already seen that each window has its own Minimize, Maximize, Restore, and Close buttons. So why do we need the Program Control menu as well? That's a good question, and I'd guess that Microsoft was probably trying to please all the people, all the time. The Program Control menu does come in handy, however, when your mouse decides to quit. Press the Alt key plus the Spacebar to access the Program Control menu. You can then make your choices from the menu.

*Tip*

You can also position the mouse pointer anywhere on the title bar of a window and click with the right mouse button to access the Program Control Menu.

*Note*

**If the Minimize, Maximize, and Restore buttons are too small for you to click easily, you can make them bigger. Right-click on the Windows 98 Desktop and select Properties to open the Display Properties dialog box. Click on the Appearance tab and then select Caption Buttons from the Item drop-down list. Increase the Size and look at the preview sample to see the resulting buttons. Click on OK when you are satisfied with the size.**

## Moving a Window

Sometimes a window doesn't appear on the screen exactly where you want it. You can move a window to a new position as long as the window is not maximized or minimized. The window must be in a restored state to be moved.

The title bar of a window is the handle for moving the window around. Position the mouse pointer at the title bar, hold down the mouse button, and drag the mouse. Release the mouse button when the window is in the desired location.

*Tip*

Make sure the mouse pointer remains a single arrow when pointing to the title bar. If it turns into a double-headed arrow, you will be resizing the window instead of moving it.

# Resizing a Window

Almost any window can be manually resized if it is not the right size for you. The window must be in a restored state to be resized. It cannot be minimized or maximized.

## Hands On: Resizing a Window

1. Open the My Computer window.
2. Move the mouse pointer to a border of the window. The mouse pointer will change to a double-headed arrow (see Figure 3.4).

If you position the mouse over any corner of the window you will be able to resize both the height and width of a window at the same time. The lower right corner has three lines through it which represent a size handle.

3. Click and hold the left mouse button.

**Figure 3.4**
You can resize all four sides of a window.

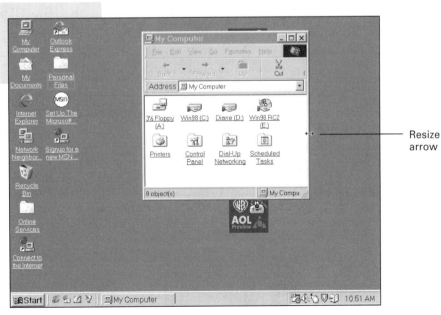

Resize arrow

4. Drag the border to the size you want. As you drag the border, the window will expand or contract.

5. Release the mouse button when the window is the desired size.

## Using Scroll Bars

The scroll bars are the bars located on the right side and bottom of most windows. Each vertical scroll bar has an up arrow at the top of the bar, a down arrow at the bottom of the bar and a small square box in the middle. A horizontal scroll bar is similar to the vertical scroll bar except the arrows point to the left and right.

Suppose you are working on a letter in your word processing program. Picture the scroll bar as an elevator. When you're on the elevator if you want to go up, you press the up arrow, right? The same goes for a window. If you want to move the view on your screen up a line at a time, click on the up arrow. Each time you click, your view moves up one more line. So . . . guess what the down arrow does? You're right, of course; it moves your view down a line at a time. Figure 3.5 shows a window with vertical and horizontal scroll bars. Other scrolling movements include clicking above the scroll box to move up a screen at a time, clicking below the scroll box to move down a screen at a time, or dragging the scroll box up or down the scroll bar, which rapidly moves the screen.

Press and hold the mouse pointer on the arrows to rapidly move up or down the screen.

**Figure 3.5** Scroll bars enable you to view other items in a window.

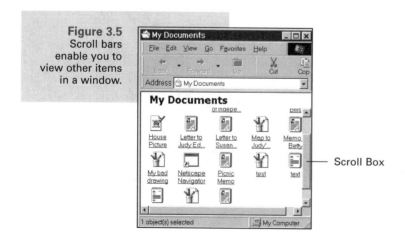

# Using the Menu Bar

Another common component on most windows is the menu bar. When you go into a restaurant, the first thing you usually do is to select what you want to eat from a menu. If you go into the restaurant in the morning, you'll usually read breakfast menu; at lunch you are more likely to check the lunch menu, and so forth. The same is true for a computer window. If you are working with File type stuff (as you'll learn about later in this chapter), then you'll be using the File menu, but if you're working with Format type stuff, then, of course, you'll need the Format menu.

You can access the menu bar with your mouse by simply clicking on the desired choice. The desired menu will open, and you'll be able to choose from it. (Just like at Denny's!) You can choose from the menu in one of three ways:

1. Move the mouse to the desired choice and then click.

2. Press the up or down arrow keys until you reach a desired command and then press the Enter key.

3. Type the mnemonic (underlined) letter in the name of the command.

If you choose a menu in error, click on the menu choice again or press the Escape key to cancel out of the menu.

Several possible actions can occur when you make a selection from a menu. Figure 3.6 illustrates a menu from the My Computer window.

- The requested action occurs.

  I see no problem here. Ask and you shall receive! The "Line Up Icons" selection in Figure 3.6 is an example. Also, do you notice that some items have a check mark beside them (such as Status Bar) and some have a small dot beside them (like Large Icons)? The check mark means that choice is currently being used. If you choose that item again, the check mark disappears. The check mark is like a light switch—toggle it on or off. The small dot to the left of a menu selection also means that choice is currently being used, but that multiple choices are available for this item; you must choose one (and only one) of these choices.

- A submenu appears for you to choose from.

  Some menu items are followed by a small triangle, which indicates that you have to make more choices. If you've used the Start menu, you've probably seen this type of menu item. The correct name for it is a *cascading menu*. In Figure 3.6, the Toolbars choice has a cascading menu.

Figure 3.6
A sample menu
with several
types of menu
selections.

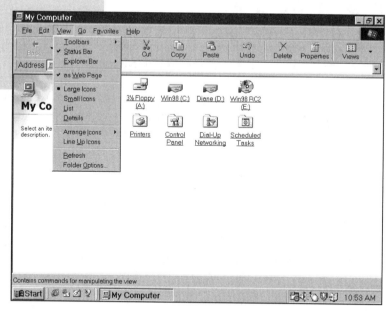

- A dialog box asks you for more information.

    When you choose a menu selection that has a series of three dots next to it, *(an ellipsis),* you need to provide further information. If you select Folder Options in Figure 3.6, a dialog box opens. Dialog boxes are discussed in the next section.

- Windows simply ignores your request.

    OK, we've all been here before! When a menu is opened, sometimes you will notice a choice that's grayed out or dimmed. Windows is telling you that a particular feature is currently unavailable. It's like going into Denny's at breakfast time and trying to order a baked potato. Baked potatoes aren't available until dinnertime, so that choice would be grayed out on a computer menu. When that particular choice is applicable, it will become black and you can then select it from the menu. Figure 3.7 illustrates a menu with unavailable items.

## Making Choices with Dialog Boxes

Dialog boxes are boxes that appear when you select a menu item with the ellipsis after it. These boxes are used to collect more information necessary to fulfill your menu request and vary in the type of information required. Windows 98 uses

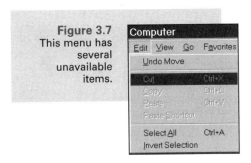

**Figure 3.7**
This menu has several unavailable items.

several techniques to ask for information in a dialog box. We'll take a look at each of these methods:

- Check boxes
- Option buttons
- Text boxes
- List boxes
- Drop-down list boxes
- Command buttons

Also, some dialog boxes contain several tabs or pages. That's Windows' way of keeping things organized. As you click on the various tabs, the choices in the dialog box change. The dialog box in Figure 3.8 has several tabs.

*Check boxes* are the small square boxes. When you look at Figure 3.9 (the Options box from the Solitaire game), you will notice small check boxes next to the

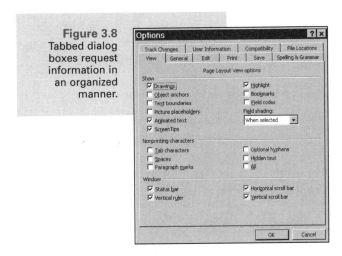

**Figure 3.8**
Tabbed dialog boxes request information in an organized manner.

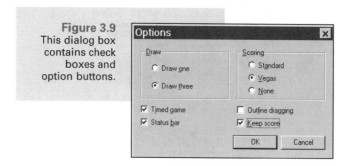

**Figure 3.9**
This dialog box contains check boxes and option buttons.

choices for Timed game; Status bar; Outline dragging, and Keep score. You can select as many of these options as you want. It's like ordering a sandwich with lettuce, pickles, and mustard, but no tomato.

*Option buttons*, sometimes called radio buttons, are the small round circles. From a group of option buttons, you can pick one option. Again looking at Figure 3.9, the Scoring section has option buttons. You can elect Standard, Vegas, or None. If you were in the restaurant, the waiter might ask whether you want soup, salad, or cole slaw.

*Text boxes* ask you to type information in the white rectangular box. In Figure 3.10, the dialog box is asking you to type a page number. If the insertion point is not blinking in the text box, you must click your mouse in the text box before you can type in it. Occasionally, Windows will supply a suggestion; you can accept it, or you can type in your own choice. If a suggestion appears in the box and you don't want it, press the Delete key to remove that choice; then type your own information.

*List boxes* show you a list of choices from which you can select. If the list box is too small to display all the choices at one time, you can use the box's scroll bar to view more selections. When you find the choice you want, click on it with your mouse. Windows will highlight your selection, and in some cases it will also appear in a small box above the list box.

*Drop-down list boxes* are like regular list boxes except they have a small arrow to the right of the box. The current choice is displayed in the box, but when you click on the down arrow a list of choices appears. For example, the drop-down list box in Figure 3.11 displays a list of folders and disk drives from which you can open a file.

*Command buttons* are the rectangular buttons in all dialog boxes. The most common command buttons are the OK and Cancel buttons, which handle the final step when you are working with a dialog box. Clicking on the OK button tells

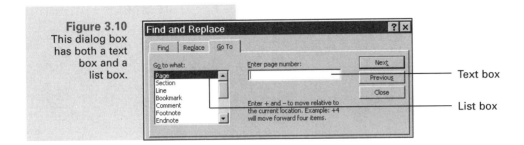

**Figure 3.10**
This dialog box has both a text box and a list box.

Windows to accept the choices you made in a dialog box and to carry out the command. Clicking on the Cancel button tells Windows to ignore any choices you made in the dialog box and to return to whatever you were doing previously. Figure 3.11 shows examples of other types of command buttons. This dialog box does not have an OK button, but instead has an Open button and a Cancel button. It also has an Advanced button and a few others. The Advanced button has an ellipsis, so if you click on it, another dialog box appears.

Most dialog boxes have several different sections, and you need to be able to move between them. The fastest way is to click the mouse on the desired section of the dialog box. You could also use the Tab key on your keyboard to move from section to section. If you go too far, you can press and hold the Shift key while you press the Tab key to move backwards.

Another type of Windows dialog box provides information. These boxes are called alert boxes, and they display an *I* or an *X* (as shown in Figure 3.12) or even occasionally an exclamation point (!). Most alert boxes have only one button—an OK button. Because the alert box is telling you something, the only response needed from you is to acknowledge that you've seen the message, thus the OK button. You cannot continue with your program until you click on the OK button.

**Figure 3.11**
Microsoft Word's Look In: box is an example of a drop-down list box.

**Figure 3.12**
You must click
the OK button to
continue with
your work.

# Using Toolbars

Many windows include *toolbars,* which usually appear under the Menu bar. The toolbar icons represent some of the most commonly used features in that window or program. With the advent of the Web style Desktop in Windows 98, most windows have some type of a toolbar. Figure 3.13 shows the toolbar from the Windows Explorer window.

Selections are made from a toolbar with a single click. Some buttons on the toolbar are pressed to activate a feature. Other buttons are like toggle switches. Click once to turn the feature on, and click again to deactivate the feature. Some toolbars, such as the one in Figure 3.14, have drop-down lists for you to select from, and some programs display multiple toolbars.

**Figure 3.13**
Toolbars are
shortcuts to
selections on
the menu.

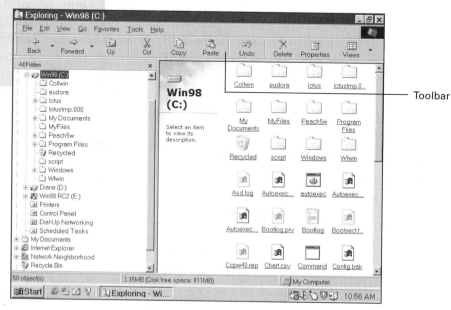

Toolbar

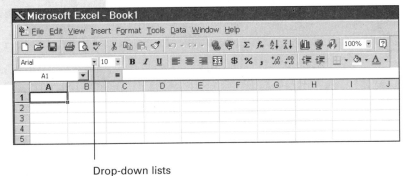

**Figure 3.14**
Microsoft Excel
has many
different
toolbars.

Drop-down lists

# File Operations

As mentioned at the beginning of this chapter, software commands are fairly consistent throughout all Windows programs. Features like saving, closing, opening, and printing files are easier than ever to use. In most programs, you use these features by accessing the menu, using a shortcut key, or clicking a choice on a toolbar.

## Saving a File

After you've created a file in your favorite software application, you'll probably want to retain that file. One reason to save it is so that you can use it again in another project. Another reason to save a file is so you can start it and then complete or modify it at a later time. All Windows programs use the same method to save a file.

### Hands On: Saving a File

1. Click on the File menu; then choose the Save command or press Ctrl+S. The Save As dialog box appears.

*Note*

If the file was previously saved, the Save As box does not appear and the file is resaved with no questions asked. You won't need to continue with steps 2 through 4.

• • • • • • • • • • • • • • • • • • • • • • • • • • • • • • • • • • • • • • • • • • • •

If your application has a toolbar, you can also click on the Save button to save your file.

• • • • • • • • • • • • • • • • • • • • • • • • • • • • • • • • • • • • • • • • • • • •

2. Choose a folder from the Save In: drop-down list box in which to save the file.

3. Enter a descriptive name for the file in the File Name section (see Figure 3.15).

**Figure 3.15**
Descriptive file names can include spaces and most special characters.

Most newer software programs allow file names of up to 256 characters including any characters for the folders the file is to be stored in. If you happen to be using an older (pre-Windows 95) version of an application software, the file name itself is still limited to eight characters.

• • • • • • • • • • • • • • • • • • • • • • • • • • • • • • • • • • • • • • • • • • • •

If you are using one of the older versions of your application, now might be a good time to consider upgrading that software!

• • • • • • • • • • • • • • • • • • • • • • • • • • • • • • • • • • • • • • • • • • • •

4. Click on Save or OK. (The button you see depends on the software program you are using.) Windows stores your file on the disk for future use.

## Closing a File

When you are finished working on a file, you should put it away. This operation is called closing a file. When a file is closed it is released from the computer memory and that memory is freed up to do other things. Closing is not the same as saving a file, but you should know that when you do close a file, if it has not been saved, the application will ask you if you want to save it. If you want to save the file, the Save command does its job and then the Close command will be completed.

Not all applications have a Close command. Some programs, WordPad or Paint, for example, only allow you to have a single file open at a time and don't need a Close command. Other programs such as Calculator or Internet Explorer don't have a Close command because the application doesn't create a file to close.

To close a file:

1. Click on the File menu and then choose the Close command. If the file has already been saved, you will not need to continue with steps 2 and 3.

• • • • • • • • • • • • • • • • • • • • • • • • • • • • • • • • • • • • • • • • • • • • • • • • • • • • •

Many applications also use Ctrl+W as a shortcut to close a file.

• • • • • • • • • • • • • • • • • • • • • • • • • • • • • • • • • • • • • • • • • • • • • • • • • • • • •

2. Click on Yes or No if Windows asks you whether to save the file (see Figure 3.16).

3. Continue with the steps to save a file that you learned in the preceding section.

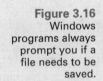

**Figure 3.16** Windows programs always prompt you if a file needs to be saved.

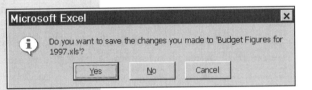

# Opening a File

You've created a file, saved a file, and closed a file. Now it's time to go back and work on that file again. When you open a file, a copy of the saved file is pulled into the computer memory and is displayed on your screen, ready for you to modify or do whatever you want to it.

## Hands On: Opening a File

1. Choose File, Open, or press Ctrl+O. A dialog box similar to the one displayed in Figure 3.17 appears on your screen.

2. Choose the folder from the Look In: drop-down list box to which the file had been saved.

3. Click on the file name you want to open. The file name appears in the File Name box. Click on OK.

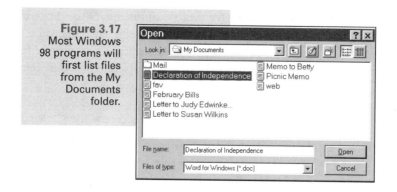

**Figure 3.17**
Most Windows
98 programs will
first list files
from the My
Documents
folder.

*Tip*

Double-click on the file name (instead of clicking it once and then clicking on the OK button).

# Printing a File

A few years back a popular business topic was the arrival of the so-called paperless office. Because that day has not yet arrived, you will probably want a hard copy of the file you created. Windows prints in the background and has a print queue to handle all of your printing jobs so you can print multiple documents without waiting for each one to finish printing before choosing to print another job.

## Hands On: Printing a Document

1. Choose File, Print, or press Ctrl+P. A Print dialog box similar to the one seen in Figure 3.18 appears on your screen.

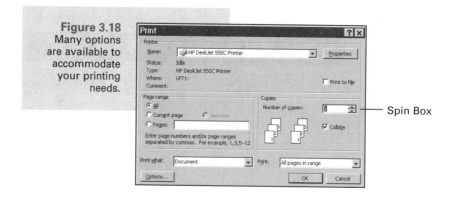

**Figure 3.18**
Many options
are available to
accommodate
your printing
needs.

— Spin Box

*Tip*

For more
information
on faxing, see
Chapter 16.

Many windows have a toolbar with a Printer button.

**2.** To select a different printer than the one displayed in the Print dialog box, open the <u>N</u>ame list box. This list contains all the printers available to you, including any fax "printer" that you have installed. Click on the desired printer.

**3.** Click in the Spin Box to specify how many copies of the document you want in the Number of <u>C</u>opies box.

**4.** Specify any other desired options from the Print dialog box and then click on OK. The document will be sent to the printer you specified.

When Windows 98 begins printing, a small printer icon appears in the System Tray in the lower-right corner of your screen. Double-click on this printer to view or change the status of any unprinted print job. This window displays the name of the document being printed, the current print status of the job, the owner—or whoever asked for the job to be printed—the size of the print job, and the time the job was sent to the printer. You can also select print jobs and delete or pause them.

*Note*

**Windows will issue a warning box if your printer is unavailable or out of paper when someone tries to print to it.**

# Editing Operations

Windows programs are wonderful in that if you make a mistake or change your mind about something—no problem, you can change it.

Cut, Copy, Paste, and Undo are some of the most common Windows editing commands. Each of these commands has a shortcut key, and I recommend you memorize them. You never know when you might need them.

The reason I suggest you memorize the shortcut keys is that I was recently working with a very popular accounting program and needed to use some Windows editing commands. The problem was that those choices were not on the application's menu, and in one case I couldn't even get to the menu! I was panicking, until I tried the shortcut keys. They worked—and saved me a ton of time! The moral of the story is that although there is a lot of consistency between Windows programs, you will occasionally run across a program that doesn't exactly follow the rules.

# Discovering the Windows Clipboard

Windows includes an electronic version of a clipboard. This *Clipboard* is a temporary holding area for information, which can be a word, a phrase, a picture, a file, or a bunch of files. Information on the Clipboard is actually stored in a special section of computer memory. Because the storage location is in memory, the information is nonspecific to the program you are using. Therefore you can use the Clipboard to transfer information from one program to another. You'll learn about that a little later in this chapter. The Clipboard involves three commands: Cut, Copy, and Paste.

The Windows Clipboard holds one piece of information at a time. If you cut or copy information to the Clipboard, that information remains on the Clipboard until you cut or copy something else to the Clipboard. (Or until you turn off your computer.)

## Cutting Information

The Cut command removes information from the current location, say, for example, a paragraph of text in a word processing document. Cutting is not the same as deleting the information, however, because even though Windows removes the information from the document, the paragraph (in this case) didn't go into never-never land. Instead, it went to the Clipboard. Picture, if you will, a pencil sitting on a desk. Picking up the pencil and holding it in your hand is analogous to cutting it to the Clipboard (that is, your hand is like the Clipboard). You'll use the Paste command to place the information in the new location.

To cut information to the Clipboard:

1. Select the information to be cut.
2. Choose Edit, Cut (or press Ctrl+X).

## Copying Information

The Copy command is similar to Cut except that Copy leaves the selected information in the current location instead of removing it. The information still goes to the Clipboard and waits for you to tell it what to do next.

To copy information to the Clipboard:

1. Select the information to be copied.
2. Choose Edit, Copy (or press Ctrl+C).

### Pasting Information

The Paste command is used when information has been copied or cut to the Clipboard and then needs to be relocated to a specified place. Recall the picture of the pencil in your hand; you are now going to place the pencil on the other side of the desk. That action is the same as using the Paste command. With one exception . . .

When you actually put down the pencil, you no longer have it in your hand. The Windows Clipboard does it just a little bit differently. Instead of releasing the information to the new location, it places a *copy* of the information in the specified location and retains the original on the Clipboard. This approach enables you to Paste that information a second, third, fourth or a hundred more times. The information remains on the Clipboard until you cut or copy something else or you turn off the computer.

To paste information from the Clipboard:

1. Position the mouse pointer where the information is to be relocated.

2. Choose <u>E</u>dit, <u>P</u>aste (or press Ctrl+V).

• • • • • • • • • • • • • • • • • • • • • • • • • • • • • • • • • • • • • • • • • • • • • • • •

Most windows have a toolbar with Cut, Copy, and Paste buttons.

• • • • • • • • • • • • • • • • • • • • • • • • • • • • • • • • • • • • • • • • • • • • • • • •

## Switching between Programs

Windows 98 can run multiple programs at the same time. Older versions of Windows also had that capability but with each Windows upgrade, the operations become smoother and easier, especially when the application software you use has been designed to take advantage of Windows features. Software such as Microsoft Office 97, Lotus SmartSuite 97, or WordPerfect 8 are 32-bit applications, which simply means the information can travel faster and easier from place to place and that the software traffic signals are coordinated so the information flow is smoother.

Even if you have already started an application, Microsoft Word, for example, the Start button on the Taskbar is easily available for you to launch another program, perhaps, Microsoft Excel. You can keep launching programs until your computer runs out of memory. A word of advice, however: if you really don't need a program, don't waste your computer's resources. Running unnecessary applications slows down your computer.

To switch between active applications, click on the Taskbar button for the desired application. You can switch between applications as much or as often as you desire.

Another way to cycle between open applications is to press the Alt+Tab keys.

# Linking and the Clipboard

Linking is a major feature of Windows! Before you can understand linking, you need to know about a limitation of using the standard Paste command and the Windows Clipboard. When you use the Edit Paste command, Windows is actually pasting a *copy* of whatever you had on the Clipboard into the new location. If the original information changes, the pasted copy does not change. You would need to go back to the original information, select it again, copy it again, and then paste it again. Each time the original or source information changes, you would need to repeat this procedure. That's not a problem unless you are trying to keep a report up-to-date with current information. Enter linking into the picture.

Linking is the process of tying together pieces of information. Instead of simply copying text when the paste command is used, linking places the pasted information into the new document as an object that is tied to the original location. When the original information is modified, the pasted object of information gets updated as well. You should know however, that not all Windows applications support linking.

If an application supports linking, a Paste Special command will be available from the Edit menu (see Figure 3.19).

**Figure 3.19**
In a link, changes to the source file are reflected in your document.

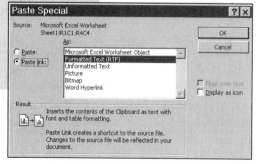

What is the benefit of linking? Besides the fact the pasted object is always up-to-date, if you need to edit the original information, all you need do is double-click on the object. The originating program will be launched, with the linked information opened. When you edit the information, both the originating document and the linked document will reflect the changes.

This process isn't really as confusing as it sounds. For example, suppose you are creating a document called Sales Report in WordPerfect, and you have included some spreadsheet figures from a Lotus 1-2-3 worksheet called Sales By Month. While you are working on the Sales Report, you notice that some of the Sales By Month figures were entered incorrectly. In this case, you can double-click on the linked object to launch Lotus 1-2-3; the Sales By Month spreadsheet will be open and ready for your changes, and your WordPerfect document will automatically reflect every change you make in your 1-2-3 spreadsheet.

One final note about Linking. You may run into the occasional program that does not support Linking. Although their numbers are dwindling, a few such programs still linger on. You'll know that a program doesn't support linking because Paste Special and Paste Link will not be available.

## Reversing an Action with Undo

Most, but maybe not all, menus contain an Undo command. This command is sometimes called the "OOPS!" command. The Undo command reverses the last action you took.

Be aware, however, that occasionally the Undo command cannot undo the last action you took, but most simple editing commands can be reversed. One type of step that cannot be undone is the File Save command. The file has already been written to the disk and cannot be reversed. Also, some programs such as Microsoft Word or WordPerfect have multiple levels of undo that enable you to keep undoing. So if you made a mistake 10 steps ago, you could revert back to that step and start over. Now THAT'S handy!

To reverse an action:

Choose Edit, Undo (or Press Ctrl+Z).

OK, bear with me as I get a little stupid here. Some people tell me they cannot remember the keystroke command for Undo, so here's a little analogy I use. When you're asleep, you're "catching some zzzz's," right? So—think to yourself: "Gee, I must have been asleep when I did that one!" Ctrl+Z—get it? All right, I said it was stupid—but try it—it works!

As a review of this chapter, you've noticed that most Windows programs have a common format. You've also seen that most Windows programs enable you to use a shortcut keystroke to access many of the menu commands. Table 3.1 lists some of the common shortcuts. They appear in alphabetical order.

## Table 3.1  Shortcut Key Combinations

| Key Combination | Command |
| --- | --- |
| Ctrl+A | Select All |
| Ctrl+C | Copy |
| Ctrl+F | Find |
| Ctrl+H | Replace |
| Ctrl+N | New |
| Ctrl+O | Open |
| Ctrl+P | Print |
| Ctrl+S | Save |
| Ctrl+V | Paste |
| Ctrl+X | Cut |
| Ctrl+Z | Undo |

# 4

# Using Windows Explorer to Manage Files, Drives, and Folders

## IN THIS CHAPTER

- **Working in the Explorer Environment**
- **Switching Drives**
- **Using Folders to Organize Drives**
- **Finding Files**
- **Moving and Copying Files**
- **Renaming Files**
- **Deleting Files**
- **Formatting and Copying Floppy Disks**

Windows Explorer is an application with which you'll become extremely familiar as you become more of a power user. Windows Explorer helps you keep your disk drives organized by providing easy ways to make folders in which you store files, move and copy files between folders or drives, find files, and more.

# Understanding the Windows Explorer Environment

Windows Explorer is a program that helps you organize and manage your computer. To open Windows Explorer, choose Start and highlight Programs. From the bottom of the Programs menu, choose Windows Explorer. In Figure 4.1, you see a fairly traditional view of Windows Explorer. If you're upgrading to Windows 98 from Windows 3.1, Windows Explorer replaces the File Manager program.

You can open Windows Explorer by right-clicking on the Start button and choosing Explore from the shortcut menu that appears.

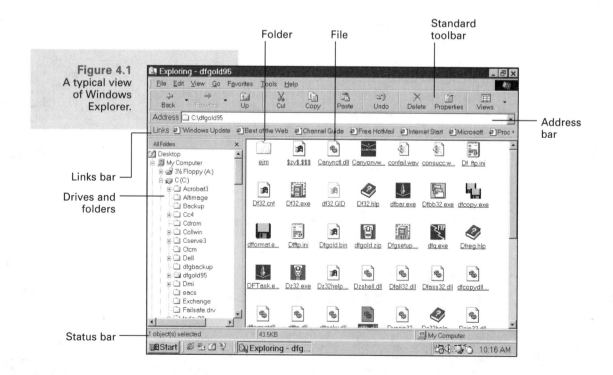

**Figure 4.1**
A typical view of Windows Explorer.

*Note*

**You can, if you prefer, use the Windows 3.1 File Manager. Use the techniques you'll learn later in this chapter to find WINFILE.EXE. If you double-click that file, you'll start Program Manager. To make using the File Manager more convenient, you'll probably want to create a shortcut for it and place it either on your Desktop or on the Programs menu.**

See Chapter 5 to learn how to create a shortcut.

In this fairly traditional view of Windows Explorer, all the drives on your computer and all the folders on those drives appear in the left pane. The right pane displays the contents of the drive or folder selected in the left pane. Because folders can contain folders, you may see both folders and files in the right pane.

*Tip*

If you come from an MS-DOS background, folders are the same as directories—just a different name for the same thing.

# Changing What You See

While you are working in Windows Explorer, you have control over what you see—and don't see. You can hide or display all toolbars and the status bar. You also can change the information that appears in both the left pane and the right pane of Windows Explorer. Last, you can customize the appearance of folders in the right pane.

## Hiding and Displaying Toolbars

In Figure 4.1, you see the Standard toolbar, the Address bar, and the Links bar. You can, however, hide or display any of these screen elements.

Also, you can control the appearance of the Standard toolbar by hiding or displaying text labels. Compare Figure 4.1, which includes text labels on the

*Note*

**Use the Address bar and the Links bar to select Web sites to visit. You also can use the Address bar to specify locations on your computer (drives or folders) to open.**

**Figure 4.2**
Windows
Explorer toolbars
do not include
text labels.

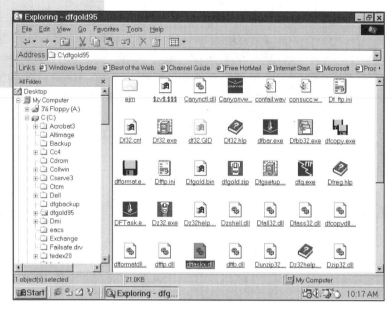

Standard toolbar, with Figure 4.2, which does not include text labels on the Standard toolbar.

• • • • • • • • • • • • • • • • • • • • • • • • • • • • • • • • • • • • • • • • • • • • • • • • •

When you exclude text labels from the Standard toolbar tools, you can point at a tool to display a screen tip that describes the tool's purpose.

• • • • • • • • • • • • • • • • • • • • • • • • • • • • • • • • • • • • • • • • • • • • • • • • •

## Hands On: Hiding and Displaying Windows Explorer Toolbars

To control the appearance of Windows Explorer toolbars, follow these steps:

1. Open the View menu.

2. Highlight the Toolbars command. A submenu opens (see Figure. 4.3), and all elements you see onscreen also display a check mark on the submenu.

3. To hide an element, choose an element that displays a check mark on the submenu. Similarly, to display an element, choose an element that *doesn't* display a check mark on the submenu.

**Figure 4.3**
From this menu,
hide or display
toolbars and
text labels.

## Hiding and Displaying the Status Bar

The status bar at the bottom of the screen provides information about the selected drive, file, or folder. In Figure 4.1, the status bar showed information about the file selected in the right pane; the file was 78.5 KB. In Figure 4.4, the status bar shows information about the folder selected in the left pane; it contains 25 objects (folders and files). Because no file or folder is selected in the right pane, you see the amount of disk space occupied by the folder selected in the left pane (5.44 MB) and the amount of free disk space on the selected drive (719 MB).

To hide the status bar (or display it if it doesn't appear on your screen), choose View, Status Bar. If, when you open the View menu, a check appears next to the Status Bar command, choosing the command will hide the status bar. If you don't see a check next to the Status Bar command when you open the View menu, choosing the command will display the status bar.

## Changing the Contents of the Explorer Bar

The left pane of the Windows Explorer window is also called the Explorer bar. In addition to viewing the drives and folders on your computer in the Explorer bar, you can view other information. To switch to a different view, choose View,

**Figure 4.4**
When you don't
select a file or
folder in the
right pane, the
status bar shows
information
about the space
available on the
selected drive.

<u>E</u>xplorer Bar. A submenu, with your choice of views, will open. Choose the view you want to display in the left pane.

*Note*

**For information to appear in the right pane when you make a choice in the left pane while viewing anything other than drives and folders, you must be connected to the Internet. In addition, when you first switch to another view, you need to focus on the left pane of Windows Explorer because the right pane does not, initially, relate to the left pane. The right pane will relate to the left pane after you switch to the view *and* make a choice in the left pane. In Figures 4.5, 4.6, and 4.7, no choices were made in the left pane, so the right pane remained empty. In Figure 4.8, the Internet was actually searched— and, after choosing one of the search results, the information appeared in the right pane.**

In Figure 4.5 your Favorites list appears in the Explorer bar; the list you see is the same list that appears when you click on the Start button and choose Favorites.

**Figure 4.5**
Viewing your
Favorites in
Windows
Explorer.

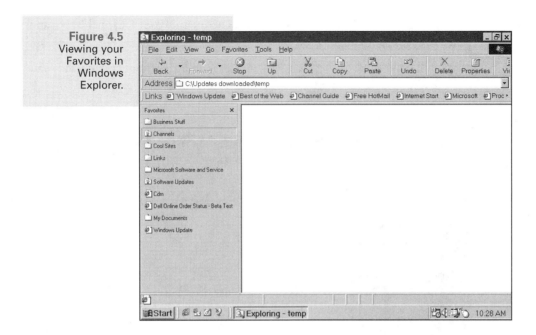

In Figure 4.6, you see a history of the Web pages you have visited—and you can revisit them by selecting them in Windows Explorer.

**Figure 4.6**
Viewing a
history of the
Web sites you
have visited
recently.

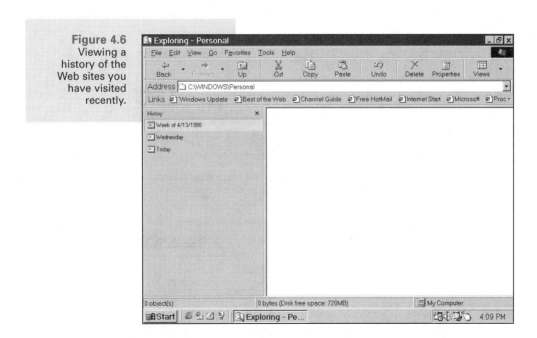

In Figure 4.7, you see the list of channels contained in your Channel bar—and, you can access a channel by selecting it in Windows Explorer.

If you are connected to the Internet, you can search the Internet from the Windows Explorer by choosing the Search view (see Figure 4.8).

**Figure 4.7**
Viewing the Channel bar in Windows Explorer.

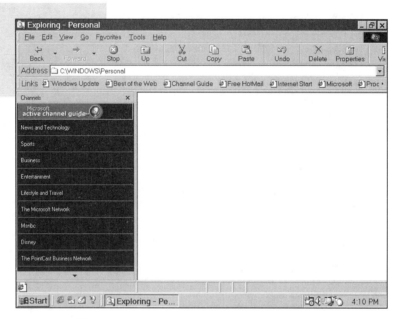

**Figure 4.8**
Searching the Internet from Windows Explorer.

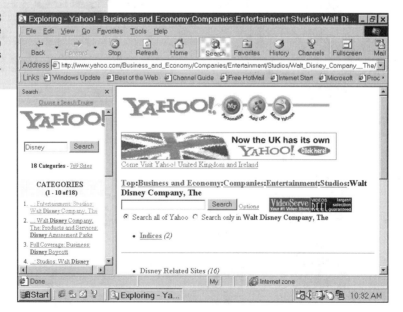

# Changing the Information that Appears in All Folders View

Most people use Windows Explorer to work with drives, folders, and files, so you'll concentrate on that view. For the rest of this chapter, you'll make sure that you see folders and drives in the Explorer bar. Choose View, Explorer Bar and, from the submenu that appears, choose All Folders.

You can adjust the size of the left and right panes by dragging the bar that divides them. As you move the mouse pointer over the bar, the pointer becomes a two-headed arrow (see Figure 4.9). Drag to the left to enlarge the size of the right pane and reduce the size of the left pane. Drag to the right to achieve the opposite effect.

In the opening screens in this chapter, you saw the information in the right pane displayed as what Windows Explorer calls "large icons." You can change the appearance of the right side of your screen in a number of ways. Note that the changes you make affect all folders, not just the selected folder in the left pane.

To display small icons, as shown in Figure 4.10, choose View, Small Icons.

When you view small icons, Windows Explorer arranges the objects in the right pane alphabetically within groups (folders and then files) across the screen by default.

**Figure 4.9**
Changing the size of the panes in Windows Explorer.

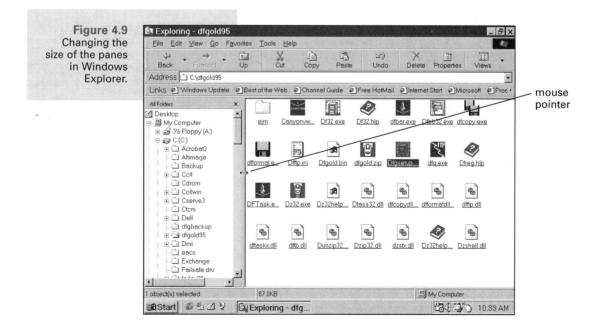

mouse pointer

**Figure 4.10**
Small icons enable you to see more of the contents of a folder that contains many objects.

To view the objects in the right pane in a list format, as shown in Figure 4.11, choose View, List.

**Figure 4.11**
In List format, the objects appear alphabetically down the right pane.

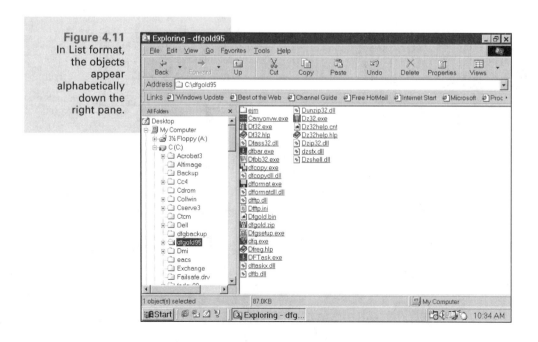

If you need more information, choose View, Details to display the size, file type, last modification date and time, and attributes of the objects in the right pane (see Figure 4.12).

By default, the objects will appear alphabetically down the pane. You can, however, quickly sort the objects in the right pane by any of the columns displayed. Simply click on the column heading. For example, to sort the objects by size, click on the title of the Size column. And, clicking any of the column headings twice toggles the sort between ascending and descending order.

Suppose you like large icons, but you need to know details. In this case, the Web page format is for you. Choose View, As Web Page. Then choose View, Large Icons. To see the details of any object in the right pane, select that object (see Figure 4.13).

## Customizing a Folder

OK, this one is for fun. You can customize a folder so that it contains a background image in the right pane when you view it (see Figure 4.14). You need to be careful, however, not to choose a background pattern that will block the actual contents of the folder.

**Figure 4.12**
The Details view provides the most information about the objects in the right pane.

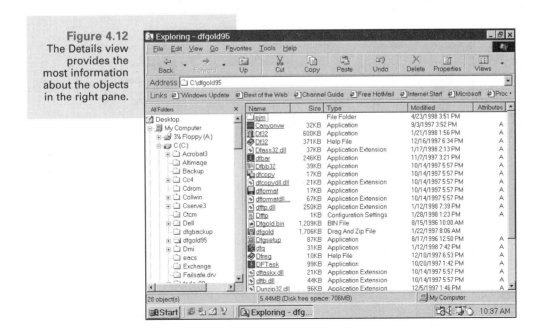

**Figure 4.13**
In Web page format, you can highlight an object in the right pane to see its details.

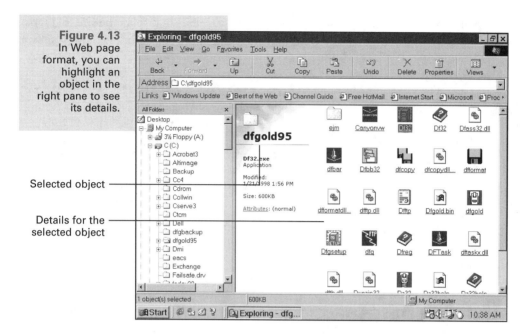

Selected object

Details for the selected object

**Figure 4.14**
This folder was customized to display a background.

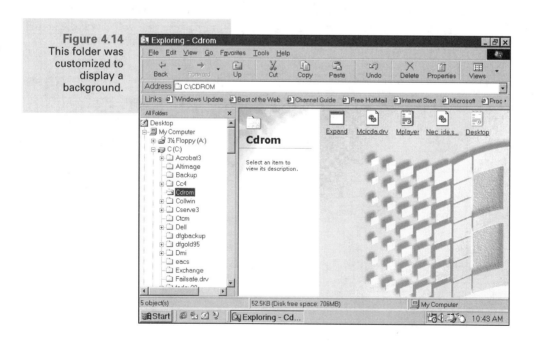

In Chapter 5, you'll learn how to give all the folders on your computer the same look as the selected folder.

## Hands On: Adding a Background Image to a Folder

1. In the left pane, click on the folder to which you want to add a background image.

2. Choose View, Customize This Folder. The Customize This Folder Wizard starts (see Figure 4.15).

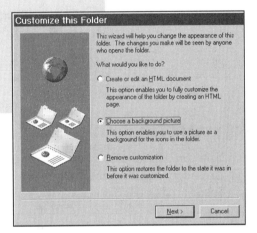

**Figure 4.15**
The first box of the wizard that helps you add a background image to a folder.

3. Choose the second option button in the box—Choose a Background Picture—and click on Next.

*Tip*

If you really want to control the appearance of the folder and you're adept at HTML, use the Customize This Folder Wizard to create an HTML document that you can then modify.

4. In the second dialog box of the wizard, select a background image from the list on the right. A sample of the image appears in the left pane (see Figure 4.16). If the image you want to use doesn't appear in the list, you can click the Browse button to navigate around your computer and find the image.

5. Click on Next. The wizard congratulates you and tells you that you have chosen to change the background picture.

6. Click on Finish. The background you selected appears in the right pane for the folder selected in the left pane.

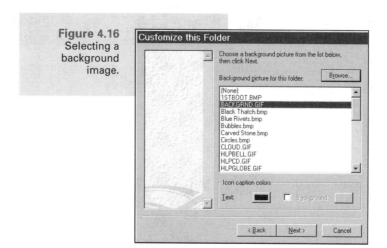

**Figure 4.16**
Selecting a
background
image.

# Working with Drives

Your computer contains both hard and floppy disk drives—and some of you may have additional equipment that behaves like a disk drive, such as a Zip drive or a Syquest removable hard disk drive. You can use Windows Explorer to access information on those drives and to create folders in which you can store information—and simultaneously keep the drive organized so that you can find things when you need them.

## Switching Drives

This section takes a more detailed look at how you use the left pane of Windows Explorer. First of all, any folder preceded by a plus sign (+) contains additional folders. You can open the folder to see the additional folders by clicking on the plus sign. When you do, the additional folders in the left pane are indented slightly and the plus sign changes to a minus sign (see Figure 4.17). The right pane doesn't change.

• • • • • • • • • • • • • • • • • • • • • • • • • • • • • • • • • • • • • • • • • • • •

The indentation of folders is a visual aid to help you remember that one folder contains other folders. This indentation effect is often referred to as a *tree structure* because a tree has branches and those branches also have branches.

• • • • • • • • • • • • • • • • • • • • • • • • • • • • • • • • • • • • • • • • • • • •

To display the contents of a drive (or a folder) in the *right* pane, click on the name of the drive or the icon that appears immediately to the left of the drive's name in the *left* pane (see Figure 4.18).

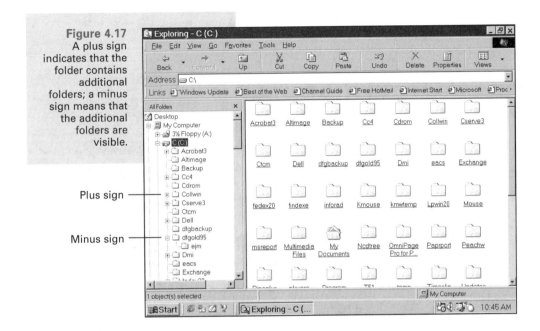

**Figure 4.17**
A plus sign indicates that the folder contains additional folders; a minus sign means that the additional folders are visible.

Plus sign ——

Minus sign ——

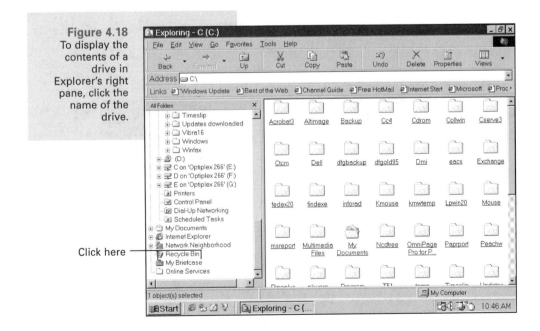

**Figure 4.18**
To display the contents of a drive in Explorer's right pane, click the name of the drive.

Click here ——

When you need to use your floppy disk drive, you use the same technique—but be sure you insert the floppy disk into the drive before you click on the drive. You may be used to the terminology "change to the floppy drive" or "switch to the floppy drive"; in Windows, clicking on the drive in the Explorer is the same as changing or switching to the drive.

# Creating Folders to Organize a Drive

You use folders to organize files on your disks the same way you use folders in your file cabinet to store papers related to the same subject. A folder on a computer might contain files with similar purposes; for example, you might create a folder to hold all your Microsoft Word documents. Or if you're really into the concept of organizing, you might create several different folders to hold your Word documents, based on the subjects of the documents.

## Hands On: Creating a New Folder

To create a new folder, follow these steps:

1. Click on the folder in which you want to place the new folder. If you simply want to add a folder to a drive without placing the new folder inside an existing folder, click on the drive.

2. Choose File, New. From the submenu that appears, choose Folder. A new folder appears in the right pane (see Figure 4.19).

**Figure 4.19**
A new folder, currently named New Folder.

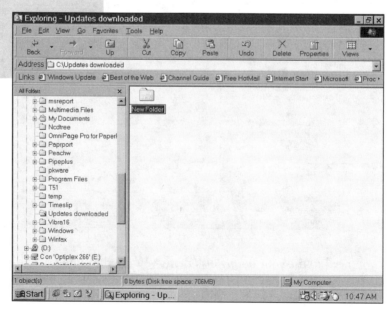

3. While the text New Folder is highlighted (selected), type a name for the folder you are creating.

If you type while text is selected, the text you type replaces the selected text. That way, you don't have to delete the existing text—you can simply type over it.

4. Press Enter. The new name—I called mine Temporary—becomes the name of the folder, and a plus sign appears to the left of the folder you originally selected in step 1.

5. To see your new folder in the left pane, click the plus sign next to the folder that contains the new folder (see Figure 4.20).

**Figure 4.20**
Viewing, in the left pane, the new folder you created.

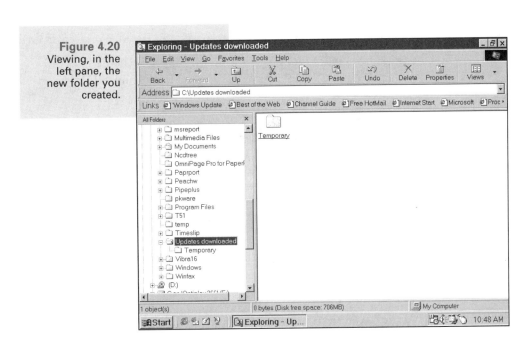

# Working with Files

Now that you know how to organize files, you'll find occasions where you can't find them even though you organized them. Don't worry—this section explains how to search for a file. You'll also learn how to copy and move files between folders and drives, and you'll learn how to rename files and delete files you no longer need.

# Finding Files

So, theoretically, having done your homework and organized your files, you shouldn't need to "find" a file—except when it isn't where you're sure you put it. It happens to everyone—or maybe it doesn't happen to you because you're an organization god. But suppose that some technical support person is trying to help you resolve a conflict on your computer, and the technical support person believes that multiple copies of the same file, located in different folders, could be the source of all evil on your computer. *Now* you do need to search for files.

## Hands On: Searching for Files

To search a drive for files, follow these steps:

1. In Windows Explorer, select the drive you want to search.

2. Choose <u>T</u>ools, <u>F</u>ind. From the submenu that appears, choose <u>F</u>iles or Folders. The Find: All Files dialog box appears (see Figure 4.21).

**Figure 4.21**
Use the Find: All Files dialog box to search for either a file or folder.

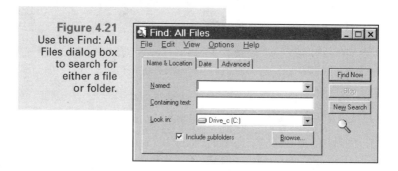

3. Use the first two boxes to specify your search. If you put information in *both* boxes, you're limiting the search, since Windows will return files that contain *both* sets of information. To make your search more global, supply only one of the following:

   ■ In the <u>N</u>amed box, type a file or a folder name.

      or

   ■ In the <u>C</u>ontaining Text box, type text for which you want to search every file.

4. If necessary, open the <u>L</u>ook In list box and change the starting place for the search.

*Note*

**You can use DOS wildcard characters such as * and ? to perform a global search. For example, searching for Win*.* would return both Win.ini and Winword.ini. Searching for 04FIG??.pcx would return all files that begin with 04FIG, have two additional characters, and end with a PCX extension—such as 04FIG01.PCX, 04FIG02.PCX, 04FIG03.PCX, and so on.**

5. Click on F̲ind Now. If Windows Explorer finds any files or folders that match your search criteria, their names will appear at the bottom of the Find window (see Figure 4.22). If Windows Explorer finds no matches, you'll see an informational message at the bottom of the window.

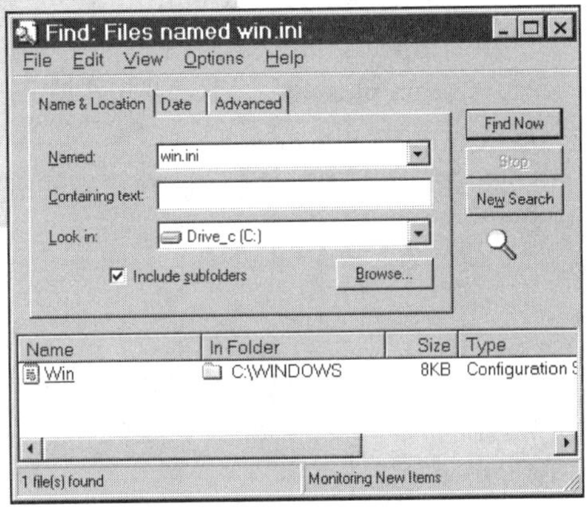

**Figure 4.22**
The results of the search appear in the bottom of the Find window.

> **Find: Files named win.ini**
>
> File   Edit   View   Options   Help
>
> Name & Location | Date | Advanced
>
> Named: win.ini                      F̲ind Now
>
> Containing text:                     Stop
>
> Look in: Drive_c (C:)                New Search
>
> ☑ Include subfolders      Browse...
>
> | Name | In Folder | Size | Type |
> | --- | --- | --- | --- |
> | Win | C:\WINDOWS | 8KB | Configuration S |
>
> 1 file(s) found          Monitoring New Items

*Tip*

You don't need to open Windows Explorer to search for files or folders. Click on the Start button and choose F̲ind from the Start menu. From the Find submenu, choose F̲iles or Folders.

# Copying or Moving Files

You will find occasions where you need to copy or move a file from one folder to another or from one drive to another. For example, you may need to copy a file onto a floppy disk to give to a colleague.

## Hands On: Copying and Moving Files from One Folder or Drive to Another

To copy or move files from one folder to another, follow these steps:

1. In Windows Explorer, open the folder containing the file you want to copy or move.

2. Select the file you want to copy or move.

---

Remember, if you're using the Active Desktop, you select a file by pointing at it. If you're using the Standard Desktop, you select a file by clicking on it.

---

3. Take one of these actions:

- **Move**—Drag the file from the right pane into the left pane onto the folder where you want to place it.

- **Copy**—Press and hold Ctrl while dragging. When you copy a file, you'll see a plus sign (+) attached to the mouse pointer during the operation (see Figure 4.23).

4. Release the mouse button to drop the file onto its new location.

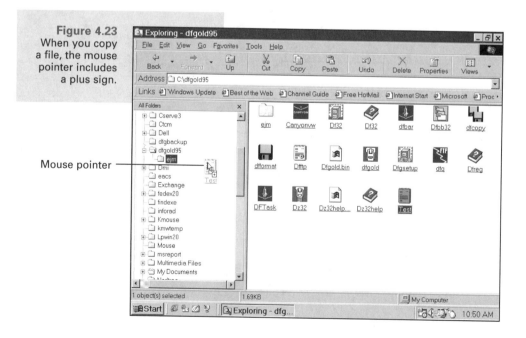

**Figure 4.23** When you copy a file, the mouse pointer includes a plus sign.

Mouse pointer

Some notes about copying and moving:

- If a file with the same name exists at the target location, you'll see a Confirm File Replace dialog box (like the one in Figure 4.24); you can stop the operation if necessary.

- You can use exactly the same technique to copy a file to a different drive—simply drop the file onto the desired drive. You would use this method to copy or move a file to a floppy disk. If you want to move a file to a different drive—that is, you don't want the file stored on both drives—you must delete the file from one drive.

- If you want to place a file inside a folder on a different drive, click on the plus sign (+) in front of the drive containing the folder so that you can see the folders on the drive. Then drag the file onto the folder.

- You can use exactly the same technique to copy an entire folder. In this case, the object you drag from the right pane is a folder. You can also drag the folder exclusively in the left pane—click on plus signs so that you can see the folders in the left pane. Then drag one folder in the left pane onto another folder in the left pane.

- If you're uncomfortable with dragging and dropping, you can move and copy files using menu commands. In the right pane, select the file you want to move or copy. Right-click that file. From the shortcut menu that appears, choose Copy to copy the file or Cut to move the file. Then, in the left pane, point at the folder or drive where you want to place the file and right-click. From the shortcut menu, choose Paste.

**Figure 4.24**
If you're about to overwrite an existing file, Windows Explorer warns you.

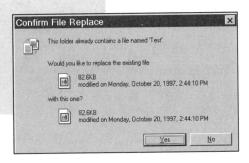

# Renaming Files

Occasionally, after you name a file you change your mind and want to name it something else. You could save it under a new name, but then you'd have a file you need to delete. *Renaming* a file requires fewer steps than saving it under a new name and deleting the original.

## Hands On: Renaming a File

To rename a file, follow these steps:

**1.** In Windows Explorer, find the file you want to rename.

If you use the techniques explained earlier in this chapter to find the file, be aware that you can follow the rest of these steps to rename the file in the Find window.

**2.** Select the file.

Remember, if you're using the Active Desktop, you select a file by pointing at it. If you're using the Standard Desktop, you select a file by clicking on it.

**3.** Press F2. The file name appears selected (see Figure 4.25).

**4.** Type the new name for the file and press Enter.

**Figure 4.25**
When you press F2 to rename a file, the file name appears selected.

# Deleting Files

> **See Chapter 2 for more information on emptying the Recycle Bin.**

Everyone deletes files. In Windows 98, you can delete files, folders, or shortcuts from the Desktop by dragging them onto the Recycle Bin. For example, you can delete files in the My Documents folder on the Desktop by dragging them onto the Recycle Bin. To finish the deletion process, you empty the Recycle Bin.

## Hands On: Deleting Files

Rather than dragging unwanted files to the Recycle Bin, you may find it easier to use Windows Explorer or the Find window to delete files.

1. Find the file you want to delete in either Windows Explorer or the Find window.

2. Select the file you want to delete. You can select a series of files that appear contiguously in the window by selecting the first file, holding down the Shift key, and selecting the last file. Similarly, you can select multiple files that *do not* appear contiguously by holding down the Ctrl key as you select each file.

3. Click on the Delete button on the toolbar or press the Del key on your keyboard. A message similar to the one in Figure 4.26 will appear.

**Figure 4.26** Windows asks you to confirm the deletion.

4. Choose <u>Y</u>es or <u>N</u>o, as appropriate.

*Tip*

If you find, after moving, copying, or deleting files, that the right pane of Windows Explorer seems messy, select an icon in the pane and choose <u>V</u>iew, Arrange <u>I</u>cons. From the submenu, make sure a check appears next to the <u>A</u>uto Arrange command. If it does not, choose that command.

# Managing Floppy Disks

Now that you know how to manage your hard disks, it's time to talk about managing floppy disks. All the techniques you've learned so far about moving, copying, deleting, and renaming work on floppy disks the same way they work on hard disks. You have only two new techniques to learn with respect to managing floppy disks:

- Formatting a floppy disk
- Copying a floppy disk

## Formatting Floppy Disks

Although most floppy disks come formatted these days when you buy them, you may want to format a disk if you plan to recycle it and use it for something other than its original intended purpose.

*Caution*

> Typically, formatting a floppy disk destroys all information on that disk. Make sure that you select a disk to format that *doesn't* contain any information you want to keep.

### Hands On: Formatting a Floppy Disk

Use the My Computer icon and follow these steps to format a floppy disk:

1. Place the disk you want to format in the floppy drive; we'll assume your floppy drive is named A.
2. On the Desktop, open the My Computer icon.
3. Select the floppy drive.

*Caution*

> Warning: You *can* format hard disks—and doing so destroys all information on them. Make sure you select the floppy drive before continuing.

4. Choose File, Format. The Format dialog box appears (see Figure 4.27).

**Figure 4.27**
Use the Format dialog box to format a floppy disk.

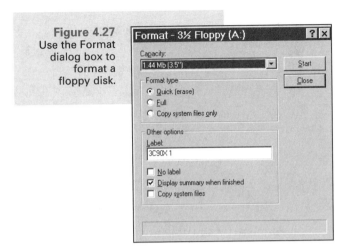

5. Choose a Format Type:

   - **Quick**—Deletes all the files on the disk, and standard disk utility programs could recover these files. Choose this option if the information on the disk is not sensitive. Windows performs this operation very quickly—hence its name.

   - **Full**—Destroys all information on the disk, and no standard disk utility could recover any of the files that were on the disk. Choose this option if the information on the disk *is* sensitive. This operation takes approximately 2 minutes (which seems like an eternity when you're working at a computer).

   - **Copy System Files Only**—Creates a disk that you can use to start your computer. This option *does not* destroy existing files on the disk; it simply adds the files needed to start your computer.

6. Select any other options:

   - Choose not to allow the operating system to label the disk. In most cases, the computer label is not essential; it's just a nice touch. If you do allow the operating system to label the floppy disk, type the label you want in the Label box. The label can be up to eleven characters long, but contain no spaces or periods.

   - If you choose to display a summary when the format operation completes, you'll see a dialog box similar to the one in Figure 4.28. Choose Close to close this box after you read it.

   - When you choose Copy System Files, Windows copies the files you

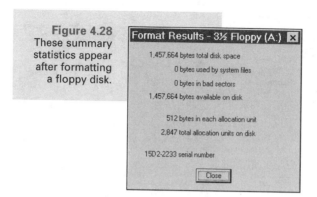

**Figure 4.28**
These summary
statistics appear
after formatting
a floppy disk.

Format Results - 3½ Floppy (A:)

1,457,664 bytes total disk space

0 bytes used by system files

0 bytes in bad sectors

1,457,664 bytes available on disk

512 bytes in each allocation unit

2,847 total allocation units on disk

15D2-2233 serial number

Close

need to start your computer to the floppy disk *after* formatting the disk. In this case, any files that were on the disk originally will be destroyed, and then the system files will be added to the floppy disk.

7. Choose Close to close the Format dialog box.

## Copying Floppy Disks

For those of you who remember the DOS command, we're talking about diskcopying. When you copy a floppy disk, you make an exact duplicate of its image. You'll most often need to copy a floppy disk if a software vendor has told you to make a backup copy of your program on floppy disks.

When you copy a floppy disk, you use one floppy drive and two floppy disks: the one you want to copy and the one on which you want to place the copy.

### Hands On: Copying a Floppy Disk

Use the My Computer icon and follow these steps to format a floppy disk:

1. Place the disk you want to copy in the floppy drive; we'll assume your floppy drive is named A. The disk you want to copy is called the *source disk*.

2. On the Desktop, open the My Computer icon.

3. Select the floppy drive containing the disk you want to copy.

4. Choose File, Copy Disk. The Copy Disk dialog box appears (see Figure 4.29).

5. Make sure that the drive in the Copy From box is the same as the drive in the Copy To box.

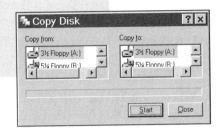

**Figure 4.29**
Use this dialog
box to copy a
floppy disk.

*Note*

**If your computer contains only one floppy drive, you will see only one drive in the box. If, however, your computer contains two floppy drives or any removable hard drives (such as Zip drives or Syquest drives), you will also see those drives in the Copy Disk box. However, to copy a disk, you must use the same drive. You cannot, for example, copy a 3½ inch floppy disk in Drive A to a 5¼ inch floppy disk in Drive B.**

6. Click on <u>S</u>tart. As the copy operation progresses, you'll see a message in the Copy Disk box that Windows is reading the source disk. Eventually, when Windows has read the source disk, you'll see the dialog box shown in Figure 4.30.

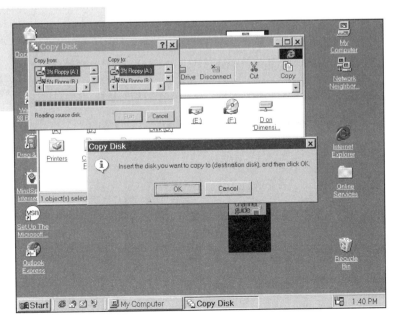

**Figure 4.30**
When
appropriate,
Windows
prompts you to
change the disk.

7. Remove the source disk from the drive and replace it with the disk onto which you want to copy the information—the *destination disk.*

8. Click on OK. Windows copies the information onto the destination disk. While the operation takes place, a message in the Copy Disk box reports that Windows is writing to the destination disk.

9. When the operation completes, you'll see an informational message in the Copy Disk dialog box (see Figure 4.31).

**Figure 4.31**
Windows informs you when the copy operation is complete.

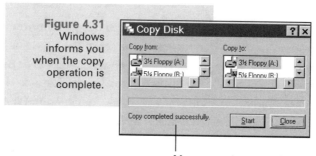

Messages about copying appear here.

10. Click on Close.

# PART II
# Setting Up and Customizing Windows

# 5

# Changing What's on the Desktop

## IN THIS CHAPTER

- **Working with Icons on the Desktop**
- **Understanding Display Properties**
- **Customizing the Desktop**
- **Making the Desktop "Active"**

The Desktop is your main work place—you start on the Desktop when you first boot your computer. Some icons on the Desktop come, by default, with Windows. For example, you'll always see a My Computer icon and a Recycle Bin. And if you're connected to a network, the Network Neighborhood icon appears. You can make the Desktop look the way you want it to look, arranging the Desktop to suit your work style.

*Note*

**In this chapter, we've hidden the Taskbar to make figures easier to understand. In Chapter 7, you'll learn how to hide the Taskbar.**

# Working with Icons on the Desktop

You can move the icons around on the Desktop to place them in locations that may work better for you, and you can add icons to the Desktop to make starting particular programs easier.

## Arranging Icons

Moving an icon is as simple as dragging it. But when you drag, usually things don't line up the way you would like. So, use the Line Up Icons command. Drag your icons until they appear in the approximate location where you want them. Then, point at a blank spot on the Desktop and click on the *right* mouse button. A shortcut menu appears (see Figure 5.1). Choose Line Up Icons to place the icons in orderly lines.

*Tip*

• • • • • • • • • • • • • • • • • • • • • • • • • • • • • • • • • • • • • • • • • •

The Arrange Icons command enables you to automatically arrange icons on the Desktop by Name, Type, Size, or Date. The Auto Arrange command on the Arrange Icons submenu lines up all the icons on the Desktop from top to bottom in the order they currently appear—but it arranges them neatly starting at the left side of the screen.

• • • • • • • • • • • • • • • • • • • • • • • • • • • • • • • • • • • • • • • • • •

## Changing the Appearance of Desktop Icons

In Windows 95, the operating system automatically placed the My Computer icon and the Recycle Bin on the Desktop. If you had a network, you also saw a Network Neighborhood icon. The icons that appeared for these items were stan-

**Figure 5.1**
Use the shortcut menu to reorganize the icons on your Desktop.

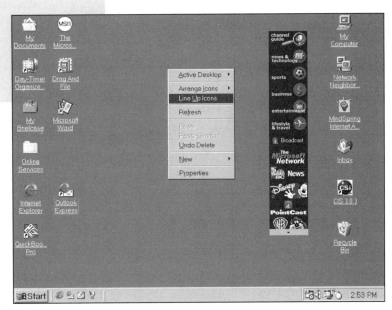

dard—and you couldn't change them. But in Windows 98, you can change them. Right-click on a blank spot on the Desktop and choose the Properties command from the new shortcut menu. You'll see the Display Properties dialog box. Click on the Effects tab (see Figure 5.2).

**Figure 5.2**
From the Effects tab, you can change the appearance of standard Windows icons.

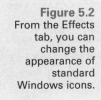
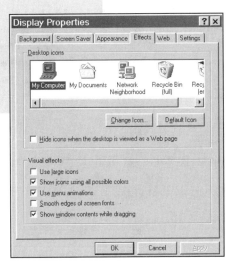

**Figure 5.3**
Choose a new icon from the Change Icon dialog box.

In the <u>D</u>esktop Icons box, click on the icon you want to change. Then click on the <u>C</u>hange Icon button. From the Change Icon dialog box (see Figure 5.3), select the icon you want to appear on your Desktop. Choose OK twice to close the dialog boxes.

*Note*

**The contents of the Change Icon dialog box will change, depending on the icon you selected.**

*Tip*

Use the D<u>e</u>fault Icon button on the Effects tab of the Display Properties dialog box to return these icons to the default pictures supplied with Windows.

# Adding and Deleting Shortcuts

When you use a program on a regular basis, placing a shortcut to launch the program on your Desktop saves you a lot of time. And creating a shortcut is easy. Here's how to create a shortcut on the Desktop for the Windows 3.1 File Manager (if you prefer it to Windows Explorer).

## Hands On: Creating a Desktop Shortcut from the Find Window

Placing a shortcut on your Desktop from the Find Window is easy. You need to know the name of the file that runs the program for which you want to create a shortcut. The Windows 3.1 File Manager file is called WINFILE.EXE.

1. Choose Start, Find, Files and Folders to display the Find: All Files dialog box (see Figure 5.4).

**Figure 5.4**
Using the Find: All Files dialog box to locate files on your computer.

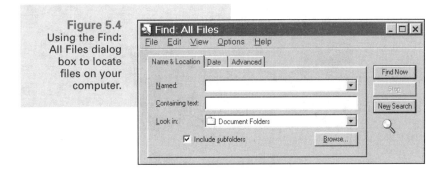

*Tip*

When you don't know the exact file name, you can search using the Browse button.

2. Type **WINFILE.EXE** in the Named box. Case doesn't matter, so you can use all uppercase, all lowercase, or a combination.

3. Change the Look In drop-down list box to search the C drive—where Windows is typically stored in the Windows folder. Make sure that the Include Subfolders check box contains a check or the file won't be found.

4. Click on the Find Now button. The bottom of the Find window expands to display the files that match your search.

5. Right-click on the file for which you want to create a shortcut to display a shortcut menu (see Figure 5.5). In this example, right-click on WINFILE.EXE.

6. Choose the Send To command and, on the submenu that appears, choose Desktop as Shortcut command on the shortcut menu. Windows will place the shortcut on your Desktop.

**Figure 5.5**
Use the Send to
Desktop as
Shortcut
command to
create a shortcut
icon to launch
this program.

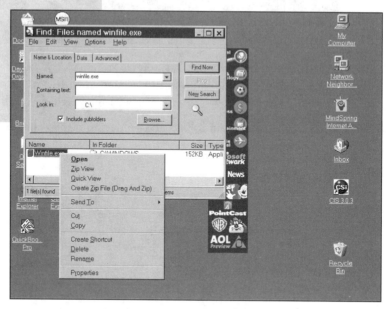

*Note*

You also can drag the file out of the Find window and onto the Desktop to create a shortcut. And, you may be wondering why I didn't tell you to choose Create Shortcut. If you do, you'll see a message telling you Windows cannot create a shortcut in the Find window—and the message will ask you if you want to place the shortcut on the Desktop. So, to avoid a step, I chose a different method.

7. Choose Yes and close the Find window by clicking the X in the upper-right corner of the window. On your Desktop, you'll find an icon that looks like a file cabinet; its name is Shortcut to Winfile.exe (see Figure 5.6).

8. To change the icon's name to something meaningful—like File Manager—highlight the icon and press F2. The current name of the icon appears selected.

9. Type the new name you want for the icon and press Enter when you finish typing. The text you type replaces the selected text, and the name will be changed.

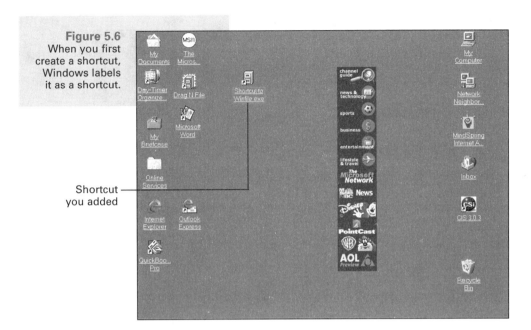

**Figure 5.6**
When you first create a shortcut, Windows labels it as a shortcut.

Shortcut you added

*Note*

**If you are using the Web style Desktop, highlight by simply pointing at the icon—but don't click. If you are using the Classic Desktop, point and click to highlight the icon. If you are unsure, right-click on the icon and choose Rename from the shortcut menu.**

Placing a shortcut on your Desktop is nice, but your Desktop can become cluttered very quickly. An alternative arrangement is to keep only those shortcuts you use many times each day on the Desktop and to place shortcuts on the Programs menu.

## Hands On: Placing a Shortcut on the Programs Menu

Suppose you decide you'd rather have the File Manager icon on the Programs menu—because you use it sometimes, but not enough to clutter up your Desktop. You can drag the shortcut onto the Programs menu.

1. Drag the shortcut you want to move onto the Start button. The Start menu will open.

**Figure 5.7**
Dragging a
shortcut onto the
Programs menu.

Drag here first —

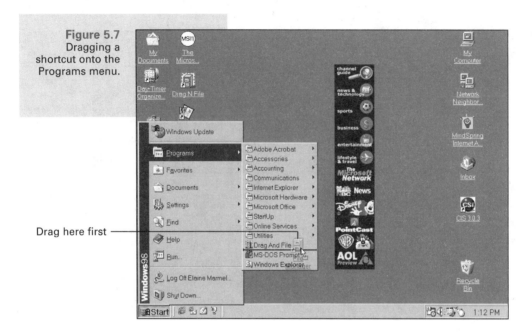

**2.** Continue dragging the shortcut up the Start menu to point to the Programs menu, which will also open.

**3.** Continue dragging down the Programs menu until you see a horizontal bar at the place where you want the File Manager to appear (see Figure 5.7).

**4.** Release the mouse button. A copy of the shortcut appears on the Programs menu.

*Note*

**You may need to click on the Start button again to make the Start menu behave in its typical fashion.**

When you drag a shortcut from the Desktop to the Programs menu, the shortcut appears on both the Programs menu and on the Desktop. Because you don't really need two copies, you can delete one copy of the shortcut. Drag either copy—the one on the Desktop or the one on the Programs menu—into the Recycle Bin. When the Recycle Bin's title becomes highlighted, release the mouse button. You'll see the Confirm File Delete dialog box shown in Figure 5.8.

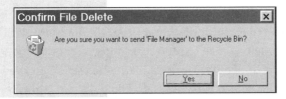

**Figure 5.8**
Windows asks
for confirmation
when you place
an item in the
Recycle Bin.

*Tip*

You can easily place any shortcut on the Quick Launch toolbar. Simply drag the short-cut from its current location—on your Desktop or on the Programs menu—onto the Quick Launch toolbar at the place where you want the shortcut to appear. Windows places a copy of the shortcut on the Quick Launch toolbar, and you can then delete the other copy of the shortcut by dragging it to the Recycle Bin. If any of the icons on the Quick Launch toolbar seems to disappear after you add a shortcut, resize the toolbar by dragging its right edge to the right.

# Shortcuts and DOS Programs

For the most part, you can install and use DOS programs in Windows 98. Because most DOS programs were not created to run in Windows, you'll need to create appropriate shortcuts. You can use the same technique you used to create a shortcut for a Windows program, or you can use Windows Explorer.

*Note*

**I've noticed that some DOS programs simply won't install or run on some faster Pentium machines. If you have trouble with a DOS program, talk to the program's manufacturer to determine whether the speed of your machine might be affecting your ability to run the program.**

**Hands On:   Using Windows Explorer to Create a Desktop Shortcut**

This technique works best if the Windows Explorer window is *not* maximized—that is, you can see a portion of the Desktop behind Explorer.

1. Open Windows Explorer by choosing Start, Programs, Windows Explorer.
2. Open the folder that contains the program.
3. Highlight the program file.

*Note*

By default, Windows doesn't display extensions such as EXE, which can make the job of finding the program file more difficult. To display these extensions, use Explorer's menus to choose View, Folder Options. In the Folder Options dialog box, click on the View tab. Remove the check from the Hide File Extensions for Known File Types check box—it's the third box in the Advanced Settings list.

4. Right-click to display a shortcut menu.
5. Choose Send To. From the submenu that appears, choose Desktop as Shortcut (see Figure 5.9). Windows places the shortcut on your Desktop.

**Figure 5.9**
When you create a shortcut in Explorer, you can still place it on your Desktop.

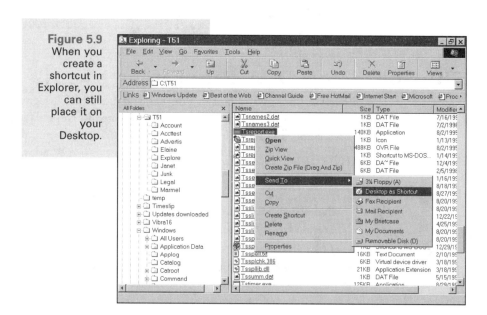

## Working in a DOS Window versus Working in a Full Screen

Once you create a shortcut for a DOS program, Windows typically runs that program in a DOS window—which is smaller than your full screen and may be difficult to see (see Figure 5.10).

**Figure 5.10**
A DOS program running under Windows in a DOS window.

You don't need to suffer—you can tell Windows to use the entire screen for your DOS program when you run it. Right-click on the shortcut you created and choose Properties. In the Properties dialog box, click on the Screen tab (see Figure 5.11). Click on the Full-screen option button and set the Initial Size to Default. Then click on OK. The next time you run the program from the shortcut, it will fill your entire screen.

**Figure 5.11**
Modify the shortcut for your DOS program so that the program fills your screen.

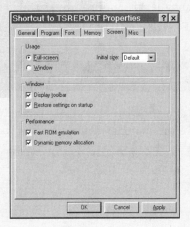

# Understanding Display Properties

Using the Display properties of your video card and Windows 98, you can make changes to what you see and how things behave onscreen. You can enable a screen saver, change the background appearance and color scheme, and change the resolution at which your monitor displays information.

*Note*

**The tabs in your Display Properties dialog box may differ from those shown in the figures in this book. The tabs that appear in the Display Properties dialog box depend on the video card that is installed in your computer.**

## Using a Screen Saver

Screen savers help you avoid burning in images on your monitor. If an image remains onscreen for too long a period of time—several hours without changing—you may begin to see "ghosts" of that image in the background when you use other programs on your computer. For example, in the days of DOS, people often used menu programs to make starting programs easier. The menu program would reappear when you exited from a program. Often, the menu program's image would remain, for hours, on the monitor—and its image would "burn in" the monitor.

A screen saver is an image that appears onscreen after a delay during which no action occurs on the computer. Many third-party vendors sell screen saver programs that predominantly provide entertainment. Windows 98 comes with its own set of screen savers.

### Hands On: Enabling a Windows 98 Screen Saver

1. Right-click on a blank spot on your Desktop and choose Properties from the shortcut menu. The Display Properties dialog box appears.
2. Click on the Screen Saver tab and open the Screen Saver list box (see Figure 5.12).
3. Choose a screen saver. A sample of that screen saver appears on the monitor image in the Display Properties dialog box (see Figure 5.13).

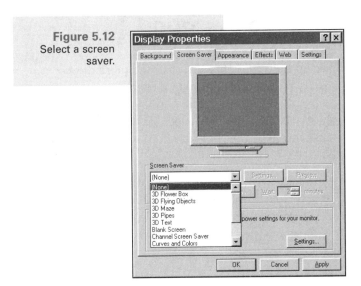

**Figure 5.12**
Select a screen saver.

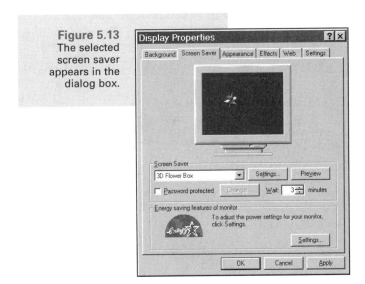

**Figure 5.13**
The selected screen saver appears in the dialog box.

4. Use the <u>W</u>ait spin box to set the amount of time Windows should allow to pass with no action at the computer before displaying the screen saver.

5. Click on the <u>A</u>pply button.

If you don't intend to make any other Display changes, click on OK.

# Controlling the Background of Your Desktop

Spice up the appearance of your computer's display using wallpaper. Wallpapers provide backgrounds on your Desktop—they won't be visible unless you are viewing the Desktop. In the Display Properties dialog box, click on the Background tab. From the Wallpaper list box, select an HTML document to serve as a wallpaper. A sample of your selection appears in the monitor in the dialog box.

*Note*

**If you closed the Display Properties dialog box after the last section, right-click on a blank spot on your Desktop and choose Properties from the shortcut menu.**

Depending on the document you choose, the monitor on the dialog box may be filled or may contain only a portion of the wallpaper. To change the way the wallpaper appears on your monitor, use the Display drop-down list box (see Figures 5.14, 5.15 and 5.16).

**Figure 5.14**
This wallpaper is centered on the monitor.

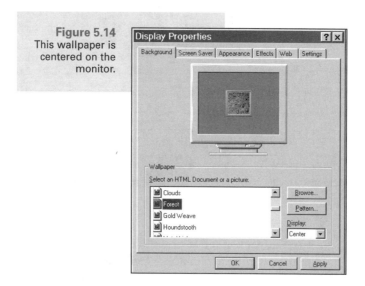

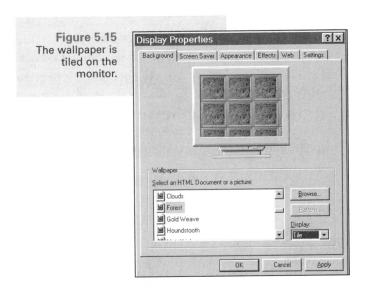

**Figure 5.15**
The wallpaper is tiled on the monitor.

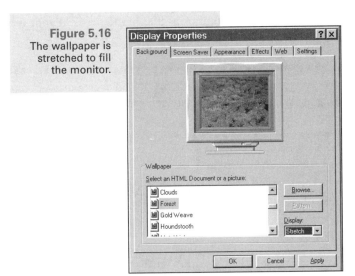

**Figure 5.16**
The wallpaper is stretched to fill the monitor.

# Setting Resolution and Colors

Depending on the age of your monitor and video card, you may be able to change the resolution of the image you view onscreen. The typical resolution for older hardware is 640 × 480 pixels. A pixel is a small dot, and, with a resolution of 640 × 480, images use 640 pixels across the monitor and 480 pixels down the monitor. New monitors and video cards will support 800 × 600 pixels, 1024 × 768 pixels, 1152 × 864 pixels, and 1280 × 1024; some of the newest monitors and

*Caution*

Changing the display resolution can have unexpected results; you may not want to mess with this unless you're certain that both your monitor and your video card are new enough to support setting a higher resolution. Typically, if a resolution setting appears in the dialog box, you can use it. When you change the resolution or the number of colors, you should restart your computer. If Windows doesn't prompt you to restart, you should shut down and restart from the Start menu.

video cards will display a resolution of 1600 × 1200. The higher the resolution you choose, the more information you can view onscreen, but the smaller the information gets. With lower resolutions, such as 640 × 480, images do not appear as crisp as they appear in higher resolutions, but the image is larger. A fairly nice working resolution is 800 × 600 pixels, if your monitor and video card support it.

*Tip*

If you choose a resolution of 800 x 600 and decide that text appears too small, consider using one of the large color schemes in Windows. See the next section for more information.

*Note*

If the Display Properties dialog box is not open, right-click on a blank spot on your Desktop and choose Properties from the shortcut menu.

To change resolution, use the Settings tab of the Display Properties dialog box (see Figure 5.17). Change the resolution by sliding the bar in the Screen Area box to the left or right. Sliding to the left lowers the resolution; sliding to the right increases it.

You also can control the number of colors your monitor displays using the Colors drop-down list box. Open the drop-down list box and choose the number of colors you want your computer to display. Be aware that, although the scheme may be available, some programs may not work properly if you choose a higher

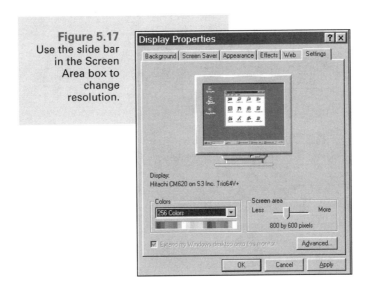

**Figure 5.17**
Use the slide bar
in the Screen
Area box to
change
resolution.

number of colors. Most software today will work fine with 256 Colors; depending on the software you use, you may be able to choose High Color or True Color.

# Choosing Color Schemes

*Note*

**If the Display Properties dialog box is not open, right-click on a blank spot on your Desktop and choose Properties from the shortcut menu.**

Color schemes determine the colors of dialog box title bars and text, the background of your Desktop if you haven't selected a wallpaper, scroll bars, and other screen elements. To choose a color scheme, use the Appearance tab of the Display Properties dialog box. Open the Scheme drop-down list box (see Figure 5.18) and select a scheme; a sample of the color scheme will appear on the tab.

By customizing one of the existing color schemes, you can create your own color scheme. Open the Item drop-down list box and select the element you want to customize. Depending on the item, you can control its color and size as well as the font used for it, the font color, the font size, and the font attributes (regular, bold, or italic type).

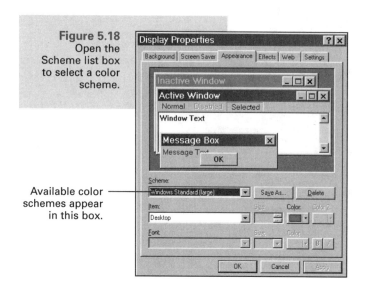

**Figure 5.18**
Open the
Scheme list box
to select a color
scheme.

Available color
schemes appear
in this box.

# Customizing the Desktop

In Windows 98, you can customize your Desktop in several ways. You can view Internet content directly on your Desktop. You also can set options for the way you view folders in Windows 98, and you'll find some new toolbars in Windows 98.

## Viewing the Desktop as a Web Page

The expression *viewing your Desktop as a Web page* is synonymous with "using the Active Desktop." Both mean that you can set up your Desktop so that it displays the content of an Internet Web page. The Web page can act as wallpaper, and if you are always linked to the Internet, your Desktop will be updated as often as the Web page is updated.

*Note*

**If you are not always linked to the Internet, you must connect to the Web to update a Web page wallpaper.**

Although you can load an entire Web page, you can, instead, load just certain elements, such as a stock ticker, weather information, or news headlines. To enable the Active Desktop, right-click on a blank spot on the Desktop, highlight the Active Desktop command, and choose View as Web Page (see Figure 5.19).

**Figure 5.19**
Use this menu to
turn on the
Active Desktop.

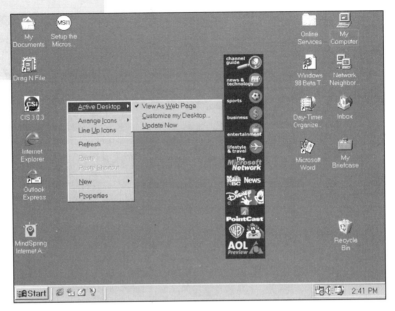

## Choosing an Active Desktop

Microsoft maintains an Active Desktop Gallery from which you can choose an
Active Desktop for your computer. If you right-click on the Desktop and choose
Active Desktop, Customize the Desktop, you'll see the Web tab of the Display
Properties dialog box. Click on New to display the dialog box shown in Figure
5.20 that helps you log on to Microsoft's Active Desktop Gallery Web site (see
Figure 5.21), where you can choose Active Desktops for your computer.

**Figure 5.20**
Use this dialog
box to navigate
to the Active
Desktop Gallery
Web page.

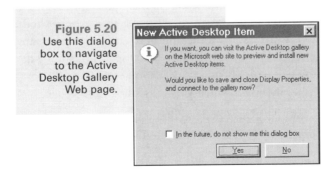

Figure 5.21
Use the Gallery
Index on this
Web page to
select Active
Desktop items
for your
computer.

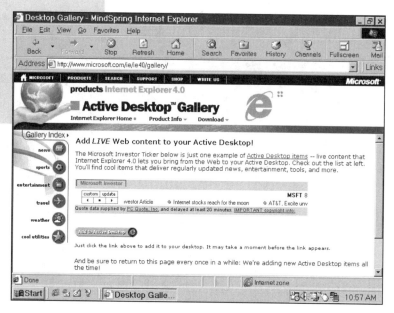

Click on one of the icons in the Gallery Index to see the choices for that category. In Figure 5.22, I chose News and then CNET. To add an item to your Desktop, click on the Add to Active Desktop button.

*Note*

**You may see security alerts while adding an item to the active desktop. To complete the add process, you'll need to accept the content.**

**For more information on customizing a subscription, see Chapter 17.**

Typically, you'll see a confirmation dialog box and then a message box that indicates that you have chosen to subscribe to a channel and add it to your Active Desktop. You'll also have the option to customize your subscription to determine how often information on your Desktop is updated. The information on your Desktop will typically update when you connect to the Internet, based on the settings you established when you subscribed to the page.

When you click on OK, you'll see documents downloading. When the download finishes, you'll have, on your Desktop, your own personal version of the

Figure 5.22
Add an item to
the Active
Desktop.

Click here

item you selected. It will show live information as long as you are connected to the Internet. Because the Desktop is "active," you can click on links that appear on the Active Desktop item (see Figure 5.23) and load associated Web pages (see Figure 5.24).

# Viewing Folders as Web Pages

You can make folders appear in Web page format; when you choose this option, you'll see additional information about the items in a folder as you highlight them.

The default view for the contents of My Computer looks like the one in Figure 5.25. To view the contents of My Computer as a Web page, choose View, As Web Page; the Web page view looks like Figure 5.26. When you select an item in a folder viewed as a Web page, information about the item appears graphically at the left edge of the folder.

Suppose you decide you really like viewing folders as Web pages—and that, while you work in Windows Explorer, you'd like all folders to look like Web Pages.

**Figure 5.23**
You can hyperlink from your Desktop to a Web page.

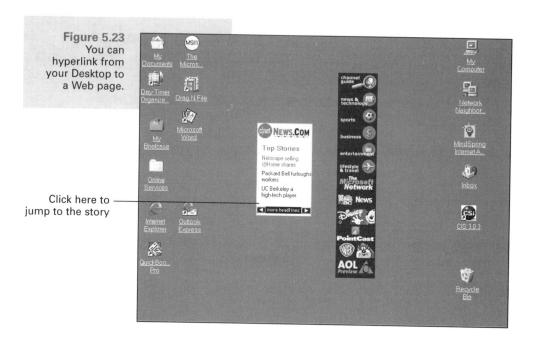

Click here to jump to the story

**Figure 5.24**
The Web page displayed from the Desktop hyperlink.

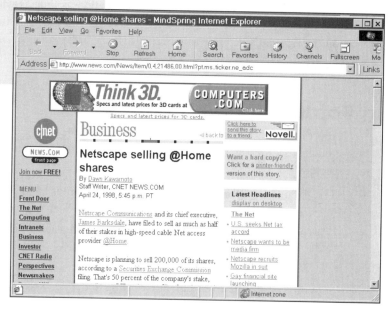

**Figure 5.25**
The default view
of My Computer.

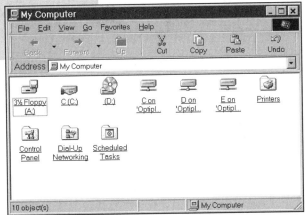

**Figure 5.26**
My Computer
when viewed as
a Web page.

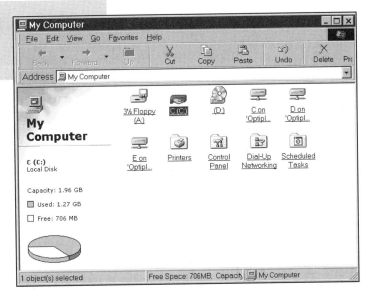

## Hands On: Viewing All Folders in Windows Explorer as Web Pages

1. Right-click on the Start button and choose <u>E</u>xplore. Windows Explorer will appear.

2. Open any folder to select it.

3. Choose <u>V</u>iew, As <u>W</u>eb Page. The folder appears in the right pane of Windows Explorer as a Web page (see Figure 5.27).

*Tip*

• • • • • • • • • • • • • • • • • • • • • • • • • • • • • • • • • • • • • • • • • • • • • • • • •

If you change your mind, you can return all folders to the classic Windows style using the same technique. Select one folder and repeat steps 1–3.

• • • • • • • • • • • • • • • • • • • • • • • • • • • • • • • • • • • • • • • • • • • • • • • • •

**Figure 5.27**
Viewing a folder in Windows Explorer as a Web page.

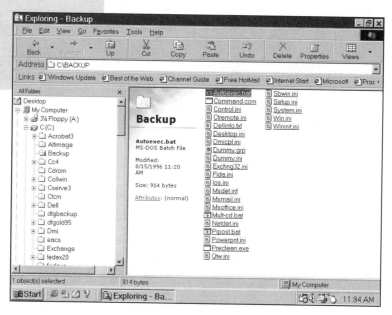

# Windows 98 and Toolbars

For more information on the Quick Launch toolbar, see Chapter 2.

In the past, the Windows Taskbar was a useful tool for switching between open programs. Now you can make it more useful by adding toolbars to the Windows Taskbar; these toolbars can help you open programs, files, folders, or even Web pages. If you prefer, you can place toolbars on any part of your Desktop.

Windows contains four predefined toolbars that you can add to the Taskbar: the Quick Launch toolbar, the Address toolbar, the Links toolbar, and the Desktop toolbar. In addition, you can create your own toolbars.

*Note*

**By default, these toolbars are added to the Taskbar. You can, however, drag the toolbar onto your Desktop and leave it there. You can even resize it by dragging its edges.**

## Address Toolbar

If you are connected to the Internet already, you can use the Address toolbar to go to a Web page address (URL) without first opening Internet Explorer: simply type the address and press Enter. Windows will launch Internet Explorer and go to the URL you typed. You can also search for Web sites just by typing **Find**, **Go**, or **?** before the word for which you want to search.

*Note*

**If you are not already connected to the Web, you must connect first before trying to use the Address toolbar.**

To add the Address toolbar to your Taskbar, right-click on an empty space on the Taskbar. A shortcut menu appears (see Figure 5.28). Highlight Toolbars and choose Address. Windows adds the Address toolbar to the Taskbar (see Figure 5.29).

**Figure 5.28**
Adding the
Address toolbar
to the Taskbar.

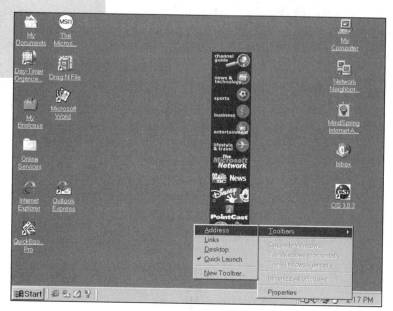

**Figure 5.29**
Use the Address
toolbar to type
URLs and
connect to
Web pages.

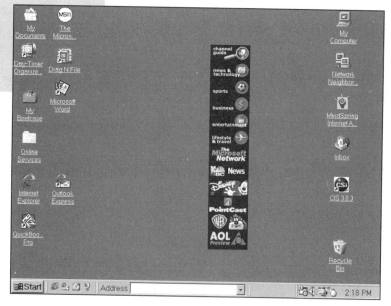

You can resize the toolbar by dragging one of the light gray vertical bars that appear at either edge of the toolbar. The mouse pointer shape changes to a pair of black vertical bars as you drag.

## Links Toolbar

If you choose to display the Links toolbar on the Taskbar, you'll see a list of the Internet links stored in the Links subfolder of the Favorites folder (choose Start, Favorites to see the Links subfolder). When you display the Links toolbar, you give yourself an easy way to open a URL without first opening your browser—assuming you are connected to the Internet when you click on the link.

To add the Links toolbar to your Taskbar, right-click on an empty space on the Taskbar. A shortcut menu appears (refer to Figure 5.28). Highlight Toolbars and choose Links. Windows adds the Links toolbar to the Taskbar (see Figure 5.30).

> You can also resize the Taskbar to make the information more visible. For more information about resizing the Taskbar, see Chapter 7.

If you change your mind and don't want to display a toolbar, right-click on the toolbar and choose Close. A dialog box asks you to confirm closing the toolbar. Choose OK.

**Figure 5.30**
Use the Links toolbar to connect to URLs stored in the Links subfolder of the Favorites folder.

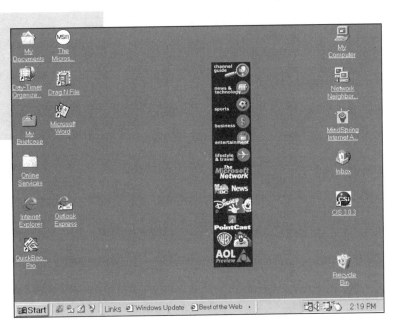

# Desktop Toolbar

Would you like a toolbar that contains all the icons on your Desktop? Display the Desktop toolbar in the Taskbar. Right-click on an empty space on the Taskbar, and a shortcut menu appears (refer to Figure 5.28). Highlight Toolbars and choose Desktop. Windows adds the Desktop toolbar to the Taskbar (see Figure 5.31).

*Note*

**Rather than using the Desktop toolbar, you may prefer to add shortcuts for programs you use regularly to the Quick Launch toolbar. Simply drag the shortcut from its current location—on your Desktop or on the Programs menu—onto the Quick Launch toolbar at the place where you want the shortcut to appear. Windows places a copy of the shortcut on the Quick Launch toolbar. You can then delete the other copy of the shortcut.**

**Figure 5.31**
The Desktop toolbar contains all the icons that appear on your Desktop.

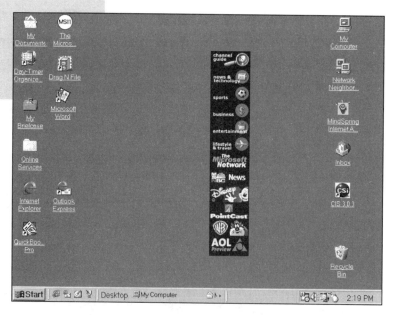

## Creating Your Own Toolbar

Perhaps you have a set of icons you'd like to display on a Taskbar—no problem. You can create your own toolbar and place it on the Taskbar. The only requirement is that all the icons for your toolbar must appear in the same folder. So, if necessary, use Windows Explorer to create a folder and then copy shortcuts for the programs you want on your toolbar into that folder. Then right-click on an empty space on the Taskbar, highlight Toolbars, and choose New Toolbar. Windows displays the New Toolbar dialog box (see Figure 5.32).

Navigate to the folder containing the icons you want on your toolbar and choose OK. Windows places your new toolbar on the Taskbar.

You can create a toolbar that contains Control Panel icons if you use the Control Panel frequently. Just choose the Control Panel folder in the New Toolbar dialog box.

**Figure 5.32**
Use this dialog box to select a folder containing icons you want on your toolbar.

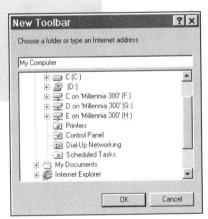

# 6

# Installing and Configuring Printers

## IN THIS CHAPTER

- **The Basics of Printing**
- **Using a Printer Other Than the Default Printer**
- **Printing to a File**
- **Deleting a Printer**
- **Installing a New Printer**
- **Setting the Default Printer**
- **Printing to a File**

By default, when you installed the operating system, Windows walked you through installing a printer. But times change, and so do printers. Perhaps you switched to a different printer, or perhaps you added a second (or third) printer. The purpose of this chapter is to examine printer issues.

# The Basics of Printing

In the days of DOS, you needed to install a printer for each program, but Windows changed that unhappy situation. In Windows 98, as in previous versions of Windows, you set up your printer only once—and then each application uses that printer. When you "install a printer," you take two basic steps. First, you physically attach the printer to your computer; then you tell the operating system about your printer by installing drivers for the printer. (*Drivers* are software programs that tell the operating system which printer is attached to your computer and how that printer behaves.) With this information, the operating system is ready to handle printing jobs.

When you print, you do so from inside some software program. The program sends the print job to the printer, and the operating system takes over and controls the printing process. Therefore, because the operating system controls the printer, typically, printer problems are *not* related to the program from which you are printing.

*Note*

If you find that you have problems printing, try using the Print Troubleshooting wizard. To run any Troubleshooting wizard, refer to Chapter 2.

When you buy a new printer, you may notice that disks come in the box along with the printer. These disks contain drivers that will make the printer behave correctly. Often the disks contain drivers that were created *after* the operating system was created. If you find disks in the box along with your printer, you should use the drivers on those disks instead of letting the operating system install its version of the drivers. You may also want to check the printer manufacturer's Web site for updated drivers. You will be less likely to encounter printer problems if you use drivers supplied by the printer's manufacturer than if you use the operating system drivers.

For information on setting up a network printer, see Chapter 14.

# Installing a New Printer

Suppose that you buy a new printer. You need to tell the operating system about your printer by installing printer drivers. Even in this day of Plug and Play, the operating system will not automatically "find" many printers if you simply plug them in. You must actually go through an installation process.

You may also need to add a new printer driver for an existing printer. For example, the HP LaserJet 5 prints, by default, at 600 dpi (dots per inch). You may want that kind of resolution most of the time, but at other times, you may want only 300 dpi. You can switch the resolution of the HP LaserJet 5 to 300 dpi, but then you need to remember to switch it back to 600 dpi as appropriate. As an alternative, you can use the HP LaserJet III driver, which prints only at 300 dpi, to print on your HP LasetJet 5 printer at 300 dpi. Although this arrangement may sound strange, the HPLaserJet 5 will use the HP LaserJet III driver and print at 300 dpi. In a case like this, you install both printer drivers.

## Hands On: Installing Printer Drivers

1. Close all programs so that nothing is running before you start installing drivers.
2. Choose Start, Settings, Printers to display the Printers folder (see Figure 6.1).

**Figure 6.1**
From the Printers folder, you can view printers currently installed as well as add a new printer.

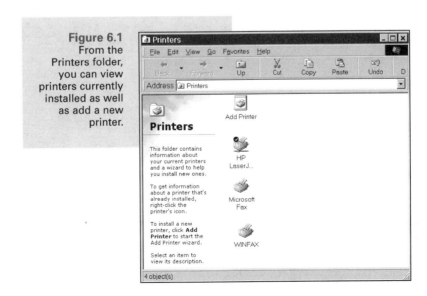

To learn how to install a network printer—a printer *not* attached directly to your computer—see Chapter 14.

3. Click on the Add Printer icon to start the Add a Printer Wizard. The first dialog box of this Wizard explains that it will help you install your printer.

4. Click on Next. In the dialog box shown in Figure 6.2, choose Local Printer to install a printer that is directly attached to your computer.

5. Click on Next. Windows builds the list of printer drivers it can use to install a printer (see Figure 6.3).

**Figure 6.2**
Choose Local Printer to install drivers for a printer that is attached directly to your computer.

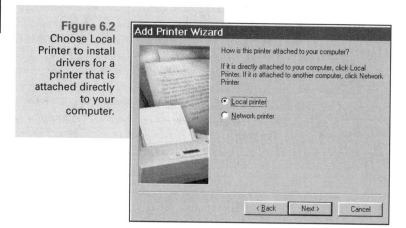

**Figure 6.3**
The list of printer drivers available from Windows.

*Tip*

If you have floppy disks for your printer, complete only steps 1-5; then insert the first disk in your floppy drive and click on the Have Disk button you see in Figure 6.3. Windows launches the printer installation routine provided on the disk, and you'll see a wizard that walks you through the rest of the installation process.

6. From the Manufacturers list, select the manufacturer of your printer. The available printers from that particular manufacturer appear in the Printers list. Select the correct printer.

7. Click on Next. Select a port to attach when you see the dialog box shown in Figure 6.4. Most of the time, printers are attached to LPT1.

8. Click on Next. Supply a name for the printer you're installing or use the one suggested. In the dialog box shown in Figure 6.5, you also can specify whether you want to make this printer the default printer.

9. Click on Next. On the last screen of the Add a Printer Wizard, you can choose to print a test page (see Figure 6.6).

10. Click on Finish. Windows prompts you to insert your Windows CD-ROM so that it can copy the appropriate printer driver to your computer (see Figure 6.7).

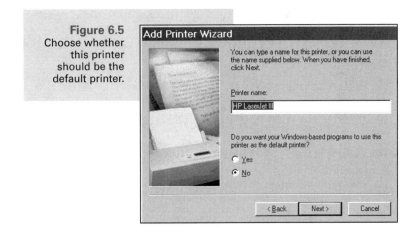

**Figure 6.4** Select the port to which your printer is attached.

**Figure 6.5** Choose whether this printer should be the default printer.

11. Click on OK. Windows copies the correct files to your computer and places an icon for the printer in the Printers folder (see Figure 6.8).

**Figure 6.6**
Print a test page to make sure the printer prints correctly.

**Figure 6.7**
Insert the Windows CD-ROM to allow Windows to copy the correct printer driver to your computer.

**Figure 6.8**
After Windows copies the driver files, an icon for the new printer appears in the Printers folder.

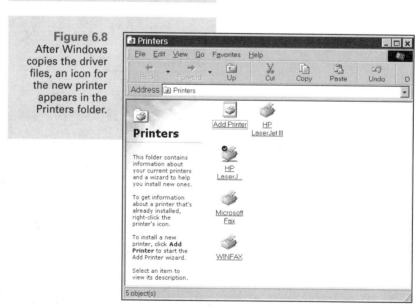

# Setting the Default Printer

As you saw, you can choose to make the new printer you're adding the default printer during printer installation. But what if you decide, after installation, that you want to set a different printer as the default printer? Open the Printers folder (choose Start, Settings, Printers) and highlight the printer you want to use as the default printer. Right-click to display a shortcut menu (see Figure 6.9) and choose Set as Default. You can always identify the default printer because Windows places a check mark next to it (see Figure 6.9).

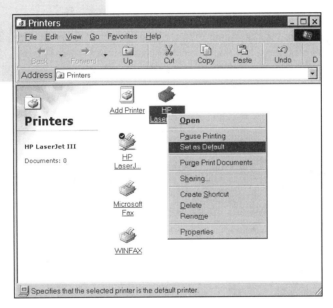

**Figure 6.9**
Selecting a new printer as the default printer.

*Note*

**Each printer has a set of specific options. You can access the options for a printer by right-clicking on the printer's icon and choosing Properties to display the Properties dialog box. The default setup for most printers is the one you'd typically use: 8-1/2 by 11 paper with portrait orientation. If you need to change these options for all programs, use the printer's Properties box. If you need to make a "one-time" change for a particular document that you're printing, use the application from which you're printing to make the change.**

# Using a Printer Other Than the Default Printer

Suppose you're working in an application and you want to print to a printer that is not the default printer. Do you have to change the default printer to the printer you want? No. You simply select the printer to which you want to print while working in the application.

For example, to print a Microsoft Word document to a printer other than the default printer, don't click the Print button on the Standard toolbar; instead, choose File, Print to open the Print dialog box. Click on the arrow next to the Name list to select the printer to which you want to print (see Figure 6.10).

If you save the document with a printer selection other than the default printer, some programs, like Word, will remember that setting—and always print to the selected printer rather than to the default printer.

**Figure 6.10**
Select the printer to which you want to print.

# Printing to a File

Occasionally, you may want to print a document to a file. This action works well when you need to create a file containing specific data and the application in which you're working won't let you create a text file. This task is easy to accomplish using a Generic printer.

Start the Add Printer Wizard (from the Printers folder, click on the Add Printer icon). Click on Next in the first dialog box and select Local Printer in the second dialog box. When the list of printers appears, select Generic in the Manufacturers list and Generic / Text Only in the Printers list (see Figure 6.11). Click on Next to display the available ports and choose FILE: (see Figure 6.12).

**Figure 6.11**
Select the Generic printer.

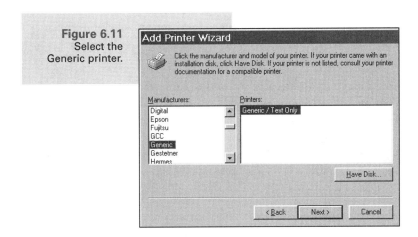

**Figure 6.12**
Place the Generic printer on the FILE: port.

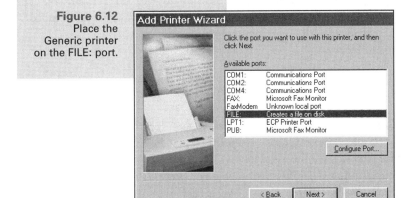

Click on Next to assign a name and determine whether this printer should be the default printer—typically, it should *not* be the default printer. Click on Next. In the dialog box you see, choose to skip printing a test page and click Finish. Insert the Windows 98 CD-ROM and allow Windows to install the drivers necessary for the Generic printer.

Use the Generic printer the same way you would use any non-default printer. Open an application and prepare something to print. Then choose File, Print. In the Print dialog box, select the Generic printer. When you choose OK, Windows displays a dialog box that resembles the Save As dialog box. When you print to a file, you actually create a file; and whenever you create a file, either by saving or by printing, you must supply a file name. Windows suggests a printer file extension of .PRN (see Figure 6.13).

The file that you create by printing to a Generic printer does not contain printer codes that tell a printer how to behave when printing a file. Nor does it contain any formatting that might have been applied originally. For this reason, you can open and view a file you "printed" to a Generic printer using the Windows Notepad or WordPad. In either case, you won't see any formatting.

# Deleting a Printer

If you no longer need a particular printer, you can easily delete it. Right-click on the printer's icon and choose <u>D</u>elete. If no other printer needs the files used by the printer you deleted, Windows deletes those files as well. If you delete the default printer, Windows automatically assigns a new default printer—and if Windows assigns a printer you don't want as the default, you need to select a new default printer.

# Customizing the Start Menu and Taskbar

## IN THIS CHAPTER

- **Organizing the Programs Menu**
- **Modifying the Start Menu**
- **Working with the Taskbar**

You don't have to settle for the default views of the Programs menu, the Start menu, or the Taskbar. Typically, you want your computer Desktop to accurately reflect the way you work. So you should make these tools work for you. You can organize the Programs menu and the Start menu to help you work more efficiently, and you can move the Taskbar to a location other than the bottom of your screen (or you can hide it altogether).

# Organizing the Programs Menu

Every time you install a new program on your computer, that program adds a something—either an icon or a group—to the Programs menu. In Windows 98, new items appear at the bottom of the Programs menu, which can make finding things even more difficult.

But you don't have to settle for the default placement of items on the Programs menu. You can move items around, and you can organize items on the Programs menu so that they appear the way you want them to appear.

## Rearranging Entries

Whenever you install a program, the program typically creates either an icon or a folder containing several icons that you need to run the program. The icon or the folder appears at the bottom of the Programs menu. A typical Programs menu can look like the one in Figure 7.1.

**Figure 7.1**
As you install software, each new program adds an icon or a folder to the Programs menu.

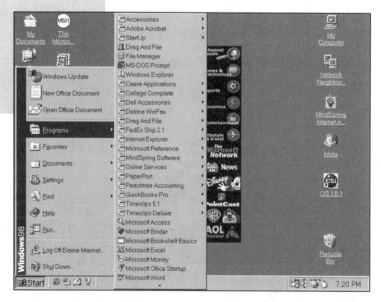

But suppose you want to move an entry on the Programs menu so that it appears in a different location. Suppose, for example, that you decide you'd like Microsoft Word to appear at the top of the menu. You can move the entry simply by dragging and dropping it.

## Hands On: Changing the Position of a Program Menu Entry

1. Click on the Start button and highlight <u>P</u>rograms.
2. Point at the entry you want to move.
3. Press and hold the left mouse button to select the entry.
4. Move the mouse up or down. As you move the mouse, several things happen (refer to Figure 7.2):
   - A box surrounds the item you selected.
   - The mouse pointer changes to an arrow with a box attached.
   - A horizontal line marks the position of the entry if you were to drop it.
5. Move the mouse until the horizontal line appears at the location where you want to place the entry.
6. Release the mouse button to drop the entry at its new location.

**Figure 7.2**
The potential location of the item appears as a horizontal line while you drag the item on the Programs menu.

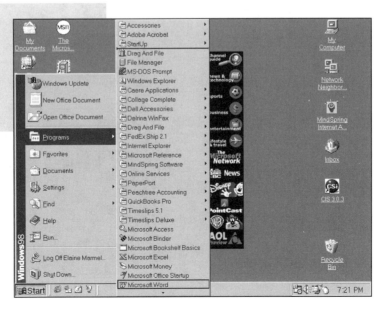

# Making Folders to Organize the Programs Menu

Moving entries around on the Programs menu can help, but as you add more and more software, the list can get so long that you'll see an arrow at the bottom (refer to Figure 7.2). If you click on the arrow, the menu will scroll down to display additional items, but you won't be able to see the items at the top of the menu. Instead, the arrow will appear at the top of the menu.

*Note*

**This arrow is a change from the way Windows 95 originally worked. In the original edition of Windows 95, Windows would display multiple panes for the Programs menu when you had so many programs that they wouldn't all fit on one pane.**

For some of us, having a list that long is just overwhelming. Folders can be useful to organize not only your hard drive, but also your Programs menu. If you use folders to organize the Programs menu, you can shorten it significantly. In Figure 7.3, I've reduced the size of the Programs menu by creating "subject" folders—and placing program folders in the correct subject folder.

**Figure 7.3**
The Programs menu reorganized using subject folders.

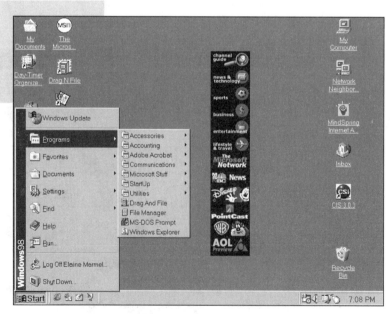

For this kind of organizational effort, you'll find it easiest to work in the Explorer view of your Programs menu. Right-click on the Taskbar and choose Properties or choose Start, Settings, Taskbar & Start Menu. Then click on the Start Menu Programs tab (see Figure 7.4).

*Note*

**The Add and Remove buttons on this tab provide an alternative method for adding and removing shortcuts. However, the method described in Chapter 5 is shorter.**

Click on the Advanced button to display the contents of the Start Menu folder stored in the \Windows folder (see Figure 7.5). This view might seem familiar; you could have gotten here by opening Windows Explorer and viewing the contents of the Start Menu folder stored in the Windows folder. Using the Taskbar Properties dialog box is just a faster way to get here. And, conceptually, you now know that the Start menu is a folder stored in the Windows folder of your computer; in addition, the Programs menu is a folder stored in the Start Menu folder. Because you have actually opened Windows Explorer, all the rules of Windows Explorer apply.

**Figure 7.4**
From the Start Menu Programs tab, you can customize the Start menu.

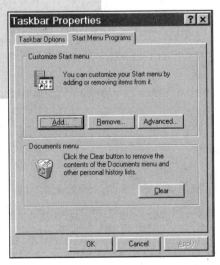

**Figure 7.5**
The contents of
the Start Menu
folder in the
Windows folder.

## Hands On: Organizing Program Menu Entries by Subject

1. Click on the Programs folder in the left pane to display the contents of the Programs menu in the right pane (see Figure 7.6).

2. Choose File, New, Folder. The new folder appears at the end of the list, with the words New Folder selected so that you can easily rename the folder (see Figure 7.7).

3. Type a name for the subject or category and press Enter. Windows renames the folder.

4. Select entries from the list in the right pane. You can use the following selection techniques:

   ■ To select multiple, contiguous entries, highlight the first entry. Then press and hold the Shift key while selecting the last entry.

   ■ To select multiple, noncontiguous entries, press and hold the Ctrl key. Then click on each entry you want to select.

*Tip*

Remember, in Web view, you only need to point—don't click—to select.

**Figure 7.6**
The contents of the Programs menu appear in folder form in the Explorer view.

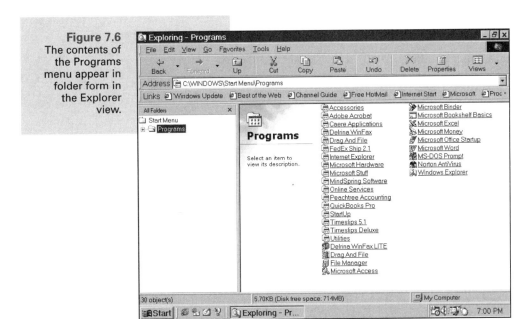

**Figure 7.7**
A new Folder waiting to be renamed.

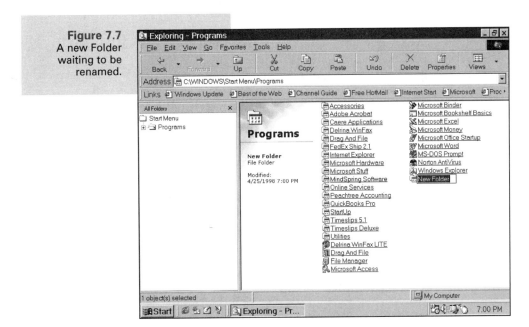

5. Drag the selected entries onto the new folder you created. Figure 7.8 shows two entries (Peachtree Accounting and Timeslips Deluxe) being

**Figure 7.8**
Select entries
and drag them
into the folder
you created.

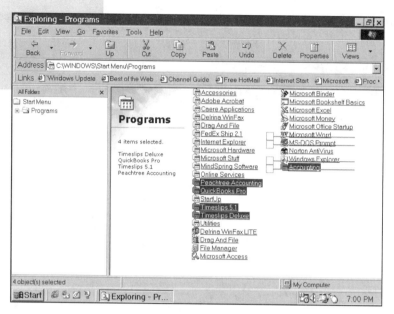

**Figure 7.8**
Select entries
and drag them
into the folder
you created.

dragged into the Accounting folder. As you drag, you'll see outlines for the selected entries. The target folder—Accounting in the example—changes colors when you move the mouse pointer over it.

6. Drop the selected entries into the folder. The entries disappear from the pane on the right.

7. To view the contents of the new folder, click on the plus sign to the left of the Programs folder in the left pane. The folders in the left pane will be re-sorted alphabetically.

8. Open the new folder you created. The entries you dropped there will appear (see Figure 7.9).

9. Repeat these steps for each subject folder you intend to create.

10. When you finish organizing, close the Explorer window, and click on OK to close Taskbar Properties dialog box.

As you can see from Figure 7.10, I created subjects for Accounting, Communications, and Utilities. I also created a group for Microsoft Stuff; inside that folder, I can place separate folders for various Microsoft products such as Office 97 or Intellimouse. Although you cannot tell from Figure 7.10, I also created a few new folders and placed them in the Accessories menu. For example, I created a folder on the Accessories menu for scanner-related applications and placed the Caere Applications and Paperport folders inside it. To get the Scanner folder inside the

**Figure 7.9**
The new folder contains the entries you dragged into it.

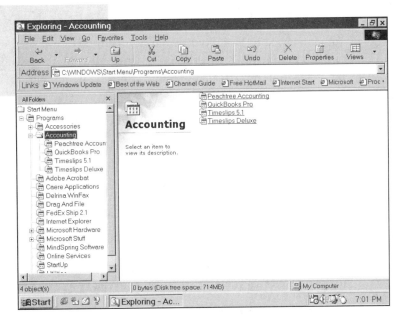

Accessories folder, I created the Scanner folder using the preceding instructions, including moving the entries I wanted inside it. Then I dragged the Scanner folder onto the Accessories folder.

**Figure 7.10**
A reorganized Start and Programs menu.

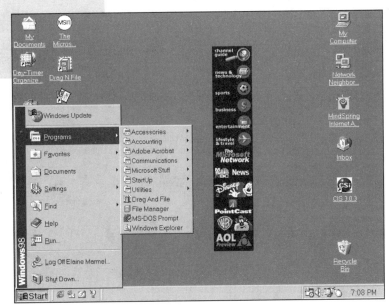

# Making Changes to the Start Menu

You don't need to limit your organization efforts to just the Programs menu; you can also modify the top of the Start menu, either by adding items to it or removing items from it. Let's first examine removing items from the Start menu.

Office 97 places two icons near the top of the Start menu: Open Office Document and New Office Document. Windows 98 places Windows Update near the top of the Start menu (see Figure 7.11).

Suppose you don't want those items at the top of the Start menu. You can move them to the Programs menu, using the same basic technique described in the preceding section. Again, open the Explorer view of the Start Menu folder by choosing Start, Settings, Taskbar & Start Menu. Then click on the Start Menu Programs tab and choose Advanced. If you want to place the elements directly on the Programs menu *without* placing them in a folder on the Programs menu, make sure the Start Menu folder is open in the left pane. Then use the right pane to drag the entries you want to move onto the Programs folder (see Figure 7.12).

To move the entries off the Start menu but into a folder on the Programs menu, first create the folder using the technique described in the preceding section. Then make sure you can see the folders in the Programs folder; if you see a plus sign to the left of the Programs folder, click on it so that you see a minus sign (see Figure 7.13).

**Figure 7.11**
You can move the entries that appear at the top of the Start Menu.

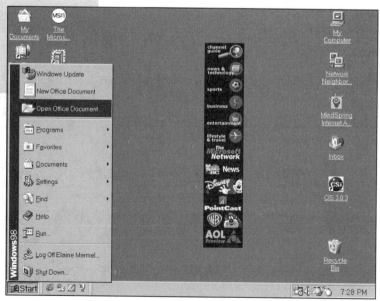

**Figure 7.12**
To move entries from the Start Menu folder directly onto the Programs menu, use the right pane to drag them to the Programs folder.

**Figure 7.13**
You'll be able to see the folders in the Programs folder when the symbol to the left of the Programs folder appears as a minus sign.

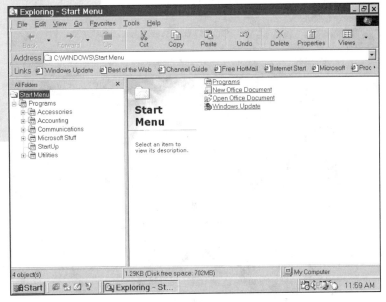

Next, click on the Start Menu folder so that its contents appear in the right pane. Last, drag the entries from the right pane into the correct folder in the left pane.

The process of adding items to the Start menu is the opposite of the process for removing items from the Start menu. You drag the item you want on the Start menu from the Programs menu—or from a folder that appears on the Programs menu.

# Managing the Taskbar

The Taskbar in Windows can be very useful, particularly if you run several programs at one time and need to switch between them often. By default, the Taskbar appears at the bottom of your screen and appears to be about 1/2 inch thick. You can, however, move the Taskbar or resize the Taskbar—or you can hide the Taskbar altogether and make it appear only when you need it.

## Moving the Taskbar

Want to try out the Taskbar in a new location onscreen? You can place it along any edge of the screen by dragging it. Click on an empty location on the Taskbar and drag it to the location of your choice. In Figure 7.14, the Taskbar appears on the right edge of the screen.

**Figure 7.14**
Move the Taskbar to any edge of your screen.

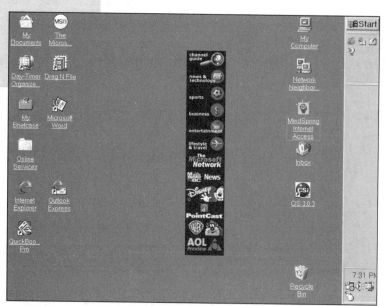

When you move the Taskbar, Windows will automatically adjust the placement of Desktop shortcuts if they will be covered by the repositioned Taskbar.

## Resizing the Taskbar

See chapter 5 for more information on these toolbars.

Resizing the Taskbar is particularly useful if you choose to display any extra toolbars, since Windows places them on the Taskbar. Suppose, for example, that you want to use the Address toolbar. If you open several programs along with the Address toolbar, you can identify only one of the programs at a time because of the lack of space on the Taskbar (see Figure 7.15).

But if you resize the Taskbar to make it larger, your view improves dramatically (see Figure 7.16). To resize the Taskbar, move the mouse pointer over the top edge of the Taskbar until the pointer becomes a two-headed arrow (see Figure 7.17). Drag in an upward motion. The Taskbar increases in size in ½-inch increments. Release the mouse button when the Taskbar reaches the desired size.

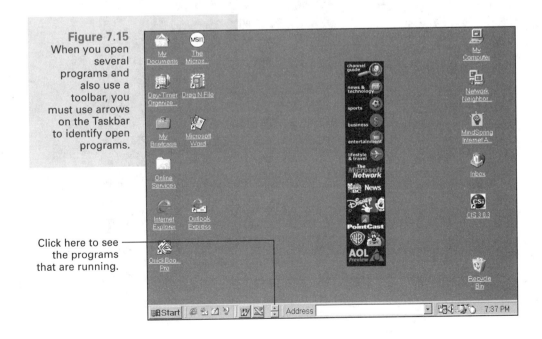

**Figure 7.15**
When you open several programs and also use a toolbar, you must use arrows on the Taskbar to identify open programs.

Click here to see the programs that are running.

**Figure 7.16**
Resize the
Taskbar to see
more entries.

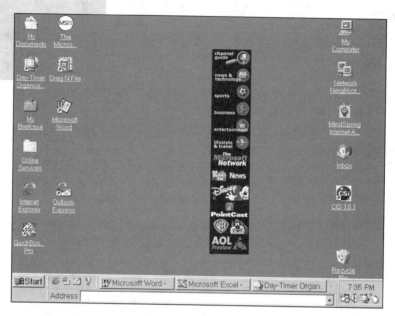

**Figure 7.17**
To resize the
Taskbar, drag
when the mouse
pointer looks like
a two-headed
arrow.

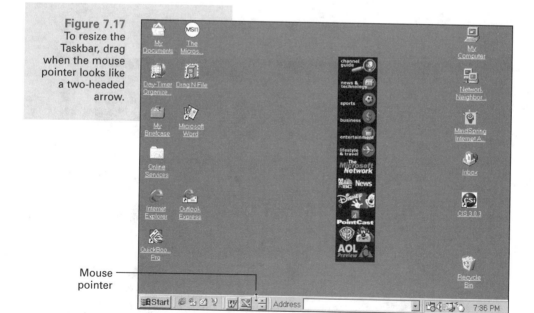

Mouse
pointer

*Note*

**When you resize the Taskbar, you lose some working space in your applications. If the ½ inch you lose is important to you, reconsider using the toolbar.**

# Hiding the Taskbar

If you tend to (a) run only one program at a time or (b) not switch between programs a great deal, viewing the Taskbar all the time may annoy you or distract you. You can use the Taskbar's AutoHide feature to display the Taskbar only when you want to see it. By using the AutoHide feature, you increase the viewing area in applications by ½ inch.

Right-click on an empty space on the Taskbar and choose Properties. The Taskbar Properties dialog box appears (see Figure 7.18).

Place a check in the Auto Hide check box and click on OK. The Taskbar disappears into the edge of your monitor and the dialog box closes (see Figure 7.19).

When you need the Taskbar, slide the mouse pointer into the area where the Taskbar would normally appear and it will reappear (see Figure 7.20).

When you move the mouse pointer out of the Taskbar area, Windows automatically hides the Taskbar again.

**Figure 7.18**
Use this dialog box to set the Taskbar to automatically hide itself.

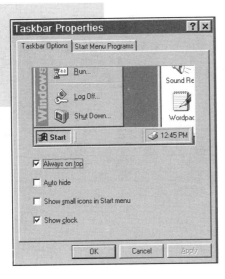

**Figure 7.19**
The Desktop with the Taskbar hidden.

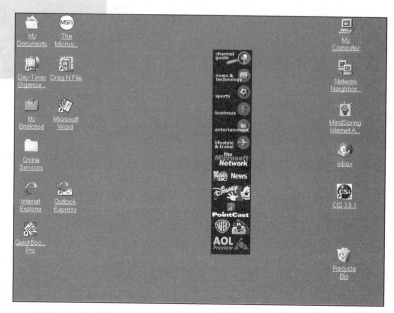

**Figure 7.20**
Slide the mouse pointer into the Taskbar area to redisplay it "on demand."

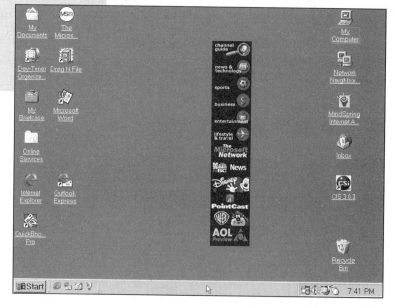

# 8

# Exploring the Control Panel

## IN THIS CHAPTER

- **Adding and Removing Software**
- **Installing Fonts**
- **Adding New Hardware**
- **Setting the Date and Time**
- **Changing Regional Settings**
- **Using Passwords**
- **Exploring System Properties**

For more information on setting Display properties, see Chapter 5. For more information on setting Printer properties, see Chapter 6. For more information on Networking, see Chapter 14. For more information on the Internet, see Chapter 17. For more information on Power Management, see Chapter 18.

The Windows Control Panel contains icons you use to change various settings and troubleshoot problems that may arise for hardware and software on your computer. Many of the icons in the Control Panel are there "if you need them," and you may never need to use them. For example, although you see a Fonts icon in the Control Panel, you may never need to use it. In this chapter, I cover the icons in the Control Panel that you are most likely to use; for other icons, I'll simply provide a brief explanation.

*Note*

Some icons in the Control Panel appear because software or hardware on your computer placed them there. For that reason, as you view figures in this chapter, you may see icons that you don't have on your computer.

# Adding and Removing Software

*Note*

The instructions and figures throughout this chapter assume that you are using a Web Style Desktop. When you use the Web Style Desktop, you click instead of double-click to open files, folders, and programs. If you are using the Classic Desktop, I've included the Double-Click icon you see in the margin next to this paragraph for your convenience. Paragraphs marked with this icon contain a "click" instruction. Classic Desktop users should double-click instead of click when they follow that instruction. When selecting files, folders, or icons, Web-Style Desktop users should point, while Classic Desktop users should click.

You're most likely to use the Control Panel to add or remove software. From the Control Panel (see Figure 8.1), you can add software applications or you can add Windows add-ons. To open the Control Panel, choose Start, Settings, Control Panel.

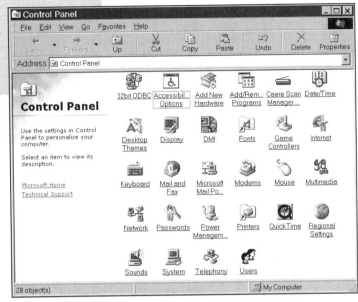

**Figure 8.1**
Use the icons in
the Control Panel
to change
settings on your
computer.

If you plan to use the Control Panel a lot, you might want to create a keyboard shortcut to open it. You can place the shortcut on your Desktop and leave it there, or if you're like me and like your Desktop clean, you can place the Control Panel on the Start menu, on the Programs menu, or even in a folder on the Programs menu.

## Hands On: Creating a Keybard Shortcut to Open the Control Panel

When you create a keyboard shortcut to open the Control Panel, you must create the shortcut and place it at its permanent home *before* you assign the key combination. That is, if you intend to store the shortcut on the Programs menu, place it there before you assign the keyboard shortcut.

1. Choose Start, Find, Files or Folders to display the Find window.
2. Type **Control.exe** in the Named box and then click on Find Now. Windows will find the file in the \Windows folder.

Control.exe is the file that opens the Control Panel.

3. Drag the Control.exe file onto the Desktop to create a shortcut on the Desktop.

4. Choose Yes to place the shortcut on your Desktop and close the Find window. If you intend to leave the shortcut on your Desktop, skip to step 9.

5. If you want to place the shortcut on the Start menu, on the Programs menu, or in a folder on the Programs menu, right-click on a blank spot on the Taskbar and choose Properties.

6. Click on the Start Menu Programs tab and then click on Advanced to open Windows Explorer in the Start Menu folder.

7. Drag the icon from your Desktop to the location where you want it to appear. You'll need to click on the plus sign next to the Programs folder in the left pane to open that folder if you want to place the Control Panel on the Programs menu. In Figure 8.2, I dragged the shortcut onto the Programs menu.

8. Click on the Programs folder in the right pane to open it. You'll see the shortcut you added in the right pane.

9. Rename the shortcut, if desired, by highlighting it, pressing F2, and typing a new name.

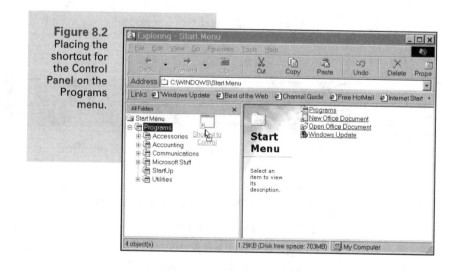

Figure 8.2
Placing the shortcut for the Control Panel on the Programs menu.

10. Right-click on the shortcut and choose Properties from the menu. The Properties box for the shortcut appears.

11. Click in the Shortcut Key box and press the letter on your keyboard that you want to assign as the shortcut. Windows will automati-cally add Ctrl+Alt to the key you select. In Figure 8.3, I chose **P**.

12. Click on Apply and Close. If you placed the shortcut on a menu instead of on your Desktop, close the Exploring window.

13. To use the shortcut, press and hold Ctrl+Alt and touch the letter you assigned as the shortcut key. The Control Panel will open.

*Note*

If the Control Panel doesn't seem to open all the way—that is, the icons don't appear—when you use your keyboard shortcut, press Ctrl+Alt+Del once. In the Close Programs dialog box, high-light the Control Panel and click on End Task. Then try your shortcut again. The Control Panel should open properly.

**Figure 8.3**
Assigning a
keyboard
shortcut.

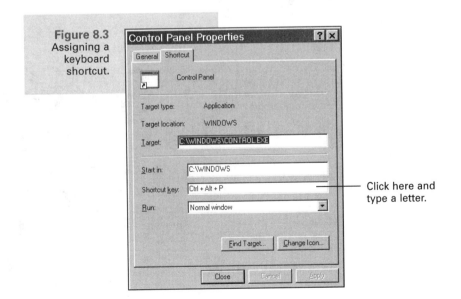

Click here and
type a letter.

# Adding a Program

Suppose you purchase a program like Office 97 or QuickBooks. The easiest way to install programs is to use the Add wizard to walk through the process.

*Note*

**Many programs that come on a CD-ROM include an "autorun" feature. When you insert the disk into the CD-ROM drive, an installation program begins automatically. In this case, follow the on-screen prompts to install your program. You may need to make some installation decisions, such as the program components that you want to install or the drive and folder into which you want to install the program. For questions about program components, read your program documentation or contact the program manufacturer. When choosing a drive and folder, your best choice typically is the default location the program suggests.**

In the Control Panel, click on Add/Remove Programs to display the Add/Remove Programs Properties dialog box (see Figure 8.4). Click on the Install button to start the Install Program wizard. The first dialog box of the Wizard appears (see Figure 8.5).

**Figure 8.4**
Use this dialog box to install a new program.

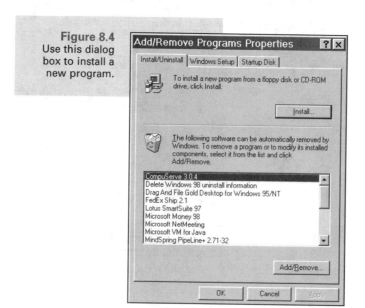

**Figure 8.5**
The first box of the Install Program Wizard prompts you to insert either the first floppy disk or the CD-ROM from which you intend to install the program.

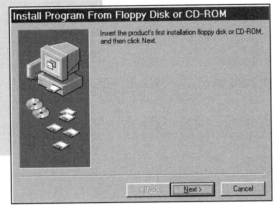

Click on <u>N</u>ext and Windows searches first your A drive and then your CD-ROM drive looking for an installation program. When Windows finds an installation program named either SETUP.EXE or INSTALL.EXE, it displays the Run Installation Program dialog box shown in Figure 8.6. If the installation program has another name, the Command Line for Installation Program box will be blank. You'll need to click on the B<u>r</u>owse button and navigate to the installation program on the appropriate disk.

Choose Finish, and the program's installation process begins. Follow the prompts that appear onscreen to complete the installation. You may need to select a location for the program—typically, the location the program suggests is your best choice—or make other program selections. For example, if you're installing Microsoft Office, you can choose the components of Office that you want to install. The installation program also creates icons for you to use to run

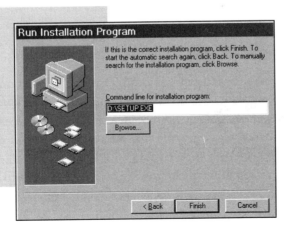

**Figure 8.6**
The Command Line for Installation Program box contains the name of the installation program that Windows will use to install your program.

the program; the location of these icons depends on the program you install. You may find icons on your Desktop, on the Programs menu, in a folder on the Programs menu, or in some combination of these locations.

# Removing a Program

In the days of DOS and Windows 3.1, you typically removed programs by deleting the directories that contained them. In Windows 95, this method is your last resort.

## Using Windows to Uninstall a Program

*Note*

**Beginning with Windows 95, you could install two types of programs: 32-bit or 16-bit. Prior to Windows 95, all programs were 16-bit programs. This fact becomes significant when you attempt to remove a program after you install it. Typically, only 32-bit programs appear in the Add/Remove Programs Properties box, although occasionally, you may find a 16-bit program in the list. When you want to remove a program, start by checking the Add/Remove Programs Properties box. For programs listed, this method of removing a program is most complete.**

Although this method may not be an option, you should first try to remove a program using the Add/Remove Programs Properties box. If you see the program in the list, you'll be able to remove the program using Windows. This process removes not only files stored on your hard disk but also entries the program makes in the Windows 98 Registry.

*Note*

**The Windows Registry stores configuration information about the software and hardware installed on your computer. If you don't use the Add/Remove button to remove a program that appears in the Add/Remove Programs Properties box, information about the program remains in the Registry and could cause conflicts at a later date. For more information about the Registry, see Chapter 14.**

Highlight the program and click on the Add/Remove button. What you see next on-screen depends on the program you are removing. Technically, the program launches its own version of an "uninstall shield," which serves as a wizard to walk you through the process of removing the program. You may be instructed, as in the case of Microsoft Office, Professional Edition, to insert your original program CD-ROM. Simply follow the prompts you see. If you aren't sure how to answer a question, contact the program's manufacturer before continuing.

## Using the Program's Uninstaller

If you don't find an entry for the program you want to remove in the Add/Remove Programs Properties box, next check the program's folder on the Start menu to see whether the program has its own "uninstaller" (see Figure 8.7).

After you start the uninstaller program, what you see onscreen depends on the program, but a wizard will start and prompt you, as necessary, for any information it needs to remove the program.

In some cases, using either the Windows removal method or the program's uninstaller, the removal process may not succeed in completely removing the program. If that happens, you need to finish the process using the techniques described in the next section.

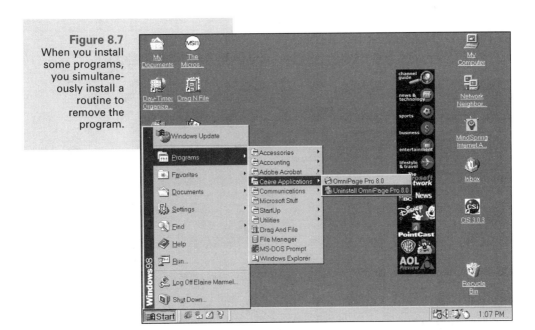

**Figure 8.7**
When you install some programs, you simultaneously install a routine to remove the program.

# Using Windows Explorer to Remove a Program

For a program that doesn't appear in the Add/Remove Programs Properties box and also doesn't include an uninstaller in the program's folder, you have only one option. You can remove the program by deleting it from your hard disk using Windows Explorer.

Right-click on the Start button and choose Explore. Windows Explorer appears (see Figure 8.8).

In the left pane, highlight the folder containing the program to open it. Then press the Del key on your keyboard. You'll see the Confirm Folder Delete dialog box shown in Figure 8.9.

Choose Yes to delete the folder and all its contents, including the program file. Then empty the Recycle Bin to finish removing the program from your computer. Be aware that this method does not remove any icons for the program that appear on either the Programs menu or your Desktop. Also, this method *does not* remove any Registry entries the program may have made during its installation.

• • • • • • • • • • • • • • • • • • • • • • • • • • • • • • • • • • • • • • • •

To remove Desktop icons or Programs menu entries, drag them to the Recycle Bin.

• • • • • • • • • • • • • • • • • • • • • • • • • • • • • • • • • • • • • • • •

**Figure 8.8**
Use Windows Explorer to delete programs you can't delete any other way.

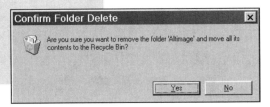

**Figure 8.9**
Deleted files are
typically stored
temporarily in
the Recycle Bin.

# Adding Windows Components

A typical installation of Windows 98 installs a default set of Windows components—also called *applets*, or small applications—that make your work easier. By default, if you install Windows 98 as an upgrade to Windows 95, any previously existing Windows components are also upgraded. You may find that you want to add a component that was not included when you installed Windows 98, such as Windows Backup.

## Hands On: Adding Windows Components

The Clipboard Viewer is a handy tool; you can use it to view anything currently stored on the Windows Clipboard—and you can even save that information to a text file.

1. Choose Start, Settings, Control Panel to open the Control Panel
2. Click on Add/Remove Programs to display the Add/Remove Programs Properties dialog box.
3. Click on the Windows Setup tab to display the components you can add to your Windows configuration (see Figure 8.10).
4. Highlight the component you want to add. To add the Clipboard Viewer, highlight System Tools in the Components list box.

*Tip*

The component list is actually a list of categories; to see the names of the components in any category, highlight the category and click on Details.

5. Click on Details. Windows displays the components associated with the item you highlighted in step 4 (see Figure 8.11).
6. Place a check in the box next to the component you want to add and choose OK.

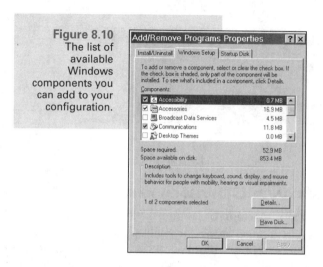

**Figure 8.10**
The list of available Windows components you can add to your configuration.

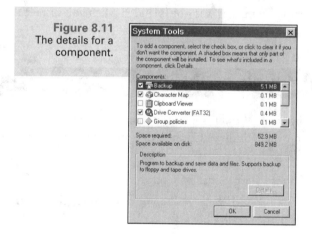

**Figure 8.11**
The details for a component.

**Tip**

If the Windows 98 files came preinstalled on your computer, you do not need to insert your Windows 98 CD-ROM; instead, you can use the Copying Files dialog box that appears to navigate to the \Windows\Options\Cabs folder.

7. Click on <u>A</u>pply. Windows prompts you to insert your Windows 98 CD-ROM.

8. Choose OK. The Copying Files dialog box appears, and you'll see a bar indicating the progress for installing the component. Then, Windows will take a moment to set up the component. Last, Windows will redisplay the Windows Setup tab of the Add/Remove Programs Properties box.

9. Click on OK.

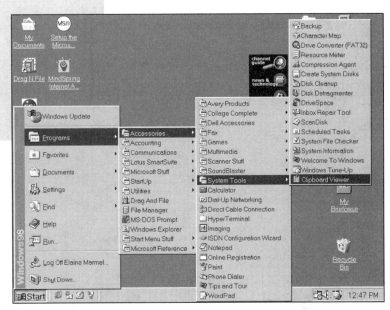

**Figure 8.12**
Windows places shortcuts for Windows components on the Accessories menu, sometimes in a folder.

Whenever you install a new Windows component, you'll find it on the Accessories menu. Choose Start, Programs, Accessories. Windows may have stored the component in a folder on the Accessories menu; the Clipboard Viewer appears on the System Tools folder unless you move it (see Figure 8.12).

# Installing Fonts

By default, Windows installs some standard fonts on your computer. As you add other software, that software may also add fonts to your computer. You can view all the fonts installed on your computer from the Fonts window, which you can open from the Control Panel. Choose Start, Settings, Control Panel. Then click on the Fonts icon (see Figure 8.13).

In this section, you'll learn how to

- View and print a font sample
- Find fonts that are similar to each other
- Add and delete fonts
- Understand the difference between computer fonts and printer fonts

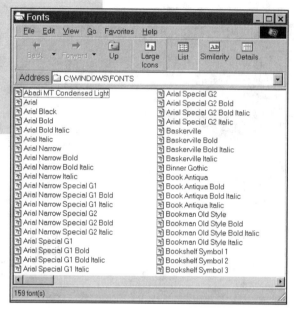

**Figure 8.13**
Fonts installed on your computer appear, by default, in alphabetical order in the Fonts window.

If you need a special character that you can't find in the font you're using, try using the Windows Character Map applet to insert the character into a document. The applet is easy to use; if you need to install it, see the directions earlier in this chapter for adding a Windows component. To use the Character Map, open it, find the character you want to use, and copy the character to the Windows Clipboard. Then switch to the application where you need the character and paste the character.

# Viewing and Printing a Font Sample

You can view or print a sample of any font that you see in the Fonts window by double-clicking on the font. Windows displays the entire alphabet in the selected font, along with sample a phrase in several sizes (see Figure 8.14). If you click on the Print button in the window, you can print the font sample.

**You cannot view Type 1 fonts, which are scalable fonts designed to work with PostScript devices.**

*Note*

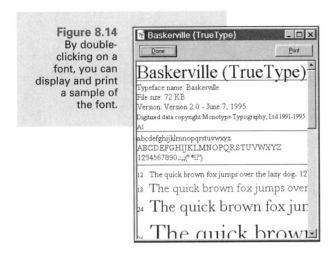

# Finding Fonts That Resemble Each Other

As you double-click on various fonts in the Font window, you'll notice that many of them look alike. You can list the fonts in the window so that similar fonts appear grouped together.

In the Fonts window, choose View, List Fonts by Similarity. Windows reorders the list to display fonts based on their similarity to the first font in the list (see Figure 8.15).

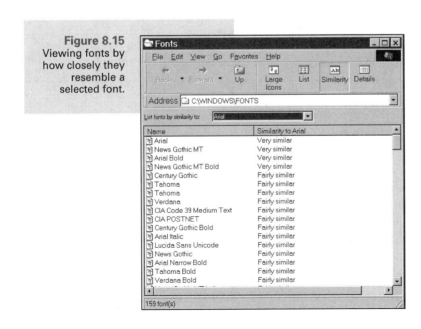

**Figure 8.16**
Select the font
to which you
want to compare
all others.

To determine how closely installed fonts resemble a specific font, open the List Fonts by Similarity To list box and select the specific font. Windows reorders the list to compare all fonts to the one you selected (see Figure 8.16).

Windows uses Panose font-mapping information to compare fonts. Panose information is stored with the font and includes characteristics such as serif or sans serif, normal, italics, or bold. If no Panose information is stored with the font, you'll find the font at the bottom of the list with a notation in the Similarity column.

# Adding Fonts

Typically, software programs install fonts for you. But suppose, for example, that you buy a new computer and find that it doesn't have on it a font you used on your old computer. You can install the font on your new computer. Copy the font from your old computer onto a floppy disk and place the disk in your new computer. You'll need to use Windows Explorer to copy the fonts, and you'll be copying font file names, not the names you see in the Fonts window. To determine a font's file name, right-click on the font and choose Properties. In the Properties dialog box, at the top, you'll see the name for the font file (see Figure 8.17).

**Figure 8.17**
Identifying a
font's file name.

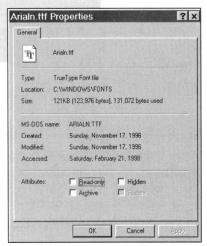

If the font is a TrueType, Raster, or Adobe Type 1 font, you don't need to use the
Add Fonts dialog box. You can use Windows Explorer to copy the font directly into
the \Windows\Fonts folder.

In the Fonts window, choose File, Install New Font to display the dialog box you
see in Figure 8.18. Navigate to the drive containing the font(s) you want to add
and select the font(s). You can select individual fonts by holding Ctrl as you click;
you can select a list of fonts by clicking on the first font and holding Shift while
you click on the last font. Click on OK. Windows installs the fonts.

**Figure 8.18**
Add fonts using
this dialog box.

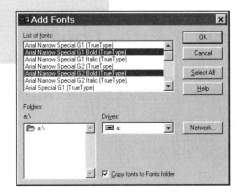

*Tip*

If you want to use TrueType or Raster fonts stored on a network drive without actually copying the fonts to your computer, remove the check in the Copy Fonts to Fonts Folder check box.

## Deleting Fonts

To delete fonts, open the Fonts window by clicking on the Fonts icon in the Control Panel. Select the fonts you want to delete. You can select individual fonts by holding Ctrl as you select each font, or you can select a contiguous list of fonts by selecting the first font and holding down the Shift key as you select the last font. Choose File, Delete (or right-click and choose Delete from the shortcut menu). Windows asks you to confirm the deletion (see Figure 8.19).

**Figure 8.19**
Deleting a font.

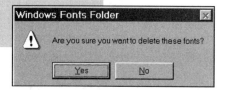

*Note*

**If you are using the Recycle Bin, Windows places the file for the deleted font into the Recycle Bin. You can restore the font if you accidentally delete the wrong font by selecting the font file in the Recycle Bin and choosing File, Restore.**

## Computer Fonts versus Printer Fonts

When you install a printer, the printer's installation program may install some printer fonts. These fonts appear in the font lists for various Windows programs, but they do *not* appear in the Fonts window of the Control Panel.

To specify font settings for your printer, you use the Printer icon in the Control Panel. Choose Start, Settings, Control Panel. Click on the Printers icon to open the Printers window. Right-click on the printer for which you want to specify font settings and choose Properties. In the Properties dialog box, click on the Fonts tab and choose the settings you want (see Figure 8.20).

**Figure 8.20**
Use the printer's
Properties box to
specify font
settings for
printer fonts.

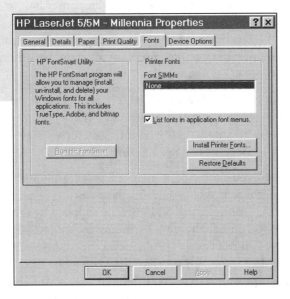

# Adding New Hardware

Typically, you add new hardware to your computer under two conditions:

- You are adding a new type of device to your computer, such as a Zip drive or a tape drive.
- You are replacing an existing piece of hardware, such as a mouse or video card.

If you are adding a new type of device, you only need to make sure that your computer is turned off and unplugged while you add the device and then follow the manufacturer's instructions for installation. Your new hardware may come with a disk from the manufacturer that contains drivers for the device. As a rule, you should use the manufacturer's supplied drivers, since they probably will be later versions than those drivers that come with the operating system.

You should turn your computer off and unplug it to avoid static electricity charges that can damage the computer.

If you are replacing an existing hardware device, you should remove the software for the existing device before you shut off your computer and remove the hardware. Use the Add/Remove Programs Properties box to check for software related to the hardware you are replacing. If you find software, remove it, shut off and unplug the computer, replace the existing hardware item with a new hardware item following the manufacturer's installation instructions, and restart your computer.

 Much of today's new hardware is of the "plug and play" variety. That is, with your computer shut off, you install the hardware. When you then turn on your computer, Windows 98 automatically "detects" the new hardware and sets it up for you. And that may be all you need to do.

But sometimes, you need to get involved because the operating system doesn't find what you think it should find. In these cases, you use the Add New Hardware icon in the Control Panel and software supplied by the manufacturer of the device. After you install the new hardware and restart your computer, choose Start, Settings, Control Panel. Then click on the Add New Hardware icon to start the Add New Hardware Wizard. The first dialog box of the Wizard tells you to close any open programs before continuing. When you click on Next, a dialog box tells you that Windows will begin searching for any new Plug and Play devices on your system (see Figure 8.21).

Click on Next. Windows begins searching and asks you to wait. If your screen goes black, don't worry. That's normal. Eventually, Windows displays a list of potential devices and asks you whether the device you want to install appears in the list. Typically, the device *won't* appear in the list; if it did, Windows would have found it and set it up when you restarted your computer after installing the device—and you wouldn't be running the Add New Hardware Wizard. But if the device does appear in the list, choose Yes, the Device Is in the List; click on the device; and choose Next. Windows proceeds to install the device. If the device

**Figure 8.21**
When Windows searches for new hardware, the process can take a few minutes.

does not appear in the list, choose <u>N</u>o, the Device Isn't in the List; then click on Next, and Windows displays the dialog box you see in Figure 8.22.

If you let Windows search, it starts the process again; this time, you'll see a progress indicator. During this type of search, your computer may stop responding. If the indicator doesn't move for a long time, you'll need to restart your computer, start this process again, and choose to select your hardware from a list. Typically, this search is a waste of time because if Windows was going to find your hardware, it would have found it the first time. So, you might want to skip this process and choose to select your hardware from a list.

If you choose to select your hardware from a list, Windows displays a dialog box like the one in Figure 8.23, where you see various categories of devices. Select a category and choose Next. Insert the disk supplied for the hardware by the manufacturer and click on <u>H</u>ave Disk (see Figure 8.24). Then choose Next.

**Figure 8.22**
You can let Windows search for hardware that is not Plug and Play compatible, or you can choose the hardware from a list.

**Figure 8.23**
Select a hardware category.

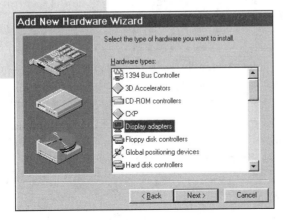

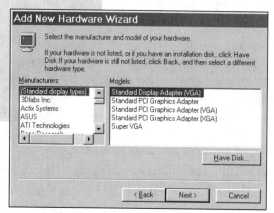

**Figure 8.24**
Tell Windows to use the information supplied by the manufacturer to set up your hardware device.

If after installing new hardware, you think that a conflict exists, see "Exploring System Properties" later in this chapter, "Troubleshooting Wizards" in Chapter 2, and "System Troubleshooter" in Chapter 13.

The manufacturer of your hardware device controls what appears on the screen. Follow the prompts you see to finish the installation process.

# Setting the Date and Time

Windows and many Windows programs rely on the date and time stored in your computer's system clock; you'll see the time displayed in the lower-right corner of the screen in the System Tray. If you place the mouse pointer on the time, you'll also see the date (see Figure 8.25).

You can change the date or time from the Date/Time Properties box. To open the Date/Time Properties box (see Figure 8.26), open the Control Panel and click on the Date/Time icon.

As a shortcut, you can open the Date/Time Properties box by double-clicking on the time that appears in the System Tray.

Use the list box to select a month and the spinner box to select a year; select a date on the calendar. To change the time, click in the time box and either use the spinner box arrows or type the correct time. If you move and your time zone changes, click on the Time Zone tab, open the list box at the top, and select the correct time zone (see Figure 8.27).

**Figure 8.25**
The time, based on your computer's system clock.

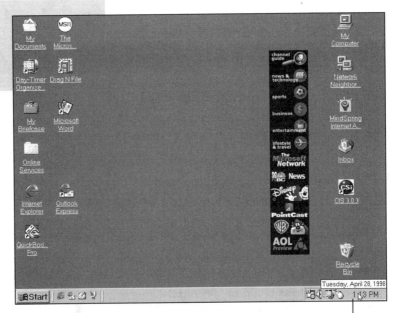

Point here to see the date.

**Figure 8.26**
Use this box to change the date or time on your computer system's clock.

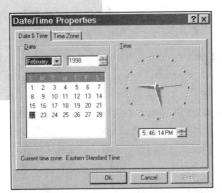

**Figure 8.27**
Windows can automatically adjust your computer's clock for daylight savings changes.

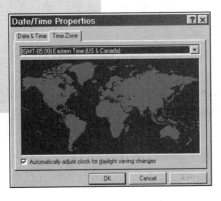

# Windows and the Year 2000

The year 2000 has been in the headlines for many months now, and computer users should rightfully be concerned that the software they are using is year 2000-compliant. The premise behind the problem is that, when the date rolls over from 1999 to 2000, the computers of the world will suddenly think that it is 1900.

The majority of people who will experience problems associated with the year 2000 are people running mainframe systems and large corporate databases because, for efficiency reasons, many mainframe applications were written to store only two digits of a year. If these systems are not updated to handle four-digit dates, serious consequences are possible. For example, electronic inventory systems could place orders for stock that is not really needed. In the financial world, mortgage calculations could be inaccurate.

Microsoft has published a "Statement of Compliance", which you can read at their Web site, http://microsoft.com/ithome/topics/year2k /y2kcomply/y2kcomply.htm. It states:

"A Year 2000 Compliant product from Microsoft will not produce errors processing date data in connection with the year change from December 31, 1999 to January 1, 2000 when used with accurate date data in accordance with its documentation and the recommendations and exceptions set forth in the Microsoft Year 2000 Product Guide, provided all other products (e.g., other software, firmware and hardware) used with it properly exchange date data with the Microsoft product. A Year 2000 Compliant product from Microsoft will recognize the Year 2000 as a leap year."

*Note*

For more information on Microsoft's products and the Year 2000 problem, visit http://www.microsoft.com/year2000/

All of Microsoft's operating systems prior to Windows 98 meet Microsoft's standard of compliance with some disclosed exceptions that constitute minor date issues.

Even though Windows 98 won't be affected, you may still experience problems with the year 2000 either because of your computer's BIOS or because of individual applications that you use.

If your computer system's BIOS is unable to correctly record the date change from December 31, 1999, to January 1, 2000, it will boot with an incorrect date following December 31, 1999. To fix this problem, you can take one of two approaches:

1. Set the date manually in the system BIOS. After you make the correction, the system will function normally. You can manually correct the system date by entering the computer's CMOS setup program—you'll need to read the computer's instruction manual to determine how to enter the CMOS program. If, however, you're not comfortable making the change, you can hire a computer professional to show you how to make the change or even make the change for you.

2. You could obtain an updated BIOS for your system. To obtain this upgrade, you will need to contact the hardware manufacturer of your PC.

For more information on Microsoft products and the year 2000, visit http://www.microsoft.com/cio/articles/year2000faq.htm on the World Wide Web.

You may experience some problems with the year 2000 at an application level, if you enter the year using a two-digit shortcut, because there is no industrywide standard on how to interpret these entries. For this reason, you may need to type in all four digits (for example, type **2000** instead of **00**) to specify the correct year. You can, however, use Windows Regional Settings to help you specify the year correctly.

# Changing Regional Settings

The Regional Settings icon in the Control Panel helps you control how numbers, currency amounts, dates, and times appear in various applications. You can take advantage of Regional Settings options to check how each application you use stores a two-digit date in relation to the year 2000 problem.

Open the Control Panel (use your keyboard shortcut or choose Start, Settings, Control Panel) and click on the Regional Settings icon. From the Regional Settings tab (see Figure 8.28), you can select a region; if programs you use support international settings, the programs will change the way they display and sort numbers, currency, dates, and times to conform with the region you select.

Use the Number tab (see Figure 8.29), the Currency tab (see Figure 8.30), the Time tab (see Figure 8.31), and the Date tab (see Figure 8.32) to control the way numbers, currency, times, and dates appear in various applications.

Set the Short Date Style on the Date tab to M/d/yyyy to help you confirm that dates you enter are accurate. By making this change, you can enter a two-digit date in an application, but the application will display the four-digit date onscreen. If the application shows the wrong century, you can immediately reenter the date as a four-digit date.

**Figure 8.28**
Select an appropriate region.

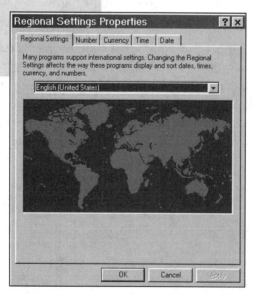

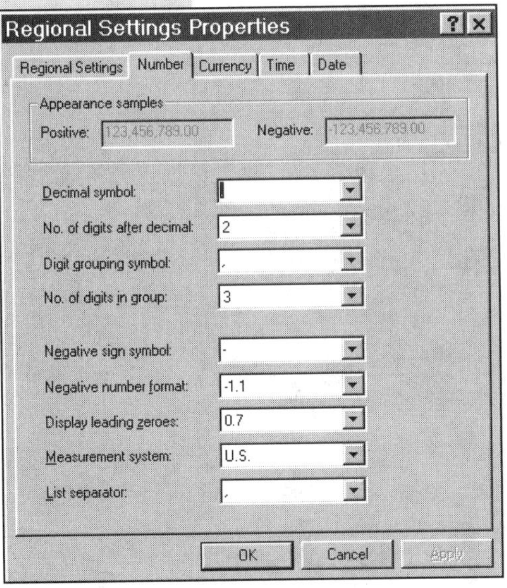

**Figure 8.29**
**The Number tab.**

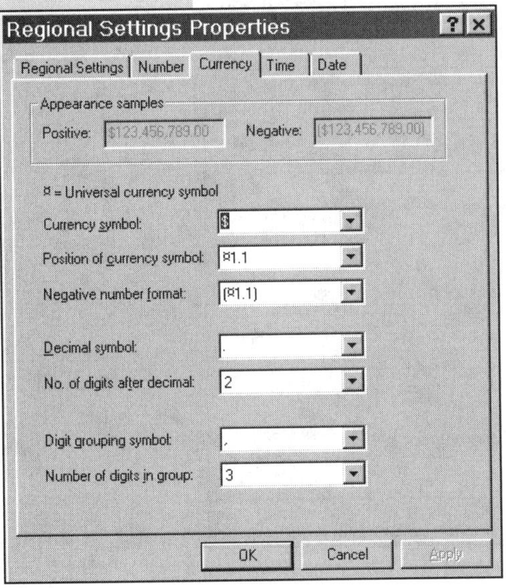

**Regional Settings Properties**

Regional Settings | Number | Currency | Time | Date

Appearance samples

Positive: 123,456,789.00    Negative: -123,456,789.00

| | |
|---|---|
| Decimal symbol: | . |
| No. of digits after decimal: | 2 |
| Digit grouping symbol: | , |
| No. of digits in group: | 3 |
| Negative sign symbol: | - |
| Negative number format: | -1.1 |
| Display leading zeroes: | 0.7 |
| Measurement system: | U.S. |
| List separator: | , |

OK    Cancel    Apply

**Figure 8.30**
**The Currency tab.**

**Regional Settings Properties**

Regional Settings | Number | Currency | Time | Date

Appearance samples

Positive: $123,456,789.00    Negative: ($123,456,789.00)

¤ = Universal currency symbol

| | |
|---|---|
| Currency symbol: | $ |
| Position of currency symbol: | ¤1.1 |
| Negative number format: | (¤1.1) |
| Decimal symbol: | . |
| No. of digits after decimal: | 2 |
| Digit grouping symbol: | , |
| Number of digits in group: | 3 |

OK    Cancel    Apply

**Figure 8.31**
The Time tab.

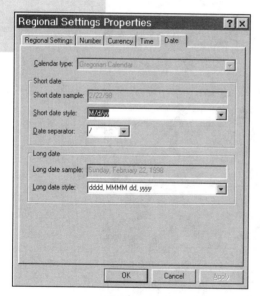

**Figure 8.32**
The Date tab.

# Adding Sounds When You Click

If your computer is equipped with a sound card and speakers, you've already heard some sounds from Windows 98—particularly the sound when you start Windows 98 and the sound when you shut down Windows 98.

If you like sounds, you don't have to settle for just those sounds; you can add sounds that you'll hear for actions you take regularly, such as starting programs, closing programs, maximizing or minimizing windows, or opening menus. Windows refers to these actions as *events*.

If you don't like sounds, you can shut them off.

Open the Control Panel (use the shortcut you created earlier in this chapter or choose Start, Settings, Control Panel) and click on the Sounds icon. The Sounds Properties dialog box opens (see Figure 8.33).

You can apply sounds to individual events, or you can use a sound scheme that assigns sounds to most major events. If you like sound, choosing a sound scheme is a good approach because it assigns sounds to most events; if you don't like a particular sound, you can change that sound. To select a sound scheme, open the Schemes list box and select a scheme (see Figure 8.34).

**Note**

**Some programs install sound schemes on your computer; you may have noticed MindSpring Sound Scheme in Figure 8.34. The Internet service provider MindSpring provided this scheme. Most of the scheme's sounds apply to on-line events.**

**Figure 8.33**
Use this dialog box to add, change, or remove sounds associated with actions you take on your computer.

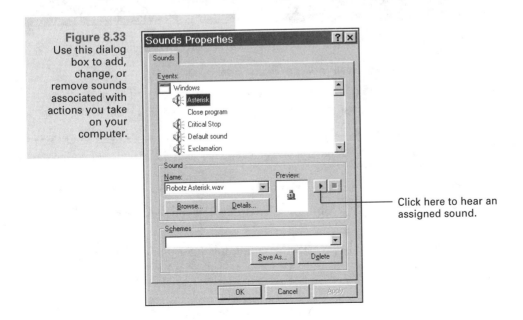

Click here to hear an assigned sound.

**Figure 8.34**
Use a sound scheme to quickly assign sounds to most of the actions you take on your computer.

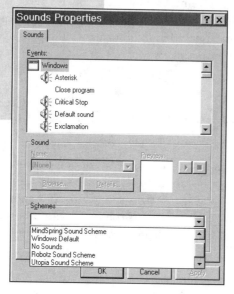

*Tip*

To quickly remove sounds from events, choose No Sounds as your sound scheme.

## Hands On: Changing the Sound for an Event

Suppose you don't like the sound assigned to a particular event.

1. Open the Sounds Properties dialog box.
2. Highlight the event whose sound you want to change. The sound currently assigned to it appears in the Name box (see Figure 8.35).

*Tip*

To hear the sound already assigned to an event, highlight the sound and click on the Preview button.

3. Click on the Browse button. The dialog box you see in Figure 8.36 appears.
4. Select a sound. To preview the sound, highlight it and click on the Preview button.

**Figure 8.35**
Highlight an
event to change
its sound.

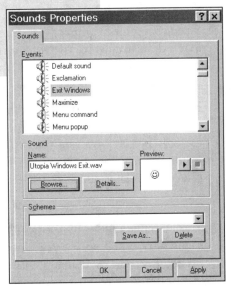

**Figure 8.36**
By default,
Windows
displays sound
files stored in the
\Windows\Media
folder.

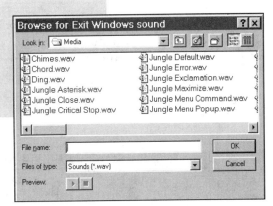

5. Choose OK. When the Sounds Properties dialog box reappears, the sound you selected appears in the <u>N</u>ame box for the highlighted event.

6. Repeat steps 2 through 5 until you have assigned sounds to each event for which you want to hear a sound.

7. Click on OK. Windows redisplays the Control Panel. You'll hear the sounds you selected each time you take the action associated with the sound.

# Using Passwords

Windows comes equipped to store two passwords: a network password and a Windows password. Network passwords are useful to make sure that only authorized users have access to information stored on a network; if you haven't set up a network, you'll never see the Network Password dialog box.

By using a Windows password, different people can use the same computer and each person can have his or her own preferences and desktop settings. If you are the only person who uses your computer, you may not need a Windows password. You establish passwords when you first install Windows, but you can change them later on.

*Note*

**To change a network password, you must be logged on to the network. If you're working in any network besides a Windows network, you must use your network's software to change a network password.**

To change a password, open the Control Panel (using a keyboard shortcut or by choosing Start, Settings, Control Panel) and click on the Passwords icon. The Passwords Properties box appears (see Figure 8.37).

Click on the top button on the tab to change your Windows password. If available, click on the bottom button on the tab to change a network password. The

**Figure 8.37**
On the Change Passwords tab, you can change your Windows password or a Windows network password.

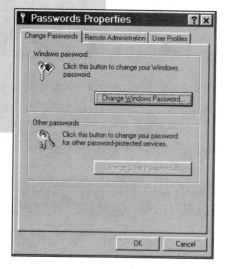

dialog box you'll see after clicking on either button is similar to the one shown in Figure 8.38.

Type your current password in the Old Password box. Type the password you want to start using in the New Password box and retype it in the Confirm New Password box. Then choose OK.

The Remote Administration tab (see Figure 8.39) pertains to computers in a network. Use the Remote Administration tab to allow someone working at a different computer, usually a network administrator, to establish shared files on your computer and shared printer(s) attached to your computer. If you check the box on this tab, you'll need to supply a password and confirm it.

On the User Profiles tab (see Figure 8.40), you can allow different people who use the same computer to have different Desktop settings such as wallpapers, screen savers, Desktop icons, and even Start and Program menu choices. If you select the second option button on the tab, you can place checks in appropriate boxes to establish the settings each user profile can store.

**Figure 8.38**
Use the Change Windows Password dialog box to change a password.

**Figure 8.39**
Set up remote access to your computer by placing a check in the box on this tab.

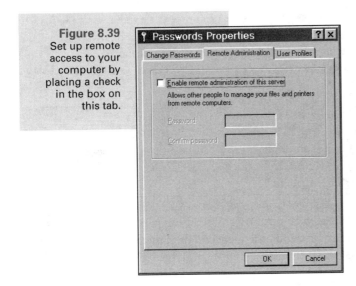

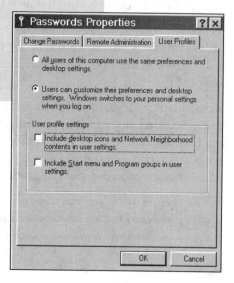

**Figure 8.40**
Select the second option button on this tab to set up user profiles.

# Exploring System Properties

When you work with System Properties, you basically work with the hardware installed on your computer. To open the System Properties dialog box, open the Control Panel (choose Start, Settings, Control Panel) and click on the System icon.

As a shortcut, you can open the System Properties box by holding down the Windows key while you press the Pause/Break key on your keyboard.

*Caution*

**Messing around with the System Properties box can cause your computer to function improperly. If you are not certain about what you're doing, consult a professional.**

General information about your operating system, the person to whom it is registered, and the computer appear on the General tab of the System Properties dialog box (see Figure 8.41).

**Figure 8.41**
From the
General tab, you
can identify the
version of
Windows that
you're using.

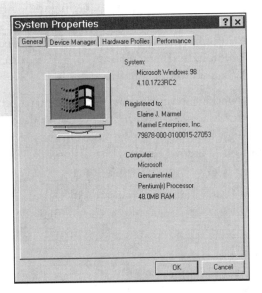

Use the Device Manager tab (see Figure 8.42) to help you identify the hardware installed on your computer. You can also identify conflicts and problems by checking the Device Manager. If you see a red X or a yellow exclamation point (!) next to any device, that device has a problem of some sort. Typically, red Xs indicate more serious problems.

**Figure 8.42**
The Device
Manager shows
the hardware
installed on your
computer—and
devices that
have problems.

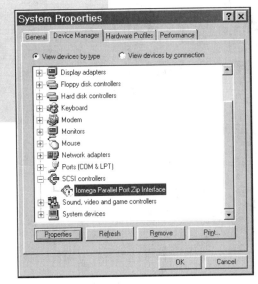

To get more information about the problem, highlight the item with the red X or yellow ! and click on Properties (see Figure 8.43). Windows displays the properties for the device; information concerning the problem appears in the center of the General tab. If you have trouble figuring out how to solve the problem, try using one of the Windows troubleshooting wizards.

> See Chapter 2 for help on running a trouble-shooting wizard.

If your system is working properly, you might want to print the information stored in the Device Manager—just in case you ever need to refer to what settings you were using when things worked fine. On the Device Manager tab, click on the Print button. Windows displays the dialog box you see in Figure 8.44. Choose to print All Devices and System Summary.

On the Hardware Profiles tab (see Figure 8.45), you can set up multiple hardware configurations so that, depending on the configuration you choose, drivers

**Figure 8.43**
Check the device to determine the source of the problem.

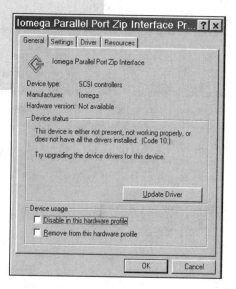

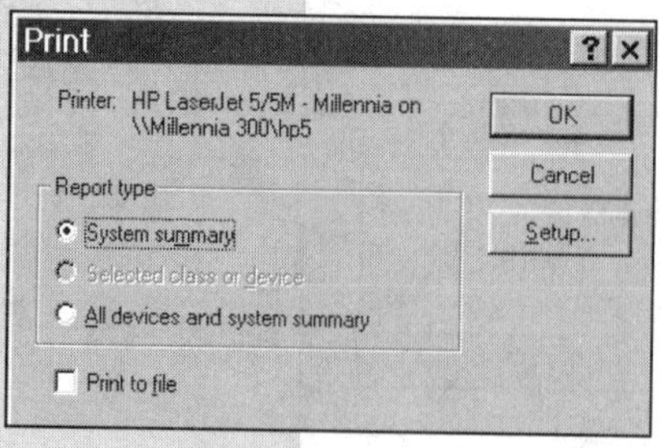

**Figure 8.44**
Print detailed information for the Device Manager when your computer is working well; that information can help you troubleshoot at a later date.

for some hardware devices will load while drivers for other hardware devices won't load. Be careful here: this operation is tricky. Before you try it, consult a professional.

From the Performance tab (see Figure 8.46), you can check status information about your computer, such as the amount of memory Windows is recognizing

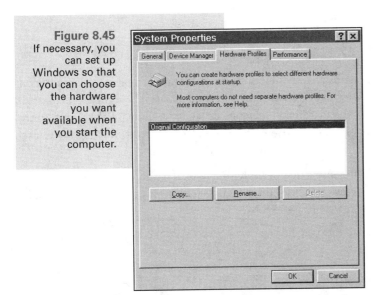

**Figure 8.45**
If necessary, you can set up Windows so that you can choose the hardware you want available when you start the computer.

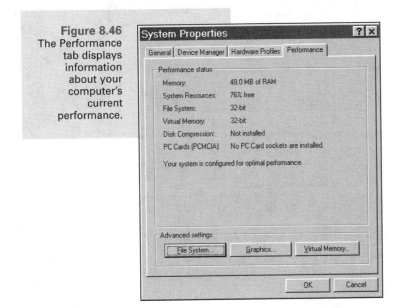

**Figure 8.46**
The Performance tab displays information about your computer's current performance.

and the amount of system resources that are free. You'll also see information about whether your computer is configured for optimal performance. The buttons in the bottom of the box can help you if your computer *is not* configured for optimal performance, but if you are not an advanced user, you should *not* change any of these settings without guidance.

# Control Panel Icons You Might Find Interesting

In addition to the icons already described, your Control Panel may contain icons that you don't see in the figures, and the figures may contain some icons that you don't see in your Control Panel. The icons differ from Control Panel to Control Panel because software and hardware place icons in the Control Panel—and each computer has installed different hardware and software.

You may also notice some icons in both your Control Panel and the one you see in Figure 8.47 that have not been discussed. This section provides a brief description of the icons you see in Figure 8.47.

**Figure 8.47**
A typical Control Panel contains icons you may never need to use.

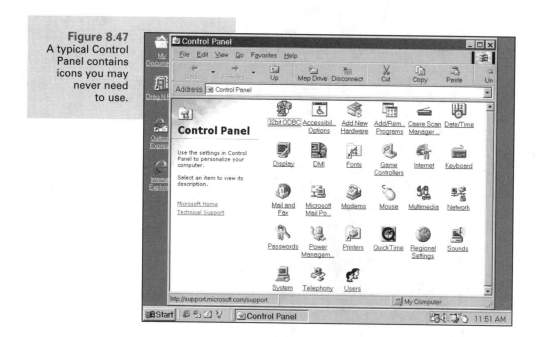

# 32bit ODBC

Microsoft Office users will find this icon, along with Find Fast, in the Control Panel. ODBC is a programming interface that helps different database application software "talk" to each other. In particular, ODBC helps database management software access data in systems that use Structured Query Language (SQL) as the standard data access method. Because most popular database software programs use SQL, ODBC enables developers to build databases using any software they choose without worrying about accessing data in a database written in some other database language.

●●●●●●●●●●●●●●●●●●●●●●●●●●●●●●●●●●●●●●●●●●●●●●●●●●●●●●●●●●●●●

*Tip*

Find Fast is a file indexing application that Microsoft Office uses to speed up searches through files.

●●●●●●●●●●●●●●●●●●●●●●●●●●●●●●●●●●●●●●●●●●●●●●●●●●●●●●●●●●●●●

# Accessibility Options and Tools

The Accessibility Options and Accessibility Tools icons appear in the Control Panel if you have installed them. If you don't see them and want them, click on the Add/Remove Programs icon and then select the Windows Setup tab. Highlight the first component and click on Details. Place checks in both components in the Accessibility window (see Figure 8.48) and choose OK. Click on OK in the

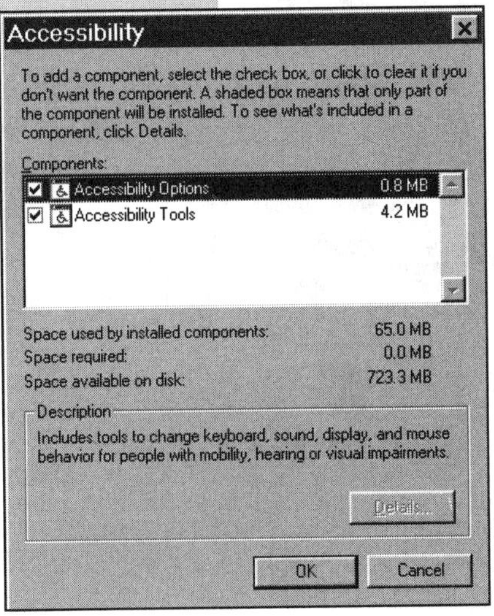

**Figure 8.48**
Installing
Accessibility
Options and
Accessibility
Tools.

**Accessibility**                                          ⊠

To add a component, select the check box, or click to clear it if you don't want the component. A shaded box means that only part of the component will be installed. To see what's included in a component, click Details.

Components:

☑ 🖰 Accessibility Options                          0.8 MB
☑ 🖰 Accessibility Tools                             4.2 MB

Space used by installed components:          65.0 MB
Space required:                                      0.0 MB
Space available on disk:                         723.3 MB

Description
Includes tools to change keyboard, sound, display, and mouse behavior for people with mobility, hearing or visual impairments.

                                                    Details...

                            OK              Cancel

Add/Remove Programs box, and Windows prompts you to insert your Windows 98 CD-ROM. After you insert it and click on OK, Windows copies the necessary files to your hard disk. If you click on the Accessibility Options icon, you'll see the dialog box shown in Figure 8.49.

Usually, people with disabilities such as poor eyesight or hearing find it necessary to install specialized software to make using a computer easier. In Windows 98, accessibility options try to eliminate the need to install specialized software to make using a computer easier for people with disabilities. For example, using Accessibility options, you can display captions for sounds made by both the operating system and application software.

• • • • • • • • • • • • • • • • • • • • • • • • • • • • • • • • • • • • • • • • • • • • • •

All you mouse haters might want to take a look at the Mouse tab of the Accessibility Properties box. The options on that tab enable you to substitute numeric keypad strokes for mouse movements and clicks.

• • • • • • • • • • • • • • • • • • • • • • • • • • • • • • • • • • • • • • • • • • • • • •

You can use the Accessibility Wizard to help you set accessibility options such as StickyKeys or ShowSounds. Choose Start, Programs, Accessories, Accessibility. You'll see two choices on this menu: Accessibility Wizard and Magnifier. The Wizard walks you through setting options. The Magnifier is a display utility that

**Figure 8.49**
Accessibility Options can be added as a Windows component to make using a computer easier.

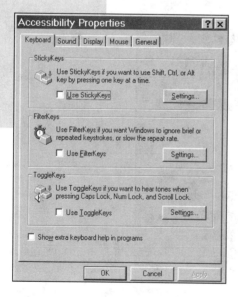

**Figure 8.50**
The Microsoft Magnifier enlarges the portion of the screen containing the mouse pointer.

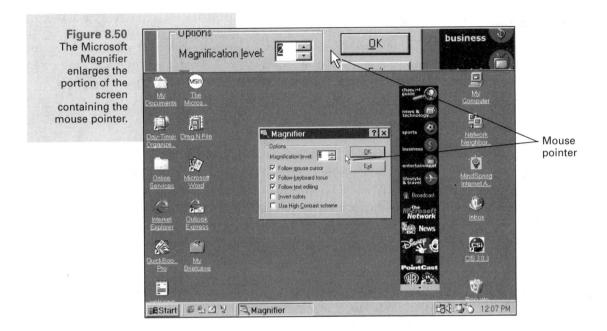

Mouse pointer

can make the screen easier to read for the visually impaired. Using it, you can magnify a portion of the screen for easier reading (see Figure 8.50).

## Caere Scan Manager

The Caere Scan Manager was installed on my computer when I installed my Visioneer PaperPort scanner. The Caere Scan Manager keeps track of the type of scanner currently attached to my computer and some driver information about that scanner.

## DMI

DMI stands for Desktop Management Interface and is software that was installed on my computer by its manufacturer, Dell. The Desktop Management Task Force, which is a consortium of hardware and software vendors, created DMI software. DMI software can identify, report, and provide information about components using a nonproprietary industry standard; the information provided by DMI software is particularly useful when trying to troubleshoot problems on computer systems that contain parts from multiple vendors.

# Game Controllers

You can use the Game Controllers icon to add, remove, or change settings for game controllers, also called "joysticks." If you play a lot of computer games, you probably have a joystick; otherwise, you may never use this icon.

# Keyboard

Have you ever experienced the situation where you find letters repeating onscreen when you didn't want them to repeat? You can increase the Character Repeat rate to lengthen the amount of time you can depress a key before the character repeats itself. Use the Keyboard Properties box (see Figure 8.51) to modify the language and behavior of your keyboard.

*Note*

**You may notice different options in your Keyboard Properties box if you have installed specialized keyboard software.**

**Figure 8.51**
From the Keyboard Properties box, you can change the behavior of your keyboard.

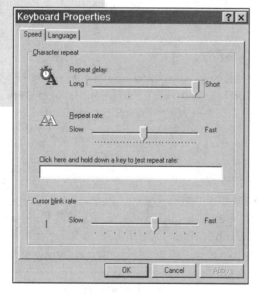

## Modems

After your modem is set up and working correctly, you shouldn't have much reason to use the Modems icon in the Control Panel. You can set your dialing properties (whether you need to dial 9 for an outside line, and so on) from the General tab of the Modems Properties box (see Figure 8.52).

From the Diagnostics tab, you can test to make sure that your computer is communicating with your modem from the Modems Properties dialog box (see Figure 8.53). Highlight the COM port on which your modem is installed and click on the More Info button.

## Mouse

The appearance of the Mouse Properties box depends on the type of mouse attached to your computer. In Figure 8.54, you see the Mouse Properties box for a Microsoft Intellimouse.

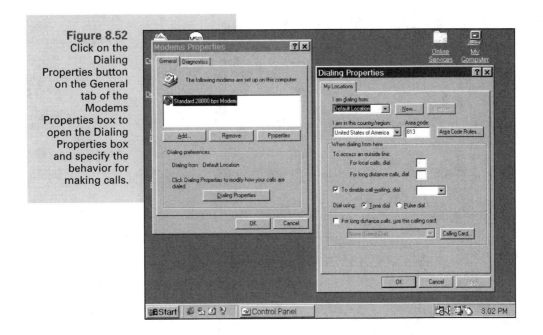

**Figure 8.52** Click on the Dialing Properties button on the General tab of the Modems Properties box to open the Dialing Properties box and specify the behavior for making calls.

**Figure 8.53**
The information at the bottom of the More Info box indicates that the computer and modem are communicating.

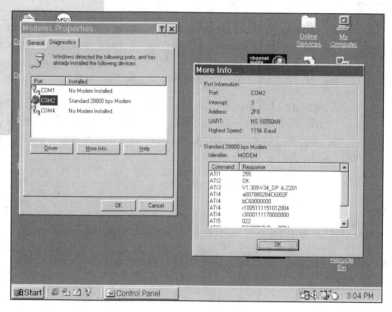

**Figure 8.54**
Your Mouse Properties box may look different, since the appearance of this box depends on the mouse you use.

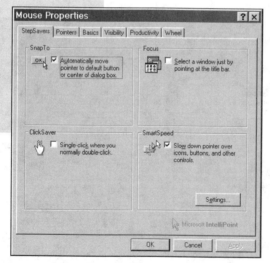

If you use a Logitech mouse, the icon for the mouse in the Control Panel looks like the animal as opposed to the mechanical mouse. It's kind of a cute icon.

From any Mouse Properties box, you can, at a minimum, switch the behavior of the right and left mouse buttons, and you can control the speed at which the mouse pointer moves compared to how much you move the mouse on your Desktop. The software your mouse uses determines the other functions you can control.

# Multimedia

You can display the Volume Control icon in your System Tray using the Audio tab of the Multimedia Properties box (see Figure 8.55). Place a check in the Show Volume Control on the Taskbar check box.

On the Video tab, you can control whether video clips play in a window or fill your entire screen. The MIDI tab helps you control the way MIDI output behaves and lets you add MIDI instruments to your computer. MIDI (which stands for Musical Instrument Digital Interface) is a communications protocol that allows electronic musical instruments such as synthesizers to interact with each other. On the CD Music tab, you can set the volume for CD music. Also, if you have more than one CD-ROM drive on your computer, you can select the letter of the CD-ROM drive that you want to use to play music. The Devices tab of the Multimedia Properties box looks very similar to the Device Manager tab of the System Properties box; in the Multimedia Properties box, however, only multimedia devices are listed.

**Figure 8.55**
From the Multimedia Properties box, you can control the behavior of the multimedia devices on your computer.

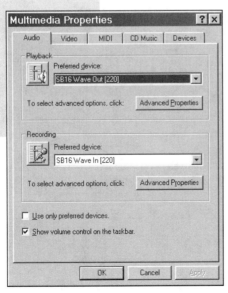

## Telephony

If you install a modem that supports voice as well as data, you'll use the Telephony box to set up the software that controls the voice portion of the modem's operation. In the Telephony box, you specify the dialing properties you need to use when making voice calls by modem, and you set up and configure Telephony drivers.

Once you finish using the Telephony box to set up your modem, you use Phone Dialer, which is a Windows accessory, to actually dial the phone number using the modem.

## Users

Earlier in this chapter, you read about different people sharing the same computer. When you click on the Users icon in the Control Panel, you start a wizard that helps you set up multiple users for the same computer. Each user will be able to save his or her own Desktop settings, including icons and wallpaper.

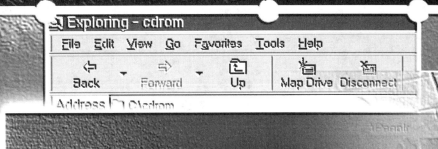

# PART III
# Windows Accessories and Tools

My
ocument

rag N Fil

CIS 3.0.3

Internet
Explorer

# 9

# Using WordPad and Notepad

## IN THIS CHAPTER

- **Creating a WordPad Document**
- **Editing a WordPad Document**
- **Formatting a WordPad Document**
- **Adding Graphics to a WordPad Document**
- **Saving and Printing a WordPad Document**
- **Creating a Text File in Notepad**

Several "freebie" accessory programs are included with Windows 98. Some are useful and some are—well, not so useful. This chapter discusses two of the more useful programs: WordPad and Notepad, both of which are text-editing programs.

The WordPad program is a scaled-down version of the popular word processing program, Microsoft Word; Notepad is a scaled-down version of WordPad.

This chapter shows you how to create documents with WordPad and Notepad and how to make efficient use of their features.

# Using WordPad

If you use your computer to write letters, proposals, memos, and other such documents, but don't need to do things like mail merge or macros, WordPad is just the program to use. It's basic—but functional. Like Microsoft Word, WordPerfect, and other well-know word processing programs, WordPad can create and edit documents of any length. It accepts graphics, as well as headers and footers, and the find-and-replace feature enables you to find text easily. It has several types of tab stops and a variety of font settings and paragraph settings. Most people use these features every day, and this chapter gives you a chance to practice using them.

## Starting WordPad

WordPad, like most Windows programs, is accessed from the Start button.

### Hands On:  Starting WordPad

1. Click on the Start button.
2. Highlight Programs, Accessories, WordPad. The WordPad program will launch and begin with a clean screen ready for you to use. You may need to maximize the WordPad window. Your screen should look like the one in Figure 9.1

The WordPad window displays two toolbars: the top bar is called the *toolbar*, whereas the bottom one is the *format bar*. The toolbar contains many of the common Window commands such as New, Open, Save, Print, Print Preview, Find, Cut, Copy, Paste, Undo, and Date/Time.

The format bar has features for selecting font, font size, color, bold, italics, underline, justification (left, center, and right), and bullets.

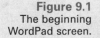

**Figure 9.1**
The beginning
WordPad screen.

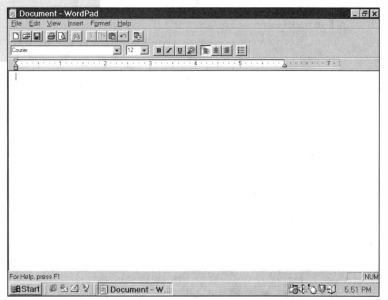

Position the mouse pointer over a tool to reveal a ScreenTip that tells the name of toolbar buttons, while the status bar displays the purpose of the button.

The WordPad screen also displays the ruler, which you can use for setting tabs. The toolbar, format bar, and ruler are shown in Figure 9.2

If any of the bars are not displayed, click on the <u>V</u>iew menu and then choose the items that do not have a check mark beside them. WordPad will then display those features.

Toolbar          Format Bar          Ruler

**Figure 9.2**
You can access
WordPad
features in a
single click by
using the toolbar
and format bar.

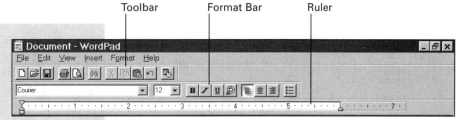

# Creating a WordPad Document

The main document area of the WordPad window contains the blinking *insertion point*. Keep an eye on that insertion point because it indicates where new text will appear.

When typing a document, WordPad monitors the lines within a paragraph. If the word you are typing will not fit entirely on the current line, WordPad goes to the next line. This feature is called *word wrap*. Press the Enter key only when you get to the end of a paragraph. You can press the key a second time if you want an extra blank line between paragraphs. A short line of text—a date or greeting like "Dear Mr. Jones"—counts as a paragraph all by itself.

While typing the text for the following exercise, if you make a mistake, press the Backspace key to delete the previously typed character. If you make other mistakes, leave them alone. You will fix them later.

## Hands On: Typing a Document

The ad in this exercise might appear in a company newsletter or on the bulletin board. Type the text according to the following steps. The paragraphs don't seem to be in the right order, but you will revise the text later.

FOR SALE

This is a home and you must see it to appreciate the beauty and elegance. Priced to sell at $830,000. Contact Barbara Jenkins at extension 4426 for more information.

Fireplace
Vaulted Ceilings
3 Car Garage

Beautiful contemporary home on 4 acres located in the rolling hills of Meadowland Creek. This home has 4 bedrooms, one overlooking a nice private lake. There are 3 bathrooms and a full surrounding deck. It also includes:

1. Type **FOR SALE** on the first line and then press the Enter key twice to move the insertion point down two lines.

*Note*

> **Remember! Don't press the Enter key at the end of a line. Wait until you have completed an entire paragraph.**

2. Type the first body paragraph, beginning with the words **This is a**. After typing **information.**, press the Enter key twice to create a new paragraph and move down two more lines.

3. Type the list of items (beginning with **Fireplace**), pressing Enter once at the end of each item. Press Enter an extra time at the end of the third item.

4. Type the second body paragraph, beginning with the word **Beautiful**, then press the Enter key twice to create a new paragraph and move down two more lines.

When your document is finished, it should look like the one in Figure 9.3.

**Figure 9.3**
The typed document as it appears in WordPad.

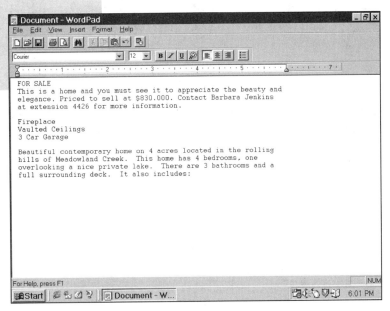

# Editing a WordPad Document

Now that you have typed your document, it's time to go back and make changes to it. Anything is changeable in a word processing document. The secret to making changes is the location of the insertion point. You need to move it to the location where a change is to be made. To move the insertion point, you can either:

- Move the mouse pointer to the location and click the mouse button.
- Use your up, down, left, or right arrow keys on the keyboard to direct the insertion point to the appropriate location.

Either method is fine to use. It's a matter of personal preference.

You can also use various keyboard combinations to move the insertion point quickly. Table 9.1 lists some of the keyboard combinations.

*Tip*

These same keyboard combinations work with most word processing programs!

*Note*

**The insertion point will not go past the text you have typed unless you press the Enter key after typing the final word.**

## Table 9.1 Keys to Move around Quickly in a WordPad Document

| Key Combination | Moves the Insertion Point |
| --- | --- |
| Ctrl + → | One word to the right |
| Ctrl+ ← | One word to the left |
| Ctrl+ ↑ | One paragraph up |
| Ctrl+ ↓ | One paragraph down |
| Ctrl+Home | Top of the document |
| Ctrl+End | Bottom of the document |
| Home | Beginning of a line |
| End | End of a line |
| Page Up | Next screen up |
| Page Down | Next screen down |

## Hands On: Editing a Document

Now that you have typed the document, you need to make a few changes.

1. Position the insertion point in front of the word *home* and begin typing the word **wonderful**. WordPad inserts the word and shoves all other text to the right to make room for it.

2. Position the mouse in front of the *8* and then press the Delete key to delete the *8*. Type a **2** to replace it.

3. Double-click the mouse on the word *nice* to select and highlight it. Press the Delete key on the keyboard to delete the selected word.

*Tip*

If at any time you need help with a WordPad feature, press F1 to display the Help window.

*Note*

**Pressing the Delete key deletes the character to the right of the insertion point; pressing the Backspace key deletes the character to the left of the insertion point. An easy way to remember which is which is that the Backspace key has an arrow pointing to the left!**

## Adding a Date or Time

Because your computer stores the current date and time, WordPad can use that information to insert the date or time into your document. This feature is really handy when you can't remember if today is the 9th or the 10th. (This happens to me frequently!)

WordPad has 12 date or time formats, ranging from short abbreviated versions such as 11/2/97 to formats that spell out the day and month as well as display the date and year. You can even display military time—down to the second. It's your choice!

## Hands On: Adding the Date

1. Press Ctrl+Home to move the insertion point to the top of the document and then press the Enter key twice to make room for the date and time. Press Ctrl+Home again to move back up to the top.

2. Choose <u>I</u>nsert, <u>D</u>ate and Time. The Date and Time dialog box (see Figure 9.4) prompts you to make a selection from the available formats.

*Tip*

• • • • • • • • • • • • • • • • • • • • • • • • • • • • • • • • • • • • • • • • • •

Another way to open the Date and Time dialog box is to click the Date/Time button (the last button on the top toolbar).

• • • • • • • • • • • • • • • • • • • • • • • • • • • • • • • • • • • • • • • • • • •

**Figure 9.4**
Add the current date to your document.

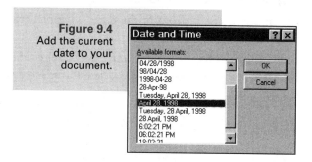

3. Choose the format you want from the <u>A</u>vailable formats list box and then click on OK. WordPad inserts the current date and/or time into your document at the location of your insertion point.

*Note*

**The date and time feature is *static*, which means that your document does not change each time you open it. If you choose 11/2/97, that date remains in the document unless you select the date and time feature again.**

## Selecting Text in a WordPad Document

Making corrections or changes when the change involves only a character or two is quite easy, but if you want to delete an entire paragraph, the steps you used earlier could take forever!

WordPad includes several special techniques for selecting a block of text that makes those types of changes simpler. Blocks can be anywhere from two characters to the entire document in length.

When you are working with a block of text, any formatting or editing changes you make in WordPad apply only to that block of text. If you don't select text before you apply changes, you may get unexpected results. Table 9.2 illustrates a few of the techniques for selecting a block of text. Some of these procedures use a mouse and some are keyboard methods.

| **Table 9.2 Block Selection Techniques** | |
|---|---|
| **Do This** | **To Select This** |
| Double-click on a word | A word |
| Triple-click on a word | A paragraph |
| Click and drag across characters | Any amount of text you drag the mouse across |
| Press Ctrl+A | The entire document |
| Press Shift+(arrow key) | Highlights one character at a time from the insertion point in the direction of the arrow key you press |

*Tip*

• • • • • • • • • • • • • • • • • • • • • • • • • • • • • • • • • • • • • • • • • • • • • •

To deselect text, click anywhere outside of the highlighted text.

• • • • • • • • • • • • • • • • • • • • • • • • • • • • • • • • • • • • • • • • • • • • • • •

## Moving a Block of Text

> **For more information on Cut and Paste, see Chapter 3.**

To change the location of a paragraph or other block of text, don't delete it and retype it in the new location. Instead, use the Windows Cut and Paste commands to move it for you.

The Windows Cut command deletes selected text from its original location and places a copy of the selected text on the Windows Clipboard. Windows then retains the text on the Clipboard, waiting for instructions on where to paste the text. When you paste the text into the new location, the text remains on the Clipboard until you either turn off your computer or copy or paste another selection to the Windows Clipboard.

### Hands On: Moving a Paragraph with Cut and Paste

In the sample ad, you typed the body paragraphs out of order. Body paragraph 2 needs to be paragraph 1. To move a paragraph, you must select it first, then you can tell WordPad where to place the text.

1. Triple-click (click rapidly three times) on the second body paragraph (the one that begins with the word *Beautiful*). The entire paragraph becomes highlighted.

2. Choose Edit, Cut—or press Ctrl+X. The text disappears and is placed on the Windows Clipboard.

You could also click on the Cut button (it looks like a pair of scissors) on the toolbar.

3. Position the insertion point in front of the word *This* in the first body paragraph, making sure the insertion point is blinking and that paragraph 1 is not highlighted.

4. Choose Edit, Paste. The paragraph is inserted, and body paragraph 1 becomes body paragraph 2 (see Figure 9.5).

You could also click on the Paste button (it looks like a small clipboard with a piece of paper on it) on the toolbar.

**Note**

**Cut, Copy, and Paste are also available by clicking the right mouse button. A shortcut menu appears, and you can make your selection with the left mouse button.**

**Figure 9.5**
The paragraph has been moved without retyping it.

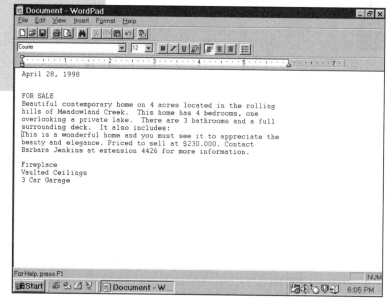

Sometimes you may need to adjust a paragraph after pasting text. For example, you may need to press the Enter key at the end of a paragraph to allow an extra line of spacing between the two paragraphs. If you need to delete an extra blank line, place the insertion point on one of the blank lines and press the Delete key. WordPad deletes the blank line and moves all subsequent paragraphs up one line.

Another method for moving text is called the *drag-and-drop* method. It's the fastest method of all, but requires a steady hand with the mouse.

### Hands On: Moving a Paragraph with Drag and Drop

1. Triple-click on the paragraph that begins with the words *This is a wonderful* and then position the mouse pointer on top of the highlighted text.

2. Hold down the mouse button and then move the mouse pointer. A small line appears at the tip of the mouse pointer. (See Figure 9.6.)

3. "Drag" the small dotted line under the list of the house's features and then release the mouse button. The text "drops" into the new location.

**Figure 9.6**
Misplaced paragraphs are easily moved with WordPad's drag-and-drop feature.

```
Document - WordPad
File  Edit  View  Insert  Format  Help

Courier                    12    B  I  U

April 28, 1998

FOR SALE
Beautiful contemporary home on 4 acres located in the rolling
hills of Meadowland Creek.  This home has 4 bedrooms, one
overlooking a private lake.  There are 3 bathrooms and a full
surrounding deck.  It also includes:

This is a wonderful home and you must see it to appreciate the
beauty and elegance. Priced to sell at $230,000. Contact
Barbara Jenkins at extension 4426 for more information.

Fireplace
Vaulted Ceilings
3 Car Garage


For Help, press F1                                              NUM
Start      Document - W...                          6:07 PM
```

*Tip*

If you drop the text where you did not want it, choose <u>E</u>dit, <u>U</u>ndo to reverse your most recent action.

# Formatting a WordPad Document

The document as you have typed it is not very pretty, just sort of plain and drab. Sure, it says just what you want it to, but no one will notice it as it is. The document needs to be formatted.

*Formatting* controls the appearance of a document. Some formatting commands involve a few characters, some involve an entire paragraph, and others encompass the entire document. Some examples of WordPad's formatting include:

- Font type, size, or color
- Paragraph alignment and indentation
- Bullet points
- Page orientation
- Paper size
- Margin settings

## Changing Font Attributes

WordPad applies your font type, size, and color choices to the text you select. WordPad's default font is Times New Roman 10 point, which is a relatively small font that is sometimes hard to read.

*Note*

**A 72-point font is approximately 1 inch tall when printed.**

The general rule of thumb is to not have more than two fonts on a single page. Adding attributes such as bolding or italics gives the appearance of more fonts, without adding different typefaces.

## Hands On: Changing Font Attributes

1. Select the entire document by pressing Ctrl+A.

2. Choose a point size from the Font Size drop-down list box in the format bar. For this example, select a 14-point size.

3. Open the Font Name drop-down list box, and select the font name you would like for your document. For this example, choose Arial (see Figure 9.7).

   Notice the font style of the entire document changed to Arial, and Arial is reflected in the Font Name drop-down list box.

4. Click anywhere in the body of the document to deselect it.

   Now you want to make the heading of the document larger and bolder.

5. Select the words *FOR SALE* and then change the point size to 24.

6. Click on the Bold button on the format bar or press Ctrl+B. When the Bold button is in use, it appears to be pressed in.

● ● ● ● ● ● ● ● ● ● ● ● ● ● ● ● ● ● ● ● ● ● ● ● ● ● ● ● ● ● ● ● ● ● ● ● ● ● ● ● ● ● ● ●

The shortcut key for italics is Ctrl+I and for underline is Ctrl+U.

● ● ● ● ● ● ● ● ● ● ● ● ● ● ● ● ● ● ● ● ● ● ● ● ● ● ● ● ● ● ● ● ● ● ● ● ● ● ● ● ● ● ● ●

7. Click anywhere in the body of the document to deselect the heading.

**Figure 9.7**
Your font choices
will vary
depending upon
installed
software.

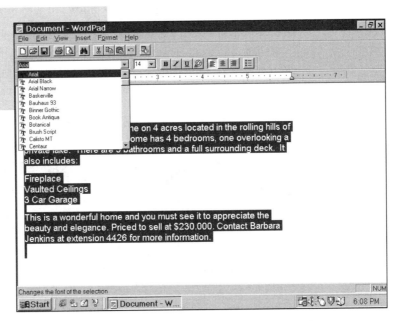

*Note*

> If you want to change the font attributes all at one time, plus have the ability to preview a sample before changing it, choose Format, Font. The Font dialog box contains all the font attribute choices.

## Changing Paragraph Attributes

The most common change made to paragraph formatting is the alignment of text. By default, WordPad documents are justified (aligned) on the left side of the document. Other choices include centered and right justified. You cannot change justification for part of a paragraph. An alignment change affects the entire paragraph.

Here are samples of paragraphs with various justification choices applied.

> This example shows left-justified text. Notice the left edge of the paragraph is even. The shortcut key to left-justify text is Ctrl+L. You cannot change justification for part of a paragraph. An alignment change affects the entire paragraph.

> This example shows center-justified text. Notice neither side of the paragraph is even. The shortcut key to center-justify text is Ctrl+E. You cannot change justification for part of a paragraph. An alignment change affects the entire paragraph.

> This example shows right-justified text. Notice the right edge of the paragraph is even. The shortcut key to right-justify text is Ctrl+R. You cannot change justification for part of a paragraph. An alignment change affects the entire paragraph.

The bottom WordPad toolbar has buttons for all three alignment choices.

### Hands On: Changing Paragraph Attributes

1. Click anywhere in the date line and then click on the Align Right button on the format bar. The entire date is even with the right margin.
2. Click anywhere in the FOR SALE heading and then click on the Center button on the format bar. The heading is centered as shown in Figure 9.8.

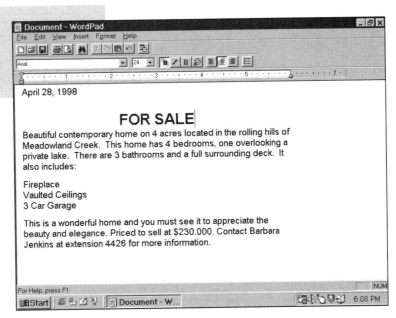

**Figure 9.8**
Heading text is
centered
between the
margins.

## Adding Bullets

A *bullet* is a small black circle or other character that precedes each item in a list. Bullets call attention to the list of items and differentiate them from the rest of the text in a document. WordPad considers bullets a paragraph attribute because a bulleted paragraph is also indented.

### Hands On: Adding Bullets

1. Click and drag to highlight the list of three items in the middle of the document.
2. Choose Format, Bullet Style. A bullet has been added in front of each item, and the text has been indented ½ inch to the right (see Figure 9.9).

*Tip*

Optionally, click on the Bullets button on the format bar to add bullets to the selected items.

**Figure 9.9**
Use bullets to
call attention
to a list.

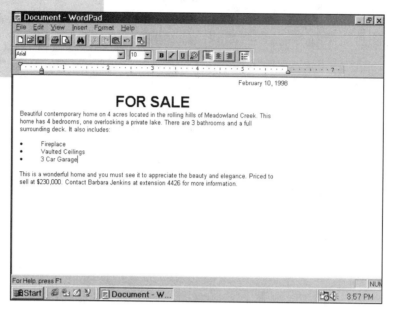

## Changing Page Attributes

Page attributes are settings that affect the layout of the text on the page. Examples of page attributes include margins, orientation, and paper size. WordPad applies one set of page settings to all pages of a document.

### Hands On: Changing Page Settings

1. Choose File, Page Setup. The Page Setup dialog box displays selections for the paper size, source, orientation, and margins available. A preview of the current settings is also displayed and will change as you make different selections.

2. Click on the down arrow next to the Size list box to select a different paper size. Your choices may vary according to the type of printer you are using.

*Tip*

If more than one printer is available for your use, click on the Printer button at the bottom to select another printer.

3. Click on the down arrow next to the Source list box to choose the paper tray you want to use. Your choices may vary according to the type of printer you are using. Figure 9.10 illustrates options for the HP LaserJet III.

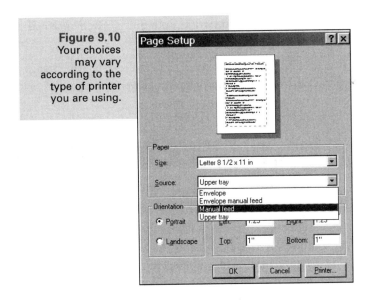

**Figure 9.10**
Your choices may vary according to the type of printer you are using.

4. Choose Portrait or Landscape for the Orientation of text on the page. Portrait orientation prints with the narrow edge of the paper at the top, whereas Landscape prints with the wide edge at the top.

5. Choose the margin settings you want for your document. Margins are measured in inches, although you are not required to put the inch mark next to the measurement in the text box. WordPad inserts that character for you. You are only required to specify the numeric measurement.

*Tip*

Press the Tab key to quickly move from margin setting to margin setting.

6. Press the Enter key or click on OK when you are satisfied with the page settings.

## Saving a WordPad Document

As you work on a document, that document is stored only in the computer memory area. As soon as you start a different document in WordPad or exit the Word-Pad program, unless you save your document, you will not be able to edit or print it again.

You've put a lot of time and effort into creating and modifying your document, so you certainly don't want to lose it! The general rule of thumb is to save your work every 10 to 15 minutes. In the event the computer quits functioning, you will not lose all of your work, only that portion that had been completed since the last time the document was saved.

WordPad documents are saved by default to the My Documents folder located on your Windows 98 Desktop. You can save a file to a different folder; however, you cannot change the default location.

## Hands On: Saving a File

1.  Choose <u>F</u>ile, <u>S</u>ave—or press Ctrl+S. Also note that the third button on the top toolbar is the Save command.

2.  If you are saving a file for the first time, the Save As dialog box prompts you to give the file a name. By default, WordPad tries to name the file Document, but this name is not very helpful. Instead, type a more descriptive file name in the File <u>N</u>ame text box, such as **House for Sale**, as shown in Figure 9.11.

**Figure 9.11**
File names can be up to 255 characters in length and can include spaces.

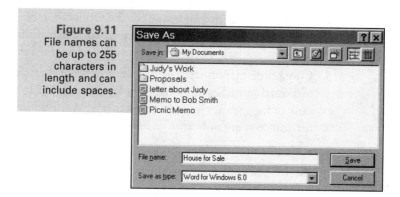

File names can be as long as you want them and can include spaces or any special characters except asterisks and question marks.

3.  Optionally, click on the arrow in the Save <u>I</u>n list box to select a different folder in which to store the document.

4.  Press the Enter key or click on OK to save the document with the specified name. The file is now safely stored for future use. The name of the document appears at the top of the screen in the WordPad title bar.

After the file has initially been saved, you can update the saved information by choosing <u>F</u>ile, <u>S</u>ave again or by pressing Ctrl+S. The Save As dialog box does not appear again. WordPad automatically resaves the file with the current file name.

# Adding Graphics to a WordPad Document

WordPad enables you to place pictures or graphics into your document. You can use this feature to add a scanned image of the house for sale.

You cannot create a graphic image with WordPad, but you can copy and paste an image from any program that does create graphics. If the graphic has been saved in a .GIF or .JPG format, you can use Internet Explorer to copy the image.

> **For more information on locating files, see "Working with Files" in Chapter 4.**

## Hands On: Adding a Picture to a Document

To add a picture to a WordPad document:

1. Locate the picture you want to insert into the WordPad document. You can use Windows Explorer or My Computer to locate the file as shown in Figure 9.12.

2. Click on the graphics file to open the program associated with it as shown in Figure 9.13.

3. Position the mouse pointer over the picture, and right-click to activate a shortcut menu, similar to the one in Figure 9.14.

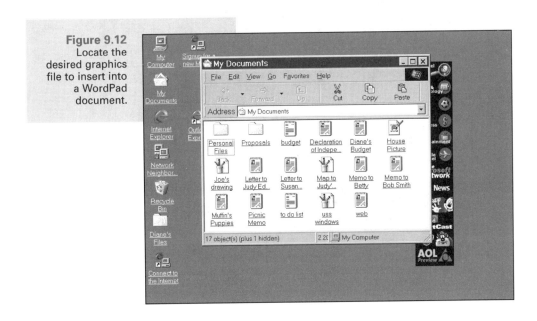

**Figure 9.12**
Locate the desired graphics file to insert into a WordPad document.

**Figure 9.13**
The program associated with a graphic begins when you click on the file icon.

**Figure 9.14**
Clicking the right mouse button activates the shortcut menu.

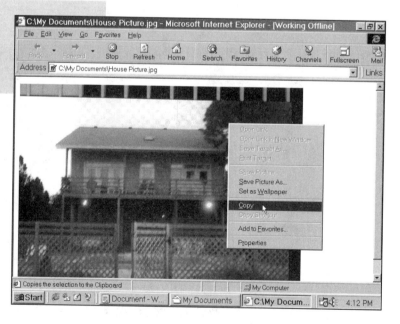

**4.** Choose <u>C</u>opy from the shortcut menu to copy the picture to the Windows Clipboard.

5. Return to the WordPad document and position the insertion point to show WordPad where to place the graphic.

6. Choose Edit, Paste. The graphic appears in the WordPad document and has eight small handles around it.

To resize a graphic, position the mouse over one of the eight handles surrounding the graphic and then click and drag the mouse until the frame of the picture is the desired size. Release the mouse button, and the picture will be resized.

## Printing a WordPad Document

Finally! You've finished the document, and now it's time to print it. Printing is a slow, expensive process and uses our natural resources, so you should always preview a document prior to printing it. Previewing a document enables you to check the overall perspective of text and graphics in relation to the paper. You can answer questions such as, Should I make the text larger? Should I center the heading? Does this document have the right look?

Print Preview enables you to look but not touch; that is, you cannot edit the document from Print Preview. You are getting a bird's eye view of the document to check the perspective only. To modify the document further, you must return to the editing screen.

To preview a document choose File, Print Preview. The document gets smaller, and seven buttons appear at the top of the screen, as seen in Figure 9.15.

- **Print**—Closes the Preview window and brings up the Print dialog box.
- **Next Page**—Previews the next page of the document.
- **Previous Page**—Previews the previous page of the document.
- **Two Pages**—Previews two pages side by side.
- **Zoom In**—Magnifies the document view.
- **Zoom Out**—Returns the document to a full page view.
- **Close**—Closes the Preview window and returns to the editing screen.

When you are actually ready to print the document, several printing methods are available. The fastest method is to click on the Print button on the toolbar. This action sends the document directly to the current printer and prints all pages of the document, no questions asked.

If, however, you want to control the printing, such as how many copies to print, which printer to use, or choose specific pages to print, you need to open the Print dialog box.

**Figure 9.15**
Print Preview
has its own set
of buttons.

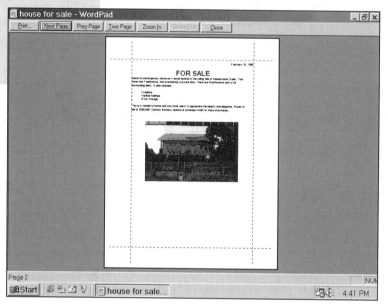

## Hands On: Printing a Document

1. Click on File, Print—or press Ctrl+P. The Print dialog box appears and is ready for you to make selections. See Figure 9.16.

2. Make any desired changes in the dialog box and then click on OK to continue with the printing process.

**Figure 9.16**
Select print
options from the
Print dialog box.

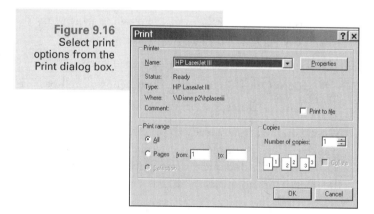

# Creating a New WordPad Document

WordPad automatically gives you a new document to work with each time you start the program. If you currently have a document on the screen and want to start a new document, you will have to create it.

> ## Hands On:  Creating a New WordPad Document:

1. Choose File, New—or click on the New button on the top toolbar.

   The New dialog box opens, which prompts you for the type of new document you want to create.

WordPad supports four types of documents:

- **Word 6 Document**—A document of this type can be opened and edited in Microsoft Word without conversion problems. This choice is the default.
- **Rich Text Document**—A document of this type can include character formatting and tabs for use in a variety of word processing programs.
- **Text Document**—A document of this type has no formatting (for example, a Notepad document).
- **Unicode Text Document**—A document of this type can include characters recognized in many other foreign languages.

2. Click on the type of document to create and choose OK.

If you need to save any changes in the current document, WordPad prompts you before it displays the new document on the screen (see Figure 9.17).

**Figure 9.17**
Click on Yes to save the current document or No to discard it.

# Opening an Existing WordPad Document

Opening a document places a copy of a saved document into the computer memory and on your screen for further editing or review.

> ## Hands On: Opening an Existing WordPad Document:
>
> 1. Choose File, Open—or press Ctrl+O. The Open dialog box shown in Figure 9.18 appears with a list of documents. The default folder is the My Documents folder.
> 2. Locate the folder that contains the file you want.
> 3. Double-click on the desired file name to open the file.
>
> The file appears on your screen ready for you to edit.

**Figure 9.18**
A list of Word type documents is displayed by default.

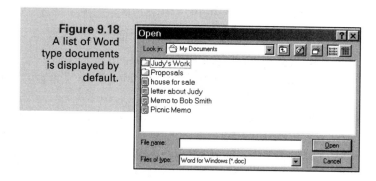

## Quitting the WordPad Program

Exiting the WordPad program when you are finished allows other programs to use the computer's resources.

To quit a program, use one of the following methods:

- Click on the Close button at the far right of the WordPad title bar.
- Choose File, Exit.

WordPad prompts you to save any open files before the program actually shuts down.

# Using Notepad

Notepad is a miniature text-only word processing program. It's very limited in comparison to WordPad or other word processors. For example, Notepad cannot center text, nor does it support multiple fonts in a document. It also doesn't allow you to add graphics to a Notepad document.

If it can't do all those things, why did Microsoft even include it?

First of all, Windows 98 has a special connection to Notepad. Some of the files that your software installs are written in plain text instead of "computerese." When one of these files needs to be edited, Notepad is the program Windows 98 uses to open the file and allow it to be edited.

Second, Notepad is fast! Because it doesn't have a lot of fluff, it doesn't need to load a lot of program files into the computer memory. So Notepad loads and runs quickly. That's handy if you have an older computer.

Notepad is a great program to create small reminder notes to yourself. The capacity of each document is somewhat limited, so you don't want to use it to create lengthy correspondence.

## Starting Notepad

Notepad is one of the accessory programs included when Windows 98 is installed.

### Hands On: Starting Notepad

1. Click on the Start button.
2. Highlight Programs, Accessories, Notepad. The Notepad program launches and begins with a clean editing screen, ready for you to use. As you can see in Figure 9.19, Notepad doesn't have any toolbars and gives you only four menu choices to select from.

## Creating a File in Notepad

When it is first installed, Notepad does not have automatic word wrap. It's available, but the first time you use the program, you must turn on the feature. It will then remain on until you turn the feature off. Wrapping text makes all the text visible on the screen, but it also affects how the text appears when printed.

If word wrap is turned off, the text you type keeps on going across the screen. The text doesn't automatically jump to the next line as it does in WordPad or other word processing programs. It does however, print correctly, according to the margin settings you specify.

If word wrap is turned on, the text you type wraps to the next line, but the way you see the text onscreen is exactly the way it prints. Notepad ignores your margin commands when word wrap is activated. This feature is especially important if you are working in a smaller-than-maximized window. You may get unexpected results when you print your document!

**Figure 9.19**
The Notepad window is very simple.

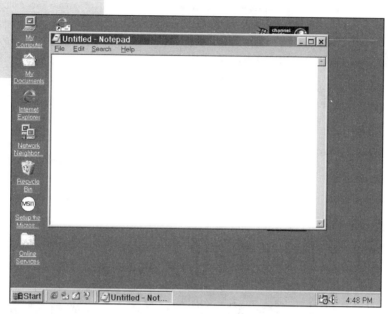

If you are going to print your document, you should activate word wrap, but turn it off before you print.

## Hands on: Formatting a Notepad File

To set up a document:

1. Choose Edit, Word Wrap.

   Next you will want to select the font to use while creating your note. Any font choice you make affects the screen display only. No matter which font you choose, the document prints in a Courier 10cpi font. Also, when you change the font, that font remains the default display font for other Notepad documents that you open or create.

To change the font:

2. Choose Edit, Set Font to display the Font dialog box.
3. Select the font and font attributes you want to use and then click on OK to close the Font dialog box.

You may also want to check the page layout to be assured the margins, paper orientation, and other settings are to your liking. These choices affect printing.

To change page layout settings:

4. Choose File, Page Setup to open the Page Setup dialog box (see Figure 9.20). From here you specify most of the options that affect the printing of your Notepad document.

   - Choose the paper size from the Size drop-down list box.
   - Select Portrait or Landscape for the orientation of the paper.
   - Adjust the Left, Right, Top, or Bottom margins.
   - Modify the Header or Footer.

   Just like many word processing programs, Notepad allows for headers and footers, but each is only one line long. You must use special print codes if you want specific information, such as the file name or page number, to print. The default header prints the file name, and the default footer prints the word *Page* and the page number. Table 9.3 displays the codes you can use.

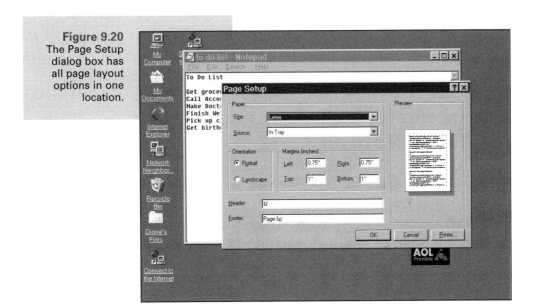

**Figure 9.20**
The Page Setup dialog box has all page layout options in one location.

| Table 9.3 Printer Codes Available for Notepad | |
|---|---|
| **Type This** | **To Get This** |
| &f | File name |
| &d | Print date |
| &t | Print time |
| &p | Page number |

*Note*

**The special print codes are only available in the header and footer. They will not work in the body of the document.**

5. Make any desired changes to the page setup and then click on OK. Notepad applies the new settings to the current document.

Now you can type and edit the note as you would in any standard word processing program.

*Tip*

You can add a date and time stamp to your Notepad document by pressing F5.

## Saving a File in Notepad

Just like other files, you must save Notepad documents if you want to keep them for future use. The difference is that the file will be saved in a text-only format.

### Hands On: Saving a Notepad File

1. Choose File, Save. The Save As dialog box as seen in Figure 9.21 prompts you to enter a file name. Descriptive file names up to 255 characters are allowed.

**Figure 9.21**
The default
folder for
Notepad is the
My Documents
folder.

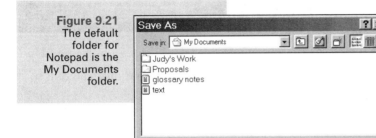

**Figure 9.21** The default folder for Notepad is the My Documents folder.

2. Enter a file name in the File Name text box.

3. Choose an optional folder location from the Save In box and then click on OK. The file will be saved.

## Opening a File in Notepad

Opening a file displays a copy of the original file on the computer screen so you can edit it.

### Hands On: Opening a File in Notepad

1. Choose File, Open. The Open dialog box appears on your screen.

2. If necessary, use the Look In box to navigate to the folder your file is stored in.

3. Double-click on the desired file to open it.

Notepad opens the file, and it is ready for you to edit.

## Printing a File from Notepad

As mentioned earlier in this chapter, you should turn off word wrap just prior to printing. The text on your screen will look a little strange, but when it comes out of the printer, the text will have been adjusted according to the margin settings you chose earlier.

## Hands On: Printing a Notepad File

1. Choose <u>E</u>dit, <u>W</u>ord Wrap to deactivate the word wrap feature.
2. Choose <u>F</u>ile, <u>P</u>rint. No print options are available. Your only choice is to print a single copy of the entire document.

# 10

# Getting Creative with Paint

## IN THIS CHAPTER

- Identifying and Using the Paint Tools
- Drawing Lines and Shapes
- Editing Attributes of Objects
- Rearranging Objects

Every drawing is made up of a series of small objects—usually one or more shapes such as circles or rectangles, combined with other objects such as lines or text. The Paint program in Windows 98 helps you make drawings. You'll find this program on the Accessories menu.

# Discovering Parts of a Paint Window

Right here at the beginning of this chapter I need to tell you that I am not now, have never been, and never will be blessed with drawing skills. You'll soon see the evidence for yourself.

### Hands On: Starting the Paint Program

1. Click on the Start button.
2. Highlight Programs, Accessories, Paint. The Paint program opens with a clean screen for you to begin your drawing. You may need to maximize the Paint window.

## Identifying the Tool Box

A feature called the Tool Box appears on the left side of the Paint window. If you position the mouse pointer on top of each tool, Windows 98 displays the name of the tool at the mouse pointer and a description of the tool in the status bar.

*Tip*

If the toolbox is not displayed, click on the View menu and choose Tool Box.

You select a tool by clicking once on its designated button. The tool button appears to be "pressed in" when a tool is active. Also, some tools display additional options at the bottom of the Tool Box when they are selected. For example, if you select the Brush tool, the various shapes, thickness, and angles will be available for you to choose from. If you select the Rectangle tool, you can choose from a rectangle with a frame only, filled with a frame, or filled only. Figure 10.1 illustrates the appearance of the Brush tool when it is selected.

These 16 tools enable you to create or edit the objects you need for your drawings:

- **Free-Form select**—Selects an irregular shaped area to edit.
- **Select**—Selects a rectangular portion of the picture to edit.

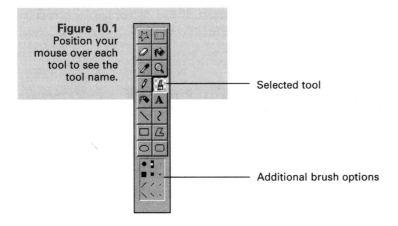

**Figure 10.1**
Position your mouse over each tool to see the tool name.

Selected tool

Additional brush options

- **Erase/Color Eraser**—Erases a portion of the picture or Replaces a color with another color.
- **Fill With color**—Fills in an enclosed area with color.
- **Pick Color**—Copies color from one area or object to another.
- **Magnifier**—Magnifies or zooms in or out on a picture.
- **Pencil**—Draws free-form lines.
- **Brush**—Draws with a brush of a selected size and shape.
- **Airbrush**—Creates an airbrush or spray can effect.
- **Text**—Inserts text into a drawing.
- **Line**—Draws a straight line.
- **Curve**—Draws a curved line with at least one but no more than two arcs.
- **Rectangle**—Draws rectangles or squares.
- **Polygon**—Draws polygons.
- **Ellipse**—Draws an ellipse or circle.
- **Rounded Rectangle**—Draws rectangles or squares with rounded corners.

# Editing the Color Box

The color box appears at the very bottom of the screen with a palette of 28 colors that you can use while making a drawing. The two small overlapping boxes directly to the left of the color box represent the currently selected colors. The front box is the foreground color, and the rear box is the background color. Clicking on a color with the left mouse button selects a color for the foreground or frame of an object. Clicking on a color with the right mouse button selects a color for the background or interior (fill) of an object. If you do not see the particular color or shade you want, you can replace existing colors from a palette of several other colors or even create your own colors.

## Hands On: Changing Color Choices

1. Click on the color in the color box you want to replace.

*Note*

> If you do not first choose a color to replace, the current selected color will be replaced.

2. Choose Colors, Edit Colors.

   The Edit Colors dialog box, shown in Figure 10.2, displays the basic colors that are available.

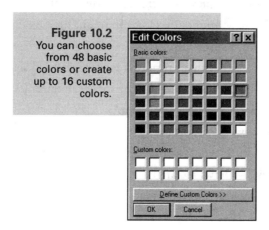

**Figure 10.2**
You can choose from 48 basic colors or create up to 16 custom colors.

3. Click on the new Basic color you want to use, then click on OK. The new color appears in the color box.

These colors are available for the current drawing only. The next drawing you create reverts to the default colors.

## Designing a Custom Color

If you can't find the exact shade you want in any of the 48 basic colors, you can design your own. Microsoft Paint enables you to create up to 16 custom colors. Like the basic colors, these colors are available for the current drawing only.

## Hands On:  Creating a Custom Color

1. Click on the color you want to replace.
2. Choose Colors, Edit Colors.
3. Click on a blank Custom colors box to designate a location for the new custom color.
4. Click on the Define Custom Colors button. The Edit Colors dialog box expands to include a color matrix.

   The fastest way to create a custom color is to use the mouse pointer. Notice in Figure 10.3 the crosshairs in the color matrix.

**Figure 10.3**
Use the mouse to move the crosshairs vertically or horizontally.

Crosshairs —

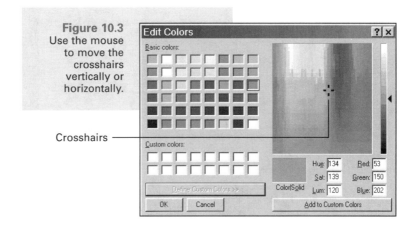

You can create a color by dragging the crosshairs horizontally or vertically. The slider bar (represented by a arrow) on the right of the matrix adjusts the brightness of the custom color. Paint displays a sample of the color you are mixing in the Color/Solid box.

5. When you are satisfied with the color, click on the Add to Custom Colors button. Paint displays the newly designed color in the Custom color box you designated.
6. Click on OK to close the Edit Colors dialog box. The new color appears in the color box.

# Resizing the Drawing Screen

You can determine the size of your Paint working area. By default, when the Paint program opens, the screen working area is rather small—just a little over 4 inches wide by 3 inches tall.

## Hands On: Resizing the Drawing Screen

1. Click on Image, then choose Attributes or press Ctrl+E.

2. From the Units area, choose Inches.

3. Enter the desired page Width and Height (measured in inches); then click on OK. In Figure 10.4, the screen was resized to 6 inches by 5 inches.

**Figure 10.4**
Enlarging the screen also means that you have a larger file to save.

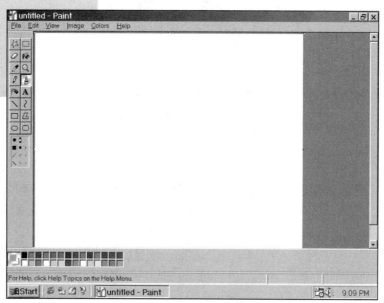

The new page size remains in effect for all new drawings. However, you can restore the default size.

## Hands On: Reverting to the Default Setting

1. Click on Image; then choose Attributes or press Ctrl+E.

2. Click on the Default button from the Attributes dialog box to restore the screen settings to the original installed size.

3. Click on OK to close the Attributes dialog box.

# Drawing with the Paint Tools

As described earlier in this chapter, Microsoft Paint includes several types of drawing tools, including a paintbrush; airbrush; text tool; and tools to draw various shapes such as lines, circles, or rectangles.

The hands-on exercise in the next section shows you how to draw the boat shown in Figure 10.5. You will need the following tools:

- The Rectangle tool
- The Polygon tool
- The Ellipse tool
- The Fill With Color tool
- The Magnifier tool
- The Pencil tool
- The Airbrush tool
- The Line tool
- The Text tool

**Figure 10.5**
It can take many different tools to assemble even a simple drawing!

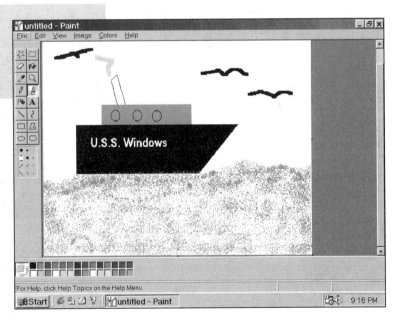

# Drawing Shapes

Shapes can be circles, squares, rectangles, polygons. You'll need two rectangles for the body of the boat and a triangle for the front. You'll also need three circles for the portholes.

### Hands On: Drawing Shapes

1. Click on the Rectangle tool. When the tool appears to be "pushed in," it is active.

2. Position the mouse on the drawing screen and click and drag the mouse until you have a rectangle approximately 3 inches long by 1 inch tall. It doesn't have to be exactly those measurements, just something similar to what you see in Figure 10.6

3. Draw a second smaller rectangle above the first rectangle to represent the upper deck. Your drawing should look like Figure 10.7.

4. Click on the Polygon tool. You'll use it to draw the front of the boat.

   To use the Polygon tool, click at the starting point of your drawing; then drag the mouse to the next point, release the mouse button, and click at the next point of the polygon.

**Figure 10.6**
If you want a perfect square instead of a rectangle, hold down the Shift key as you draw.

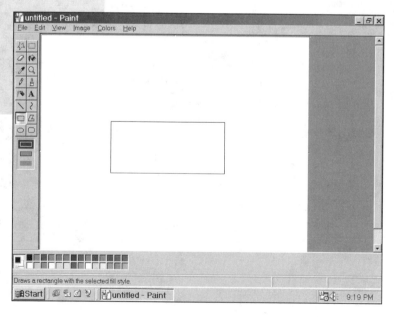

**Figure 10.7**
A tool stays selected until a new tool is chosen.

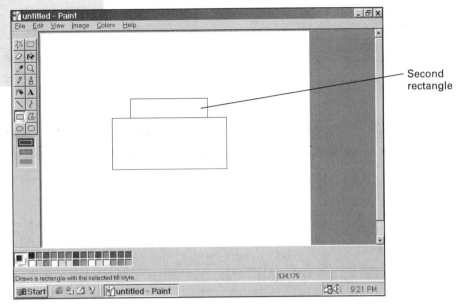

Second rectangle

5. Draw a triangle off the right edge of the rectangle (see Figure 10.8). Make sure the ends of the triangle touch the edge of the rectangle.

6. Release the mouse button. The completed triangle appears on the screen.

**Figure 10.8**
Every click of the mouse creates a new point on a polygon.

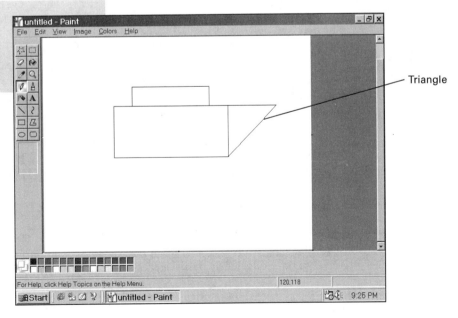

Triangle

• • • • • • • • • • • • • • • • • • • • • • • • • • • • • • • • • • • • • • • • • • • •

If you make a mistake, choose Edit, Undo to reverse up to the last three actions.

• • • • • • • • • • • • • • • • • • • • • • • • • • • • • • • • • • • • • • • • • • • • •

Finally, you need to draw the portholes on the upper deck of the boat, using the Ellipse tool. In this example, you can draw one circle and then copy and paste the other two.

## Hands On: Drawing Circles

1. Click on the Ellipse tool and move the mouse to the center of the upper deck rectangle on the boat.

• • • • • • • • • • • • • • • • • • • • • • • • • • • • • • • • • • • • • • • • • • • • •

To draw a perfect square, hold down the Shift key on the keyboard as you are drawing with the rectangle tool. Release the mouse button before you release the Shift key.

• • • • • • • • • • • • • • • • • • • • • • • • • • • • • • • • • • • • • • • • • • • • •

2. Hold down the Shift key on your keyboard and click and drag to draw a small circle in the middle of the rectangle. Holding down the Shift key assures you of a perfect circle.

3. Release the mouse button when the circle is the desired size.

4. Click on the Select tool. Click and drag to draw an imaginary box around the circle you just placed. When you release the mouse button, a dotted-line box appears around the circle, as shown in Figure 10.9.

• • • • • • • • • • • • • • • • • • • • • • • • • • • • • • • • • • • • • • • • • • • • •

If you position the mouse pointer over one of the eight small black handles on the selection box, the pointer becomes a double-headed arrow. You can resize the selected object by clicking and dragging the box to the desired size.

• • • • • • • • • • • • • • • • • • • • • • • • • • • • • • • • • • • • • • • • • • • • •

5. Choose Edit, Copy (or press Ctrl+C) to copy the object to the Windows Clipboard.

6. Choose Edit, Paste. A replica of the circle appears in the upper-left corner of the screen.

7. Position the mouse pointer over the new circle and drag it to the appropriate location next to the first one.

8. Repeat steps 6 and 7 to place the third porthole into position. Your drawing should look like the one in Figure 10.10.

**Figure 10.9**
Use the
Windows copy
and paste
commands to
save time with
your drawing!

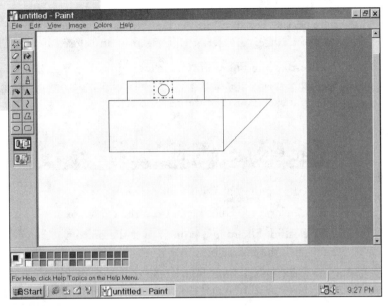

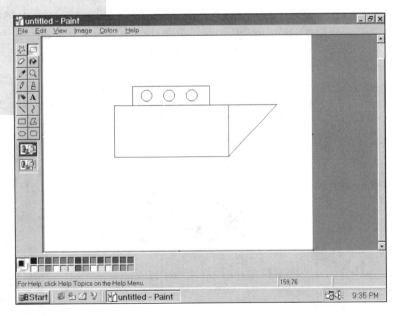
**Figure 10.10**
A combination
of circles,
rectangles, and
triangles makes
up the body of
this drawing.

*Tip*

To deselect an object or tool, click on any other area of the drawing or click on another tool.

# Using the Fill With Color Tool

The next step is to fill in the body of the boat. You can use the Fill With Color tool to change the interior (fill) color of any closed-in area.

Notice that the Fill With Color tool looks like a spilled bucket of paint. That's just what it acts like. If the edges of an object do not meet, the fill will "leak" out onto the background of the next object.

## Hands On: Coloring the Boat

1. Choose the Fill With Color tool.
2. Click on the color black from the color box.
3. Position the mouse pointer over the bottom rectangle of the boat and click the mouse button.
4. Repeat step 3 for the triangle you drew on the front of the boat. Both the bottom section and the front section of the boat are now "painted" black.
5. Click on a shade of gray for the upper deck of the boat.
6. Click in the upper rectangle. It gets filled in except for the portholes.
7. Optionally, click inside the three circles with a lighter shade of gray. Your drawing should look similar to Figure 10.11.

**Figure 10.11**
An object must be completely closed to fill it with color.

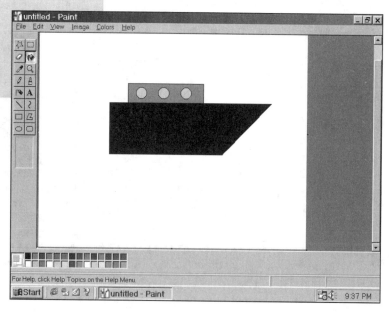

# Drawing Lines

Your boat's looking pretty good! But it needs the smoke stack. The smoke stack will be created with the Line tool. You'll find it much easier to draw the smoke stack if you zoom in and make the view of the picture a little larger.

## Hands On: Drawing Lines

1. Click on the Magnifier tool; then click on 2x of the Magnifier tool options located at the bottom of the Tool Box. This action makes the drawing seem twice as close.

2. Click on the Line tool and choose the black color from the color box.

3. Position the mouse pointer at the top of the boat and draw two slightly-angled parallel lines about ½ inch apart, with the line on the right a tiny bit longer than the line on the left, as shown in Figure 10.12.

4. Draw another line to connect the tops of the two parallel lines.

5. Click on the Magnifier tool and then click on 1x of the Magnifier tool options. The drawing screen returns to normal size, and you now have a smoke stack!

**Figure 10.12**
Zooming in on a drawing makes it much easier to see the detail.

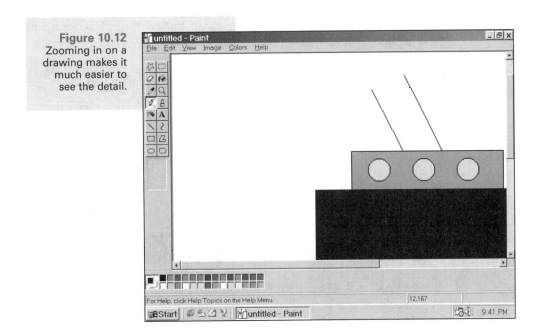

# Drawing Freehand

Microsoft Paint gives you two freehand drawing tools—the Brush and the Pencil. Both tools operate the same way, but the Pencil gives a much thinner line, and the Brush gives several options not only for thickness of the line but also for the angle of the brush.

If you click on the Brush tool, you will notice that 12 options are available. The styles vary from top to bottom, but if you look from left to right, the thickest brush line is on the left, a medium thickness brush stroke is in the middle, and the lightest brush stroke is on the right.

*Tip*

Selecting the first brush angle on the last row gives the effect of writing in calligraphy!

You'll use the freehand Brush tool to add birds to the picture.

## Hands On: Using the Brush Tool

1. Click on the Brush tool. This example uses the default thickness and angle to draw the birds.

2. Position the mouse pointer in the sky above the boat. To use the Brush tool, you click and drag the mouse. Pretend you have a regular pen in your hand. While you are pressing the mouse button, the pen is down and making lines. To release the pen, release the mouse button. Draw as many birds as you want.

3. Click on the thickest line style and the color gray; and then add the smoke coming out of the smokestack (see Figure 10.13).

# Using the Text Tool

You can use the Text tool to type words or letters on your drawing screen. You can use any font face or font size that is installed on your system. You can also change the attributes to bold, italics, or underline.

## Hands On: Using the Text Tool

1. Click on the Text tool.

2. Position the mouse pointer where you want to start typing, but don't click

**Figure 10.13**
Are your birds
singing?

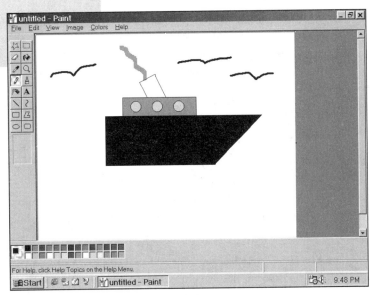

yet. You'll start by drawing a text frame in which to fit the words you're
going to type.

**3.** Create a text frame by clicking and dragging the mouse diagonally until
the imaginary box is the size you want to type in (see Figure 10.14).

**Figure 10.14**
Text can be
formatted before
or after typing.

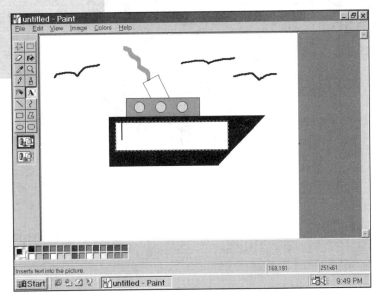

*Note*

It's particularly important to make the text frame the right width. If the box is not wide enough, you might have trouble rearranging the words.

4. Choose a color for the text from the color box at the bottom of the screen. I've selected yellow for the sample exercise.

5. Type the name of your boat, but don't click the mouse outside of the text boundaries yet. My boat's name is *U.S.S. Windows*.

6. With the blinking insertion point still in the text box, from the text toolbar shown in Figure 10.15, choose a typeface, size, and style for your text.

*Tip*

If your text toolbar does not appear, choose <u>V</u>iew, T<u>e</u>xt Toolbar.

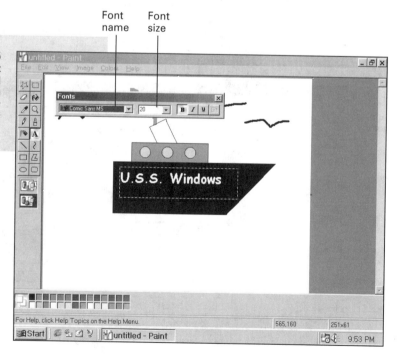

**Figure 10.15**
The exact font choices depend on the software installed on any particular machine.

You have two choices for the background of your text—transparent or solid. The background choices appear at the bottom of the toolbar; the top selection is a solid background, and the bottom choice is the transparent background.

7. Again, with the insertion point still blinking inside the text box, choose the transparent background.

*Note*

**If you didn't get the text box the right size earlier, now is your chance to adjust it. Position the mouse pointer over one of the corners of the text box until the pointer becomes a double-headed arrow. Click and drag the box until it is the desired size. The text will adjust to fit in the new size box.**

8. Select all the options for the typed text. Click the mouse pointer anywhere outside of the text box to accept the choices and deselect the typed text.

When the text is deselected, the text toolbar closes. Your picture should look similar to the picture in Figure 10.16.

**Figure 10.16**
Use a transparent background if you are placing text over a colored object.

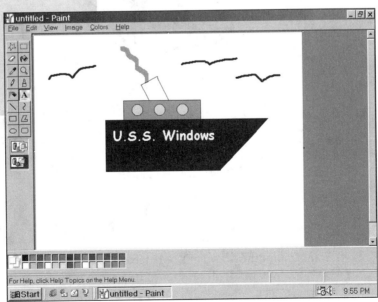

# Using the Airbrush

To complete this drawing, you need to add the water to the bottom of the screen, which you can do with the Airbrush tool. Using the Airbrush tool is like using a can of spray paint. The longer you press the nozzle and the slower you move, the heavier the covering of paint.

## Hands On: Spraying with the Airbrush Tool

1. Click on the Airbrush tool and then choose a spray size from the bottom of the Tool Box. Optionally, choose a spray color from the color box.

2. Position the mouse pointer under the boat; then press and hold the mouse button to paint the water. Your picture should now look similar to the one in Figure 10.17.

**Figure 10.17**
The longer you hold the mouse in a position, the heavier the airbrush effect.

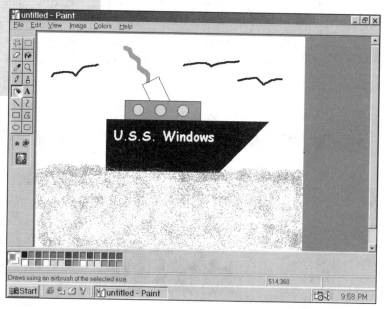

# Saving and Printing a Drawing

At this point, the drawing is only temporarily stored in the computer memory. If you want to work with or refer to it later, you must save the drawing. Although Windows 98 can work with many types of graphic formats, the Microsoft Paint program can save only in a .BMP (bitmap) format.

## Saving a Drawing

Saving a Microsoft Paint file is the same as saving any file created in a Windows program.

### Hands On: Saving a Drawing

1. Choose File, Save—or press Ctrl+S. The first time an untitled document is saved, both the Save and Save As commands display the Save As dialog box. After a document has been saved once, the Save command simply saves the document under its current name.

2. Type a descriptive name for the drawing in the File Name box and then click on Save. The name of the saved document appears at the top of the drawing window.

*Tip*

You can also save a drawing as your wallpaper for the Windows desktop by choosing File, Set as Wallpaper (Tiled) or Set as Wallpaper (Centered).

## Printing a Drawing

**For more information on Windows desktop wallpaper, see Chapter 5.**

Printing is the final step for many drawing projects. Again, Windows 98 brings more and more consistency to software programs, so printing a drawing is similar to printing a WordPad document.

### Hands On: Printing a Drawing

1. Choose File, Print—or press Ctrl+P.
2. Change any desired options such as the number of copies to print or which printer the document should print to; then click on OK.

# Discovering Other Drawing Options

In addition to drawing shapes, such as circles and squares, in Microsoft Paint, you can also flip, rotate, stretch, or skew objects that you have drawn or copied from another source.

# Flipping and Rotating an Object

In Microsoft Paint you can flip an area upside down or reverse its direction. You can also rotate an area by a specified number of degrees.

Figure 10.18 shows three identical airplanes. Airplanes 2 and 3 are just copies of airplane 1.

## Hands On: Flipping an Object

To flip an object:

1. Use the Selection tool to select the object to be flipped.
2. Choose Image, Flip/Rotate—or press Ctrl+R. From the Flip and Rotate dialog box, you can choose to flip the object horizontally or vertically, or you can choose to rotate it 90, 180, or 270 degrees.
3. Make the desired selection and then click on OK.

*Note*

**An object can be flipped both horizontally and vertically, but doing so requires two separate steps.**

**Figure 10.18**
Three identical objects appear in this drawing.

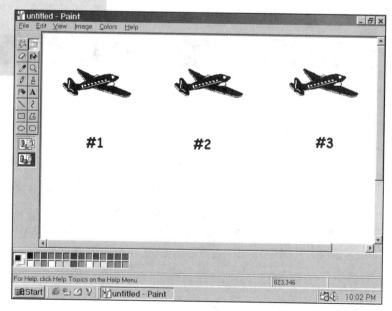

**Figure 10.19**
Flip the airplane horizontally to make it appear facing the other direction.

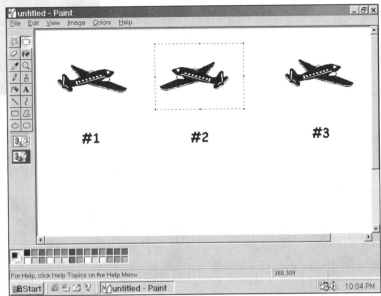

In Figure 10.19 the middle airplane is facing the opposite direction of the other two. The airplane was flipped horizontally.

# Stretching and Skewing an Object

Webster's dictionary defines the word *skew* as "to distort." Microsoft Paint enables you to skew objects, giving them a distinctly distorted appearance. Hold on to your seats—we're going to have a little fun with this one!

## Hands On: Skewing an Object

To skew an object:

1. Select the object or area to be skewed. If a specific object or area is not selected, the entire drawing will be skewed.

*Tip*

Before you skew an object, make sure the background color in the color box is the same as the background of your drawing. If not, when the object is skewed, it will pick up the currently selected background color.

2. Choose Image, Stretch/Skew.

3. Enter the number of degrees to skew the object in either the horizontal or vertical skew box. The maximum value is 89.

4. Click on OK.

The object or area is redrawn with the new settings. The third airplane in Figure 10.20 was skewed vertically 35 degrees. It appears to be flying up into the sky.

**Figure 10.20**
An object can be skewed both horizontally and vertically, but each change requires a separate step.

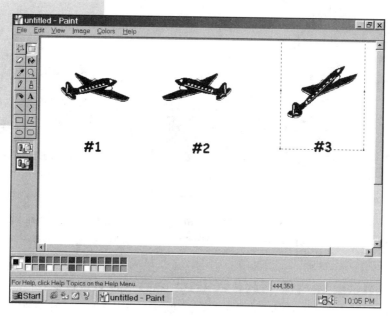

# 11

# A World of Multimedia

## IN THIS CHAPTER

- Playing a Music CD
- Using the Volume Control
- Using the Media Player
- Using the Sound Recorder
- Integrating Multimedia with Other Documents
- Introducing the DVD Player

Windows 98 brings a higher level of performance for multimedia than previous versions of Windows. It's even prepared for some of the technology still in development, so it will be able to accommodate new peripherals that you might add to your system.

See Appendix B for more information on the TV Viewer.

Multimedia is the fun part of your computer. It includes games, music, video, and other forms of entertainment. To use the multimedia capabilities Windows 98 supports, your computer must have a sound card, speakers, a CD-ROM drive, and a VGA or higher monitor. If you want to record your own sounds, you'll also need a microphone, and if you intend to use the TV Viewer you'll need a special TV video card.

With the higher graphical support Windows 98 delivers, you'll find games play faster and with a higher level of graphics capability. The architecture built into Windows 98 supports digital video, audio, and Musical Instrument Digital Interface (MIDI). This version of Windows supports 3-D interpretation and digital audio for games, which results in better animations. Thank the 32-bit multitasking architecture for these more powerful capabilities.

In the past, using multimedia clips was sometimes cumbersome and involved several steps on the part of the user. Windows 98 includes Plug-and-Play support for most of the popular sound cards and CD-ROM drivers, which means that installing or playing software from CD-ROM is easier than ever.

In Windows 98 you can even play your favorite music CDs while you are computing.

# Playing a Music CD

You can place your favorite music CD into the computer and listen while you work! Windows 98 supports a feature called Autoplay that can distinguish between a music CD and a software CD-ROM; Autoplay knows whether to start the music or to look for a file called autorun.inf. If Autoplay finds autorun.inf on the disk, Windows 98 will follow the instructions built into the file.

If your computer does not have Autoplay, you can begin the CD Player yourself. There are several methods to start a music CD. One method is from the Windows 98 Start menu.

## Hands On: Playing a Music CD

1. Place the CD you want to listen to in the CD-ROM drive.
2. From the Start menu, click on Programs, Accessories, Entertainment and then choose the CD Player.

**Figure 11.1**
The digital
display indicates
the current track.

Notice in Figure 11.1 that the CD Player has many of the same buttons as a standard CD player.

*Tip*

If Autoplay has begun, you can click CD Player on the Taskbar to open the CD Player window.

With the CD Player, you can select which track you want to play. You can choose a single track for immediate play or you can define a play list.

To choose a single track:

3. Click on the Tra<u>c</u>k drop-down arrow. From the list of available tracks, click on the track you want to play. The track will immediately begin playing.

To define a play list:

4. Choose <u>D</u>isc, Edit Play <u>L</u>ist. The Disc Settings dialog box as seen in Figure 11.2 displays the current play list, which by default is in standard numerical order. This dialog box also displays a list of available tracks.

5. Click on any track you want to remove from the current <u>P</u>lay List; then click on <u>R</u>emove.

6. Click on any track you want to add from the A<u>v</u>ailable Tracks list; then click on A<u>d</u>d.

You can also change the order of play.

7. From the <u>P</u>lay List, click on the track to be moved and drag it to the new position in the <u>P</u>lay List. A small arrow on the left side (Figure 11.3) of the <u>P</u>lay List indicates the new position.

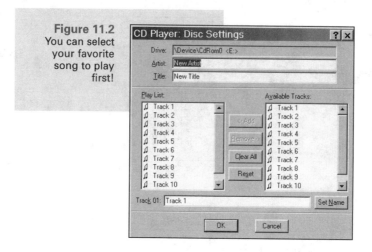

**Figure 11.2**
You can select your favorite song to play first!

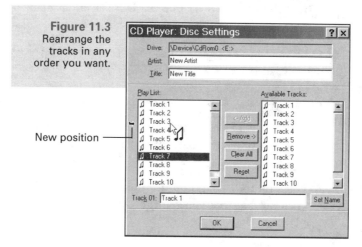

**Figure 11.3**
Rearrange the tracks in any order you want.

New position

# Labeling a Music CD

The Windows 98 CD Player does not have the ability to recognize which musical artist is on the CD, but you can add the Artist name, the name of the CD, and/or the name of individual tracks.

## Hands On: Labeling a Music CD

1. Click in the Artist text box and type the artist's name.
2. Click in the Title text box and type the title of the CD.

3. From the Available Tracks list, click any track you want to name and type a name in the Track box at the bottom of the dialog box. Then click on Set Name.

4. Click on OK when you have completed setting your play list. The tracks will play in the order you specified.

Windows 98 displays the appropriate information in the CD Player window as shown in Figure 11.4.

**Figure 11.4**
Naming your favorite tracks makes them easy to find.

*Note*

**Windows 98 remembers the labels and play list information that you provide. When you switch to a new CD, the settings return to the default (unless that CD has been named). However, when you reinsert the first CD, the CD Player will display the name information as well as the play order you previously selected.**

## Setting Other Play Options

In addition to playing your CD in track number order or according to your custom play list, three other play options are available:

- **Random Order**—Plays tracks in a random order.
- **Continuous Play**—Starts the CD again when the last track is finished playing.
- **Intro Play**—Plays the first 10 seconds of each track.

Click on Options to make a selection.

Click on Options again to discontinue any of the play options. Play will revert to the standard play according to track number.

Unless you select Continuous Play, the CD automatically stops after the last track plays. You can manually stop or pause play by clicking on the Stop or Pause button.

## Ejecting a CD

The most commonly used method to eject a CD is to push the button on the front of the CD-ROM drive, but you can also:

- Click on the Eject button from the CD Player window.
- Right-click on the CD-ROM drive from the My Computer window and select Eject.

If you want to leave the music CD in the player, you can begin play at any time by opening My Computer, right-clicking on the CD-ROM drive, and selecting Play.

# Using the Volume Control

Windows 98 includes an admirable sound control system with different settings for different types of sounds. It's almost like having a remote control right at your fingertips! There are two types of volume controls available. A very simple volume control enables you to adjust the volume only, while the volume controls window enables you to set different settings for the sounds and music you play on your computer.

Depending on the type of sound system installed in your PC, your choices may vary slightly from the ones displayed.

### Hands On: Using the Volume Controls

1. Click on the icon that looks like a speaker in the System Tray to display the simple Volume slider box (see Figure 11.5).
2. Drag the Volume slider up or down to control the overall volume level; then click anywhere on the Desktop to close the Volume slider.

   To fine-tune the sound mixture, you can use the Volume Control window.

*Note*

If the Volume Control icon does not appear in the System Tray, open the Control Panel and choose Multimedia. Make sure a check mark appears in the Show Volume Control on the Taskbar check box.

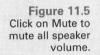

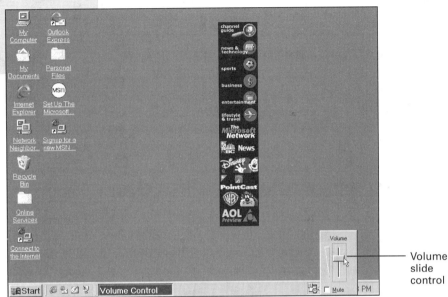

Volume
slide
control

**3.** Double-click on the speaker in the System Tray to display the Volume Control window shown in Figure 11.6. Your window may vary slightly from the one shown here.

This window enables you to set more than just volume. Additional controls are available for different types of music files such as MIDI or WAV files. Your choices depend on the devices your sound card can support. You can set the speaker balance, as well as the general volume balance, for each type of file.

**Figure 11.6**
The Volume
Control window
enables you to
adjust balance
and volume
settings.

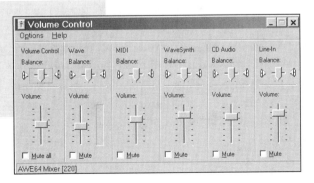

4. Drag a balance slide bar to the left to make the left speaker louder or to the right to make the right speaker louder. Drag the vertical slide bar up to make the volume louder or down to make it quieter. You can set these sliders for each type of music file.

*Tip*

You can also open the Volume Control window by clicking on Start, Programs, Accessories, Entertainment, Volume Control.

# Using the Media Player

Windows 98 and the Media Player can make beautiful music together. You can use the Media Player to play audio, video, or animation files and to control the settings for multimedia hardware devices. As with other types of multimedia, you must have a sound card installed to use the Media Player and hear sound.

## Hands On:  Using the Media Player

1. From the Start menu, click on Programs, Accessories, Entertainment; then choose Media Player.

2. Click on File, Open. Choose the media file you want to play from the Open dialog box.

3. Click on the drop-down arrow for Files of Type to display a list of file formats that the Media Player can support. Choose the file format you want. Table 11.1 lists some of the multimedia file formats you might find.

4. Locate and click on the sound or video file you want to play and then click on Open.

   The media file name is displayed at the top of the Media Player; if the clip is a video file, a video window will open as well (see Figure 11.7).

   The Media Player has a lot of buttons, much like a videotape player. Figure 11.8 points out the different button functions.

   The Media Player window also has a slide bar that indicates the total time length of the media clip. This time is generally measured in seconds. As the multimedia clip is playing, the slide bar moves to indicate the progress of the clip.

## Table 11.1 Multimedia File Formats Supported by Windows 98

| Term | Description |
| --- | --- |
| DVD | Digital Video Disk. A method of storing data digitally; includes audio, video, and computer data. |
| WAV | A file format made of digitally recorded sounds. The sounds are stored as waveforms. |
| MIDI | Musical Instrument Digital Interface. A standard format used for creating, recording, and playing back music. MIDI enables computers, synthesizers, and other equipment to communicate with each other. |
| MPEG | Moving Pictures Expert Group. A standard format for audio and video compression. |
| AVI | Audio Video Interleaved. A multimedia format for sound and moving pictures. Both the sound and video tracks are stored in the same file. |

**Figure 11.7**
Video clips are
fun on a
computer.

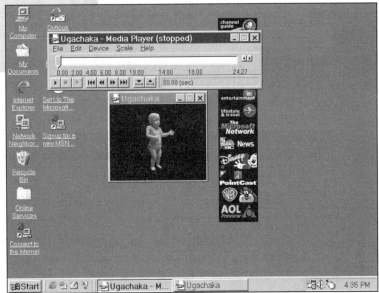

**5.** Click on the Play button to begin playing the media clip.

To stop playing the media clip before it reaches the end, click on the Stop button.

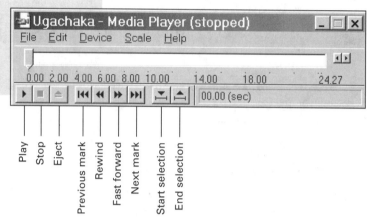

6. Close the Media Player by choosing File, Exit, or by clicking on the Close button.

# Using the Sound Recorder

One of the multimedia tools included with Windows 98 is the Sound Recorder that enables you to record and modify sound files. You need to have a microphone attached to your computer for the Sound Recorder to create WAV files from your recording.

## Hands On: Recording a Message

1. Open the Sound Recorder by clicking on the Start button and then choosing Programs, Accessories, Entertainment, Sound Recorder. The Sound Recorder window is ready to record new sounds (see Figure 11.9).

   You may have to adjust the position of the microphone to make sure it is close enough to your mouth, but not too close. The exact position varies from microphone to microphone, so you'll have to experiment a little to get it in the correct position.

2. When you are ready to record, click on the Record button. Begin speaking to record the following message:

   Hi Bob! This is (your name). Before I send out this memo, would you double-check the meeting date. I was told it had

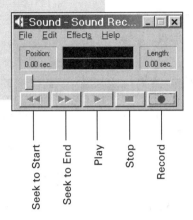

**Figure 11.9**
You can add an
echo effect to
your recording
from the
Effects menu.

been moved to the 16<sup>th</sup> instead of the 15<sup>th</sup> as originally
planned. Thanks.

3. Click on the Stop button to end the recording session.

*Note*

**If you don't click the Stop button, the Sound Recorder stops recording
at the 60-seconds mark. If your message is longer than 60 seconds,
you can click on the Record button again to continue recording. The
Sound Recorder works in 60-second increments.**

4. Click on the Seek to Start button to return to the beginning of the
   recording.

5. Click on the Play button to listen to your message.

   If you are satisfied with the message—great! If not, click on the Seek to
   Start button and rerecord your message.

   You can save your recorded message for future use or for use in a
   document.

6. Click on File, Save and enter a file name for the sound file. Optionally,
   specify a different folder to save the file. By default, Windows saves it in
   the My Documents folder.

7. Click on Save, and the sound file will be saved.

# Integrating Multimedia with Other Documents

Today's applications have the capability to embed media files in them. Your documents don't have to be boring. Adding sound or video to a file being sent electronically can add pizzaz to the file. You can add all or part of an audio or video clip to a document. The only limitation is that the person receiving the file needs multimedia capabilities (speakers and a sound card) to enjoy it.

## Selecting Part of a Multimedia Clip

The Start Selection and End Selection buttons mark the portion of the clip you want to include in your document.

### Hands On:  Selecting Part of a Multimedia Clip

1. Open the Media Player and open the media file you want to include in your document.

2. Click on the Play button to begin playing the file. When the portion you want to include begins, click on the Start Selection button.

3. When the end of the portion you want to include arrives, click on the End Selection button. A small blue bar appears in the Media Player slide bar to indicate the section you want to include (see Figure 11.10).

You can be even more precise about the selection by choosing Edit, Selection and entering the exact number of seconds you want for the clip.

Selected area

**Figure 11.10**
The Media Player allows you to edit a recording.

To place a multimedia clip in a document, you must first copy the media clip to the Windows 98 Clipboard.

4. Choose <u>E</u>dit, <u>C</u>opy (or press Ctrl+C) to copy the selection to the Windows Clipboard. You are now ready to place the clip into your document.

# Placing a Multimedia Clip into a Document

After selecting the portion of the clip you want, copy it to the Windows Clipboard.

*Note*

If you want to place the entire multimedia clip into a document, you can just copy the file name from the Windows Explorer or My Computer window. Open one of these windows and then locate the media file you want to place in the document. Click the right mouse button on the media file to open the shortcut menu and then choose <u>C</u>opy. The complete media file will be copied to the Windows Clipboard.

You can place one or more multimedia clips in any type of Windows document.

## Hands On: Placing a Media Clip into a Document

1. Make sure you have copied the media clip to the Windows Clipboard.
2. Open the program in which you want to place the media file.
3. Open the document or create any additional text you want to appear in the document.
4. Click on <u>E</u>dit, <u>P</u>aste (or press Ctrl+V) to paste the media clip into your document.

An object box will appear in the document, but the actual appearance of the object depends on the application and the type of clip. Figure 11.11 shows both a sound clip and a video clip placed into a WordPad document.

Double-click on a media clip to play it.

**Figure 11.11**
Sound clips are
usually indicated
by a bell and
video clips by a
picture.

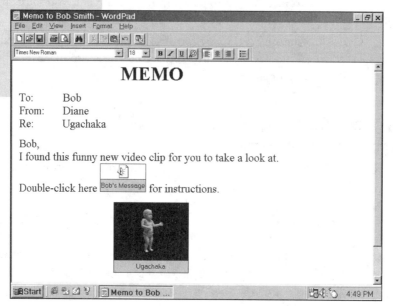

# Introducing the DVD Player

Computers traditionally have been very good at performing complex data calculations, but with multimedia being a main focus of a computer today, something had to be done about the quality of graphic and audio files. Along came DVD. DVD is not just another pretty place to store data. It was designed for multimedia applications, so it can effectively provide digital data storage that incorporates audio, video, and computer data.

Several questions surround the mystique of DVD. For example, just what is it? The letters DVD can stand for **D**igital **V**ersatile **D**isc or **D**igital **V**ideo **D**isc. That in itself isn't too important. What's important is that DVD technology can store seven times as much information as today's CD-ROM drive—almost 17 gigabytes of disk space.

A DVD disk looks similar to a music CD—it's a little more than 4-½" in diameter. However, a DVD disk can store the equivalent of 25 CDs or a full-length motion picture on just one of its four tracks, and the picture quality is superior. It can hold multichannel surround sound as well as dubbing on the other tracks in other languages. DVD is a result of the new graphic compression standard MPEG II.

Windows 98 includes support for DVD that delivers high-quality digital movies and audio to your computer monitor. With the DVD player, you can play DVD disks from a DVD drive. These disks can contain software, music, or video. And don't forget that DVD is a new storage medium as well.

The image quality of DVD movies on a Windows 98 computer will be higher than the image quality when those movies are played on a standard DVD video player. This feature is especially important for PCs used for entertainment but is also important for any multimedia hardware platform that wants to provide good quality support for playback of movies.

When will DVD replace standard CDs or videos? The technology is still new, but industry analysts expect DVD to be the dominant media format for data storage, games, software, and films within 10 years.

Here comes the problem. Because the technology is so new, the first release of Windows 98 supported only a few manufacturers' DVD cards. This situation will change in the very near future. In the meantime, the software for DVD has to come from your DVD manufacturer. Consequently, no real standard has yet developed for operating DVD on your computer.

For the time being, to learn how to operate DVD, you'll have to look to your individual manufacturer's guides for that information.

# 12

# Learning to Control the Mouse— Using Games!

## IN THIS CHAPTER

- **Playing Solitaire**
- **Changing Solitaire Options**
- **Playing Hearts across a Network**

Life is short, so have a little fun while you're at it! That seems to have been the strategy at Microsoft when it developed the Windows product. The company included a few games for you to play. These games are Solitaire, FreeCell, Hearts, and Mindsweeper. This chapter will give you an overview of two of these games—Solitaire and Hearts.

Why did Microsoft include games? I figure it's for a couple of reasons. One, lots of people have computers at home, and these games provide amusement. Haven't we all played Checkers, Poker, Monopoly, Scrabble, or Chutes and Ladders? OK, maybe not Chutes and Ladders for a long, long time, but most of us play games on occasion. They're great for relieving stress.

> For more information on adding Windows programs, see Chapter 8.

The second reason, and probably the most important one, is that the Windows games provide a wonderful instrument to practice mouse techniques.

Windows 98 does not install the games by default. If the games do not show up on your Accessories menu, you'll need to add them.

# Playing Solitaire

Solitaire is a card game designed for one player at a time. The objective is to place all the cards of the deck in the top stacks. During play, cards are placed in the seven main piles (row stacks) of the Solitaire game. Only a card that is one step lower and the opposite color can be placed on another card. For example, the only cards you can place on top of the queen of spades is the jack of hearts or jack of diamonds.

## Starting the Game

To begin playing Solitaire:

1. Click on the Start button.
2. Highlight Programs, Accessories, and then Games.
3. Click on Solitaire. The cards are dealt, and the Solitaire game opens with a screen similar to the one shown in Figure 12.1.
4. If you need to maximize your Solitaire screen, double-click on the title bar at the top or click on the Maximize button.

**Figure 12.1**
Cards are automatically dealt when the Solitaire game is started.

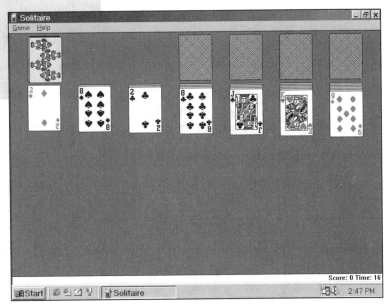

# Moving the Cards

You can move cards several ways in the Solitaire game, depending on what kind of move it is.

1. Click on the left mouse button and drag the card to be moved to the new location. The example in Figure 12.2 shows an eight of clubs being moved toward the nine of diamonds.

2. Release the mouse button when the first card is on top of the second card. The top card drops into position.

*Tip*

If the card to be moved is one of several on a row stack, position the mouse on the highest value card to be moved. That card and the lower value cards on it will be moved as well.

After moving the card from the row stack, more cards remain face down in that stack, so you want to turn over the next card.

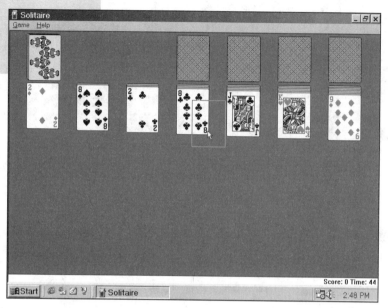

**Figure 12.2**
Moving a card is
as easy as "drag
and drop"!

*Note*

**If you try to make a move that is not permitted, the card returns to its original location.**

**3.** Click on the face down card in the row stack. The card is turned over and is ready for play.

The top row (suit stacks) is placed in ascending order from ace to king, and all cards must be of the same suit. For example, you can only play a five of spades on a four of spades.

If you have a card that can be played on the suit stacks, you have two options to get the card into position. The two of hearts in Figure 12.3 is ready to be placed into the suit stacks.

- Click and drag the card to the suit stack.

or

- Double-click on the card to go to the suit stack.

When no more cards can be played from the row stacks, you can play from the deck in the upper-left corner. Click on the back of the deck to begin turning over cards. Either three cards or a single card will be turned over, depending on the

**Figure 12.3**
Get all the cards
to the suit stacks,
and you win
the game!

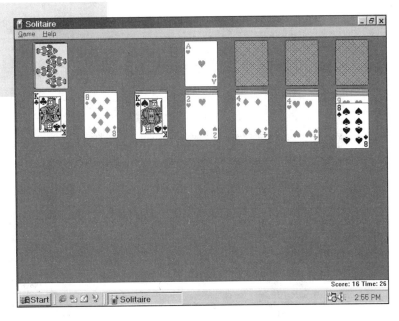

type of game you are playing. As you'll see later in this chapter there are several Solitaire game options from which you can select.

• • • • • • • • • • • • • • • • • • • • • • • • • • • • • • • • • • • • • • • • • • • •

If you play or turn over a card in error, click on the Game menu and choose Undo to reverse the last card played.

• • • • • • • • • • • • • • • • • • • • • • • • • • • • • • • • • • • • • • • • • • • •

If you look closely at Figure 12.4, you can see that a three of diamonds is available. When the three of diamonds is moved to the suit stacks, the next card in the deck (seven of clubs in this example) is available for play.

When an empty space is available in the row stacks, only a king can be moved and placed in that position. In Figure 12.5 either the king of hearts or the king of diamonds can be moved to the empty space.

The game continues until all available cards have been played. If you are playing the standard game of Solitaire, when you reach the end of the deck, you can click on the green circle where the deck was to turn them back over and begin playing the deck again. If you are playing the Vegas game of Solitaire with one card being turned over at a time (discussed in the next section), you are allowed to turn the stack over one time only. A red X appears where the deck was, indicating that the game is over.

**Figure 12.4**
Cards are moved
from the deck to
the stacks by
dragging them
to the desired
stack.

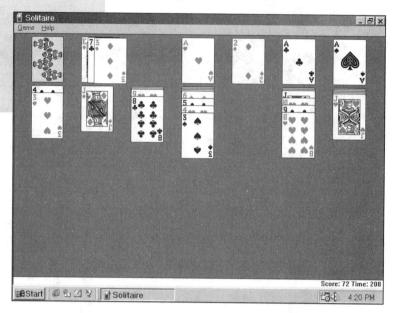

**Figure 12.5**
Put kings in the
empty spaces to
free up other
cards for
playing.

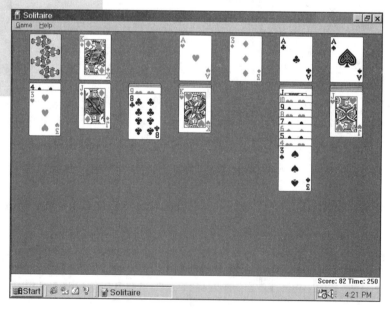

## Selecting a Different Deck

Each time you launch the Solitaire program, you may notice a different deck of cards being used. The values of the cards don't change, but the backs will vary. There are 12 different decks available with some of them being animated. If you have a favorite, you can select it at any time.

To change the deck of cards, choose Game, Deck. From the resulting dialog box, select your favorite deck.

Once you select a deck of cards, that deck will remain the default deck for future games of Solitaire. The backs will no longer be randomly selected.

## Changing Solitaire Options

If you read a book of card games, you will find there are hundreds of versions of Solitaire to play. You don't get quite that many variations with Windows 98, but you do have several alternatives.

You can also decide whether and how you want to score the game and whether you want to be timed during your play.

To change options, choose Game, Options. The Options dialog box shown in Figure 12.6 appears. Table 12.1 describes each option.

Choose the desired options and then click on OK to close the dialog box. Depending on your selections, a new game of Solitaire may begin.

**Figure 12.6**
Customize the
Solitaire game to
suit your taste.

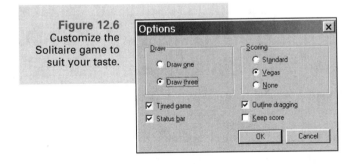

## Table 12.1 Solitaire Options

| Area | Option | Description |
|---|---|---|
| Draw | Draw One | Turn over one card at a time from the deck. |
| | Draw Three | Turn over three cards at a time from the deck. |
| Scoring | None | No scoring; the object of the game is play all 52 cards to the suit stack. |
| | Vegas | You start the game with a bet of $52. For every card played on a suit stack, you win $5. The object is to earn more money than the $52 you originally bet. Your score carries over from game to game if you also select the Keep Score box. If you choose to Draw One card at a time from the deck, you can go through the deck only once. |
| | Standard | Scoring is a little more complicated and depends on other options you have selected. The score resets with each game of Solitaire you play. |
| (Check boxes) | Timed Game | Keeps track of the time each game of Solitaire is played. If activated and used in combination with scoring, the faster you play, the higher your score. If you slow down or pause, points will be subtracted from your score. |
| | Status Bar | A bar displayed at the bottom of the Solitaire window to display the score or time played. |
| | Outline Dragging | Allows an outline of the card to be displayed as the card is being moved. |
| | Keep Score | Used only in combination with the Vegas Scoring game. When activated, the score is accumulated and does not reset a new time when a new game begins. |

## Scoring Points

If you are keeping score in your Solitaire game, you can win or lose points depending on where a card is played.

- For every card to a suit stack, you win 10 points.
- For every card from the deck to a row stack, you win five points.
- For every card turned over from a row stack, you win five points.
- For every card moved back from a suit stack to a row stack, you lose 15 points.

- If you are playing the Draw Three game, you lose 20 points for each additional pass through the deck.

- If you are playing the Draw One game, you lose 100 points for each additional pass through the deck.

- If you are playing a Timed game, you lose two points for every 10 seconds of play and receive additional bonus points at the end of the game.

Congratulations! When all the cards have been played to the suit stacks, the cards begin to cascade down the screen.

# Starting Hearts Across a Network

Another interesting game included with Windows 98 is the game of Hearts. You can play hearts alone against three fictitious players or with up to three other people across a network. The number of players in a game of Hearts is always four (real or imaginary).

The object of Hearts is to have the lowest score at the end of the game. A game is over when one player reaches 100 points.

## Hands On: Playing Hearts

To begin the game of Hearts:

1. Click on the Start button.

2. Highlight Programs, Accessories, and then Games.

3. Click on Hearts. The Hearts game opens with a welcome screen.

    The two questions shown in Figure 12.7 appear on the opening Hearts screen: What is your name? and How do you want to play?

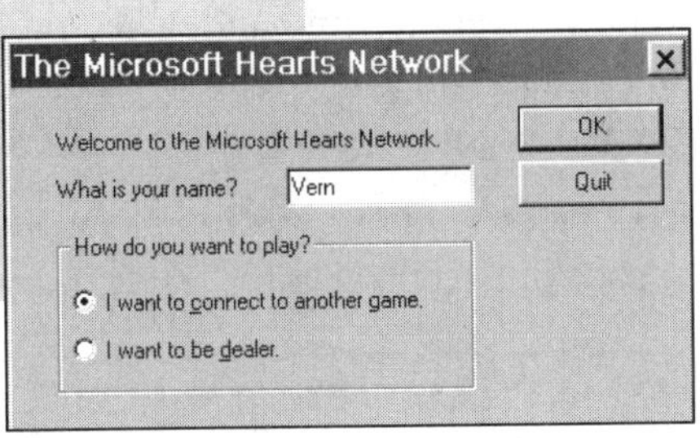

**Figure 12.7**
Use your real name, a nickname, or an imaginary name.

**The Microsoft Hearts Network**

Welcome to the Microsoft Hearts Network.

What is your name? | Vern

OK

Quit

How do you want to play?

◉ I want to connect to another game.

○ I want to be dealer.

**Figure 12.8**
Play Hearts against any player connected to your network.

You must decide if you want to join in a Hearts game elsewhere on your network or whether you want to be the dealer in a new game. If you want to play hearts alone against the computer, choose to be the dealer.

4. Enter your name and choose the method of play; then click on OK.

If you opted to connect to another game, you are prompted for the dealer's computer name. See Figure 12.8 for an example.

*Tip*

To find the name of the dealer's computer, open the Network Neighborhood icon on your desktop to see a list of all computer names in your network.

5. Enter the dealer's computer name and then click on OK.

*Note*

**A dialog box will tell you whether the dealer already has a game in progress or is not ready to play Hearts.**

If you elected to be the dealer in a new game over the network, wait for other players to join the game. Their names will appear in the green screen as they join in.

6. Press F2 to begin the game if you are the dealer.

Playing the game of Hearts follows four basic steps:

■ At the beginning of each hand, select three cards to pass to an opponent (except for every fourth hand, when no cards are passed). One of your opponents will give you three cards. Click on OK to accept the cards and begin the game.

*Tip*

Notice the three dots by each of the other players' cards. These are the cards they are intending to pass.

- The player with the two of clubs starts the play by clicking on it. The two of clubs will move to the center of the screen.

- Each player, moving clockwise, clicks a card to play. You must play a card in the same suit. If you do not have such a card and this round is not the first round of the deal, you can play any other card. If you do not have such a card and this round is the first round, you can play any card except a heart or the queen of spades.

- The person who plays the highest card of the same suit as the first card played takes the trick. That player starts the next trick by clicking a card to lead. You cannot lead a heart until a heart has been played on a previous trick.

**Note**

A *trick* is the cards collected when you play the highest card that is the same as the first card played in a round.

7. Select three cards to pass by clicking each card once. The cards you selected are sticking up from the others. To deselect a card, click it again. When you have finished your selection, click on the Pass button. The cards in Figure 12.9 have been selected to be passed to the next player.

You will then receive three cards from another player. Again, they stick up from the rest of your cards so that you can tell which ones you are receiving.

**Figure 12.9**
Pick three cards
to give to an
opponent.

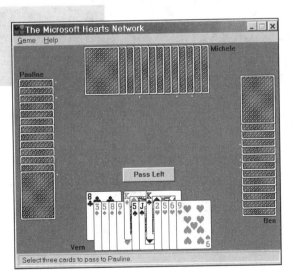

8. Click on OK to accept the cards (Sorry, you have no other choice—you can't send them back!). The received cards drop back into your hand, and play is ready to begin.

9. The player with the two of clubs begins the play by clicking on it. The two of clubs appears in the middle of the screen, and each player plays in turn according to the rules explained here.

Each hand continues until all cards have been played. The scores are then totaled and displayed on the screen.

## Scoring Your Points

At the end of each hand, you score 1 point for each heart in your hand and 13 points for the queen of spades. If you win all the hearts and the queen of spades in one hand, then you don't get any points and each of the other players gets 26 points. This is called "shooting the moon."

As shown in Figure 12.10, the computer totals your points and displays the results as well as your standing in the game.

Click on OK to acknowledge the score. The computer deals the next hand, and the game continues.

The game continues until one player gets 100 or more points or until the dealer quits the game. In Hearts, the lowest score wins.

**Figure 12.10**
Don't forget!
The lowest
score wins!

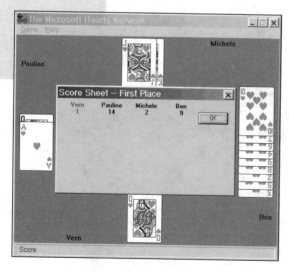

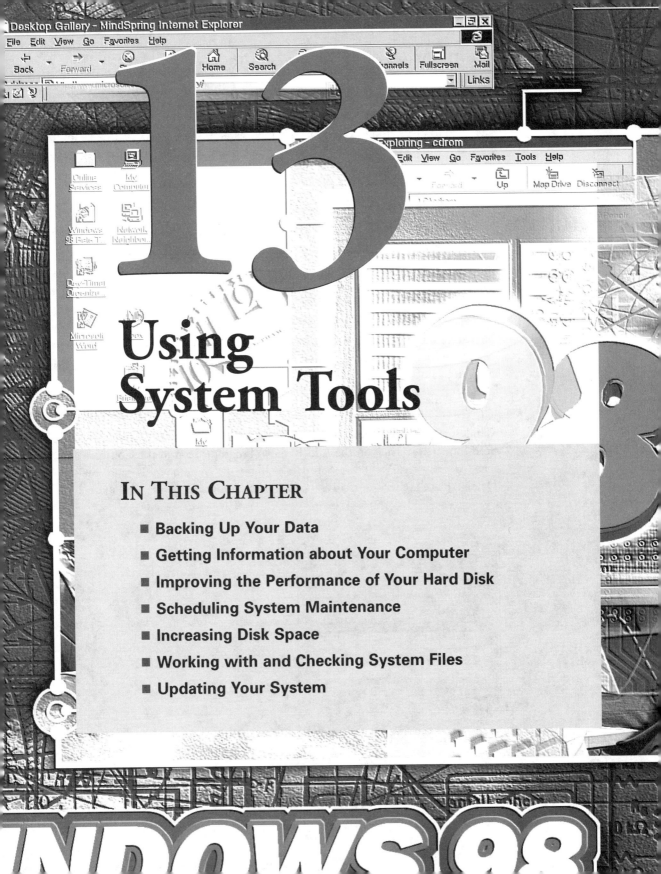

# 13

# Using System Tools

## IN THIS CHAPTER

- **Backing Up Your Data**
- **Getting Information about Your Computer**
- **Improving the Performance of Your Hard Disk**
- **Scheduling System Maintenance**
- **Increasing Disk Space**
- **Working with and Checking System Files**
- **Updating Your System**

System Tools is a broad description of the content of this chapter; in fact, almost any Windows 98 applet could be classified as a "system tool." In this chapter, however, you focus on the tools that help you maintain your computer and optimize its performance.

# Backing Up Your Data

A *backup* is a copy you make of the files on your computer; typically, you store the copy on floppy disks, tapes, or removable media such as Zip, Jaz, or SyQuest cartridges. Although backing up your computer is one of the least exciting things you can do, you really don't want to experience the excitement caused by a computer crash for which you have no backup. I could give a lecture here, but I won't. Suffice it to say, If you care about the information on your computer, back it up. If you don't care about the information on your computer, skip this section.

 Microsoft Backup is *not* installed by default along with the operating system. If you had installed it under Windows 95, Windows 98 will upgrade Backup to the Windows 98 version. Backup is available on your Windows 98 CD-ROM; if you need to install it, click on the Add/Remove Programs icon in the Control Panel. Then display the Windows Setup tab, highlight System Tools, and click on Details. Place a check next to Backup in the Components list (see Figure 13.1)

**Figure 13.1**
Backup is a component of Windows System Tools.

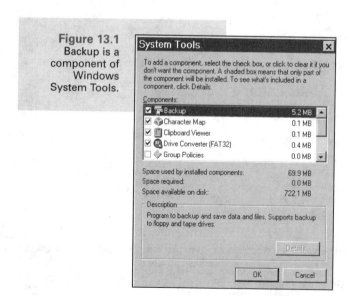

and click on OK. Windows walks you through installing Backup; you may need to insert your Windows 98 CD-ROM to complete the process.

If you use Microsoft Backup, you are not limited to backing up using floppy disks. Microsoft Backup supports drives made by Conner, Exabyte, HP/Colorado, Iomega, Micro Solutions, Seagate, Tandberg, WangDAT, and Wangtek. You can back up your data to a variety of backup media, including:

- QIC tapes, including QIC-80, QIC-80 Wide, QIC-3010, QIC-3010 Wide, QIC-3020, and QIC-3020 Wide
- TR1, TR2, TR3, and TR4 tapes
- DAT (DDS1, 2, and 3)
- DC 6000
- 8 millimeter
- Digital line tape (DLT)
- Removable media such as Iomega Zip and Jaz disks and SyQuest cartridges
- Network drives

To use Microsoft Backup, your computer's hard disk must have at least 4.9 megabytes (MB) of free space.

*Note*

**The very first time you start Microsoft Backup, it will look for a backup device, such as a tape drive. If you have a backup device and Backup doesn't find it, exit from Backup and check the Device Manager to make sure your backup device is installed.**

**Figures you see in this chapter were created on a computer that *does not* have a backup device installed.**

## Creating a Backup Job

See the sidebar on Backup Strategies for more information on backup techniques and the jobs that they require.

A backup job stores the settings for your backup, such as the files you want to back up, the media on which you want to store the backup, and when you might want to run the backup. You need to create backup jobs only for each type of backup you intend to do. For example, if you intend to make full hard disk backups and then, between full backups, back up only those files that change, you'll need to create two backup jobs: one for the full backup and one for the interim backup.

## Hands On: Creating a Backup Job

To create a backup job:

1. Start Microsoft Backup by choosing Start, Programs, Accessories, System Tools, Backup. Each time you start Microsoft Backup, you'll be prompted to create a new backup job, use an existing backup job, or restore files (see Figure 13.2). When you choose OK to create a new backup job, the Backup Wizard walks you through choosing the settings for the job.

2. Decide whether to back up your entire computer or just selected files (see Figure 13.3).

3. If you choose to back up selected files, you'll see the screen shown in Figure 13.4. If you choose to back up all files, skip to step 4.

   You can back up an entire drive by placing a check next to it in the left pane. Or, you can back up only selected files or folders. To select individual files on a drive, double-click on the icon for that drive in the left pane; then, in the right pane, select any combination of folders and files by placing a check next to those items you want to back up. A black check indicates you're backing up all files in the selected folder or drive; a gray check indicates you're backing up only some files.

**Figure 13.2**
To back up the first time, choose to create a new backup job.

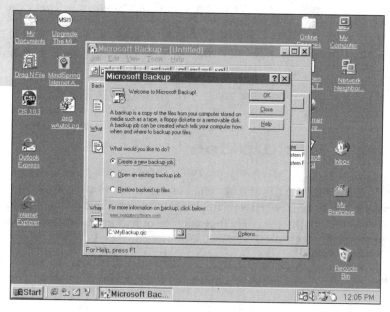

**Figure 13.3**
Choose what
you want to
back up.

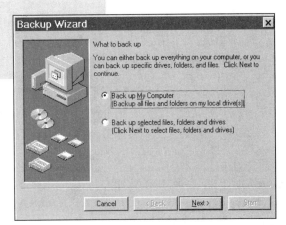

**Figure 13.4**
If you choose to
back up selected
files, you'll see
this dialog box,
where you can
select the files
you want to
back up.

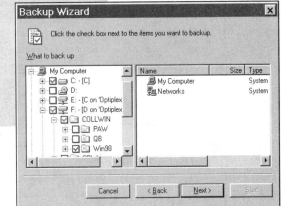

**See Chapter 14
for more
information on
network drives
and password
protection.**

4. Click on <u>N</u>ext and then decide whether to back up all the files you selected or only the files that have changed since your last back up (see Figure 13.5); this dialog box is the same as you'd see if you chose, previously, to back up all files.

5. Click on <u>N</u>ext and then choose where to back up your files. In Figure 13.6, I chose to back up to a network drive.

*Tip*

You may get an error message if you attempt to back up to a network drive that you protected with a password. To solve the problem, connect to the network drive and supply the password *before* you attempt to back up to it.

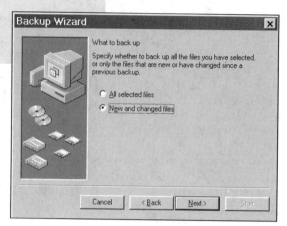

**Figure 13.5**
Decide what to back up.

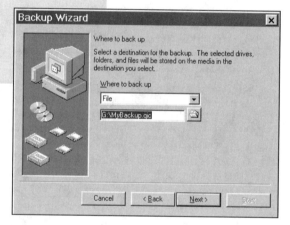

**Figure 13.6**
Choose where you want to store the backup that you make.

# Backup Strategies

You can choose to back up your entire computer every day. If you use this approach, you'll only need to create one backup job that backs up all files on your computer. If you need to restore—either your entire system or selected files—use your last backup. We suggest that you retain a few "old backups"; that is, don't make a new full backup using the same media you used for your last full backup. Rotate the media so that you keep at least five backups. Why? For two reasons:

a. When you back up, the information on the backup media is deleted at the beginning of the backup job. If something goes wrong while you're backing up and you used the media from your last backup, you no longer have a valid backup. If, however, you kept your last backup and started the next backup with new media, any problem during backup won't hurt you because you'll still have a good backup to use if you need it.

b. If you need an older version of a file, you can go back up to five days to find it.

Making a full backup everyday can be very time-consuming. You can, instead, use the *incremental* approach. Using this approach, you make a complete backup of all files on a regular basis—typically, once each week. Then each day between complete backups, you can back up only the files that have changed since your complete backup, saving you time. If you use this approach, you'll need to create two backup jobs: one for the full backup and one to back up only those files that have changed. If you find yourself in the position of needing to restore your entire computer system and you chose this approach, you'll restore, first, your last complete backup. Then you'll restore, one at a time, each *interim* backup, which will bring your system up-to-date. If you simply need an older version of a file, you can look back through the interim backups until you find the older version.

If you use the "complete backup/interim backup" approach and the media you use has sufficient room, you can store both a full backup and interim backups on the same media. For example, if you're using a tape drive, you may need just one tape for the complete backup and several interim backups—depending on the amount of information you need to back up. However, as with the daily- complete-backup approach, you should *not* make a new full backup using the media containing your last backup; instead, you should keep your last backup and start a new backup on a different set of media. That way, if something goes wrong during a backup, you still have a good backup to use.

6. Click on the Next button and then choose whether to compress and verify your backup (see Figure 13.7). When you compress a backup, you save space on the media that will hold the backup; in some cases, depending on the backup device you're using, compressing the data may also increase the time the backup job takes to complete.

   When you verify, Microsoft Backup completes the backup process and then compares the files stored on the backup media with the original files. If Microsoft Backup finds files that don't match, it will notify you; when you verify a backup, you confirm that the copy you made is a valid copy that will be useful if you need it. Verifying your backup increases the amount of time the backup job takes to complete.

7. Supply a title for the backup job (see Figure 13.8). Make the job title something descriptive—such as Full Backup or Interim Backup—so you won't have trouble selecting the correct backup job to use.

8. Click on the Start button in the final dialog box of the wizard. Backup starts the backup job; when it completes the job, you'll see a notification. When you click on OK to close the notification, you'll see a dialog box like the one in Figure 13.9.

If you encounter errors, you can click on the Report button to see a list of the problems Backup encountered.

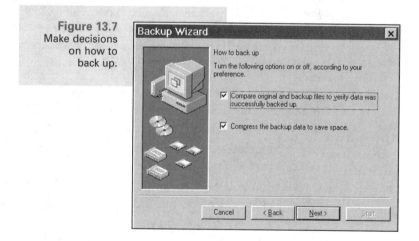

**Figure 13.7**
Make decisions on how to back up.

**Figure 13.8**
Provide a title
for your new
backup job.

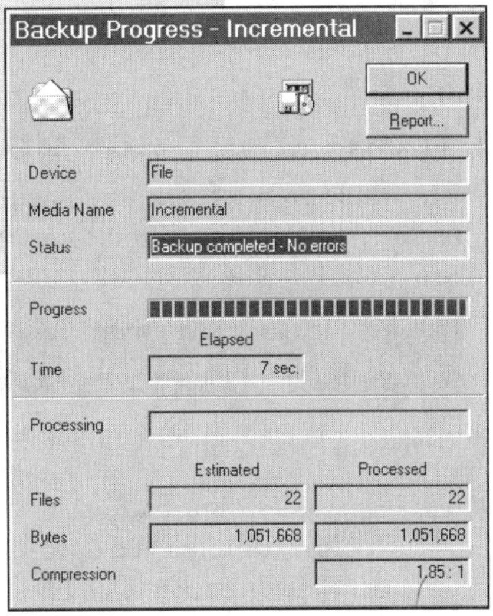

**Figure 13.9**
When the job
completes, the
Status box will
tell you whether
the job
encountered
any errors.

Once you have created backup jobs, you can choose the second option on the opening Backup screen (refer to Figure 13.2) to select the backup job you want to run. Choose a job and then click on the Start button on the Backup tab of the Microsoft Backup window (see Figure 13.10); Backup will use the settings stored in the job to make your backup.

**Figure 13.10**
The Backup tab
of the Microsoft
Backup window.

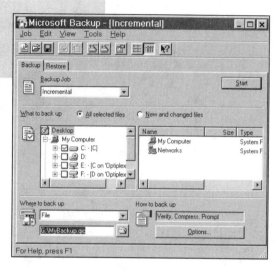

# Restoring from the Backup

The whole point of making backups is to ensure that you can—if you need to—restore a file (or your entire computer) to the last time you used it.

## Hands On: Restoring Backed Up Files

To restore backed up files:

1. Open Microsoft Backup by choosing Start, Programs, Accessories, System Tools, Backup. In the opening dialog box (refer to Figure 13.2), choose the Restore Backed Up Files option button and click on OK. Microsoft Backup starts the Restore Wizard (see Figure 13.11).

2. If you have a backup device installed, you'll see choices other than File in the Restore from list. Select the location that contains your backup.

3. Click on Next to select the backup set that contains the information you want to restore and then click on OK (see Figure 13.12).

4. Select the files you want to restore. Double-click on the drive or folder icons on the left to display the files you can restore on the right. Place checks next to the files you want to restore (see Figure 13.13).

5. Select the location for the restored files (see Figure 13.14). If you choose Alternate Location, you'll be prompted to specify a drive and path name.

**Figure 13.11**
Specify the
location of the
backup files.

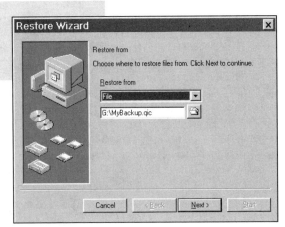

**Figure 13.12**
Check the
backup set that
contains the
information you
want to restore.

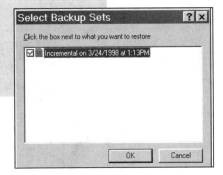

**Figure 13.13**
Select the files
you want to
restore.

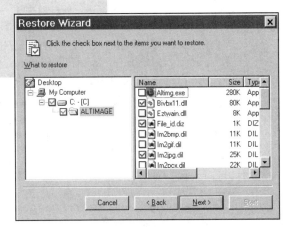

**Figure 13.14**
Specify the
location for the
restored files.

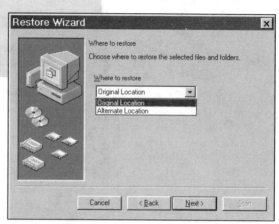

**Figure 13.15**
Specify how to
handle cases
where restoring
a file would
overwrite an
existing file.

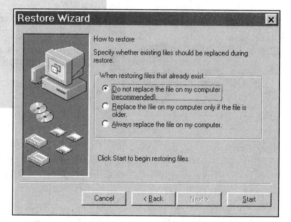

**6.** Click on <u>N</u>ext and then tell Backup how to handle cases where files already exist in the location you chose in step 4 with the same names as the files you are restoring (see Figure 13.15).

**7.** Click on <u>S</u>tart. Backup restores the files using the settings you provided. You'll see a dialog box very similar to the one shown in Figure 13.9. The Status box tells you what Backup did, and you can click on the <u>R</u>eport button to see the details.

*Note*

**Be aware that program files restored from a backup rarely work correctly. Typically, if you have accidentally deleted a file that a program needs to run, you should reinstall the program.**

# Improving the Efficiency of Your Hard Disk

Windows offers three ways you can improve the efficiency of your hard disk:

- You can run ScanDisk to check drives, files, and folders for errors.
- You can run Disk Defragmenter to reorganize files and unused space to make programs run faster.
- You can run Disk Cleanup to let Windows find and delete unnecessary files.

## Checking Drives, Files, and Folders for Errors

ScanDisk is a tool that lets you scan your hard disk to check for physical and logical errors—and fix them if you encounter them.

You can run ScanDisk in two modes: Standard and Thorough. The Standard method typically runs in just a few minutes, but does not check the physical disk for errors; instead, it checks files and folders for errors. The Thorough method can take several hours to run; it checks files and folders for errors, and it checks the surface of your hard disk as well. Plan on using the Thorough method only when you're not working—at night, perhaps.

### Hands On: Scanning Your Hard Disk for Errors

Although you can work while ScanDisk runs, you'll notice ScanDisk starting over. For best results, don't use your computer while running ScanDisk. Also, consider turning off screen savers.

1. Choose Start, Programs, Accessories, System Tools, ScanDisk. Windows displays the ScanDisk window (see Figure 13.16).

2. Select Standard to check files and folders only or Thorough to check your hard disk's surface as well as files and folders. If you choose Thorough, you can click on the Options button and change the settings ScanDisk will use during a thorough examination of your hard disk (see Figure 13.17).

3. Place a check in the Automatically Fix Errors check box to let ScanDisk repair any errors it finds without prompting you.

4. In the ScanDisk window, click on Start. As ScanDisk works, a progress

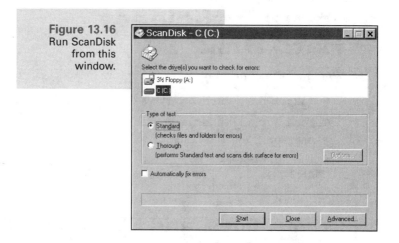

**Figure 13.16**
Run ScanDisk from this window.

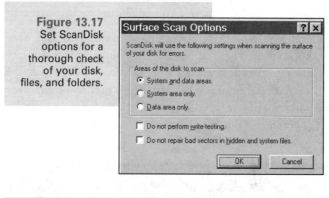

**Figure 13.17**
Set ScanDisk options for a thorough check of your disk, files, and folders.

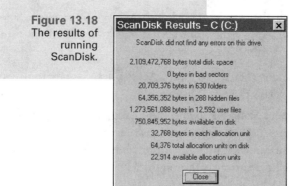

**Figure 13.18**
The results of running ScanDisk.

bar appears at the bottom of the window, showing you what ScanDisk is doing. When ScanDisk finishes, it displays a dialog box like the one shown in Figure 13.18, showing the results.

# Optimizing Performance

As you store information on your computer, files are allocated space. As you edit or add information to files and save them again, the file doesn't always fit in the original space. The operating system may place pieces of the file in many different locations on your hard disk, attaching pointers to connect the pieces of the files. The pointers tell the operating system where to look for more of a particular file when a program tries to open the file.

If you follow this discussion to its logical conclusion, it is possible for one file to be scattered all over your hard disk. Opening a file that is scattered all over the hard disk will take longer than opening a file that resides in one place on the hard disk. So, to speed up processing on your computer, you'll want to consider using Disk Defragmenter to reorganize the files on your hard disk.

*Note*

**The size of your disk and its current fragmentation will determine how long Disk Defragmenter will take to complete its job. This task can be quite lengthy.**

If you use your computer while Disk Defragmenter is running, Defrag assumes the contents of the drive have changed and continuously starts over. For that reason, you should allow your computer to remain idle while you run Disk Defragmenter; also, consider turning off screen savers while running Disk Defragmenter.

## Hands On: Optimizing Space Utilization on Your Hard Disk

Disk Defragmenter optimizes your hard disk by *defragmenting* it; that is, Disk Defragmenter collects all the pieces of a file and places them together on the disk; in addition, Defrag minimizes wasted empty space on your disk.

1. Choose Start, Programs, Accessories, System Tools, Disk Defragmenter. Disk Defragmenter opens and the Select Drive dialog box opens on top of it.

2. Select a drive to defragment (see Figure 13.19).

3. Click on OK. Disk Defragmenter starts optimizing your drive (see Figure 13.20).

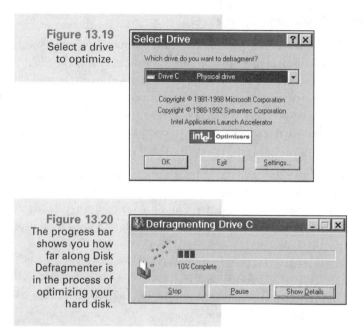

**Figure 13.19**
Select a drive to optimize.

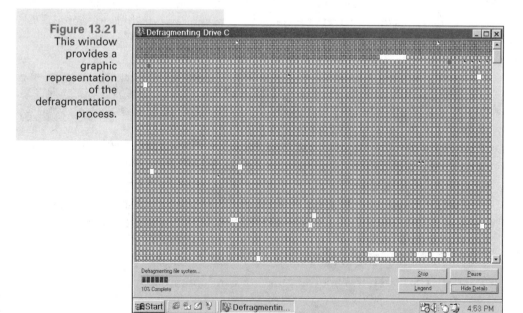

**Figure 13.20**
The progress bar shows you how far along Disk Defragmenter is in the process of optimizing your hard disk.

4. Click the Show Details button to display the view you see in Figure 13.21. When Disk Defragmenter finishes, it will notify you.

**Figure 13.21**
This window provides a graphic representation of the defragmentation process.

# Eliminating Unnecessary Files

The Disk Cleanup utility helps you eliminate "unnecessary files." It will look through your hard disk for temporary files, Internet cache files, and program files it identifies as unnecessary. Disk Cleanup then gives you the opportunity to delete some or all of the files it finds.

*Note*

**Exercise caution about deleting unneeded files, since they may not really be unneeded. Use the following rule of thumb: If you're not sure, *don't* delete. You cannot "undo" a deletion made by Disk Cleanup; that is, Disk Cleanup *does not* place files in the Recycle Bin so that you can restore them. You may want to back up your computer before you use the Disk Cleanup utility.**

## Hands On: Using Disk Cleanup to Eliminate Unneeded Files

Use Disk Cleanup to search for and, if you want, to delete temporary files, Internet cache files, and downloaded program files. Programs create temporary files and usually delete them, but sometimes things happen and the temporary files remain. Internet cache files are images of Web pages stored on your computer to help you load Web pages faster.

1. Choose Start, Programs, Accessories, System Tools, Disk Cleanup.
2. Choose a drive to clean up from the dialog box that appears. Disk Cleanup begins working (see Figure 13.22).
3. Disk Cleanup displays the results of its search in a dialog box like the one you see in Figure 13.23.
4. Highlight a category and click on the View Files button to view the list of files Disk Cleanup suggests for deletion (see Figure 13.24).

**Figure 13.22**
Disk Cleanup searches your hard disk for files to delete.

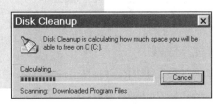

**Figure 13.23**
Disk Cleanup
lists types of files
it found that you
might want to
delete.

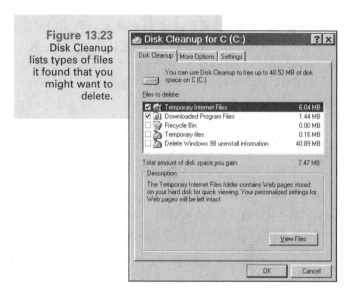

**Figure 13.24**
A window
displays the list
of files Disk
Cleanup wants
to delete.

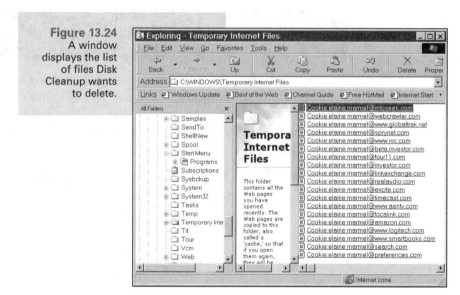

5. Close the window using the X in the upper-right corner to return to the Disk Cleanup dialog box.

6. To delete all the files in a category, leave the check next to the category. To avoid deleting all the files in a category, remove the check next to the category.

7. Click on OK to accept the settings you made. Disk Cleanup removes the files you identified.

CHAPTER 13 • USING SYSTEM TOOLS  **295**

**Later in this chapter, you'll learn more about converting to FAT 32.**

The More Options tab of the Disk Cleanup dialog box suggests additional ways you can free up disk space, such as removing Windows components, installed programs, or converting to FAT 32 (if you haven't already made that conversion). The Settings tab contains one check box that lets you tell Windows to automatically run Disk Cleanup if you are getting low on hard disk space.

# Scheduling System Maintenance

Performing maintenance can be very helpful, but we sometimes get so caught up in work that we forget. Windows 98 contains two utilities, Maintenance Wizard and Task Scheduler, that enable you to schedule maintenance so that it occurs at regular intervals.

## Hands On: Using the Maintenance Wizard

Using the Maintenance Wizard, you can schedule ScanDisk, Disk Defragmenter, and Disk Cleanup to run at intervals you designate.

1. Choose Start, Programs, Accessories, System Tools, Maintenance Wizard. On the first screen of the Wizard, you can choose to use Express settings or make selections on your own (see Figure 13.25). The rest of these steps show you the settings you can choose if you use the Custom option.

2. Click on Next. Select a maintenance schedule for the time you want to run the maintenance tasks (see Figure 13.26). Click on Next.

**Figure 13.25** Choose Express or Custom maintenance.

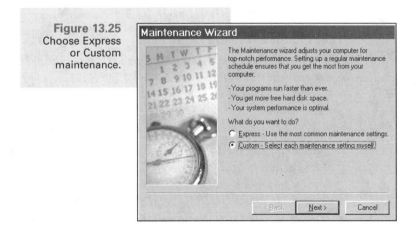

**Figure 13.26**
Specify when
you want
maintenance
to occur.

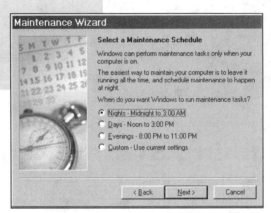

**Figure 13.27**
Speed up
Windows
starting process
by removing
items from the
Startup group.

3. Select check boxes for the items you want to avoid loading in your Startup group. Loading fewer items will speed up the Windows boot process (see Figure 13.27). Click on Next.

*Items in the Startup group load and run behind the scenes every time you start your computer. If you remove them from the Startup group, you will need to start them manually when you want to use them.*

4. Choose whether to run Disk Defragmenter (see Figure 13.28). If you decide to run the Disk Defragmenter, the Settings button and the Reschedule button become available. If you click on the Settings button, you can select the drive to defragment (refer to figure 13.19). If you click on the Reschedule button, you'll to display the Reschedule dialog box you see in Figure 13.29. From this dialog box, you can specify how often to

**Figure 13.28**
Choose whether
to run Disk
Defragmenter.

**Figure 13.29**
Specify when to
run Disk
Defragmenter.

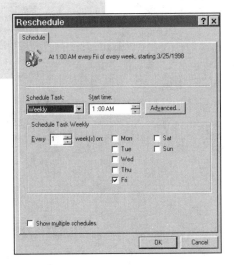

schedule the task. Choose OK to return to the Maintenance Wizard. Click on Next.

5. Specify whether to run ScanDisk (see Figure 13.30). As with Disk Defragmenter, choose Settings to specify the drive to scan and choose Reschedule to specify when to scan the disk. Click on Next.

6. Click on Next to determine whether and how Disk Cleanup should run (see Figure 13.31). Choose the Settings button to specify the types of files Disk Cleanup should delete (refer to Figure 13.23). Choose Reschedule to specify when to run Disk Cleanup. In the Maintenance Wizard, click on Next.

7. Review the maintenance tasks you scheduled (see Figure 13.32). If you

**Figure 13.30**
Choose whether
to run ScanDisk.

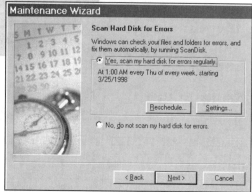

**Figure 13.31**
Tell Disk Cleanup
whether to
delete
unnecessary
files.

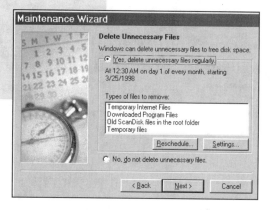

**Figure 13.32**
The Maintenance
Wizard displays
your
maintenance
schedule.

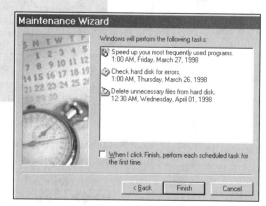

want to run all of the scheduled task immediately after completing the
Maintenance Wizard, place a check in the check box at the bottom of the
Maintenance Wizard. Click on Finish to accept the schedule.

## Hands On: Using the Task Scheduler

Task Scheduler does not restrict you to scheduling maintenance; with the Task Scheduler, you can schedule *almost anything* to happen on your computer.

1. Click on the My Computer icon.
2. Click on Scheduled Tasks. The Scheduled Tasks window opens (see Figure 13.33).
3. Click on Add Scheduled Task. The Scheduled Task Wizard starts to help you set up a scheduled task.
4. Click on <u>N</u>ext. The Wizard displays a list of programs you can choose to schedule (see Figure 13.34).

• • • • • • • • • • • • • • • • • • • • • • • • • • • • • • • • • • • • • • • • • • •

*Tip*

If you don't find the program you want to run in the list, click on B<u>r</u>owse and navigate to it.

• • • • • • • • • • • • • • • • • • • • • • • • • • • • • • • • • • • • • • • • • • •

5. Highlight the program you want to run and click on <u>N</u>ext.
6. Type a name for the scheduled event and select a frequency for Windows to perform the task (see Figure 13.35).
7. Click on <u>N</u>ext and choose a time for the scheduled task (see Figure 13.36). Be aware that the frequency you chose in the previous steps

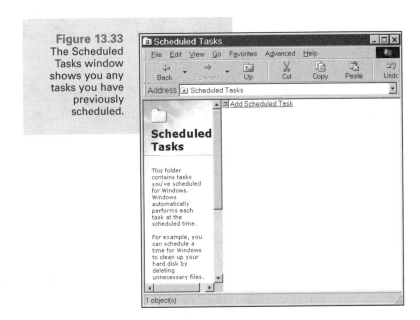

**Figure 13.33**
The Scheduled Tasks window shows you any tasks you have previously scheduled.

**Figure 13.34**
Highlight a program you want to schedule.

**Figure 13.35**
Set the frequency for Windows to run the scheduled task.

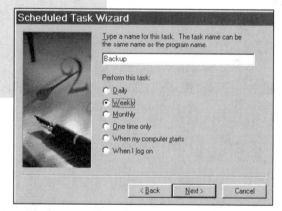

**Figure 13.36**
Set the time Windows should run the scheduled task.

determines the appearance of the screen you use to set the time for the scheduled task; if you didn't choose "Weekly" for the frequency in step 6, your screen will look different than the one shown in Figure 13.36.

8. Click on Finish to complete setting up a scheduled task.

You can set advanced options for the scheduled task by placing a check in the check box on the last screen of the Wizard. You can open the same dialog box to set advanced options by right-clicking on the scheduled task and choosing Properties.

# Increasing Disk Space

Windows provides two ways to increase the amount of available disk space:

- You can convert your hard disk from FAT (also called FAT 16) to FAT 32
- You can compress your hard disk

## Converting to FAT 32

The FAT 16 file system, which was originally conceived in 1976, long before high-capacity disk drives, uses 16-bit file allocation table entries and has some limitations:

- It cannot recognize hard disks larger than 2.1 gigabytes (GB).
- Its cluster size can be quite large and waste a lot of space on the drive.

The FAT 32 file system uses 32-bit file allocation table entries. It can support hard disks up to 2 terabytes, and its cluster size is much smaller, saving lots of space. Some notes on FAT 32 before you start this process:

- You cannot use Windows 98 to return to FAT 16 after you convert to FAT 32 unless you repartition and reformat your hard disk. If the drive also contains Windows 98, you would then need to reinstall Windows 98.

You can, however, use Partition Magic from Power Quest Corporation to return to FAT 16 without repartitioning and reformatting your hard disk. This tool can also help you easily eliminate partitions you may already have on your hard disk. For more information on PartitionMagic, visit Power Quest's Web site at www.powerquest.com.

- Most disk compression software is not compatible with FAT 32; if you have compressed your disk (see the next section for more information about compressing disks), you may not be able to convert to FAT 32.

- You can convert removable disks to FAT 32, but remember, you won't be able to read them on any operating system that does not employ the FAT 32 file system.

- If you upgraded to Windows 98 from DOS, Windows 3.1, or an older version of Windows 95, you will not be able to uninstall Windows 98 after you convert to FAT 32.

- Some disk utilities that depend on FAT 16 won't work on a FAT 32 drive. If you're running one of these utilities, Windows 98 will display a message.

To convert a drive to the FAT 32 file system, choose Start, Programs, Accessories, System Tools, Driver Converter. The Drive Converter Wizard starts. Click on Next to select a drive to convert (see Figure 13.37).

When you click on Next, Drive Converter searches for and lists installed anti-virus programs and disk utilities that depend on FAT 16 and won't work on a FAT 32 drive. When you click on Next, Drive Converter lets you launch Microsoft Backup to back up your computer before converting. When you click on Next, Drive Converter indicates that it will boot the computer in MS-DOS mode and begin the conversion, which might take a few hours. Click on Next to start the process.

**Figure 13.37**
Drive Converter lists the drives you can convert.

When Windows reboots, you won't notice any visible difference; you can check, however, to see that the conversion took place by displaying the properties tab for the disk drive. Open the My Computer window, right-click on the drive you converted, and choose Properties from the shortcut menu. On the General tab, you'll see the file system the drive is using (see Figure 13.38).

# Creating Free Space on Your Hard Disk

You can use DriveSpace 3 to compress both hard and floppy disks. When you compress a disk, you create more free space for files on the disk. DriveSpace 3 compressed drives can be as large as 2GB.

*Note*

You may be familiar with DoubleSpace, which was included in MS-DOS versions 6.0 and 6.2, or with DriveSpace for MS-DOS version 6.22 and DriveSpace for Windows. DriveSpace 3 supports drives that were compressed by using DoubleSpace or DriveSpace. If you have drives that were compressed by using either DoubleSpace or DriveSpace, you can use DriveSpace 3 to configure their compression.

**Figure 13.38**
The File system used by a drive is listed on the General tab of the drive's Properties box.

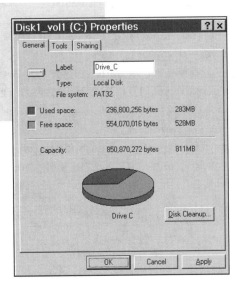

# FAT 16 and FAT 32

To understand the value of converting to FAT 32, you need to under-stand how its predecessor, FAT 16, works. The operating system uses a file system to organize and keep track of the files on your disks. Several file systems exist, but the most widely used file system is the File Allocation Table (FAT, also called FAT 16) file system. Typically, DOS- and Windows-based PCs use the FAT file system. Windows 95 uses a variation of the FAT system called VFAT; VFAT functions the same way FAT functions but also supports longer file names.

Why do you care about this? Because the combination of the size of your hard disk and the file system can actually affect the amounts of wasted space and free space on your computer.

Formatting a disk divides the disk into storage units called clusters. In the FAT (and VFAT) system, any single disk can contain a maximum of 65,535 clusters (the industry generally rounds the number to 64,000). So clusters vary in size according to the size of the disk, but due to FAT limitations, clusters can never be larger than 32,768 bytes (again, the industry rounds the number to 32K). If you multiply a 32,768 byte clus-ter by 65,535 clusters on the disk, you determine the maximum size for a disk drive: 2.1GB (2,147,483,648 bytes).

"But," you say, "I can buy a new computer today with a 6.4-GB hard disk." And we answer, "If you're going to use a FAT 16-based operat-ing system (DOS, Windows 3.1, or early versions of Windows 95), you must *partition* the disk to use all 6.4GBs; the operating system simply can't recognize more than 2.1GB at a time." When you partition a disk, you divide it into *logical* partitions that are no bigger than 2.1GB. The disk in the computer is physically one component, but the operating system uses several drive letters (C, D, E) to look at it, and each drive is called a logical drive.

Partitioning has been around for a long time. Prior to 1989, the operating system could support only one partition on a disk, and that partition could not be larger than 32MB because the FAT file system used a fixed 512 byte cluster size. Making two changes to the operating system solved this problem. First, the operating system was changed to use larger cluster sizes to support bigger partitions. Then the operating system was changed to support using multiple partitions on a single drive.

Now let's take a quick look at what happens to FAT 16 cluster sizes as the size of the partition gets larger.

| Total Partition Size | Minimum Required Cluster Size |
|---|---|
| 16 to 127 Megabytes | 2 Kbytes |
| 128 to 255 Megabytes | 4 Kbytes |
| 256 to 511 Megabytes | 8 Kbytes |
| 512 to 1,023 Megabytes | 16 Kbytes |
| 1,024 to 2,048 Megabytes | 32 Kbytes |

Again, why do you care? Because a file that is only 1 byte long will use an entire cluster regardless of its size. For example, an average AUTOEXEC.BAT file or CONFIG.SYS file might be 500 bytes or 0.5KB. One of these files uses an entire cluster, regardless of the size of the cluster. The rest of the cluster remains empty. So, larger cluster sizes waste more space on the partition.

Later versions of Windows 95 and Windows 98 support FAT 32, which is a file system based on 32-bit file allocation table entries. FAT 32 can support much larger disks (up to 2 terabytes) and uses smaller clusters than FAT 16 (the clusters on an 8GB drive would be only 4KB). So FAT 32 can save you lots of space.

*Tip*

You cannot use DriveSpace 3 to compress a disk that uses the FAT 32 file system.

When you view the contents of your computer by using My Computer or Windows Explorer, the host drive is hidden unless it has more than 2MB of free space. If it has more than 2MB of free space, the host drive is visible, and you can work with it as you would with any other drive.

Notes:

- You cannot compress a FAT 32 drive.
- You can uncompress a disk after compressing it, but only if you have sufficient space to do so.
- It is wise to back up drives before you compress them.
- You cannot use your computer while DriveSpace 3 is compressing a disk.

## Hands On: Using DriveSpace 3 to Compress a Disk

Because compressing a disk can take a few hours, you might want to compress a disk at the end of your day.

1. Choose Start, Programs, Accessories, System Tools, DriveSpace. The DriveSpace window opens, showing you a choice of the drives you can compress (see Figure 13.39).

2. Choose Drive, Compress. The Compress a Drive dialog box appears (see Figure 13.40).

3. When you click on Start, you see the dialog box shown in Figure 13.41.

**Figure 13.39**
Choose a drive
to compress.

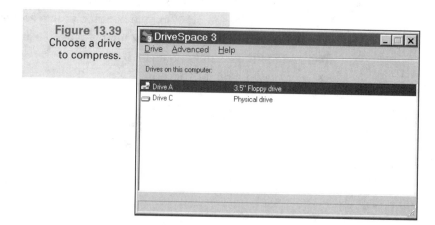

**Figure 13.40**
This dialog box estimates how much free space the disk will contain after compression.

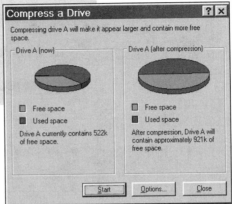

**Figure 13.41**
Windows gives you the opportunity to back up the files on the disk before you compress it.

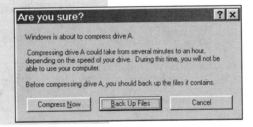

**Figure 13.42**
This Compress a Drive screen displays the results of compression.

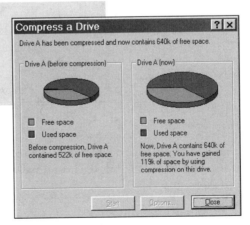

4. Click on Compress Now to start the compression process. Windows first checks the disk for errors and then compresses it. When the compression process is complete, you'll see a screen similar to the one shown in Figure 13.42.

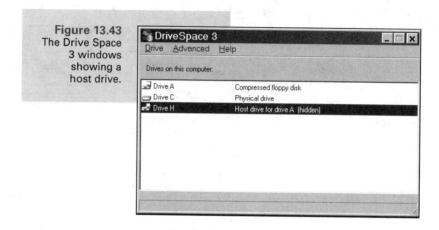

**Figure 13.43**
The Drive Space 3 windows showing a host drive.

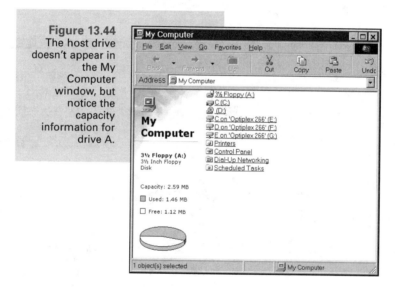

**Figure 13.44**
The host drive doesn't appear in the My Computer window, but notice the capacity information for drive A.

In the DriveSpace 3 window, you'll see the host drive along with the other drives (see Figure 13.43), but the host drive won't appear when you open My Computer (see Figure 13.44).

Once a drive is compressed, you can use the Compression Agent to modify compression information. For example, you may want to increase the compression of certain files you never access. Choose Start, Programs, Accessories, System Tools, Compression Agent. The dialog box shown in Figure 13.45 appears.

Figure 13.45
The Compression Agent dialog box.

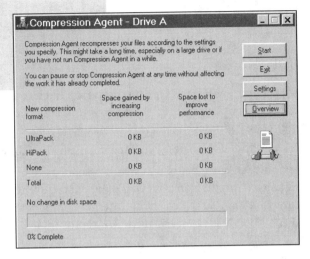

# Updating Your Computer's Drivers with Windows Update

Drivers that contain code that tell the operating system how to use devices attached to your computer ship with the operating system. With earlier versions of Windows, that was the last time you got drivers—unless you got them directly from a hardware vendor either on disk or by downloading them from a bulletin board or a Web site. With Windows 98, you can update your system whenever you want using the Windows Update feature.

As a registered user of Windows 98, you can use Windows Update to connect to a Web site; a Wizard helps you obtain driver and system updates.

*Note*

**You must be a registered user of Windows 98 to use the Update Wizard. If you are not registered, the Update Wizard prompts you to register and walks you through the update process the first time you use it.**

## Hands On: Using the Windows Update Wizard

The Windows Update Wizard scans your computer and generates a list of files that can be updated.

1. Click on Start, Windows Update. If you are not already connected to the Internet, the Update Wizard prompts you to connect. Once connected, you'll see the Windows Update Web page (see Figure 13.46).

2. Click on Product Updates. You'll see the dialog box shown in Figure 13.47.

3. Click on Yes. Active Setup scans your system to identify the Internet components installed on your computer. Then, a list like the one in Figure 13.48 appears, identifying Internet components already installed and components not yet installed (see Figure 13.48).

4. Click on an item to select it. To the right of the item, you'll see a description of the update and information on how long it should take to download.

*Note*

At the bottom of the page, you'll see a link to check for device driver updates. You must complete Internet component downloads before you update device drivers.

**Figure 13.46**
The Windows Update Web page.

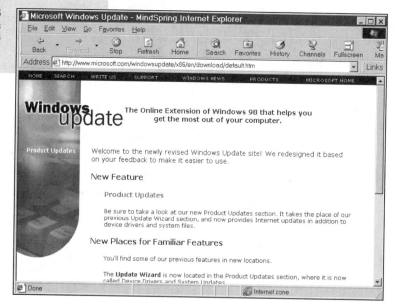

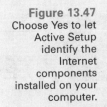

**Figure 13.47**
Choose Yes to let Active Setup identify the Internet components installed on your computer.

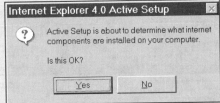

**Figure 13.48**
Possible system updates for Internet components appear onscreen.

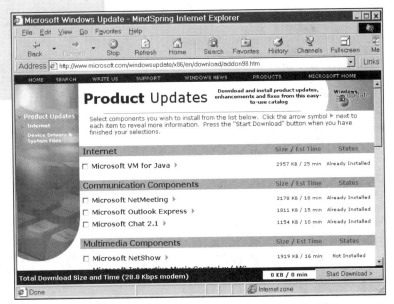

5. Click on Start Download in the lower-right corner of the window. A Web page appears, asking you to select a download site. After selecting from the list, click on the Install Now button. After the download completes, you'll be redirected to the Windows Update home page you saw in Figure 13.46.

6. To check for a download device driver and system file updates, click on Product Updates and click on No to avoid having Active Setup check for Internet components. Then, scroll to the bottom of the page and click on "Click here" (see Figure 13.49).

7. The Web page you see in Figure 13.50 appears. Click on Update. The Update wizard scans your system, looking for updates to system and device files you might want to load. Be patient, the scanning process takes

**Figure 13.49**
Check for device
driver and
system file
updates using
this Web link.

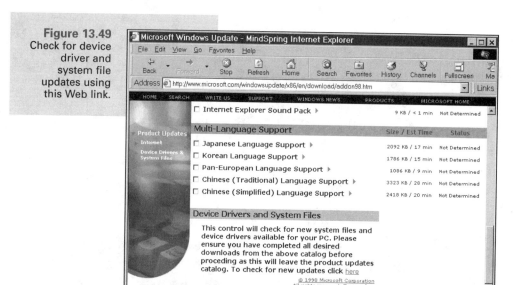

**Figure 13.49**
Check for device
driver and
system file
updates using
this Web link.

**Figure 13.50**
You can update
your system; if
your system fails
to work properly
afterward, you
can use the
Update Wizard
to restore.

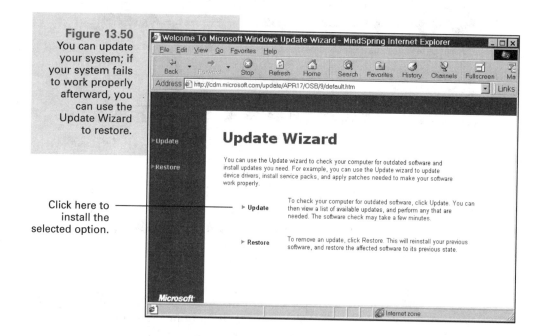

Click here to
install the
selected option.

a few minutes. You may see a security warning; if you do, choose Yes to
load the Windows 98 Update Wizard. When the process is complete,
possible updates appear in the window (see Figure 13.51).

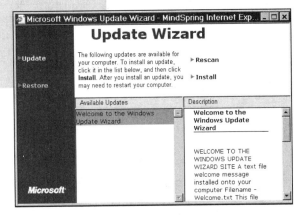

**Figure 13.51**
Possible system
updates appear
in the Available
Updates pane.

*Tip*

If you see an option to install an update to the Update Wizard, install it. You'll need
the latest version to update or restore any system files.

8. Click on an update to select it to install. The right pane displays a
   description of the update and information on how long it should take to
   download.

9. Click on Install. A dialog box appears, indicating that you have chosen to
   install an update.

10. Click on OK to install the update. A progress bar helps you monitor
    progress while you download the file (see fig. 13.52). When the process is
    complete, you'll see a message from Internet Explorer informing you.

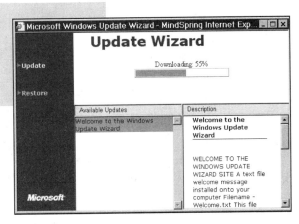

**Figure 13.52**
The progress bar
helps you
monitor the
progress of the
download.

**11.** Click on OK to clear the message. You may see a message that informs you that you need to restart your computer. To complete the update process, restart your computer. Then follow any instructions you see onscreen.

• • • • • • • • • • • • • • • • • • • • • • • • • • • • • • • • • • • • • • • • • • • •

You may want to disconnect from the Internet before you restart your computer. If you use a phone connection, you should be able to right-click on the Connection icon in the System Tray and choose Disconnect.

• • • • • • • • • • • • • • • • • • • • • • • • • • • • • • • • • • • • • • • • • • • •

*Note*

To restore your computer after installing an update, use the Windows Update command to reconnect to the Windows Update Web site. First, choose Product Updates. Click on No to stop the Active Setup wizard from running. Then, scroll to the bottom of the screen and click on the Web link that takes you to the driver and system file update Web page shown in Figure 13.50. Choose Restore. The Wizard presents a list of updates previously installed. Select one to uninstall. Or use the System Information utility you'll read about in the next section.

# Obtaining System Information for Troubleshooting

Windows 98 comes with a utility that provides information commonly requested by technical support personnel. The System Information Utility contains tools you can use to obtain information about your system and even correct problems. In this section, we'll cover some of the tools you'll be more likely to use.

To see the System Information utility, Choose Start, Programs, Accessories, System Tools, System Information. The Microsoft System Information window appears (see Figure 13.53).

In the left pane, you choose the type of information you want to view in the right pane. To look at hardware information, click on the plus sign next to hardware to display a list of hardware categories (see Figure 13.54).

Click on the plus sign next to Components to examine information about the various components on your system (see Figure 13.55).

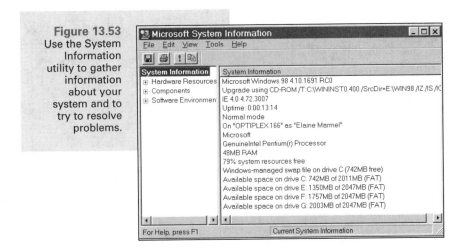

**Figure 13.53**
Use the System Information utility to gather information about your system and to try to resolve problems.

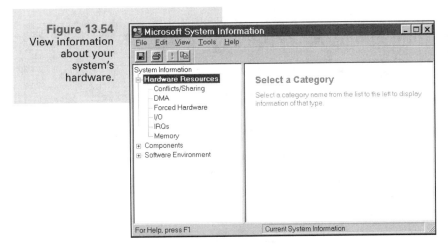

**Figure 13.54**
View information about your system's hardware.

Click on the plus sign next to Software Environment to examine information about the software on your system (see Figure 13.56). From the Tools menu, you can use various tools to try to identify and correct hardware, software, and component problems on your system.

## Updating Wizard Uninstall

When you choose Tools, Update Wizard Uninstall, you'll see the Update Wizard Uninstall dialog box shown in Figure 13.57. Select an update to uninstall and click on the Uninstall button. You'll restore the previous version of the item.

**Figure 13.55**
View information about the components on your system.

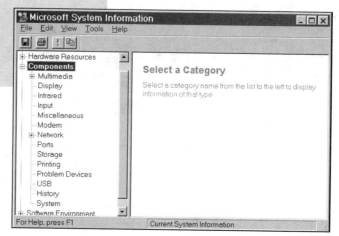

**Figure 13.56**
View information about the software on your system.

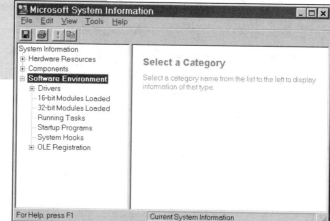

**Figure 13.57**
This tool helps you uninstall updates you previously installed using the Windows Update Wizard.

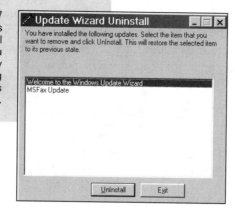

# Windows Report Tool

If you're having a problem on your system, use the Windows Report tool to collect information and send it to Microsoft. The Windows Report tool is a Wizard that walks you through the process of preparing a problem report and sending it to Microsoft. Choose Tools, Windows Report Tool to start the Windows Report Tool wizard (see Figure 13.58).

When you click on Next, the Windows Report Tool Wizard presents a box that contains a Send button. When you click on Send, the Wizard sends your report to Microsoft.

# System File Checker

The System File Checker helps you verify the integrity of operating system files or expand compressed files stored on your installation disk(s) or CD-ROM. Choose Tools, System File Checker to display the System File Checker dialog box shown in Figure 13.59.

If the System File Checker finds a problem with your operating system files, it will help you restore them. By default, the System File Checker will prompt you to back up existing files before restoring any files.

System File Checker notifies you when it finishes. You can view the results (see Figure 13.60) by clicking on the Details button that appears in the notification dialog box.

**Figure 13.58**
This Wizard helps you send information to Microsoft about a problem you're experiencing.

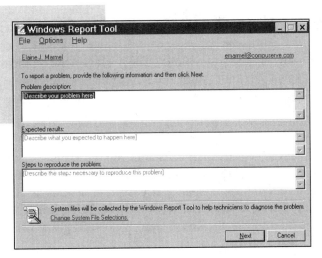

**Figure 13.59**
Use the System
File Checker to
verify the
integrity of
system files.

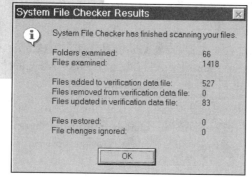

**Figure 13.60**
A typical
"results" dialog
box from System
File Checker.

# The Registry and the Registry Checker

Whenever you make a change to your system—add or delete hardware or software—the Registry gets modified. The Registry is the central database for all Windows 98 configuration information. Read that sentence twice. Yes, the Registry is *very* important to the proper running of your computer under Windows 98.

But the Registry is a collection of files, and files do get corrupted. So it's very important to have a backup of the Registry. Windows automatically makes a backup of the Registry once daily after you successfully start your computer. And the Registry Checker automatically scans the Registry for invalid entries and empty blocks of data. If the Registry Checker detects invalid entries, it will automatically restore a previous day's backup of the Registry. If, for some reason, no valid backup of the Registry is available, the Registry Checker will attempt to repair the Registry.

Typically, Windows runs the Registry Checker automatically if Windows suspects a problem with the Registry; if you want to check the Registry, however, you can run the Registry Checker by choosing Tools, Registry Checker from the System Information window. You won't see a dialog box unless the Registry Checker finds errors. Instead, Windows reports that the Registry has no errors. In the message box, Windows asks whether you want to back up the Registry again today (see Figure 13.61). Windows tells you when the backup is complete.

Provide a name for the backup copy of the Registry in the File Name box and click on the Save button. Windows places a copy of the Registry on your Desktop. Then you can edit the Registry as needed. If, after making a change to the Registry and rebooting, you find that your computer isn't working as you expected, restore the backup copy of the Registry by opening the Registry Editor and choosing Registry, Import Registry File. Select the file you placed on your Desktop.

The Registry Editor window works very much like Windows Explorer. On the left side, you see *Registry keys*. When you select a Registry key, you'll see its values in the right pane (see Figure 13.62).

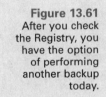

**Figure 13.61**
After you check the Registry, you have the option of performing another backup today.

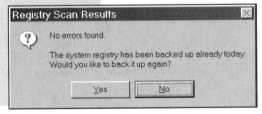

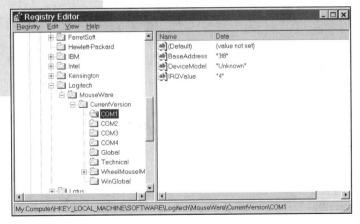

**Figure 13.62**
Registry keys appear in the left pane, and their values appear in the right pane.

# Guidelines for Editing the Registry

Under most circumstances, you don't need to edit the Registry. When you add or remove programs or hardware, Windows edits the Registry for you to reflect the changes. Occasionally, you'll need to edit the Registry. To open the Registry, choose Start, Run. In the Run dialog box, type **regedit** and click on OK. The Registry Editor appears (see Figure 13.63).

**Figure 13.63**
The Registry Editor window.

We suggest that you make a backup copy of the Registry before you make any changes. And you can do that by copying the file to your Desktop. Choose Registry, Export Registry File. A "save as" dialog box appears (see Figure 13.64).

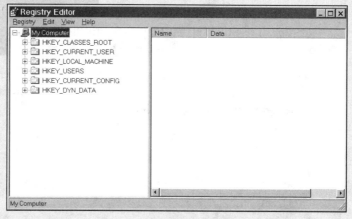

**Figure 13.64**
Backing up the Registry by exporting it.

See Chapter 8 for more information on using the Control Panel.

If you know the name of the key you want to modify or delete, you can search for it. Choose Edit, Find in the Registry window and then type some information to identify the key.

Remember, editing the Registry should be a "last resort" activity. Typically, you can modify the Registry using the appropriate Control Panel icon.

## Automatic Skip Driver Agent

The Automatic Skip Driver Agent is an informational tool; when you choose Tools, Automatic Skip Driver Agent, you'll see information about drivers that Windows may have had trouble loading and therefore did not load (see Figure 13.65).

## Dr. Watson

Dr. Watson is a diagnostic tool that logs the events that happen on your system whenever a system fault occurs. Dr. Watson identifies the software that faulted and offers a detailed description of the cause. Dr. Watson can often offer a suggested course of action.

To start Dr. Watson, open the System Information utility and then choose Tools, Dr. Watson. The Dr. Watson icon appears in the System Tray in the lower-right corner of your screen (see Figure 13.66).

To generate a system snapshot, right-click on the Dr. Watson icon and then choose Dr. Watson from the shortcut menu. Dr. Watson takes a snapshot of your

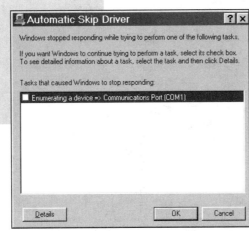

**Figure 13.65** The Automatic Skip Driver dialog box shows you drivers that caused problems for Windows.

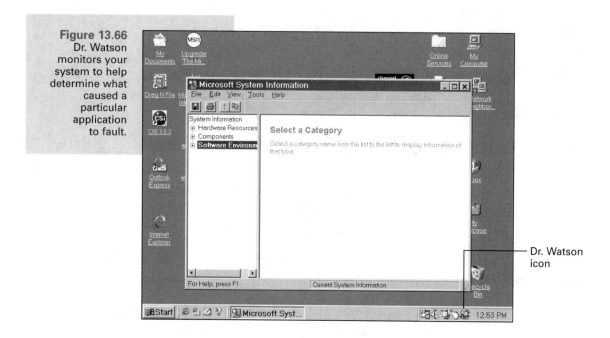

**Figure 13.66**
Dr. Watson monitors your system to help determine what caused a particular application to fault.

Dr. Watson icon

system by scanning it and presents a diagnosis (see Figure 13.67). To help technical support staff with their evaluation, type steps that describe what you were doing when the problem occurred and save the information by choosing File, Save As and typing a file name.

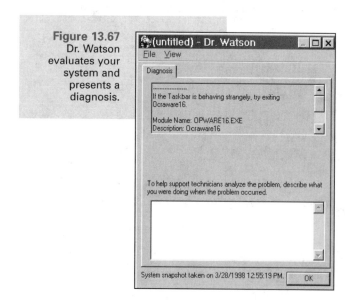

**Figure 13.67**
Dr. Watson evaluates your system and presents a diagnosis.

# System Configuration Utility

The System Configuration Utility automates the typical troubleshooting steps that Microsoft Technical Support engineers take when they diagnose a Windows configuration problem. You can use the System Configuration Utility to help you diagnose problems that occur when you start Windows normally. For example, you may be able to use the System Configuration Utility to determine the source of a problem that does *not* occur when you start your computer in Safe mode. The System Configuration Utility also can help you determine the cause of error messages, system "stops" (also called "hanging"), or loss of functionality.

If you've ever called a Microsoft Windows engineer for help, you've found that they follow a pattern to help you diagnose and resolve the problem. First, they typically ask you whether you have a backup of your system files. (Most people don't, but the engineers always ask.) Then they have you restart your computer and perform a step-by-step loading of files and drivers; usually they tell you to skip loading the AUTOEXEC.BAT file and the CONFIG.SYS file but to load everything else. This way, they can begin to isolate the source of the problem.

The System Configuration Utility automates this process. When you choose Tools, System Configuration Utility from the System Information window, you see the General tab of the System Configuration Utility (see Figure 13.68).

**Figure 13.68**
Use the System Configuration Utility to isolate and solve problems.

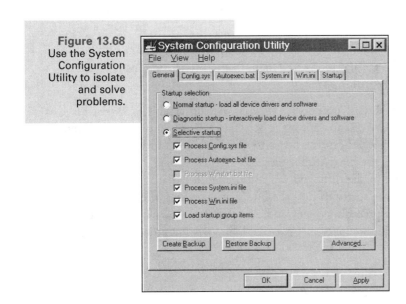

Remember that backup about which the support engineers always ask? Click on the Create <u>B</u>ackup button on the General tab to make it. Then click on the <u>Diag</u>nostic Startup option and click on OK.

For those of you who experienced the troubleshooting process in Windows 95, this choice replaces pressing F8 when you see Starting Windows as you boot your computer.

Windows then prompts you to restart your computer. You'll see a menu from which you can choose Step-By-Step confirmation. As Windows loads, it will ask you if it should load each file it normally processes. Typically, you load everything except your AUTOEXEC.BAT and your CONFIG.SYS. If the problem still occurs, you may want to consider the following:

- Faulty settings in your computer's CMOS; see the manual that came with your computer to find out how to view and modify, if necessary, the computer's CMOS settings.

- Missing or corrupted system files; see the "System File Checker" section earlier in this chapter.

- Protected mode device driver configurations; the Microsoft Knowledge Base contains an article, Q156126, that can help you with this.

- A corrupted Registry; see the "The Registry and the Registry Checker" section earlier in this chapter.

- Viruses; consult the vendor of your anti-virus software or purchase anti-virus software and follow the manufacturer's instructions for installing it and cleaning your system.

If the problem doesn't occur with normal Startup disabled, reopen the System Configuration Utility and choose the <u>S</u>elective Startup option on the General tab. Then remove checks from the boxes to selectively load files while starting Windows and isolate the file that may be causing your problem. When you isolate the problem to one of the files, you can use the tab for that file to add and remove lines from the file to try to find the line that is causing the problem (see Figure 13.69). Checks preceding a line indicate that Windows is processing that line when starting. Removing a check makes Windows *not* process the line.

Figure 13.69
Use the System
Configuration
Utility to avoid
typing errors
when editing
system files to
resolve
problems.

*Note*

**When you finish using the System Configuration Utility, be sure to redisplay the General tab and choose the Normal Start option to tell Windows to start your computer normally from this point forward.**

## Version Conflict Manager

The Version Conflict Manager runs automatically when you install drivers on your system. During the installation process, the Version Conflict Manager will notify you if you are about to install an older version of a file that already resides on your computer. Usually, you want to keep the latest version.

When you choose Tools, Version Conflict Manager in the System Information utility, you see a Version Conflict Manager dialog box, similar to the one in Figure 13.70, which lists all the files that had a more recent version before Windows 98 was installed.

**Figure 13.70**
You can view
and restore the
files that were
actually newer
than the files
Windows 98
installed when
you upgraded to
Windows 98.

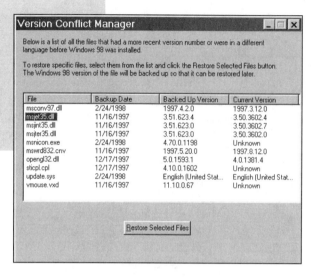

**Figure 13.70**
You can view and restore the files that were actually newer than the files Windows 98 installed when you upgraded to Windows 98.

If you are experiencing problems on your system and suspect that the source of your problem is a newer file that was replaced by Windows 98 when you upgraded, you can restore that file by selecting it from the list and choosing Restore Selected File. The Version Conflict Manager will back up the Windows 98 version of the file before restoring so that you can restore the Windows 98 version later if it turns out that reverting to your version did not solve your problem.

If you don't want to restore any files, close the Version Conflict Manager by clicking on the X in the upper-right corner of the window.

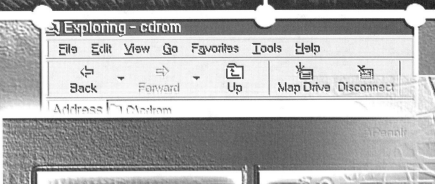

# PART IV
# Your Window to the World

# 14

# Networking and Windows 98

## IN THIS CHAPTER

- **Understanding Networking Basics**
- **Setting up a Windows 98 Network**
- **Sharing a Printer across a Network**
- **Sharing Files across a Network**

Networking, as a topic, has filled volumes. We're not going to attempt to teach you everything you need to know about networking; instead, we're going to examine the networking capabilities of Windows 98. In this chapter, you'll learn how to set up Windows 98 to operate in a peer-to-peer network.

# A General Discussion of Networking

> Suppose you need to "network on the fly"; that is, you don't have network hardware and software, but you *really* need a temporary connection. Try a direct cable connection. See Chapter 15 for more information.

When you *network* computers, you connect them so that they can share resources—both hardware and software. For example, if you place several computers and one printer in a network, each computer can print to the printer. And each computer can access information stored on the hard disks of the other computers in the network. To make these common elements available, you share devices such as printers and hard disks—and even CD-ROM drives.

You've probably heard of LANs and WANs. A *LAN* is a local area network and generally refers to computer equipment that is connected and relatively close together—in the same room, on the same floor, or in the same building. A *WAN* is a wide area network. Basically, a WAN is just a bigger LAN; the computers in a WAN are physically farther apart.

How do you connect computers? You use a combination of hardware and software; specifically, you consider five elements: LAN technology, the topology of the computers in the network, network cards for each computer in the network, the wiring you intend to use to connect the computers, and the network operating system.

## Network Hardware Considerations

The most popular LAN technology in use today is Ethernet; as an alternative, you can choose the Token-Ring technology or Fiber Distributed Data Interface (FDDI). Although I'm over-simplifying, the most basic difference between the technologies is the speed at which they transmit data.

The *topology* of the network refers to the physical arrangement of the components, which are called *nodes*, in the network. For example, in an Ethernet network, you can use a basic bus topology, which connects network nodes directly to each other. Or you can set up a star network, where all the nodes of the network are connected, by wire, to a central unit called a *hub*. You must use a hub if you intend to connect more than two computers in a network. The hub is the network equivalent of a multiple plug; in your home, when you need to plug in a hair dryer, curling iron, electric toothbrush, and electric shaver in a bathroom plug with only two sockets, you use a multiple plug adapter to convert one socket into several sockets. In a network, a hub provides multiple network connectors so that you can connect multiple network nodes. In a Token Ring network, the star configuration is called a "ring," and the device that serves the purpose of a hub is called a Multistation Access Unit (MAU). FDDI uses a ring configuration like the Token Ring network and hubs.

Each computer in a network must contain a network card; this piece of hardware contains a socket into which you insert a network cable; the other end of the cable connects to another computer's network card or to a hub. The type of network card you choose depends largely on the type of network technology you choose.

The three popular types of cabling you can use to connect network nodes are shielded or unshielded twisted pair cable, coaxial cable, and fiber optic cable. Ethernet and Token Ring networks can use any of these types of wiring; originally, FDDI could use only fiber optic cable, but today FDDI also can use unshielded twisted pair cables. Twisted pair cable, which closely resembles telephone wiring, is by far the most common cabling method.

## Network Software Considerations

Network operating systems also come in many flavors and varieties; Novell, Lantastic, Windows NT, Windows 95, and Windows 98 are just a few of the most popular. Each, of course, has its own requirements, restrictions, and methods for achieving the common purpose of monitoring the activity on your network to ensure smooth operation. The type of network operating software that you choose will also affect whether you set up a client/server network or a peer-to-peer network.

In a client/server network, one computer acts as the server and manages requests from the other computers—the clients—in the network. You could say that the client node makes a request and the server node provides the solution. Under optimal circumstances, people don't sit at the server computer and work; instead, the server is allowed to simply field requests from the client computers in the network. The client computers in the network that make the requests are often called workstations. To set up a client/server network, you need special operating system software for the server. Windows 98 can be the client for just about any network operating system server software: Novell, Windows NT, or even UNIX, but Windows 98 typically does not perform the functions of a server in a client/server network.

A peer-to-peer network contains no server; instead, all network nodes are workstations that share everything. Peer-to-peer networks run well in small environments of just a few network nodes. In these cases, the volume of traffic on the network is low; that is, requests for network resources don't happen often. Because a peer-to-peer network contains no server, you don't need any special server software; you can use Windows 98 on every machine in a peer-to-peer network.

# Setting Up a Windows 98 Network

In the rest of this chapter, we'll examine how you set up Windows 98 to function as the operating system software in a peer-to-peer network. Because we're going to focus on the software side of networking, we'll assume that you've already installed all the hardware you need. That is, you've selected a network technology such as Ethernet, and you've installed network cards into each computer that will be a part of the network. If you're connecting more than two computers, we'll assume that you also have a hub. Last, we'll assume that you have wired the computers so that they are connected, either to each other or to the hub.

*Note*

**Although printers are considered network nodes, you do not insert a network card into a printer, nor do you connect a printer to a hub. Instead, you can connect your printer directly to one of the computers in the network; later in this chapter, you'll learn how to share the printer so that other computers in the network can use it.**

For each computer running Windows 98 that you intend to use in a network environment, you must specify a network adapter, a network client, and at least one protocol.

## Adding Network Adapters

A network adapter is the hardware component that enables you to physically connect your computer to a network. As with most hardware, you need software to describe how the hardware should behave. So to completely install a network adapter, you must not only place it in the computer, but also make sure that software for it is set up.

When you turn on your computer after installing a network card, Windows 98 attempts to set up the software for the network card in your computer. If Windows recognizes the network adapter, then, when you first see the Network dia-

Figure 14.1
The Network
dialog box after
installing a
network card in
your computer.

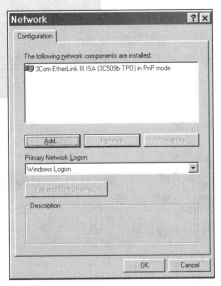

log box (see Figure 14.1), you'll see the software entry for your network adapter—and the chances are quite good that you won't need to make any changes. If Windows doesn't recognize your network adapter automatically, you will need to it set up.

To display the Network dialog box, choose Start, Settings, Control Panel. Then click on the Network icon. To add your adapter, click on the Add button. The Select Network Component Type dialog box appears (see Figure 14.2). Highlight Adapter and click on the Add button to display the Select Network Adapters dialog box (see Figure 14.3).

*Note*

**If you previously installed an Internet connection, you will see an entry for Dial Up Adapter in the Network dialog box along with your network adapter. And if your Internet service provider supports virtual private networking, you will also see two entries—one for an adapter and one for a protocol—for the Microsoft Virtual Private Networking Adapter. Virtual private networking is a new networking technology that allows you to access your corporate network securely across the Internet. Virtual private networking is particularly useful for people who travel. They can log on to the Internet and then access their corporate network.**

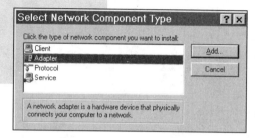

**Figure 14.2**
Choose a network component to add.

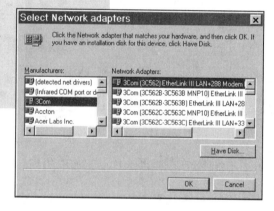

**Figure 14.3**
Choose a network adapter that matches the one you inserted in your computer.

See Chapter 8 for more information on using the Add New Hardware Wizard to install hardware not recognized by Windows.

From the list on the left, choose the manufacturer of your network adapter. In the list on the right, find your adapter. Then click on OK. Windows adds your adapter to the Network dialog box.

*Tip*

Each time you make a change in the Network dialog box, Windows prompts you to insert the Windows 98 CD-ROM so that Windows can copy files. Then Windows prompts you to restart your computer so that the new settings can take effect. Because you still have other network components to set up, don't close the dialog box yet.

*Note*

If your adapter does not appear, you'll need to use the disk that the network adapter manufacturer supplied; insert the disk into a disk drive and click on Have Disk. Then follow the on-screen prompts. This process is very similar to adding new hardware that Windows doesn't recognize.

# Adding a Client

In addition to a network adapter, you need to define client software for your computer. *Client software* describes the way your computer can behave in the network and interact with a server, if your network also contains a server. You need to select a network client that is compatible with your network configuration. For a peer-to-peer network, set up the Client for Microsoft Networks.

You can set up as many clients as you need; for example, if you need to log on to both a Windows NT server and a Novell server, set up both the Client for Microsoft Networks and the Client for NetWare Networks.

## Hands On: Adding a Network Client

If you closed the Network dialog box, reopen it by choosing Start, Settings, Control Panel. Then click on the Network icon.

1. Click on the Add button to display the Select Network Component Type dialog box (refer to Figure 14.2).

2. Highlight Client and click on the Add button. The Select Network Client dialog box appears (see Figure 14.4).

3. From the list of Manufacturers on the left, select the manufacturer of your network client software. If you're setting up a peer-to-peer network and intend to use Windows networking, choose Microsoft.

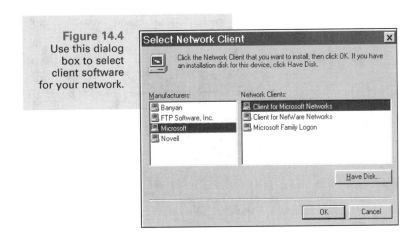

**Figure 14.4**
Use this dialog box to select client software for your network.

4. From the list of Network Clients on the right, choose the client software you want to install. For our peer-to-peer network, choose Client for Microsoft Networks.

*Note*

**The Client for NetWare Networks is Microsoft's version of the client software used in a Novell network. The Microsoft Family Logon client supports multiple users working on the same computer; this client works in conjunction with the multiple user profiles you can create when you choose the Users icon in the Control Panel. See Chapter 8 for more information on the Users icon.**

5. Click on OK. Windows adds the client to the Network dialog box, along with a protocol entry for TCP/IP (see Figure 14.5). You'll learn more about protocols in the next section.

*Tip*

Each time you make a change in the Network dialog box, Windows prompts you to insert the Windows 98 CD-ROM so that Windows can copy files. Then Windows prompts you to restart your computer so that the new settings can take effect. Because you still have other network components to set up, don't close the dialog box yet.

**Figure 14.5**
The Network dialog box after adding a client.

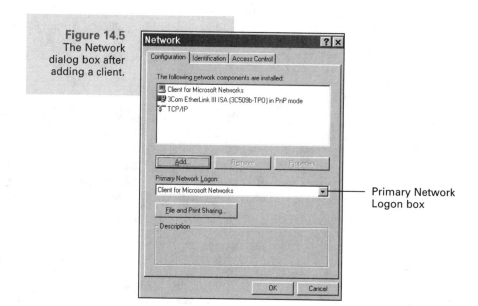

Primary Network Logon box

Repeat these steps to add other clients. If you add more than one client, you can select the client you want to use by default. Suppose, for example, that you log on to a Windows NT server most of the time, but occasionally, you need to log on to a Novell server. Install both the Client for Microsoft Networks and the Client for NetWare Networks, but set the default to Client for Microsoft Networks by opening the Primary Network Logon list box and choosing that client.

To specify the Windows NT server to which you want to connect, highlight the Client for Microsoft Networks and choose Properties. On the General tab, place a check in the Log on to Windows NT Domain check box and specify the domain for the Windows NT server (see Figure 14.6). Specify the Novell server in a similar fashion; highlight the Client for NetWare Networks and, on the General tab, specify the preferred server.

## Adding a Protocol

Network protocols are much like protocols in politics. A *protocol* is a language that participants in a conversation agree to use; it provides a means to communicate that all participants understand. A *network protocol* is the language a computer uses to communicate over a network. As in politics, all computers in the network must use the same protocol to communicate with each other.

You can, however, install several protocols. For example, TCP/IP is the protocol that computers use to communicate on the Internet. However, in a local network you may wish to use another protocol, such as NetBEUI or IPX/SPX.

**Figure 14.6**
Specify the server to which you want to connect.

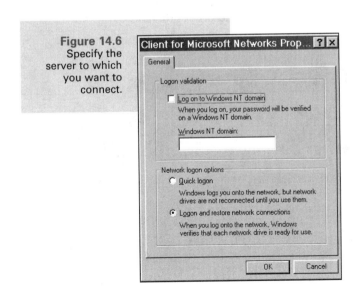

Windows, by default, installs a version of each protocol you install for each adapter you have installed. For example, if you have both a network card and a dial-up adapter installed and you install NetBEUI, Windows installs *two* NetBEUI entries—one for each adapter.

## Hands On: Adding Protocols

You can install as many protocols as you want; your computers will communicate over your network as long as you install *one common* protocol on each computer. If you closed the Network dialog box, reopen it by choosing Start, Settings, Control Panel. Then, click on the Network icon.

1. Click on the Add button to display the Select Network Component Type dialog box (refer to Figure 14.2).

2. Highlight Protocol and click on Add. The Select Network Protocol dialog box appears (see Figure 14.7).

3. From the list of Manufacturers on the left, select the manufacturer of the protocol you want to install. If you're setting up a peer-to-peer network and intend to use Windows networking, choose Microsoft.

4. From the list of Network Protocols on the right, choose the protocol you want to install. For our peer-to-peer network, choose IPX/SPX-compatible Protocol.

5. Click on OK. Windows adds the protocol to the Network dialog box (see Figure 14.8). Repear these steps to add other protocols.

**Figure 14.7**
Use this dialog box to add network protocols.

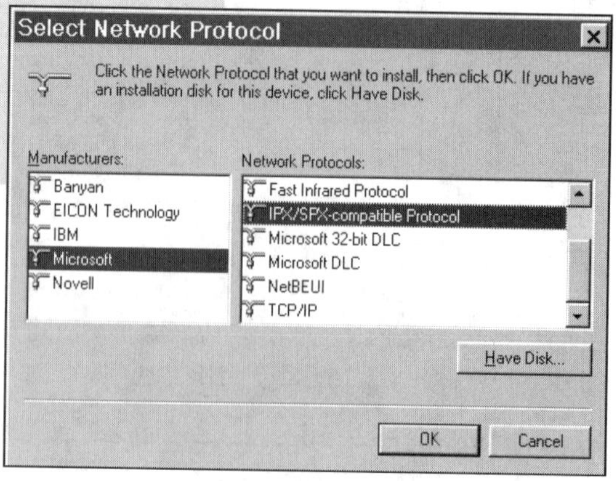

**Select Network Protocol**

Click the Network Protocol that you want to install, then click OK. If you have an installation disk for this device, click Have Disk.

Manufacturers:
- Banyan
- EICON Technology
- IBM
- **Microsoft**
- Novell

Network Protocols:
- Fast Infrared Protocol
- IPX/SPX-compatible Protocol
- Microsoft 32-bit DLC
- Microsoft DLC
- NetBEUI
- TCP/IP

Have Disk...

OK     Cancel

**Figure 14.8**
The Network
dialog box after
adding a
protocol.

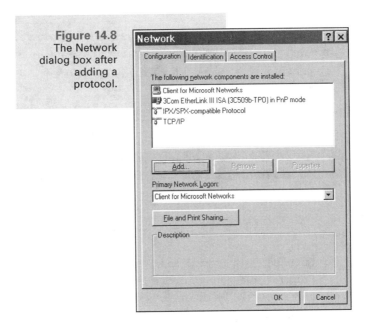

*Tip*

Each time you make a change in the Network dialog box, Windows prompts you to insert the Windows 98 CD-ROM so that Windows can copy files. Then Windows prompts you to restart your computer so that the new settings can take effect. Because you still have other network components to set up, don't close the dialog box yet.

## Checking Bindings

Network adapters must be "bound" to protocols. *Binding* is the process of establishing the protocols your network adapter will recognize and use. You can, in fact, allow your network adapter to use all the protocols you install, which is the default installation Windows selects. Or you may want certain adapters to use specific protocols while other adapters use other protocols. For example, you may want the Dial Up Adapter to use only the TCP/IP protocol—the protocol used on the Internet—while setting your network card's protocol to anything *but* TCP/IP.

*Note*

Typically, Windows default settings work fine. However, modifying bindings can help you resolve networking conflicts that may arise, so consider changing bindings if you experience problems on your network.

## Hands On: Checking Bindings

If you closed the Network dialog box, reopen it by choosing Start, Settings, Control Panel. Then, click on the Network icon. The Network dialog box appears (see Figure 14.9).

1. Highlight your network adapter and click on the Properties button. The Properties dialog box for your network adapter appears. It contains three tabs. Select the Bindings tab (see Figure 14.10).

2. Remove checks for any protocols you don't want your network adapter to use.

3. Click on OK to redisplay the Network dialog box.

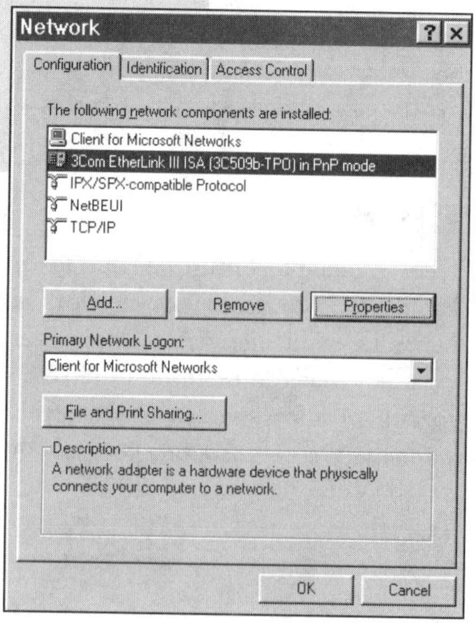

**Figure 14.9**
Use the Network box to check your adapter's binding settings.

| Network | ? X |
| --- | --- |

Configuration | Identification | Access Control |

The following network components are installed:

- Client for Microsoft Networks
- 3Com EtherLink III ISA (3C509b-TPO) in PnP mode
- IPX/SPX-compatible Protocol
- NetBEUI
- TCP/IP

Add... | Remove | Properties

Primary Network Logon:

Client for Microsoft Networks

File and Print Sharing...

Description
A network adapter is a hardware device that physically connects your computer to a network.

OK | Cancel

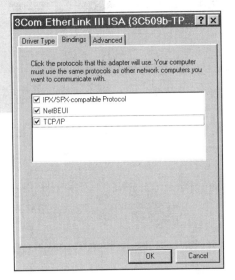

**Figure 14.10**
The Bindings tab shows the protocols your network adapter will recognize and respond to.

*Tip*

Each time you make a change in the Network dialog box, Windows prompts you to insert the Windows 98 CD-ROM so that Windows can copy files. Then Windows prompts you to restart your computer so that the new settings can take effect. Because you still have other network components to set up, don't close the dialog box yet.

## Identifying Your Computer

In a network, you need to provide information that will identify each computer. Part of the identification information includes the workgroup to which the computer belongs. A *workgroup* is nothing more than a name you establish to identify a collection of computers that should be allowed to share information and hardware on the network. It is important to understand that, if you want particular computers to be able to share with each other, those computers must be part of the *same* workgroup.

## Hands On: Identifying the Computer in the Network

Be sure to assign the same workgroup name to each computer you want to share information on the network. If you closed the Network dialog box, reopen it by choosing Start, Settings, Control Panel. Then click on the Network icon.

1. Click on the Identification tab (see Figure 14.11).

2. Assign a name for the computer; this name will appear in the Network Neighborhood window when you open it, and it will also appear in the Windows Explorer.

3. Assign a workgroup name; this name can be anything you want as long as you make it the same name for each computer in the network that you want to share files and devices.

4. Supply a computer description; this description is optional.

**Tip**

Each time you make a change in the Network dialog box, Windows prompts you to insert the Windows 98 CD-ROM so that Windows can copy files. Then Windows prompts you to restart your computer so that the new settings can take effect. Because you still have other network components to set up, don't close the dialog box yet.

**Figure 14.11**
Identify your computer for the network.

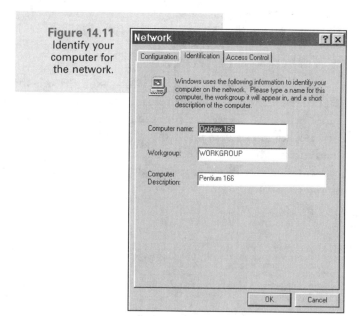

# Networking Printers

If you want to share printers across your network, first you must permit printers to be shared on your network. Then, you identify the printers that you want to share.

## Permitting Sharing

When you permit printer sharing, you also have the option to permit file sharing. Because most people use networks for the purpose of sharing both hardware and software, we'll enable both file and printer sharing in our peer-to-peer network.

> ### Hands On: Allowing File and Printer Sharing on the Network

You can enable both file and printer sharing at the same time. If you closed the Network dialog box, reopen it by choosing Start, Settings, Control Panel. Then click on the Network icon. The Network dialog box appears (see Figure 14.12).

1. Click on the Configuration tab.

2. Click on the File and Print Sharing button. The File and Print Sharing dialog box appears (see Figure 14.13).

**Figure 14.12**
Click here to establish file and printer sharing.

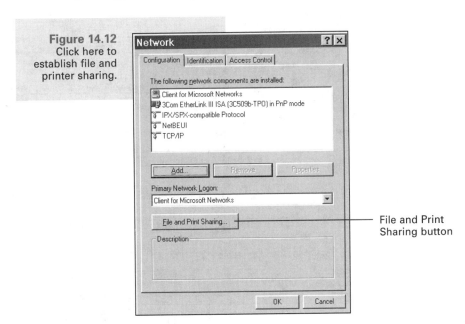

File and Print Sharing button

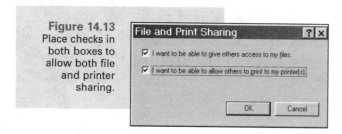

**Figure 14.13**
Place checks in both boxes to allow both file and printer sharing.

3. Place checks in both boxes to allow other network users to have access to your files and printer.

4. Click on OK to save your settings. Windows redisplays the Network dialog box, which contains an entry for file and printer sharing (see Figure 14.14).

5. Click on OK to save all your network settings. Windows 98 may prompt you to insert the CD-ROM to find the files it needs to complete the process. After Windows copies the files, it prompts you to restart your computer for the settings to take effect. Follow the instructions you see onscreen.

You can determine whether things are working as expected by opening the Network Neighborhood window on your Desktop. You should see an icon for the

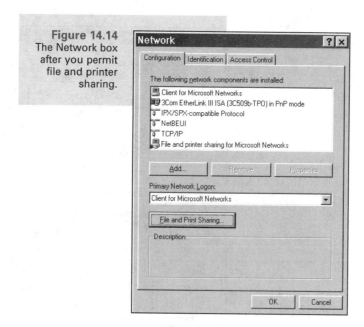

**Figure 14.14**
The Network box after you permit file and printer sharing.

Figure 14.15
The Network
Neighborhood
window shows
all computers in
the network.

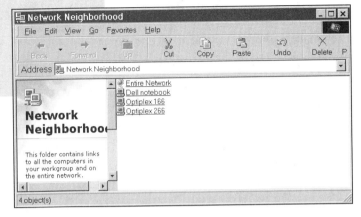

Entire Network, your own computer, and any other computers already set up to work in the network (see Figure 14.15).

If you don't see your own computer and any other computers already set up in the network, run the Network Troubleshooting Wizard to help you chase down your problem. Click on Start, Help and then select the Contents tab. Click on the Troubleshooting book, the Windows 98 Troubleshooters book, and the Networking troubleshooter.

# Sharing a Local Printer

As we mentioned earlier, printers are considered network nodes, but they don't connect directly to the network. Instead, you may connect the printer directly to one computer in the network and then allow the other computers in the network to print to it by sharing it. The printer must be installed as a local printer on the computer to which it is physically attached.

*Note*

**If all the computers in the peer-to-peer network use the printer extensively, you may experience conflicts as each computer tries to share the resource. To alleviate this potential problem, you may want to invest in a print spooler, which is a device that specifically manages the printer in the network to help avoid conflicts. The printer plugs into the print spooler, and the print spooler plugs into the network. The print spooler comes with software that tells each computer in the network how to find the printer.**

## Hands On: Sharing the Local Printer

To make a printer available to all computers in the network, share it.

1. On the computer to which the printer is attached, open the My Computer window.

2. Open the Printers folder.

3. Highlight the printer and right-click to display a shortcut menu (see Figure 14.16).

4. Choose Sharing. The printer's Properties box appears, displaying the Sharing tab (see Figure 14.17).

**Figure 14.16**
Use the shortcut menu to open the printer's Properties box to the Sharing tab.

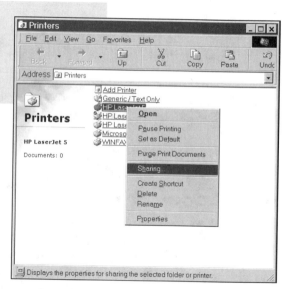

**Figure 14.17**
Setting up a printer to share it.

5. Choose the <u>S</u>hared As option button.

6. Supply a Share <u>N</u>ame; this name will appear whenever you choose the printer.

If you intend to share more than one printer and they are both the same model, make sure the Share Name uniquely distinguishes one from the other so that you can easily identify the printer to which you are sending a print job.

7. (Optional) Supply a comment; other people can see the comment if they look at your printer on the network.

8. (Optional) Supply a password; other people will need to supply this password to use your printer.

9. Click on OK. After you share the printer, its icon in the Printers window changes to include a hand (see Figure 14.18).

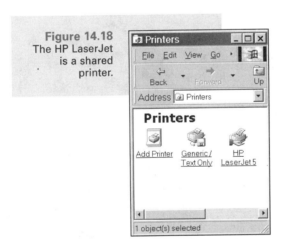

**Figure 14.18**
The HP LaserJet is a shared printer.

## Setting up a Network Printer

Once you share a local printer, other computers in the network can print to it—after each computer not attached to the printer sets up a printer that represents the shared printer.

### Hands On: Creating a Network Printer

At each computer that is not directly connected to the shared printer, add a network printer.

1. Open the My Computer window.

2. Open the Printers window.

3. Click on the Add Printer icon to start the Add Printer Wizard.

4. Click on the Next button to begin the installation.

5. Choose to install a Network Printer and click on the Next button (see Figure 14.19).

6. Supply the network path for the printer. To avoid making mistakes, click on the Browse button and navigate to the printer (see Figure 14.20).

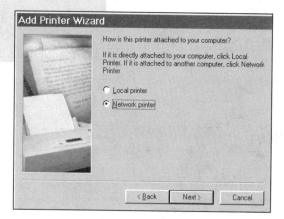

**Figure 14.19**
Install a network printer.

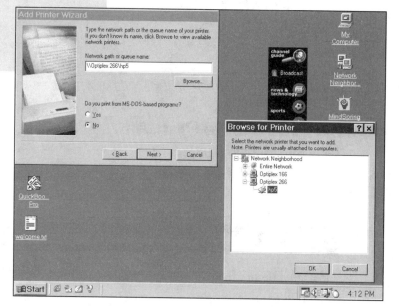

**Figure 14.20**
Supply the network path to the printer.

7. Click on OK in the Browse for Printer box to enter the printer's path in the Network Path or Queue Name box of the Add Printer Wizard.

8. If you print from MS-DOS programs, choose the <u>Y</u>es option button in the Add Printer Wizard box and click on the Next button.

9. If necessary, install a driver for the shared printer and click on the Next button.

10. Supply a name for the printer (see Figure 14.21); the name you choose will be the name you'll see in the Print dialog box of your programs.

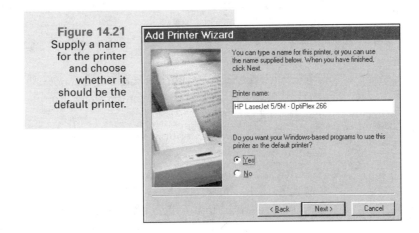

**Figure 14.21**
Supply a name for the printer and choose whether it should be the default printer.

11. Click on the <u>Y</u>es option button if you want this printer to be the default printer for the computer.

12. Print a test page to make sure that everything works as it should work. When the test page completes, the printer will be installed and ready for use.

# Sharing Drives, Folders, or Files

The last step in setting up your computer to work in the network is to share drives, folders, or files. If you want to provide access to everything on your computer, you'll find it easiest to simply share the drives on your computer. If, however, you want to restrict access, you can specify folders or files you want to share. By sharing folders or files, you provide access to only those folders or files.

You also can require a password for access to your computer; users who try to access your computer will need to supply the password to gain access.

## Hands On: Sharing Drives, Folders, or Files

You use the same technique to share drives, folders, or files.

1. Open the My Computer window.
2. Highlight the drive you want to share.

*Note*

**To share a folder, open the drive containing the folder and highlight that folder. To share a file, open the folder containing the file and highlight the file.**

3. Right-click to display a shortcut menu and choose Sharing (see Figure 14.22). A Properties box where you set sharing options appears (see Figure 14.23).
4. Click on the Shared As option button and provide a Share Name. The Comment is optional.
5. Specify the amount of access you want to supply; to allow people to look but not touch, choose Read-Only. To allow people to make changes to the information stored in the file, folder, or drive, choose Full. Choose Depends on Password if you want to provide different kinds of access for different people.

**Figure 14.22**
Use the shortcut menu to open the Properties box and specify sharing information.

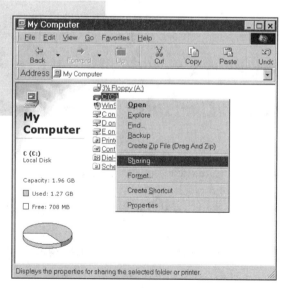

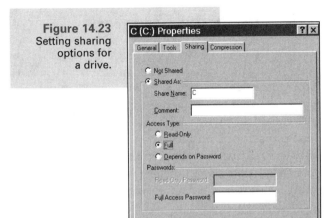

**Figure 14.23**
Setting sharing
options for
a drive.

6. (Optional) Use the Passwords portion of the tab to require passwords, regardless of the access you gave. For example, you can require a password for Read-Only access or Full Access. If you chose Depends on Password in step 5, provide both a Read-Only password and a Full Access password; then give the appropriate password to each person in your network.

7. Click on OK. When the My Computer window reappears, the icon for the drive, folder, or file will change to include a hand (see Figure 14.24).

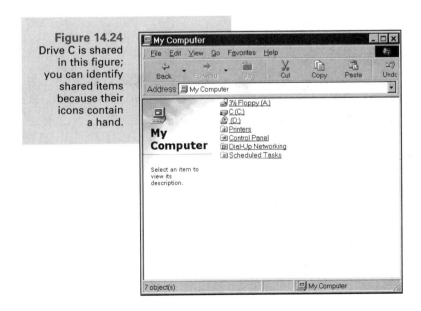

**Figure 14.24**
Drive C is shared
in this figure;
you can identify
shared items
because their
icons contain
a hand.

# Mapping Network Drives

When drives, folders, or files are shared and you need to access them on a regular basis, you'll find it easiest to map a network drive. When you *map* a network resource, you assign it a drive letter on your computer. Assume that Mary shares her drive C on your peer-to-peer network. On your computer, you have your own drive C and a CD-ROM drive to which you refer as D. Suppose that you need files on Mary's drive C on a regular basis. You'll find it easiest to map Mary's drive C and assign it a letter on your computer such as drive E. When you map a drive, you can choose to reconnect the mapped drive each time you start your computer so that you always have access to shared drives—and never have to map again.

## Hands On: Connecting to a Network Drive by Mapping

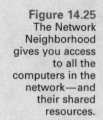

1. Open the Network Neighborhood window on your Desktop. You'll see all the computers in the network (see Figure 14.25).

2. Click on the computer containing the drive you want to map.

3. Highlight the drive you want to map and right-click to display a shortcut menu (see Figure 14.26).

4. Choose Map Network Drive.

5. In the Map Network Drive dialog box, select the letter you want to assign to the drive you are mapping and choose whether you want to always maintain a connection to that drive. If you do, check Reconnect at Logon (see Figure 14.27).

**Figure 14.25**
The Network Neighborhood gives you access to all the computers in the network—and their shared resources.

**Figure 14.26**
Use the shortcut menu to choose the Map Network Drive command.

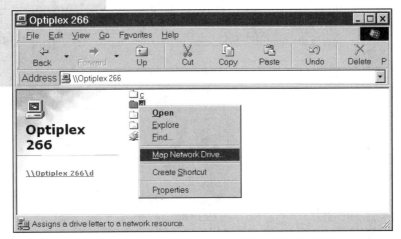

**Figure 14.27**
If you choose Reconnect at Logon, Windows will look for the mapped drive each time you start your computer.

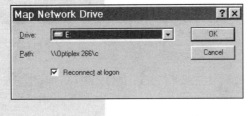

*Note*

**If the computer containing the drive you're mapping is off and you attempt to "reconnect at logon," Windows will display a message telling you the drive is not available and asking if you want to try again the next time you log on.**

6. Click on OK to establish the connection. Windows opens the drive you mapped. You can close it.

Repeat these steps for any other drives you want to map. You can view mapped drives in the My Computer window or in Windows Explorer. The icon for a mapped drive looks like a box attached to a wire. A mapped drive name contains the letter and name of its original computer. However, on your computer you refer to the mapped drive by the letter you assigned to it, which appears in parentheses at the end of the mapped drive's name (see Figure 4.28).

**Figure 14.28**
Drives E, F, and G are mapped.

These drives are mapped drives.

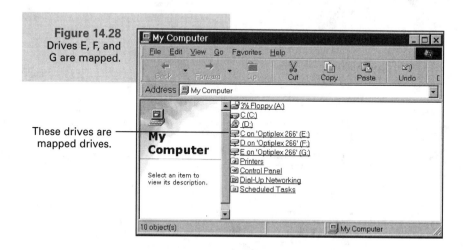

# 15

# Connectivity Tools

## IN THIS CHAPTER

- **Using the Online Services Folder**
- **Signing Up for an Online Service**
- **Establishing Dial-Up Networking**
- **Connecting with HyperTerminal**
- **Using the Phone Dialer**
- **Configuring a Direct Cable Connection**

One of the most popular uses for a computer today is to connect to the world. Whether you're jumping on the on-ramp to the Internet or just need to send an e-mail message to a co-worker, you need to get connected. Windows 98 provides several tools to assist you with your connectivity needs.

# Using the Online Services Folder

When you install Windows 98, a folder called Online Services is placed on your desktop. This folder contains setup icons to connect to several online services or Internet service providers (ISPs).

By selecting an online service or an ISP from this folder, you are establishing an account directly with that company and agreeing to pay a service fee. The fee varies with the plan you subscribe to, but the current average is between $10 and $30 per month. The service you select will provide payment instructions. Many of the services also offer a free trial period.

The following services are included in the Online Services folder:

- America Online
- CompuServe
- The Microsoft Network
- Prodigy Internet
- AT&T WorldNet

Microsoft Windows 98 does not provide technical support for any of these services. If you have any questions you should contact the service directly.

Table 15.1 lists the technical support and/or customer service telephone numbers for the online services and ISPs included with Windows 98.

All the setup routines are similar, but each has slight variations. For the example in this book, we'll subscribe to Microsoft Network (MSN).

To set up an online service, you need to provide a credit card number. You won't be billed for free trial hours, but you can't even sign up for the trial offer without a credit card.

If you elect to use a different service provider than those included with Windows 98, that provider will supply you with any necessary software to connect to its service.

Of course, before you can connect to any of these services, you must have a modem in your computer connected to a telephone line.

## Table 15.1  Technical Support Phone Numbers for Online Service Providers

| SERVICE PROVIDER | CONTACT | TELEPHONE |
| --- | --- | --- |
| America Online (US) | Tech Support | 800-827-3338 |
| | Sales & Billing | 800-827-6364 |
| America Online (UK) | Technical Support | 0800-279-7444 |
| | Customer Service | 0800-279-7444 |
| | General Inquiries | 0800-376-5432 |
| America Online (Canada) | Technical Support | 888-265-4357 |
| | General Inquiries | 888-265-4357 |
| AT&T WorldNet Service (US) | Technical Support | 800-400-1447 |
| | General Inquiries | 800-967-5363 |
| CompuServe (US & Canada) | Customer Service | 800-848-8990 |
| | Signup Support | 800-336-6823 |
| CompuServe (UK) | Customer Service | 0990-000-400 |
| | Signup Support | 0990-134-819 |
| | Technical Support | 0990-000-100 |
| Microsoft Network (US) | Customer Service | 800-386-5550 |
| Microsoft Network (US) | Technical Support | 425-635-7019 |
| Microsoft Network (US-TTD) | Customer Service | 800-840-9890 |
| Microsoft Network (US-TTD) | Technical Support | 425-635-4948 |
| Microsoft Network (Australia) | Customer Service | 02-9934-9000 |
| Microsoft Network (Australia) | Technical Support | 02-9934-9000 |
| Microsoft Network (Canada-English) | Customer Service | 800-386-5550 |
| Microsoft Network (Canada-English) | Technical Support | 425-635-7019 |
| Microsoft Network (Canada (French) | Customer Service | 800-952-1110 |
| Microsoft Network (Canada (French) | Technical Support | 425-635-7020 |
| Microsoft Network (UK) | Customer Service | 0345-000-111 |
| Microsoft Network (UK) | Technical Support | 0345-000-111 |

## Hands On: Subscribing to MSN

1. Insert the Windows 98 CD-ROM into the CD-ROM drive.

2. Click on the MSN icon or open the Online Services folder and click on the service you want to set up.

3. Click on Next to continue to the next screen. MSN setup checks to make sure no other programs are currently running. Click on Next again so that MSN can identify the country you are in.

4. Select your country from the drop-down list and then click on Next. Read the MSN member agreement carefully and then click on I Agree. MSN is now ready to start the installation.

5. Click on Next to continue to the software installation process. Be patient. This process takes a few minutes.

   Next, MSN wants to know whether you have an existing account and whether you want to dial in using the MSN network or an existing Internet connection.

6. Click on the appropriate choices and then click on Next. The Internet Connection Wizard will now connect you to MSN or to your ISP.

   The MSN Sign Up Wizard will prompt you for personal information such as name, address, and phone number.

7. Fill in the appropriate text boxes and then click on Next. You will be advised of the available membership plans and their fees.

8. Click on Next to continue. Enter your credit card information when prompted. Don't put any dashes or spaces in the credit card number. Click on Next to continue.

   MSN displays information on the membership rules.

9. Click on I Agree and then click on Next.

10. Enter a User Name and password. Your User Name will be the name you want others on the Internet to know you by (see Figure 15.1). You'll need to type the password twice and then click on Sign Me Up! Your information will be validated and a final sign-up screen will appear confirming your sign up.

11. Click on Exit to exit the MSN SignUp Wizard.

    You're now ready to log on to MSN, but you need to find a phone number to dial in to.

12. Click on the MSN icon. The MSN sign-in screen prompts you to enter the User Name and password you specified in step 10 (see Figure 15.2).

**Figure 15.1**
Your password appears in asterisks so no one can look over your shoulder as you are typing it.

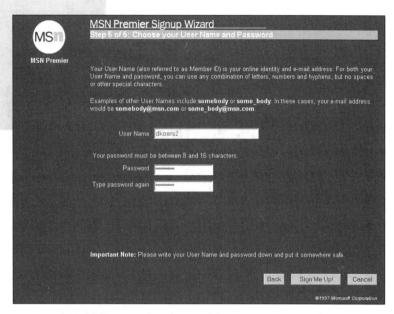

**Figure 15.2**
Click on Remember Password, and you won't have to type it in each time, but this shortcut also gives anyone who uses your computer free access to your Internet account.

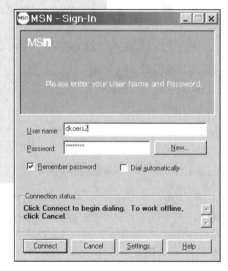

13. Click on Settings to open the Connection Settings dialog box.

14. Click on Phone Book to open the MSN Phone book.

15. Click on your state from the State or Region drop-down list box. A list of access phone numbers will be displayed as shown in Figure 15.3.

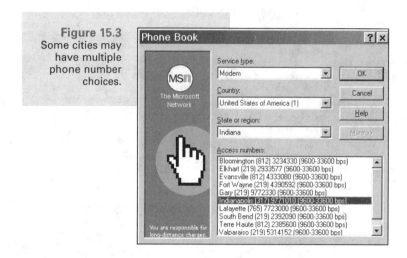

**Figure 15.3**
Some cities may have multiple phone number choices.

16. Click on the Access number that is closest to you or does not require a long distance connection and then click on OK.

*Tip*

If you have the Call Waiting feature on your modem line or if you need to dial 9 or another number to access an outside number, click on Dialing Properties and change any necessary settings.

17. Click on OK to close the Connection Settings dialog box and return to the MSN Sign-In dialog box. Now you're ready to enjoy MSN!

18. Click on Connect to dial into MSN.

# Establishing a Dial-Up Connection

Whether you need to connect to your home office when you're away or whether you're trying to access the Internet, you'll need to establish a Dial-Up Networking (DUN) connection. Even if you already have a direct ISP, you'll need to tell Windows 98 how to connect to the ISP. Information about all your connections is stored in a folder called Dial-Up Networking.

With Windows 98, DUN has been updated to support Dial-Up Scripting. Scripting automates the process of connecting to online services. Many ISPs today require a scripting process to establish a connection.

DUN now also supports a feature called Multilink Channel Aggregation, which enables you to combine multiple dial-up lines. Multiple lines can transfer data faster than one line can (kind of like "two heads are better than one"). This approach provides a dramatic performance improvement when accessing the Internet or an intranet.

## Hands On: Establishing a Dial-Up Connection

1. Click on My Computer and then click on Dial-Up Networking.

2. Click on Make New Connection to launch the New Connection Wizard.

3. Type a name for the connection and then click on Next. The name should be something that you'll recognize as a connection to your ISP.

4. Enter the Area code and Telephone number of the computer you are dialing into. (Ask your ISP for this phone number.) You'll also need to select your country from the Country code drop-down list and then click on Next.

5. Click on Finish. The connection information will be saved in the Dial-Up Networking folder; however you're not quite finished. Most ISPs have other pertinent information that you'll need to enter.

6. Right-click on the connection you created and choose Properties from the shortcut menu.

   The type of information you'll need to enter here depends on the ISP. If you don't have written instructions for these steps from your ISP, call the company and have a technical person talk you through the choices you'll need to make.

7. Click on the Server Types tab. Then select or deselect the options according to your ISP's specifications.

8. Click on TCP/IP Settings and follow your ISP's instructions. Figure 15.4 illustrates a sample TCP/IP setting.

9. Click on OK twice. Your connection is now ready to use.

• • • • • • • • • • • • • • • • • • • • • • • • • • • • • • • • • • • • • • • • • • • •
To delete a connection, right-click on the unwanted connection and choose Delete from the shortcut menu. Click on Yes to confirm the deletion.
• • • • • • • • • • • • • • • • • • • • • • • • • • • • • • • • • • • • • • • • • • • •

10. Click on your new connection to connect with your ISP. The Connect To dialog box will appear. Enter your username and password when prompted.

11. Enter any required information and then click on Connect. Your computer modem will dial into your Internet service provider.

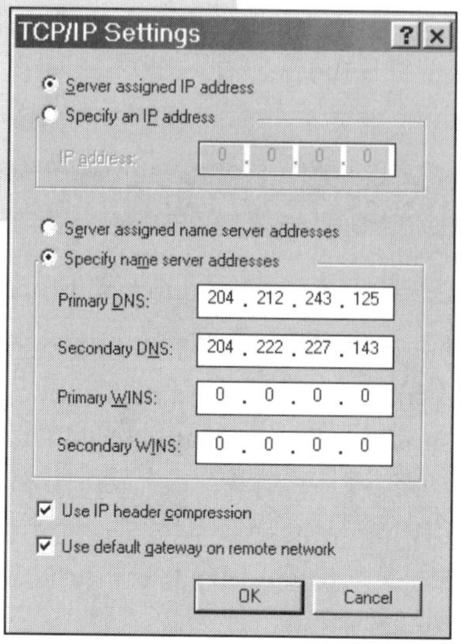

**Figure 15.4**
The settings shown in this figure depend on the requirements of your ISP.

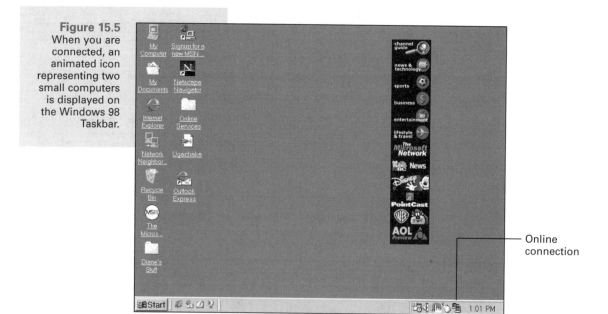

While it's connecting, you'll hear some screeching and strange noises from your computer. That's OK—it's one computer saying hello to the other, as shown in Figure 15.5.

**Figure 15.5**
When you are connected, an animated icon representing two small computers is displayed on the Windows 98 Taskbar.

*Tip*

To disconnect from your ISP, double-click on the connection icon in the task bar and then click on Dis<u>c</u>onnect.

# Connecting with HyperTerminal

> See "Adding Windows Features" in Chapter 8. The HyperTerminal program is in the Accessories, Communications section.

A modem doesn't work all by itself. A communications software program is necessary to command the modem. If you are subscribing to a service such as AOL or MSN, you can use their communications software. Sometimes, however, you just want to log on to a bulletin board or download a file from Microsoft or another computer. In this case you're forming a direct connection between your computer and someone else's, not accessing the Internet.

Windows 98 comes with a "freebie" communications program, called HyperTerminal, that enables you and your computer to contact other computers and exchange information. HyperTerminal is not installed by default with Windows 98, so you'll need to install it yourself.

To use HyperTerminal, click on Start, <u>P</u>rograms, Accessories, Communications, and HyperTerminal.

The HyperTerminal program doesn't automatically launch; instead, a window like the one in Figure 15.6 opens with selections for you to pick from.

**Figure 15.6**
Sessions are already included to connect to AT&T Mail, MCI Mail, and CompuServe.

At this point, you can either open a saved *session* or you can create a new session. A *session* is a collection of information (phone number and technical data) that's needed for calling up a specific computer. Windows 98 saves that information for future access in an icon and stores the icon in the HyperTerminal folder.

## Hands On: Creating a HyperTerminal Session

This exercise creates and saves a session to a company called Crystall Report Writer's BBS.

1. Click on the HyperTerminal icon to launch a new session.

   A New Connection Wizard helps you create a session. The first thing that's needed for the new connection is a name for it and an icon to represent it.

2. Type a name such as **Crystall BBS** in the Name box.

3. Click on an Icon for future Crystall Report Writer sessions and then click on OK. For this exercise, choose the first icon.

4. Enter the Country Code, Area Code, and Phone number of the computer you want to hook up with (see Figure 15.7) and then click OK.

5. Click on Dial to dial into the Crystall computer.

   When the two computers connect, the exact prompts you see will depend on the computer you have called and the type of BBS system that company is using (see Figure 15.8).

● ● ● ● ● ● ● ● ● ● ● ● ● ● ● ● ● ● ● ● ● ● ● ● ● ● ● ● ● ● ● ● ● ● ● ● ● ● ● ● ● ● ●
If you want to hang up a call, you can click on the Call menu and choose Disconnect.
● ● ● ● ● ● ● ● ● ● ● ● ● ● ● ● ● ● ● ● ● ● ● ● ● ● ● ● ● ● ● ● ● ● ● ● ● ● ● ● ● ● ●

**Figure 15.7**
For this exercise, United States is the Country Code, 604 is the Area Code, and the Phone number is 681-9516.

| Connect To | ? X |
| --- | --- |

Crystall BBS

Enter details for the phone number that you want to dial:

Country code: United States of America (1)

Area code: 604

Phone number: 681-9516

Connect using: Sportster 28800-33600 Internal Plu

OK    Cancel

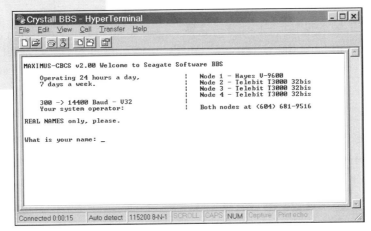

**Figure 15.8**
Follow the prompts to enter and leave the BBS system.

6. Choose File, Exit to quit the HyperTerminal program.

   When you exit the HyperTerminal program, Windows prompts you to save the session information.

7. Choose Yes to save it for future use or choose No if you don't want to keep the information (see Figure 15.9).

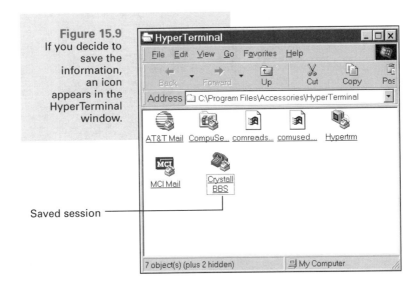

**Figure 15.9**
If you decide to save the information, an icon appears in the HyperTerminal window.

Saved session

# Using the Phone Dialer

The phone dialer is an interesting small accessory application that enables you to make phone calls using your PC. You can tell the dialer what number you want to dial by typing the number, choosing it from a speed dial list, or clicking numbers on a display keypad.

The phone dialer also keeps a call log for you, and you can quickly redial numbers from a recently dialed numbers list. The call log shows whom you called, the number, date and time, and duration of the call.

## Hands On: Starting the Phone Dialer

1. Click on Start and choose the Programs menu.
2. From the Programs menu, click on Accessories, Communications, Phone Dialer.

The phone dialer window appears as shown in Figure 15.10.

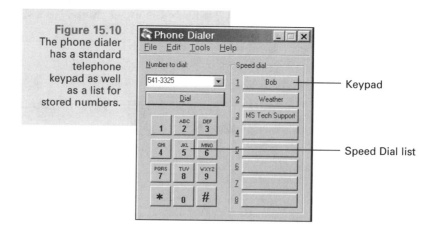

**Figure 15.10** The phone dialer has a standard telephone keypad as well as a list for stored numbers.

# Programming Speed Dial Numbers

You can store up to eight entries in the speed dial list. Having a number listed in speed dial makes calling that number a mouse click away.

## Hands On: Adding Numbers to the Speed Dial List

1. Click on Edit, Speed Dial.

   When the Speed Dial window appears (see Figure 15.11), notice the eight gray buttons on the top.

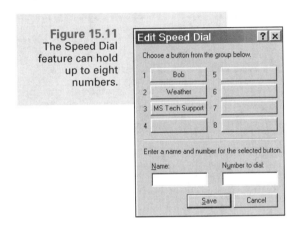

**Figure 15.11**
The Speed Dial feature can hold up to eight numbers.

2. In the Name box, type a descriptive name for the person you want to call. As you type the name, it will appear in the first available speed dial box or if you click on any button before typing, the name will appear in the selected button.

3. In the Number to Dial box, type the phone number.

   You may add dashes between the prefix and the number or parentheses around the area code. The phone dialer knows to ignore any of these of characters.

   You can, however, add any additional prefixes from your local telephone company that might be required to disable or enable one of its features. An example might be typing *67, before a phone number to enable Caller ID Blocking. In a case like that, be sure you enter both the asterisk and the comma. The asterisk tells the phone company that the next two digits are a special code, and the comma tells the phone dialer to pause before it dials the remainder of the phone number.

   Another example of using the comma in a phone number is if you have to dial 9 to access an outside line. You probably need a second or two pause before an outside line can actually be accessed after dialing the 9. Each comma you type is a one-second pause.

You'll also learn another method to set calling options in the next section.

**4.** Enter up to eight Speed Dial numbers and then click on Save.

● ● ● ● ● ● ● ● ● ● ● ● ● ● ● ● ● ● ● ● ● ● ● ● ● ● ● ● ● ● ● ● ● ● ● ● ● ● ● ● ● ● ● ● ● ● ● ●

To delete a Speed Dial number, click on the button that has the name you want to delete. Press the Delete key to delete the highlighted name, press Tab, and then press the Delete key to erase the phone number. Click on Save.

● ● ● ● ● ● ● ● ● ● ● ● ● ● ● ● ● ● ● ● ● ● ● ● ● ● ● ● ● ● ● ● ● ● ● ● ● ● ● ● ● ● ● ● ● ● ● ●

# Configuring a Phone Number

If you don't want to enter additional prefixes in the speed dial number, you can configure it using the Dialing Properties box. Dialing Properties are generic configuration choices to be used by any number you dial with the phone dialer.

**1.** Make sure that no phone number is displayed in the Number to Dial box. If a number does appear, highlight it and press the Delete key to delete it.

**2.** Click on Tools, Dialing Properties.

Figure 15.12 shows the Dialing Properties dialog box with its various options. From here you can enter the number always needed to dial an outside line or a special code to make long-distance calls.

**3.** Change any desired settings and then click on OK.

**Figure 15.12**
Disable call waiting from the Dialing Properties dialog box.

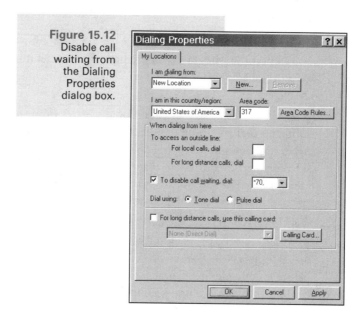

## Placing a Call

There are three methods to place a call:

- Click on the name of the person you want to dial from the Speed Dial buttons.
- Type the phone number in the <u>N</u>umber to dial box.
- Click on the drop-down arrow in the Number to dial box to select a phone number you recently called.

When you place a call through the phone dialer, the dialog box in Figure 15.13 appears. The dialog box shows the status of the call.

A Call Status window lets you know when your call goes through.

1. Click on the <u>T</u>alk button and pick up the telephone handset to transfer the call to your telephone set.

2. Hang up the telephone to end the call or click on the Hang <u>U</u>p button.

*Note*

**If the modem detects a busy signal, you will see a Call Failed window instead.**

**Figure 15.13**
The Active Call box displays the name of the person you called.

Name of person you called

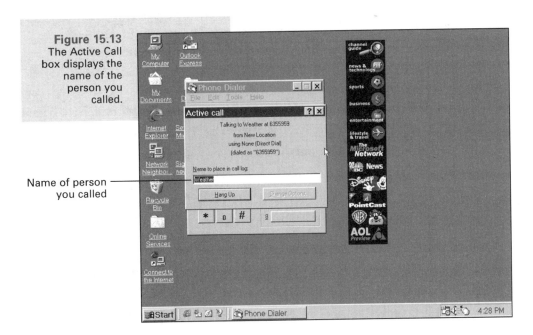

*Tip*

To view a log of calls made and the duration of the calls, choose Tools, Show Log.

# Configuring a Direct Cable Connection

Direct Cable Connection (DCC) is a feature that enables you to network any two PCs via either their serial (modem/mouse) ports or parallel (printer) ports. The connection requires neither Network Interface Cards (NICs) nor modems. DCCs are slower than traditional network connections, but great in a pinch.

DCC is wonderful for updating files, such as files in the Windows Briefcase, from a laptop computer to a desktop computer. It's also handy for accessing hardware that you may not have on your notebook, such as a CD-ROM or floppy disk drive.

> See Chapter 18 for information on the Briefcase.

The same driver that is used for the dial-up adapter is used for DCC support. If you have already installed a dial-up adapter driver, you can skip steps 1 through 7 of the following procedure and start at step 8.

*Note*

**To check whether a dial-up adapter has been installed on your PC, open the Control Panel, Networks section. If Dial-Up Adapter is already listed, you're set and ready to work with the DCC.**

If you have not already installed a dial-up adapter, you'll need to do that before you can continue. Follow these steps to install a dial-up adapter:

1. Open My Computer and then open the Control Panel folder.
2. Click on Network from the Control Panel.
3. Click on Add to add a networking component.
4. Click on Adapter and then click on Add.
5. From the list of Manufacturers, choose Microsoft; then choose Dial-Up Adapter from the Network Adapters section.
6. Click on OK. You may be prompted to insert your Windows 98 CD-ROM.
7. Click on OK to close the Network window. You may be prompted to restart your computer.

8. Click on Yes to restart Windows 98 with the new setting.

   Now you're ready to start up the Direct Cable Connection program.

9. Click on the Start menu and choose Programs.

10. Click on Accessories, Communications and choose Direct Cable Connection.

   When you start Direct Cable Connection for the first time, you have to decide whether to configure the computer you're working on as a guest or host computer (see Figure 15.14).

   If the host computer happens to be on a network, the guest machine will also have access to the same resources as the host.

11. Choose Host or Guest and then click on Next.

   The next dialog box needs to determine which port you want to use with Direct Cable Connection (see Figure 15.15). Both computers need to be

**Figure 15.14**
The guest computer is the one that will be borrowing facilities or files, and the host computer is the one that will be supplying devices such as the CD-ROM, floppy disk drive, or files.

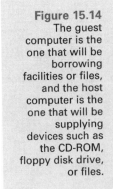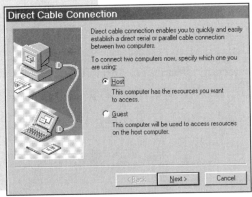

**Figure 15.15**
Data transfer is much faster through the parallel ports than it is through a serial connection.

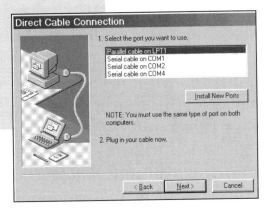

configured using the same port. For example, you can't tell Windows 98 that the host computer is going to use the serial port or COM 2 and the guest computer is going to use the parallel port or LPT1.

*Note*

**You'll need a cable that has identical connectors at both ends.**

12. Select the Port you want to use and then click Next.

    If you are setting up the host computer, you can elect to password protect the host against unwanted intrusions (see Figure 15.16).

13. To password protect the host computer, click on Use Password Protection, click on Set Password, and then enter the password twice. Both times the password will appear in asterisks. Press Enter to return to the Direct Cable Connection Wizard.

    You're now finished setting up the first computer, but you still have to set up the second computer. Repeat steps 1 through 13 to do so.

14. Click on Finish to close the Direct Cable Connection Wizard.

    Make sure the cables are attached to both computers. When the Direct Cable Connection Wizard closes, the Direct Cable Connection dialog box opens and Windows 98 will try to connect the two computers.

**See Chapter 14 for more information using a Windows 98 network.**

**Figure 15.16**
The password option does not appear if you are setting up the guest computer.

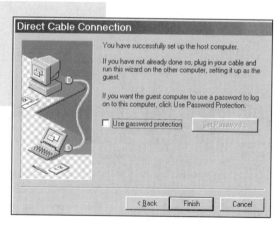

**15.** Click on <u>L</u>isten on the host computer and click on Connect on the guest computer. (Figure 15.17)

Open the Network Neighborhood icon to map drives and access files as you would in a peer-to-peer Windows 98 network.

**Figure 15.17**
When the connection is established, minimize the Direct Cable Connection dialog boxes.

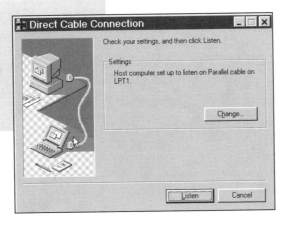

# 16

# Mailing and Faxing from Windows 98

## IN THIS CHAPTER

- Creating and Sending E-mail
- Creating Your Own Signature File
- Attaching a File to an E-mail
- Receiving and Managing E-mail
- Accessing and Using Newsgroups
- Managing the Outlook Express Address Book
- Faxing in Windows 98

Communications today must be quick. Is having a message arrive within seconds quick enough? The ability to send and receive e-mail is one of the most important functions of a computer. Just what is e-mail? *E-mail* is defined as the exchange of text messages and computer files over a communications network like the Internet or a company LAN. Windows 98 has made e-mail easy to use with a program called Outlook Express. Although it is simpler than other mail programs you may have worked with, Outlook Express is a full-featured e-mail and news reading client that works very well with most public or private e-mail systems.

Many e-mail programs limit you to text-type messages, but Outlook Express is very tightly integrated with the Internet and supports HTML, so it's easy to make your messages delightfully fun and dynamic. A single program handles both e-mail and newsgroups. You can even send Web content via e-mail with Outlook Express.

If Microsoft Office 97 is installed on your computer, you may have the Outlook 97 program installed as well. If that's the case, you should know that Outlook Express is a scaled down (but very vigorous) rendering of Outlook 97 or 98. Outlook Express includes the mail and messaging features of Outlook, but not the calendar and scheduling options.

> **See Chapter 15 for information about connecting to an Internet service provider.**

Outlook Express gives you all the messaging tools you need for easy, effective communications. Add the ability to create customizable Stationery, Signatures, and live hyperlinks, and you have an all-in-one answer to most of your communication needs.

To send or receive e-mail or access newsgroups, you must have a modem hooked up to your computer and access to some type of Internet service.

# Starting Outlook Express

The first time you open Outlook Express, the Internet Connection Wizard jumps in to assist you with setting up Outlook Express.

Figure 16.1 shows several ways to open Outlook Express:

- Click on the Outlook Express icon on the Taskbar.
- Click on the Outlook Express icon on the Desktop.
- Click on the Start button; then choose Programs, Internet Explorer, Outlook Express.

When the Internet Connection Wizard appears, it prompts you for your basic Internet access account information. The information the Internet Connection

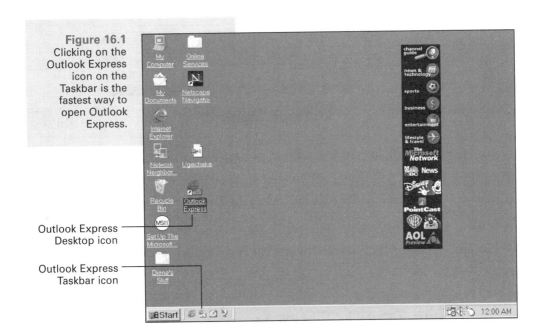

**Figure 16.1**
Clicking on the Outlook Express icon on the Taskbar is the fastest way to open Outlook Express.

Outlook Express Desktop icon

Outlook Express Taskbar icon

**See Chapter 15 for more information on the Internet Connection Wizard.**

Wizard asks for is a one-time only setup choice. You won't need it again unless you want to set up additional connections with Outlook Express.

Also, the first time you run it, Outlook Express offers to automatically import existing mail messages, address books, and account settings from a number of other e-mail products, including Netscape Mail, Netscape Communicator, Eudora Light, and Eudora Pro.

After Outlook Express has been configured, if you are not connected to your Internet service provider, Outlook Express will connect you.

The Outlook Express program opens with a plethora of things you can do. The Start page displayed on the right side of the screen (see Figure 16.2) can be your entry point to Outlook Express.

Several folders appear in the Folder list. In some ways, it's similar to the Windows Explorer folder list. For example, the top item is Outlook Express. Clicking this item displays the Start page on the right side. The folder immediately under the Outlook Express folder is the Inbox folder. When you are connected to your ISP, Outlook Express places any incoming mail in the Inbox folder. A number (in parentheses) on the right indicates the number of unread messages in the Inbox folder (see Figure 16.3).

**Figure 16.2**
The Start Screen
has links that let
you quickly jump
to the task you
need to do.

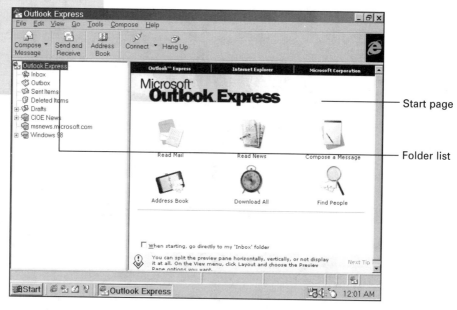

**Figure 16.3**
This user has
new messages.

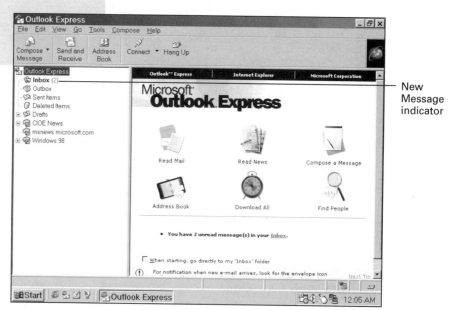

When you create mail messages, you have the option of sending them immediately or at a later time. Any messages waiting to be sent are indicated in the Outbox folder.

Other folders created by default with Outlook Express include a Sent Items folder to keep copies of any e-mail you send; a Deleted Items folder, which is similar to the Recycle Bin on the Windows Desktop; and a Drafts folder in which to keep unfinished messages. As you work with Outlook Express, you'll be adding more folders to the folder list.

# Using Outlook Express for E-mail

With the e-mail capabilities of Outlook Express, you can exchange mail with users of Microsoft Mail, Internet E-mail, and other popular e-mail packages. You will be able to do the following:

- Read e-mail messages
- Send e-mail messages
- Download e-mail and subscription information
- Locate a person's e-mail address

## Creating an E-mail Message

The saying goes, "It's the 90s". I don't particularly care for most uses of that phrase, but when it comes to communication—it IS the 90s. Now if you want to communicate with someone quickly, you *could* call the person on the telephone, or better yet, send an e-mail message.

### Hands On: Creating an E-Mail Message

1. Click on the Compose Message button on the Outlook Express toolbar.

If your toolbar is not displayed, choose View, Toolbar.

The New Message dialog box is ready to accept your information. The first line is the To line, where you need to enter the name of the recipient. Information is required on the To: line.

2. Type jsmith@smithco.com and then press the Tab key to move to the Cc line.

3. Type sjones@smithco.com as the person to whom you want to send a carbon copy (Cc) of this message. If you have more than one person to list on the Cc line, separate the e-mail names with a comma or a semicolon.

The Cc line is optional. Press the Tab key to move to the Blind Carbon Copy line.

On the Blind Carbon Copy (Bcc) line, you could optionally enter other addresses for anyone you want to receive a copy of this message without the names on the first two lines knowing about it. Again, if there are multiple recipients, separate them with a comma or semicolon.

**Tip**

If you'd like to send e-mail to multiple recipients and don't want any of them to know who else is getting the message, try this: Send the message to yourself and then use Bcc for all the recipients. This technique will get the mail to everyone, but nobody will be able to see who else was on the list.

4. Press Tab to move to the Subject line and type **New Product Announcement**. The Subject line is not required, but it is recommended. If you try to send a message without a subject, Outlook Express will ask you if you're sure you want to send it that way. Press Enter to proceed to the body of the message.

**Note**

As you type a subject in the subject line, it also appears in the title bar of the message window.

5. Type the following message in the body of the message box.

**Caution**

Don't type e-mail in ALL CAPS. That's considered SHOUTING!

Hello John!

I just wanted to tell you about the Web site that has been created to announce the distribution of our new widget production. If you have a free minute, go to http://www.koersing.com. I think you'll be impressed!

I'd like your opinion on the following issues:

Design

Content

Overall appearance

When are you free for a lunch meeting to discuss this?

(your name)

Notice in Figure 16.4 that when http://www.koersing.com was typed, it automatically became a hyperlink. Whenever you include a Universal Resource Locator (URL) in your message, Outlook Express automatically creates a live hyperlink to that address. Outlook Express recognizes HTTP and FTP locations, and formats them accordingly. When John receives this message, he only has to click the hyperlink to jump directly to that Web page.

# Formatting an E-mail Message

Let's take a moment to dress up the e-mail message. Outlook Express encourages you to bring the creativity of the Web to the mail you send. Instead of sending plain text, you can insert bullets, images, and horizontal lines and add color and style with fonts and sizes.

For birthdays or holidays, you might like to send some graphics along with a message. Outlook Express includes some graphics that you can choose from to save

**Figure 16.4**
The reader can go directly to the link location by clicking the hyperlink.

Automatic hyperlink

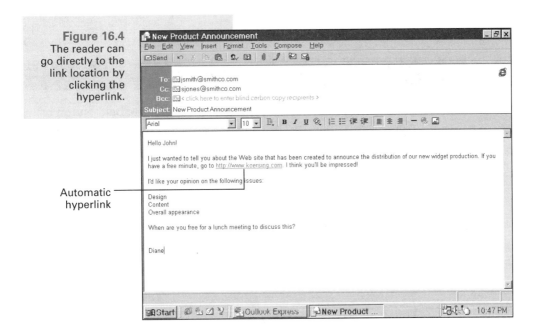

time, or you can use any GIF or JPEG graphic you have access to. The only real caution here is that some of your recipients may not be able to display the graphics. With many mail programs, they'll have no problem displaying your graphical message; however, if someone's mail program does not support HTML or graphics, Outlook Express translates graphics messages to plain text.

Formatting text in Outlook Express is almost identical to formatting text in WordPad. Figure 16.5 shows the different formatting selections available from the Outlook Express toolbar. You may have to maximize the New Message window to display all the choices.

You can change font, size, style, alignment, and even color right from the toolbar!

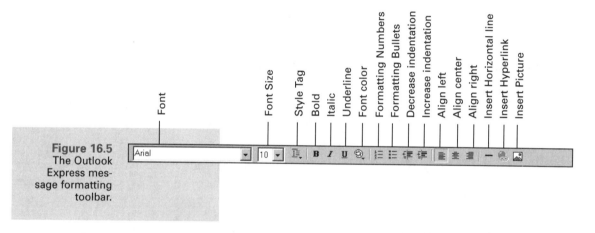

**Figure 16.5**
The Outlook Express message formatting toolbar.

## Hands On: Formatting Text

1. Click anywhere in the word *impressed;* then click on the Bold button of the New Message toolbar. The entire word appears in bold. Optionally, you could choose to italicize or underline the word as well.

2. Click and drag across the three lines *Design, Content,* and *Overall Appearance* to highlight them; then click on the Formatting Bullets button.

3. Click on <u>E</u>dit, Select <u>A</u>ll to highlight the entire document.

4. Choose a different font from the Font drop-down list and optionally a different font size from the Size drop-down list.

   Next, add a background to your message.

5. Click on F*o*rmat, App*l*y Stationery. From the Apply Stationery cascading menu, click on Chess. Click on the down arrow beside the Compose Message button to select a stationery when you first begin creating your message. The text was adjusted to fit with the background (see Figure 16.6).

You can add JPEG or GIF images to your message by choosing *I*nsert, *P*icture or by clicking the Insert Picture button. Click on the B*r*owse button to locate an image and then double-click the image you want to include. Click on OK.

6. Click on Send or press Alt+S. The message will immediately be sent to the recipients. Outlook Express also places a copy of the message in the Sent Items folder.

If you don't want to send the message immediately, click on *F*ile, Send *L*ater.

**Figure 16.6**
What do you think of your message?

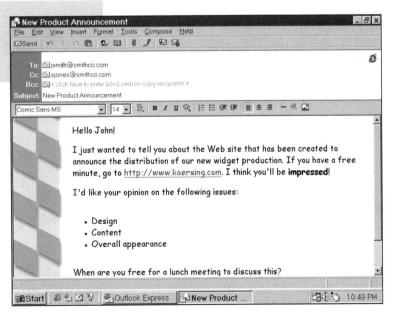

## Creating Scrolling Text

Here's an interesting way to create a scrolling text (for example, a signature) for your e-mail message. Scrolling text is created in the FrontPage Express program. It may sound tricky, but just follow the steps. It's easy!

Click on Start, Programs, Internet Explorer, FrontPage Express. When FrontPage Express begins, click on Insert, Marquee. Type your name or message in the Text line and then click on OK. Click on File, Save; then click on As File. Specify a file name and folder in which to save this file. (I used my Desktop for easiest access). Click on Save; then choose File, Exit to exit the FrontPage Express program.

Place the insertion point at the location in the Outlook Express message where you want the scrolling signature. Choose Insert, Text from File. From the Files of Type drop-down box, choose HTML Files. Locate and double-click on the FrontPage Express file.

Now when you send e-mail, if the recipients' e-mail program has HTML capabilities, they will see your message scrolling across the screen!

# Creating a Signature

You can append a signature to your Outlook Express e-mail messages or even a newsgroup posting. Your name or nickname, title and company, contact information, a favorite quote, or a disclaimer are all popular choices for a Signature.

1. From the Outlook Express window, choose Tools, Stationery.
2. When the dialog box opens, click on the Mail tab. Now click on Signature. In the Text area of the resulting Signature dialog box, type in whatever text you want to conclude your messages.

*Note*

**Follow similar steps to append your signature to newsgroup postings: Choose Tools, Stationery, but this time click on the News tab, Signature.**

Now you need to decide whether to apply the signature to all messages or only to certain ones.

3. If you want to apply it to all messages, select the Add This Signature to All Outgoing Messages check box and then click on OK. (Figure 16.7)

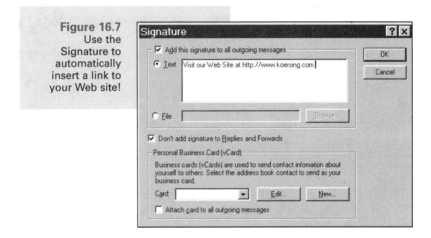

**Figure 16.7**
Use the Signature to automatically insert a link to your Web site!

4. From the Stationery dialog box, click on Apply, OK.

You can test the signature now by clicking on Compose Message. If you elected to use the signature in all messages, it will now appear in the message body.

If you decide to use the signature on selected messages, click on the body of the message and then choose Insert, Signature or press Ctrl+Shift+S. The signature that you entered will appear in the message.

## Attaching Files to an E-mail Message

You may want to include a spreadsheet or other document with an e-mail message. Outlook Express gives you several ways to include files with your e-mail messages. The easiest method works with files of any type — pictures, documents, spreadsheets, or any text or binary files.

1. Create the e-mail message as you learned in the previous section.

2. Click on Insert, File Attachment or click on the Insert File button.

3. Locate and double-click on the file to be attached to the message.

   An icon representing the attached file, like the one seen in Figure 16.8, appears at the bottom of the New Message box. Repeat steps 2 and 3 for each additional attachment.

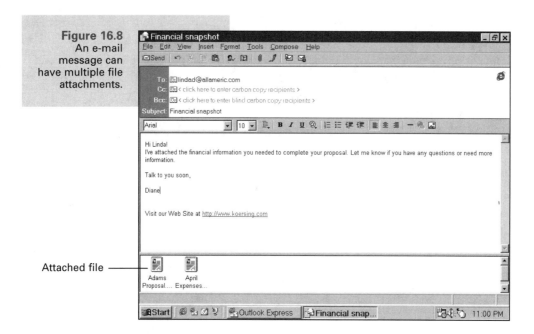

**Figure 16.8**
An e-mail
message can
have multiple file
attachments.

Attached file ——

4. Send the e-mail as usual. Outlook Express will send the file along with the message.

When a file has an attachment to it, a paper clip appears beside the message in the Sent Items folder.

# Setting Up E-mail Accounts

Do you have several e-mail addresses? That's not a problem because Outlook Express supports multiple mailboxes. Outlook Express can dial multiple ISPs separately without your having to go to each site independently. This seamless management of multiple mail accounts enables you to easily access and send messages from any of your accounts.

Outlook Express includes an Account Manager to help manage and organize all your e-mail and newsgroups. The Internet Connection Wizard quickly steps you through the process of setting up each account.

## Hands On: Setting Up E-mail Accounts

1. In Outlook Express, click on <u>T</u>ools, <u>A</u>ccounts.

2. From the Internet Accounts dialog box, click on <u>A</u>dd, <u>M</u>ail. The Internet Connection Wizard launches to assist you through the mail account setup process.

3. In the <u>D</u>isplay Name box, type the name you want others to see when you send them a message; then click on <u>N</u>ext.

4. Type your e-mail address in the E-mail address box. Don't worry if you have more than one—just pick one of them for now. You'll repeat these steps for each e-mail address you have. Click on <u>N</u>ext.

5. Choose the type of mail server (POP3 or IMAP) and fill in the incoming and outgoing mail server names in the appropriate boxes. It gets a little trickier here. When you get to this screen, my suggestion is to contact your ISP and ask for the information. The ISP will be happy to provide it.

6. Click on <u>N</u>ext.

   Most ISPs require you to log on with a password. You'll need to enter it here, as well as your logon name.

7. Enter your logon name and password in the appropriate boxes. The password will appear as asterisks on the screen. Click on <u>N</u>ext.

8. The next screen asks you to enter a "friendly name" for this e-mail account. Generally, the name of the ISP, such as CompuServe or Iquest, is used, but in reality you can call it anything you want. Instead of "CompuServe" you could type "Apples" but you'd have to remember that when "Apples" mail is received, it was sent via CompuServe. Enter a name and then click on <u>N</u>ext.

9. Now you must tell the Internet Connection Wizard what type of connection you have—whether you need to connect via your modem, a LAN, or a manual connection. Select the appropriate option and then click on <u>N</u>ext.

   Almost finished!

10. Tell the Internet Connection Wizard what kind of a dial-up connection you want to use to access this mail. Choose to <u>C</u>reate a New Connection or <u>U</u>se an Existing Connection. Click on <u>N</u>ext, Finish.

**See Chapter 15 for information on creating dial-up connections.**

The Internet Accounts box now displays the mail connection. You can add more e-mail accounts if you have them, or close the Internet Accounts dialog box.

# Retrieving Incoming E-mail

If you have upgraded from Windows 95, you should know that the Outlook Inbox replaces the Windows 95 Exchange Inbox. The Folders list helps you access messages and mail. And the Preview pane gives you a good look at mail and news content before you even open the messages.

New messages are indicated by a number next to the Inbox. In addition, you can set Outlook Express to check for new messages at specified intervals whenever you are online. See "Setting Outlook Express Options" later in this chapter to specify a time interval for checking for messages. A soft tone notifies you whenever a new message is received.

If you don't want to wait for Outlook Express to check messages automatically, you can click on the Send and Receive button at any time. Outlook Express immediately checks for new mail and sends any mail waiting in the Outbox.

## Hands On: Reading New Messages

1. Click on the Inbox. A list of new messages will be displayed, with the first message highlighted (see Figure 16.9). Optionally, you can double-click on a message to display it in its own Window.

2. Click on the next message to display it in the Preview pane.

**Figure 16.9**
Read the message from the Preview pane at the bottom.

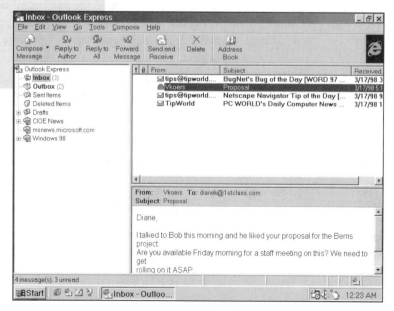

• • • • • • • • • • • • • • • • • • • • • • • • • • • • • • • • • • • • • • • • • • • •
You can print any message by pressing Ctrl+P.
• • • • • • • • • • • • • • • • • • • • • • • • • • • • • • • • • • • • • • • • • • • •

# Replying to a Message

Now that you've read the message, you may want to reply to the sender. Outlook Express enables you to answer a message immediately or later if you prefer.

## Hands On: Replying to a Message

1. Click the message you want to reply to and then click on the Reply to Author button.

• • • • • • • • • • • • • • • • • • • • • • • • • • • • • • • • • • • • • • • • • • • •
If the original message was sent to more than one person, you can click on Reply to All instead of Reply to Author. Your reply will be sent to the author and to each person who received the original message.
• • • • • • • • • • • • • • • • • • • • • • • • • • • • • • • • • • • • • • • • • • • •

A New Mail message box appears, and the sender's e-mail address is displayed in the To box. The subject box contains the same subject as the mail you received.

The original message is displayed in the body of the e-mail message.

2. Type the reply in the message body and then click on the Send button (see Figure 16.10). The reply will be sent immediately, and a copy of the reply will be placed in the Sent Items folder.

**Figure 16.10**
You can delete the text of the original message if you want to.

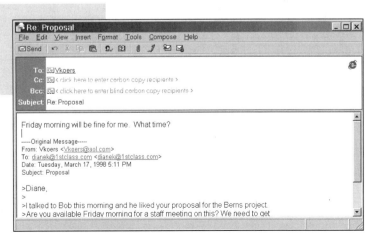

# Forwarding an E-mail Message

You can send a received message on to another person by forwarding it. You can even add your own message to the original message.

---

### Hands On: Forwarding an E-mail Message

1. Click on the message you want to forward and then click on the Forward Message button.

   A Fw:New Mail message box appears, and the e-mail address is blank in the To box. The Fw:subject box contains the same subject as the mail you received, and the original message is displayed in the body of the e-mail message.

2. Type the recipient's e-mail address in the To box.

3. Type any additional message you want to send in addition to the original message and then click on the Send button (see Figure 16.11). Outlook Express will send the message to the new recipient immediately and place a copy in the Sent Items folder.

**Figure 16.11**
When a message is forwarded, the original is retained in your Inbox.

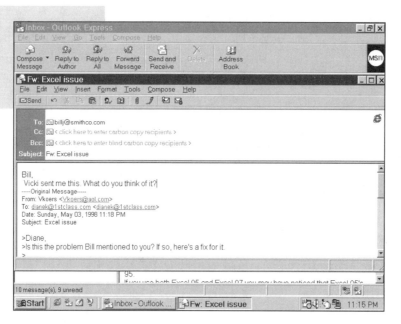

# Managing Your E-mail

Outlook Express stores incoming messages in the Inbox until you do something with them. As more and more e-mail arrives, the Inbox tends to fill up quickly. You can create new folders to organize your mail.

## Hands On: Creating a New Outlook Express Folder

1. Click on File, Folder, New Folder.
2. Type **MY MAIL** as the name for the folder in the Folder Name box; then from the lower box, click on the Outlook Express for the folder you want to place the new folder in. Click on OK.

   The new folder will be created and displayed in the Folder list. Because you opted to place the folder in Outlook Express, it is displayed in the main level of the Folder list.

   Now you'll create another folder to store personal mail in.
3. Click on File, Folder, New Folder.
4. Type **PERSONAL** as the name for the folder in the Folder Name box; then from the lower box, click on the MY MAIL as the folder you want to place the new folder in. Click on OK (see Figure 16.12).

**Figure 16.12**
The Personal subfolder is under the My Mail folder.

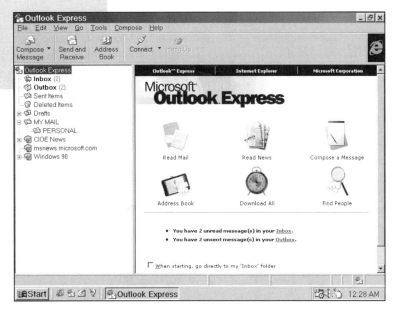

Any mail from the Inbox can now be moved to the newly created folders. Moving mail from the Inbox to new folders is similar to moving files in Windows Explorer.

To move a message, click on the message to be moved and drag it to the new folder. The message disappears from the current folder, but if you click on the new folder, you'll see the message there. Repeat this step for each message you want to move.

To delete a message, click on the message to be deleted. Then press the Delete key on the keyboard or click on the Delete button on the toolbar. Outlook Express moves the message to the Deleted Items folder.

*Tip*

If you want to "undelete" a mail message, click on the Deleted Items folder and drag the message to a different folder.

*Caution*

**If the option to empty the Deleted Items folder upon exit is active, each time you exit Outlook Express the folder will be emptied. If you want to "undelete" anything, do it before you exit Outlook Express.**

## The Inbox Assistant

You can even organize messages before you read them. With the Inbox Assistant, you can filter important messages into designated folders for easy retrieval and send unwanted junk mail straight to the trash! Create rules on a per account basis to delete, forward, move, or copy messages to desired folders—automatically.

For example, say you want to forward any message from a coworker BobS to your boss SamJ. Or maybe you're just plain tired of all the junk mail, and anything that has the word *Rich* in the subject should go straight to the Deleted Items folder. Use the Inbox Assistant to create these rules for you.

### Hands On: Using the Inbox Assistant

This exercise directs any mail from your friend Dorothy to your Personal folder.

1. Click on Tools, Inbox Assistant.
2. Click on Add.

3. Click in the From box and type **Dorothy** to specify the filtering information.

   Now you need to tell Outlook Express what to do with the filtered mail.

4. Click on Move To:; then click on Folder.

5. Click on the plus sign next to My Mail to expand it; then click on the Personal folder.

   Notice in Figure 16.13 how the folder name appears in the Properties box.

**Figure 16.13**
Enter "" in the Subject box to filter messages with no subject.

Filter information

Action to be taken

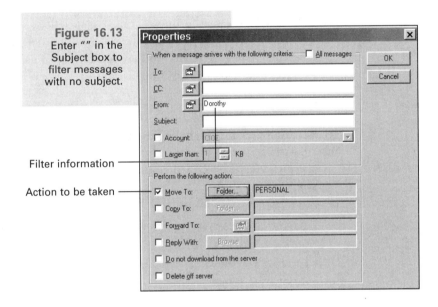

6. Click on OK to close the Properties dialog box.

7. Click on OK to close the Inbox Assistant.

Add as many rules as you want!

# Backing Up E-mail

| For information on copying files from the Windows Explorer, see Chapter 4. |
| :-- |

Finally, let's talk about backing up your e-mail. If you have a tape backup that backs up your entire hard drive frequently—wonderful! But if you don't, here's how to avoid that sinking feeling you get when you've just lost your hard drive and remember all the e-mail you had that's now gone forever.

1. Open Windows Explorer.

2. Locate the Windows\Application Data\Microsoft\Outlook Express\Mail folder.

**3.** In the Mail folder, you'll find a group of *.mbx files. (**MailBoX**—get it!) If you're only interested in what's in the Inbox, copy Inbox.mbx to a floppy disk. If you want to be *really* safe, copy all the files in the Mail folder to a floppy.

# Using Outlook Express with Newsgroups

Newsgroups are Internet forums that discuss specific subjects. A newsgroup consists of articles and follow-up posts (messages). An article with all of its follow-up posts are *supposed* to be related to the specific subject named in the original article's subject line. This series of posts is called a *thread*.

Each newsgroup has a name that consists of a series of words, separated by periods, indicating the newsgroup's subject. Say your hobby is goldfish—a newsgroup example might be rec.aquaria.freshwater.goldfish. Many software manufacturers have newsgroups for technical support. Perhaps you're having difficulty with your WinFax8 program. Contact Symantec's newsgroup at symantec.support.win95.winfax8. There are not really any set rules for naming newsgroups, but newsgroups that begin with **alt** traditionally stand for **alternative**. It's just my opinion, but you may not want your children to visit many (but not all) of these newsgroups.

All that being said, most newsgroups are very informative. Access them frequently on your favorite subject!

## Setting Up Newsgroups

You can subscribe to newsgroups to keep up-to-date with all the messages in them. But before you can subscribe to them, you must configure Outlook Express for Internet News.

Configuring a news server is very similar to configuring Internet mail. You'll probably need to contact your ISP for some of the information.

### Hands On: Configuring a News Server

**1.** In Outlook Express, click on <u>T</u>ools, <u>A</u>ccounts.

**2.** From the Internet Accounts dialog box, click on <u>A</u>dd, <u>N</u>ews. The Internet

Connection Wizard launches to assist you through the news account setup process.

3. In the Display Name box, type the name you want others to see when you post a message to a newsgroup; then click on Next.

4. Type your e-mail address in the E-mail address box. This address is where people can reply to your news messages. Click on Next.

5. In the News (NNTP) server box, type the name of your Internet news server. Get this information from your ISP. It's usually something like newsread.abccompany.com.

*Note*

**The news server for Microsoft product support is msnews.microsoft. com. If your ISP doesn't recognize that name, you can type 131.107.3.27 instead. You do not need to log on to this news server.**

6. If the news server requires you to log on, check the box next to it to select it and then click on Next.

   The next screen asks you to enter a "friendly name" for this Internet news account. You can give the news account any name you want, but for this exercise, accept the suggestions the Internet Connection Wizard gives you.

7. Enter a name and then click on Next.

8. Tell the Internet Connection Wizard what type of connection you have—whether you need to connect via your modem, a LAN, or a manual connection. Select the appropriate option and then click on Next.

9. Tell the Internet Connection Wizard what kind of a dial-up connection you want to use to access this news server. Choose to Create a new connection or Use an existing connection. Click on Next, Finish.

10. Add as many newsgroups accounts you want and then click on Close.

11. If you want to download newsgroups from the new server at this time, click on Yes. You can do so now or later.

    If you are not already online, Outlook Express connects to your ISP.

The news server is listed in the Folder list, as you can see in Figure 16.14. News servers are indicated by a small newspaper and disk drive.

**Figure 16.14**
Three news servers are configured for this user.

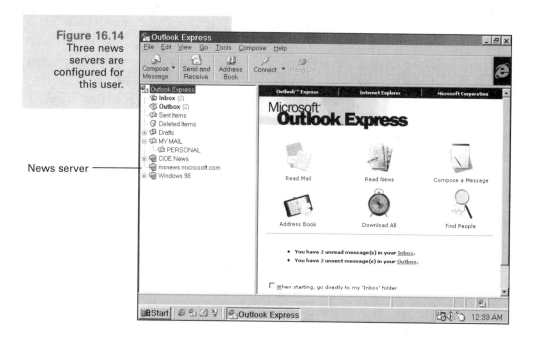

News server ———

## Accessing a Newsgroup

Now that you are connected, you can access your newsgroup. You can access the newsgroup once, or you can *subscribe* to it. Subscribing adds a newsgroup to a list where you easily get new articles. The benefit of subscribing is that the newsgroup is then included in the Folder list for easy access. You don't have to locate or type the newsgroup address over and over.

If you don't know whether a specific newsgroup is right for you, try reading some of the messages in it. If you like it, then you can subscribe.

The first time you view a newsgroup, it may take a little while (several minutes) for the messages to be downloaded.

To access a newsgroup:

1. From the Folder list, click on the news server you want to access.

2. If you are not currently subscribed to any newsgroups on that server, you'll be prompted to view a list of available newsgroups now. Click on Yes.

3. When the list of newsgroups appears, locate and click on the group you want to check into. Click on Go To or, if you want to subscribe to this group, click on Subscribe, Go To.

*Note*

**A small newspaper on the left side of the newsgroup name identifies you have subscribed to the newsgroup.**

*Tip*

To unsubscribe from a newsgroup, locate and click on the group; then click on Unsubscribe.

Optionally, you can type a word or phrase in the Display Newsgroups Which Contain box at the top of the Newsgroups dialog box to locate newsgroups about specific subjects. When you press Enter after typing the text, Outlook Express narrows down the list of newsgroups to those that contain the word you typed at the top (see Figure 16.15).

## Retrieving Newsgroup Postings

When you select a newsgroup, Outlook Express displays the headers or subject lines of a predetermined number of messages. By default, that number is 300. You can read the postings, print them, save them, reply to them, or process them in any number of ways.

Two places on the screen provide information on the number of messages a newsgroup contains. The total number of messages and how many of them you have not yet read appear at the bottom of the screen. In addition, a counter next to the newsgroup name on the Outlook Express file list gives the number of unread messages.

**Figure 16.15**
All the newsgroups in this list pertain to dogs.

Search word

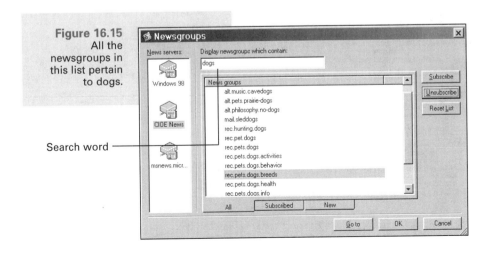

A plus sign next to a message indicates that the posting has replies. Click on the plus sign to open the "tree" and see all the replies, or the *thread* of the message.

To read a newsgroup posting, click on the posting you want to read. The message appears in the Preview pane at the bottom of the Outlook Express window. It has scroll bars for you to continue reading a longer message. If you double-click on a message, it will pop open in its own window, but I personally think that's an extra unnecessary step. Then you have to close the message window when you're finished. Why bother?

# Replying to a Newsgroup Posting

If you want to contribute to a newsgroup, you can reply to a specific message or compose a new message of your own.

To post a reply to a newsgroup message:

1. Display the message you want to reply to and click on the Reply to Author button on the toolbar. When the Reply message box opens, you'll notice that the recipient's name and subject are already filled in (see Figure 16.16).

2. Type your reply in the bottom reply area of the window.

Don't type news messages in ALL CAPS. That's considered SHOUTING! Shouting will get you *flamed* (criticized or insulted) by other users of the newsgroup.

3. Click on the Send button. Your message will be posted to the newsgroup. If an acknowledgment box appears, just click on OK.

**Figure 16.16**
Keep your response relevant to the original message.

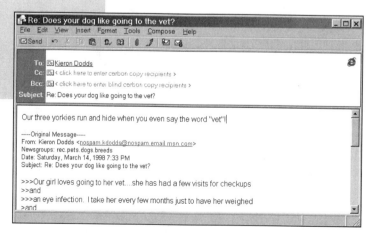

It may take a few minutes for your message to appear on the newsgroup. Check back on your newsgroup periodically for replies to your reply.

To leave a newsgroup, simply exit Outlook Express or click on another area.

# Setting Outlook Express Options

You can modify the look of Outlook Express in many ways. The default appearance of Outlook Express displays a list of all available folders on the left side of the screen, but you can change this standard layout.

## Hands On: Changing the View of Outlook Express

In this exercise, you'll change the display of the folders on the left side of the Outlook Express window.

1. Click on the <u>V</u>iew menu and choose <u>L</u>ayout. The choices under the View menu depend on which folder is currently selected.

2. In the Basic area of the Window Layout Properties dialog box, click on Outlook Bar to select it and click on Folder <u>L</u>ist to deselect it.

3. Click on OK to accept these changes. Your screen should now look like the one in Figure 16.17.

**Figure 16.17**
More folders are indicated by an arrow at the bottom of the Outlook Bar.

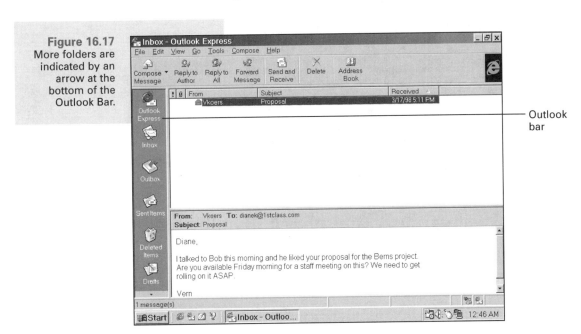

Outlook bar

You can easily experiment to get exactly the kind of layout that you like. Go ahead and try some other combinations.

You can also tell Outlook Express when to check for new mail and set other preferences by choosing Tools, Options to open the Options dialog box (see Figure 16.18).

Here are some of the features you can change from the General tab:

- Whether and at what time intervals Outlook Express should check for new incoming mail
- Whether to play a sound when any new messages arrive

You can change the sound that notifies you that you have received new mail by double-clicking on the Sounds icon in Control Panel and selecting New Mail Notification from the events list.

- Whether to delete items in the Deleted Items folder when you exit Outlook Express
- Whether to automatically add people to the Address Book

**Figure 16.18**
You can customize the way Outlook Express responds through the options.

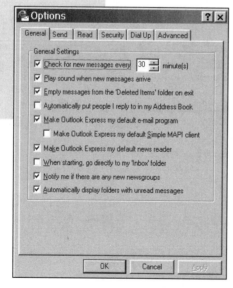

From the Send tab, you'll see the option that tells Outlook Express to include copies of mail you've sent in the Sent Items folder as well.

Did you notice earlier when you created a reply message that the text from the original message you received was included in the reply? That's because by default, the Include Message in Reply Box is checked in the Outlook Express Send options. If you don't want that feature, simply uncheck the option.

Other tabs include the Read tab that sets options for newsgroup messages, the Security tab that includes Security Zones to protect you from receiving mail with nasty (virus type) attachments included, the Dial Up tab that specifies the default dial-up connection Outlook Express should use, and the Advanced tab that specifies more options for newsgroup messages.

When you finish changing the settings, click on OK to close the Options dialog box. Some settings may not take effect until the next time you start Outlook Express.

*Tip*

You can also customize the Outlook Express toolbar by right-clicking on the toolbar and choosing Buttons. Click on any feature you want from the Available buttons and click on Add. It will be added to the Toolbar button. Repeat for as many buttons as you want to add to the Outlook Express toolbar. Click on OK to close the Customize Toolbar box.

# Managing the Address Book

The Outlook Express Address Book is a wonderful tool for storing names, addresses, fax numbers, e-mail addresses, and other personal information. It can even add e-mail addresses on-the-fly as you send and receive new mail.

If you want to backup your Address Book you can find it in Windows Explorer under \Windows\Application Data\Microsoft\Address Book. Copy the file(s) to a floppy disk for safekeeping.

## Adding Contacts to the Address Book

The Address Book lets you store information for business associates, friends, family or other address references you want to keep for future information.

## Hands On: Adding Contacts to the Address Book

1. Click on Address Book from either the Outlook Express Start window or the Outlook Express toolbar.

2. When the Address Book appears, click on the New Contact button.

3. When the Properties box appears, fill in any available information about the contact. The three tabs you will use the most are the Personal, Home, and Business tabs. There you can enter and store the contact data.

As you enter a First, Middle, and Last name, you'll notice that the Display repeats what you have typed. You can change this entry to anything you want. For example, if you enter an associate's name as Jerome Carl Jones, but he goes by "Jerry," you might enter "Jerry Jones" as the display name (see Figure 16.19).

Outlook Express allows for the fact that many people have several e-mail addresses. As you enter an e-mail address in the Add New box and then click on Add, the e-mail is added to the list in the bottom of the screen. You can then add additional e-mail addresses for this contact.

If a contact has multiple e-mail addresses, you can select one of them to be the default. Click on the e-mail address to be the default and then click on Set as Default. A small envelope appears on the side of the default address.

To add more information about the person, such as his or her home address, click on the Home tab and add the information there. As you can

**Figure 16.19**
You can also specify a nickname for this contact.

| Jerry Jones Properties | ? × |
|---|---|

Personal | Home | Business | Other | NetMeeting | Digital IDs |

Enter personal information about this contact here.

**Name**

First: Jerome    Middle: Carl    Last: Jones

Display: Jerry Jones    Nickname: Jerry

**E-Mail Addresses**

Add new: jerryj@aol.com    Add

✉ jerryj@somparther.com  (Default E-Mail)    Edit
Remove
Set as Default

☐ Send E-Mail using plain text only.

OK    Cancel

see, a number of tabs are available. Click on any of them to add information. For example, to add your new entry's business address and phone number, click on Business and make your additions there.

4. After you finish adding all the information, click on OK. Go Ahead! Add all the contacts you want!

You can also add an e-mail address for anyone you are sending messages to or receiving messages from. From the mail, reply, or newsgroup message, right-click the name of the person you want to add. When the shortcut menu opens, choose Add to Address Book. You can enter any additional information now or later. To delete a contact, open the Address Book, click on the contact you want to delete, and click on the Delete button.

Now that you've put all the information together in the Address Book, it's time to put it to good use. With the Address Book, you can send mail to anyone on the list.

## Sending Mail from the Address Book

You can send someone in your Address Book an e-mail message in one of two ways:

- Open the Address Book, click on the person you want to send to, and then click on the Send Mail button (see Figure 16.20).
- You can also look up a name when you are composing a message directly from Outlook Express. In the New Message box, click on the small icon of a file card located just to the left of the To, Cc,or Bcc lines. Click on a name from the Select Recipients window then click on the To, Cc or Bcc buttons. (see Figure 16.21).

## Sorting the Address Book

You can sort the Address Book in various ways: by Name (either First Name or Last Name), by e-mail address, Business Phone number, or Home Phone number. You can also choose to sort in ascending or descending order.

Sorting the Address Book speeds up the search for information and will affect the layout of the information if you decide to print it.

**Figure 16.20**
Double-click on a
name in the
Address Book to
display the
contact's
properties.

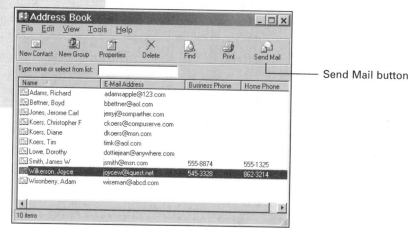

Send Mail button

**Figure 16.21**
Add multiple
recipients to the
message.

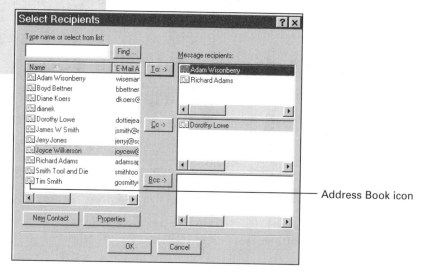

Address Book icon

## Hands On: Sorting the Address Book

1. Click on View, Sort By.

2. Choose the sort method. If you select Name, you'll then need to specify whether you want the list in alphabetical order by First Name or Last Name.

You can also sort the Address Book by clicking on the headings of the Address Book window (see Figure 16.22).

**Figure 16.22**
If you click on
Name, you may
have to click
several times
to get the
order you're
looking for.

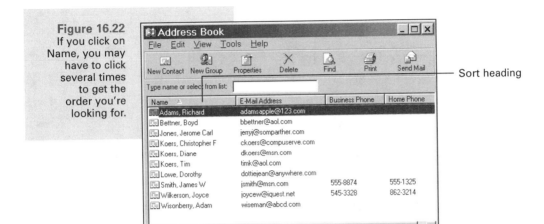

# Printing from the Address Book

As mentioned earlier, you can print the Address Book in three different formats: as a phone list, a business card list, or a memo list. The Address Book prints in the current sort order, so you might want to change that order before you print.

- **Phone list style**—Prints the name of each person in the Address Book and all telephone numbers listed for that person. A black line separates the letters of the alphabet.

- **Business card style**—Prints all available information on a contact in the current sort order. A black line separates the contacts.

- **Memo style**—Prints all available information on a contact in the current sort order. Memo style is very similar to business card style, except the layout is a little more casual. Memo style uses a larger print and leaves more space between entries. A black line separates the contacts.

## Hands On: Printing from the Address Book

1. Click on the Address Book button from the Outlook Express window.
2. Click on the Print button on the Address Book toolbar.
3. Specify which Print Style to use from the Print dialog box (see Figure 16.23).
4. Click on OK to print the document.

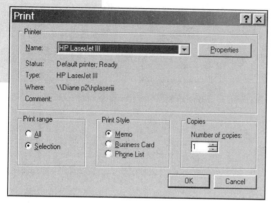

# Finding an E-mail Address

Don't have someone's e-mail address? No problem! Outlook Express supports Lightweight Directory Access Protocol (LDAP) so you can easily search for other Internet users. And when you find the person in question, simply add his or her e-mail address to your Address Book.

Outlook Express comes with Internet Accounts setup for several large personal search engines. You can find just about anyone, anywhere.

## Hands On: Using the Address Book Search Engines

1. Click on Edit, Find People, or click on Find People from the Outlook Express Start Window.

2. Click on the drop-down arrow for the Look In box to see a list of available search services.

3. Choose the service you want to search first.

4. Enter as much information as you have about the person you are searching for. Depending on whether you are searching through the Outlook Express Address Book or a search engine, you can enter the person's Name and E-mail Address. If you are searching the Outlook Express Address Book, you can also enter the person's Phone or Other information.

5. Click on Find Now to begin the search.

   Outlook Express displays any names that match your search criteria in the bottom of the Find People window.

*Note*

If you don't find the person you are looking for, try another search engine. Each one has some unique listings.

6. If you find the person you want, click on the name and then click on <u>A</u>dd to Address Book.

7. From the Address Book, you can continue to fill in other information or just click on OK to close the Address Book.

# Faxing in Windows 98

Most modems purchased today are fax/modems, meaning they can also send and receive faxes. Having a fax built right into your computer enables you to send information to someone else without having to print it first and then walk over to the fax machine and send it from there.

In reality, faxing from your computer is very similar to printing. The only difference is that the printer is a long way away—maybe across the world!

Your fax/modem software is designed to assist you in the process of faxing. Regardless of the specific software, the procedure is fairly standard.

To fax a document from your computer:

1. Open the application and document you want to fax to someone.

2. Click on <u>F</u>ile, <u>P</u>rint to open the Print dialog box. Because faxing is really just long-distance printing, you need to specify a printer.

3. Click on the down arrow to the right of the Printer text box. (The location of the Printer box depends on the specific application software.)

   A list of available printers appears.

4. Choose the fax listed in the Printer box. It could be listed, for example, as WinFax or Microsoft Fax.

5. Click on OK or <u>P</u>rint (whichever your software specifies).

   After a few seconds, a dialog box will ask you for more information. (The exact choices depend on your fax software.)

   Most fax programs ask for similar kinds of information and are very easy to use. In Figure 16.24, WinFax is the faxing software. If you have another program, the screens will look somewhat different, but you should still be able to follow along.

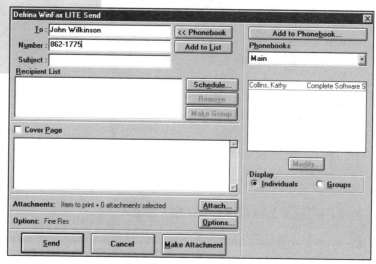

**Figure 16.24**
The WinFax Lite
faxing options
are displayed.

6. Enter the recipient's name and fax number and the subject in the appropriate locations of the dialog box, or select someone from your phonebook.

7. Click on the Cover Page box if you want to add a cover page.

8. Click on Send. The WinFax Status dialog box tells you the status of the fax. Your faxing is now complete.

# 17

# Online with Internet Explorer

## IN THIS CHAPTER

- **Browsing the Web with Internet Explorer**
- **Saving and Using Favorites**
- **Setting Parental Controls**
- **Working with Channels**
- **Using NetMeeting**
- **Using NetShow**
- **Chatting with Microsoft Chat**
- **Creating Web Pages with FrontPage Express**
- **Using Personal Web Server**

Windows 98 comes tightly integrated with a previously released product, Internet Explorer 4.0, which came with numerous tools to help you access the vast stores of information on the Internet. Not only are there are tools to access the Internet, but you can create your own information for the Internet, and there are even tools to help you meet others on the Internet.

# Browsing the Web with Internet Explorer

In Chapter 15 you learned how to establish a connection to the Internet, which is a collection of computer networks that connects millions of computers around the world.

Now that you are connected to the Internet, you'll need a program to view the HTML-type documents that have been created for the World Wide Web. These programs are called *Web browsers*. Several types of Web browsers are on the market today, and their features are updated frequently.

One of the most popular Web browsers is Microsoft Internet Explorer version 4.0, sometimes referred to as IE4. Internet Explorer is part of the Windows 98 package and is the browser demonstrated in this chapter.

Internet Explorer enables you to gain access to the vast stores of information and also has some strong controls that allow you to restrict unwanted material from being displayed.

> **See Chapter 16 for information on Outlook Express.**

But Internet Explorer is more than just a Web browser. Numerous other tools and features are included as a result of Internet Explorer 4.0 technology. These items include Channels, NetMeeting, NetShow, FrontPage Express, and Outlook Express.

You can access Internet Explorer right from your desktop by using either the Internet Explorer icon or the Quick Launch toolbar in the System Tray.

1. Click on Internet Explorer.
2. From the Dial-Up Connection dialog box, enter your Password if it is not already entered. The password will be displayed as a series of asterisks.
3. Click on Connect.

A connection to your ISP will be established and the Internet Explorer start page will be displayed. A *start page* is the first page a browser looks at when it is launched (see Figure 17.1).

**Figure 17.1**
The home.
microsoft.com
start page is
filled with news,
stock informa-
tion, and links to
many popular
Web sites.

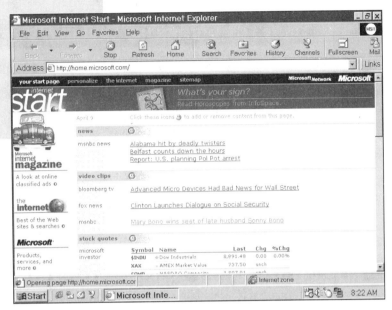

*Tip*

You can make any Web page your start page. Navigate to the Web page you want to use as the start page and choose View, Internet Options. Click on the General tab and then click on Use Current. Click on OK to save your changes.

Here's another way to change your start page. If you look closely at the Address Bar, you'll see a little E icon next to the address of the site you are currently viewing. Click on the icon and drag it to the Home icon on the toolbar. A dialog box will appear, asking if you want to make this page your start page. Click on Yes.

Screens that are accessed on the Internet are called *Web pages* or *home pages*. Web pages have *addresses*. A typical address usually starts with http://www. Then you'll need to specify an exact address such as microsoft.com or whitehouse.gov or your-company.com. Therefore a completed Web address might be something like http://www.disney.com or http://www.iupui.edu.

It's not a written rule, but most Web addresses have a suffix called an organiza-tion code. This information can help you determine what type of organization is publishing the particular Web page you're viewing. Table 17.1 lists some of the most popular organization codes and their descriptions.

## Table 17.1 Organization Codes

| Code | Description | Sample |
|------|-------------|--------|
| .com | Commercial Business | disney.com |
| .gov | Government | whitehouse.gov |
| .edu | Schools and Universities | iupui.edu |
| .net | Internet Service Providers | iquest.net |
| .org | Not-for-Profit Organizations | redcross.org |
| .mil | Military | navy.mil |

# Looking at Internet Explorer's Toolbars

The Internet Explorer window displays a toolbar with various navigation buttons.

*Tip*

If the toolbar is not displayed, click on View, Toolbars, Standard Buttons.

- **Back**—Sends Internet Explorer to the previously viewed Web page.
- **Forward**—Returns Internet Explorer to the page you were on before you clicked the Back button.
- **Stop**—Stops the loading of the current Web page.
- **Refresh**—Reloads the current Web page.
- **Home**—Returns to your Start page.
- **Search**—Displays a list of search engines to help you find a topic.
- **Favorites**—Displays a collection of Web sites you frequently access.
- **History**—Displays a list of Web sites you have previously viewed.
- **Channels**—Displays a link to Web sites used to receive information from the Internet to your computer.
- **Full Screen**—Hides the Internet Explorer menu bar and makes the toolbar smaller for larger screen space to view a Web page.
- **Mail**—Displays Internet mail options.

You can maximize your display space by clicking on the Full Screen icon, which leaves just a single toolbar with the standard buttons and the links across the top of the screen. To add the Address bar, right-click on the toolbar and select Address

Bar. If you want to retain the Links bar, adjust the Address size using the mouse. Even if all the links aren't visible, you can use the scroll arrow at the right side of the Links bar to get access to the remaining links. If you like using the menus, you can right-click on the toolbar and select Menu Bar. You'll probably have to give up something else here—with everything selected, the toolbar gets a bit crowded.

## Using Hyperlinks

Web pages can have many different elements. Some Web pages have links to other Web pages that might be of interest; others might have forms you can fill out and submit. You'll see these a lot if you are requesting information or purchasing something from the Web.

When you position your mouse on an underlined item and the mouse turns into a hand like the one seen in Figure 17.2, you are pointing to a hyperlink. If you click on the hyperlink's underlined text or picture, Internet Explorer jumps to a Web page referenced by the hyperlink. Hyperlinks are also used to submit e-mail to a specified location or to download a file from an FTP site.

*Note*

If you've ever used the Windows Help system, you've probably used hyperlinks to go from one topic to another.

Figure 17.2
As you point to a hyperlink, the actual link address appears at the bottom of the Internet Explorer window.

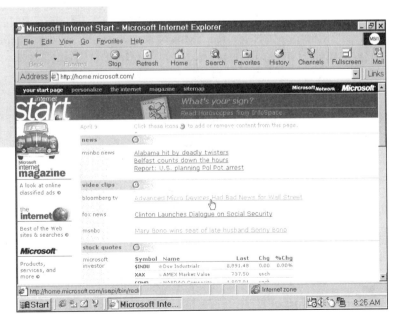

# Using Search Engines

Do you use the telephone company yellow pages to search for a specific product or service, for example, a plumber on Sunday afternoon? Of course, we all do. Your yellow pages might contain 2,000 categories with 100,000 entries. The Internet has millions of entries with tens of thousands of categories. Imagine how large a yellow pages book would be with all that data, never mind the fact that more and more entries are being added or changed daily.

The Internet's answer to the yellow pages are search engines. *Search engines* are databases with millions of listings. The various Internet search engines may have a lot of overlapping information, but they may also have unique entries. I've occasionally found totally different responses from one search engine to the next.

A company that places a page on the Internet will usually register its name with many search engines. Registration is a company's way to say to a search engine, Hello, we're here now, and if someone needs our product or information, please mention us. Most, but not all, search engines register Web pages for free. They make their revenue by advertising that also appears on search page screens.

Search engines use keywords to look up a topic of interest. For example, if you need to do some research on the works of William Shakespeare, looking in a search engine called Infoseek, you would find almost 800 Web pages that refer to William Shakespeare.

Most people tend to be brief when they specify search conditions in search engines, but brevity is not to your advantage. Don't be afraid to use multiple keywords. Most people run searches on fairly general subjects, such as "education" or "swimming" or "resume." Most search engines list pages that contain the highest number of the keyword matches first. Instead of one keyword, try to brainstorm a search string made up of multiple keywords. For example:

> Preschool education developmental early childhood
>
> Pregnancy complications women 40
>
> Marketing career services

Also, for the best possible results, search on multiple search engines.

Here's a list of some of the most popular search sites:

- Yahoo!       http://www.yahoo.com
- Infoseek     http://www.infoseek.com
- Excite       http://www.excite.com
- AltaVista    http://www.altavista.digital.com
- HotBot       http://www.hotbot.com

- Lycos          http://www.lycos.com
- Northern Light         http://www.nlsearch.com

## Hands On: Accessing a Search Engine

1. Type the search engine address in the Address bar and then press Enter; or click on the Search button on the Internet Explorer toolbar.

   If you type the address in the Address bar, Internet Explorer goes to the home page of that search engine and displays it in a full screen. If you click on the Search button, Internet Explorer chooses a search engine for you and displays it on the left side of the screen (see Figure 17.3).

2. Enter the keywords you are searching for in the search box. Each search engine has a search box, but they'll be in different locations of the Web pages.

3. Click on Search or Search Now or Go or whatever prompt your search engine displays.

   The search engine results screen (see Figure 17.4) shows how many matches to your criteria it was able to find. Most search engines also display a title or summary of the Web page(s) it found and a relevancy rating. The relevancy ratings compare the information in the site against

**Figure 17.3**
Many search engines offer predefined search categories.

Search box

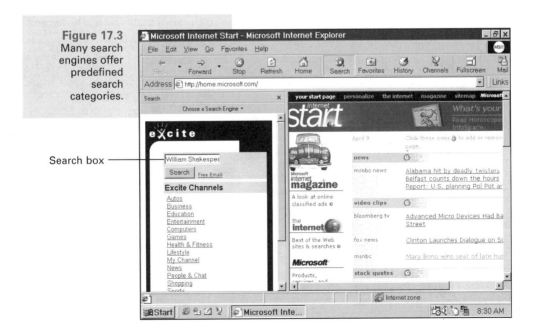

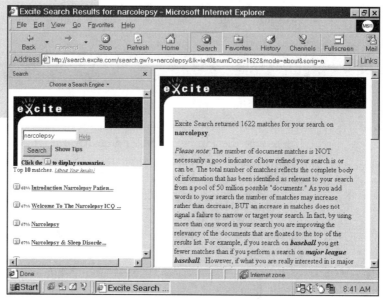

the information from the search. The higher the rating, the more likely the Web site will have the information you're looking for.

4. Click on the hyperlink you want to visit. If this site doesn't have the information you want, try the next site in the search engine results list or try searching by different keywords.

## Playing Favorites

Oh, it's dreadful to get old and forget things! One of the many things I'm finding I can't remember is Web addresses. Typing all those letters, slashes, and periods can sometimes be so difficult. Windows 98 includes a feature called *favorites* so you can save a Web address. Favorites are menu selections that act like hyperlinks to allow you to access your favorite Web page with a simple click of the mouse.

**Favorites don't have to be Web pages. They can also be file folders or files.**

*Note*

## Adding a Favorite

The more you explore the Web, the more Web sites you'll find that you want to revisit.

### Hands On: Adding a Favorite

1. Start Internet Explorer and if necessary connect to your ISP.
2. In the Address box, type **http://www.yogs.com** or type any page address you want to add to your collection of favorite pages.
3. When the page is displayed in the Internet Explorer window, click on the Favorites menu and then click on Add to Favorites.
4. Choose whether you want to subscribe to the Web page or just add a link to the page itself. (Subscriptions are discussed later in this chapter.)
5. Click on OK.

As you can see in Figure 17.5, the Web address has been added to the Favorites menu. The next time you want to access that Web page, you won't have to type a thing; just select it from the Favorites list.

You can also add a shortcut to your favorite Web site to your desktop! With the Web page displayed, click on the File menu and choose Send, Shortcut to Desktop. The shortcut appears on your Windows 98 desktop, as shown in Figure 17.6.

**Figure 17.5**
The Web page name is displayed in the Favorites menu. Point to an item to view the actual Web address.

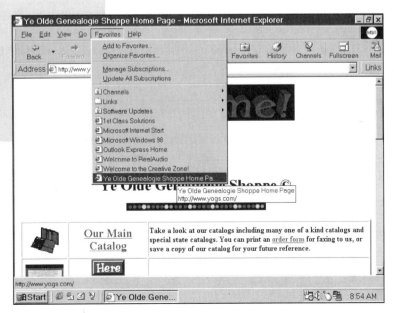

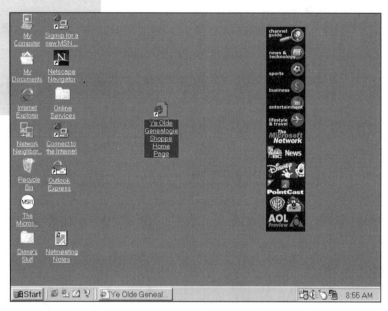

**Figure 17.6**
Click on the
desktop shortcut
to connect to
your ISP and go
to the selected
Web site.

## Accessing a Favorite

Now that you've added a Web page to your favorites, what's the easiest way to access it?

1. Click on the Favorites button to display your Favorites list on the left side of the screen or click on the Favorites menu.

2. Click on the page you want to open, and Internet Explorer will jump to the specified Web page.

## Organizing Favorites

Once you discover Favorites, you'll probably keep adding to the Favorite list. The list will just keep growing and growing so you'll need to organize it. Your favorites can be distributed into folders just like files. When you click on the Favorites menu, you'll see folders that open into submenus that list Web sites according to categories you choose.

You might want to organize your pages by topic. For example, you could create an Art folder for storing information about art exhibits and reviews and a Stocks folder for storing Web pages about stocks. Do you have several Web sites with jokes on them? Create a Funnies folder.

## Hands On: Organizing Favorites

1. Click on Favorites and choose Organize Favorites. You'll see an Organize Favorites dialog box like the one in Figure 17.7.

2. Click on the Create New Folder icon, type **FAMILY HISTORY** or a descriptive name for the folder and then press Enter.

**Figure 17.7**
Add as many
folders as you
want to keep
yourself
organized.

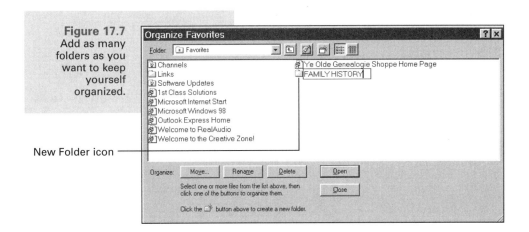

New Folder icon

3. Click on the favorite that you want to move and drag it to the new folder. In this example, drag the Ye Olde Genealogie Shoppe favorite to the FAMILY HISTORY folder.

To delete a Favorite, click on it and press the Delete key. Click on Yes to confirm the deletion. Internet Explorer sends deleted Favorites to the Recycle Bin.

4. Click on Close when you've finished organizing your Favorites.

# Setting Parental Controls

If you don't have children at home, you can just skip this section. The World Wide Web is filled with information on every imaginable topic. Therefore, you may want to monitor what type of information your children can access. With the Content Advisor options, you can screen out objectionable or offensive content by using industry-standard ratings defined independently by the Platform for Internet Content Selection (PICS) committee.

*Note*

**Not all Web pages are rated.**

## Hands On: Setting the Content Advisor

1.  Right-click on the Internet Explorer and then choose Properties from the shortcut menu.

2.  Choose Enable from the Content tab.

    When you enable the Content Advisor, a supervisor password must be assigned to prevent others from changing the settings. The settings can be modified only by people who know the password.

3.  Type a supervisor Password twice and then click on OK to open the Content Advisor dialog box.

    From the Content Advisor box, you can control the display of Web pages according to level of Language, Nudity, Sex, and Violence (see Figure 17.8).

4.  Click on the category you want to change.

5.  Drag the Rating slide bar to the desired level. A description of each rating is displayed under the rating slide bar. You'll want to select a Rating level for each category you want to restrict.

**Figure 17.8**
Each category has a five-level rating beginning with zero, the strictest, to four, which is the most lenient.

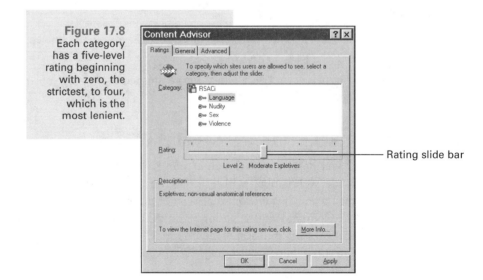

Rating slide bar

There are also a couple of options on the General tab from which you can select.

- Users can see sites that have no rating. If you activate this feature, then if a site is not rated, your child will still be able to access it.
- Supervisor can type a password to allow users to view restricted content. If you activate this feature, anyone with access to the supervisor password will be able to access a restricted Web site.

6. Choose either or both options if desired and then click on OK.

*Note*

If you want to disable ratings restrictions, return to the Content tab of the Internet Properties box and click on Disable.

7. Click on OK to close the Internet Properties dialog box.

# Working with Channels

See Chapter 5 for information on configuring the Active Desktop.

A *channel* is a Web site designed to deliver content from the Internet to your computer. You might want to subscribe to a stock market channel or a news channel so that you'll always be up-to-date with the latest information. Channel Web pages are some of the most colorful and dynamic pages you'll find, and their content is constantly changing.

To view the Channel bar that comes with Windows 98, you must have the Active Desktop configured.

## Subscribing to Channels

The Channel bar displayed on the Active Desktop has suggested categories for you to subscribe to, but you can customize the Channel bar with the topics you use the most.

Windows 98 includes the following categories:

- Entertainment channels such as Comics, AudioNet, MTV, Hollywood Online, People, NBC Daily
- News and Technology channels such as CNN, NY Times, Time, ZDNet
- Sports channels such as ESPN, MSNBC Sports, CBS SportsLine
- Travel and Lifestyle channels such as Discover, National Geographic
- Disney and Warner Brothers channels

## Hands On: Subscribing to a Channel

1. Click on a category on the Channel bar to open the Channel window.

   The first time you click on the Channel bar, a welcome message will appear. You can choose an overview of channels for more information.

2. Click on Yes or No. If you choose Yes, Internet Explorer displays the Channel overview.

*Note*

**If you are not already connected to the Internet, you will be prompted to do so now.**

The channel categories are displayed on the left side of the screen in a Channel Guide. Some of the categories have subcategories, and some are direct links to a specific Web site. If you choose a category such as News & Technology, the Internet Explorer window opens with a list of the channel sites available in that category, as shown in Figure 17.9.

3. Click on the Channel site you want to view.

   An opening view of the Web page will be displayed with a button somewhere on it marked Add Active Channel.

**Figure 17.9**
Position your mouse on the left side of the screen to see the Channel Guide or move the mouse to the right to hide the Channel Guide.

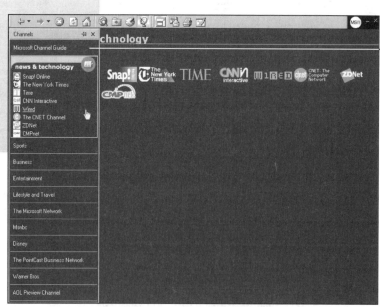

Channel Guide

4. Click on Add Active Channel.

Now you must decide whether you want to subscribe to the channel. *Subscribing* to a channel tells that Web site to send updated information to your computer at specified intervals. Figure 17.10 shows the three choices you have about updating a subscription:

- **N̲o, Just Keep It in My Channel Bar.** You want to add this channel to your Channel bar, but you do not want to subscribe to it and be automatically notified when the content changes.

- **Y̲es, but Only Tell Me When Updates Occur.** You want to subscribe to the Web site. You also want Internet Explorer to check for changes to this channel on a scheduled basis and to notify you that a change has been made.

  If you choose the above option, you can tell Windows 98 when and how to notify you by clicking on C̲ustomize.

- **Yes, Notify Me of Updates and D̲ownload the Channel for Offline Viewing.** You want to subscribe to the current channel. You also want Internet Explorer to notify you of changes to the channel and to automatically download pages from the site according to the schedule set by you or the update schedule suggested by the channel provider.

  From here you can determine whether you want to download only the home page of the channel you subscribed to or to download all the associated pages.

5. Click on your updating choice.

6. Choose the method you would prefer and then click on N̲ext.

Internet Explorer will notify you if the page has changed by adding a red dot to its icon; you can also ask to be notified by e-mail.

7. Choose whether you want to be notified by e-mail of any changes to the Web site and then click on N̲ext.

**Figure 17.10**
If you subscribe to a channel, Windows 98 will keep you up-to-date on any changes made in the Web page.

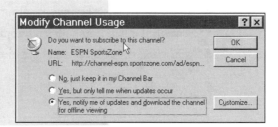

Each Channel publisher has a recommended update schedule. Depending on the type of channel, the update could be hourly, every four hours, or once a day. You can also choose daily, monthly, or weekly updates.

8. Click on the scheduled time for the updates.

The Dial as Needed option will automatically dial into the Internet for updating even if you're not at the computer. (Do remember to leave the computer on though!)

9. Click on Finish and then click on OK.

## Manually Updating a Channel

Instead of waiting for an update from the channel provider, you can manually update a channel subscription:

1. Click on Channels to open the Channels folder.

2. Right-click on the channel you want to update and choose Update Now from the shortcut menu.

# Using NetMeeting

As a writer, I'm supposed to be impartial, but I have to tell you—I think Microsoft's NetMeeting is just about the coolest program I've ever seen! My prediction is that this product will revolutionize communications.

Microsoft NetMeeting is a communication tool that offers a complete Internet (or intranet) conferencing solution for easy interchange with others. You can use NetMeeting for your work or just for fun with your friends and family.

Many companies are using NetMeeting to develop their corporate intranet into a real-time communication network because it includes six of the most-wanted collaboration tools:

- **Connection**—Calls others together for a conference
- **Audio & Video**—Enables meeting participants to see and hear each other
- **Share & Collaborate**—Shares applications and documents
- **Whiteboard**—Functions as a whiteboard for graphic representations

- **Chat**—Supports text-based chat
- **File Transfer**—Transfers files to one or all meeting participants

## Starting NetMeeting

To use NetMeeting you'll need a sound card, speakers or headphones, and a microphone.

### Hands On: Starting NetMeeting

1. Click on the Start button and choose <u>P</u>rograms.
2. Choose Internet Explorer and then choose NetMeeting.

   The first time you run NetMeeting a wizard will ask you to select a User Location Server as well as to provide information such as your e-mail address, name, city, and country.

   When the NetMeeting Wizard starts, the first screen gives you a little free advertising on NetMeeting.
3. Click on <u>N</u>ext.

   You'll now be prompted to select a directory server.

## Choosing a User Location Server

The directory server is also called a User Location Server (ULS), which is a central location for e-mail addresses. ULS servers were created to remedy a problem that occurs with modem connections. Each time you log on to the Internet with your modem, you are given an Internet address. The next time you log on, you'll be given a different Internet address. It's really hard for your friends and co-workers to keep track of you when you keep moving around! So the ULS was created. By accessing your name through the ULS, people can contact you (via NetMeeting), even though your Internet address changes constantly.

Some servers are private, but most users will use one of several public servers accessible from Microsoft. Figure 17.11 shows a list of the servers currently available for NetMeeting. This list will appear when you first start NetMeeting, but you can change your selection at any time.

**Figure 17.11**
NetMeeting
servers are so
popular that you
might have to
wait several
minutes to log
on. In this case,
try selecting a
different server.

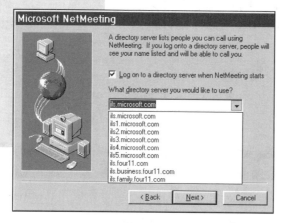

## Hands On: Beginning a NetMeeting Session

1. Pick a Directory server to start with and then click on Next.

2. Enter your Name, Address, E-mail address, and any desired comment in the appropriate boxes and then choose Next to continue.

*Note*

**In the comment section, you may want to type in something like Business Use Only or Clean Calls Only to let other users know the kind of conversation you are interested in.**

The next screen lets you categorize yourself. If you're on here searching for someone to have a conversation with, choose the personal category, but if you're going to use NetMeeting primarily for business use, use the business category. See Figure 17.12 for the selections.

3. Click on a category and then click on Next.

4. Specify the speed of your modem or connection and then click on Next.

   An Audio Tuning Wizard will help you check your microphone. Make sure your speakers or headphones as well as your microphone are connected.

5. Click on Next.

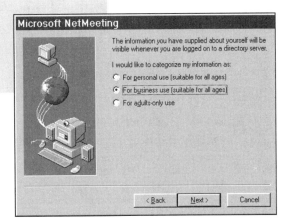

**Figure 17.12**
You'll be able to call others by the category they have selected.

6. Click on the Test button and listen to the sound played from your speakers. Adjust the volume slide button as necessary. The Test button turns into a Stop button during the test, and you can click on Stop to discontinue the test.

7. Click on Next.

8. To test the microphone, read the message on the screen into the microphone. You probably won't hear any feedback, but the Audio Tuning Wizard is recording and adjusting as necessary (see Figure 17.13).

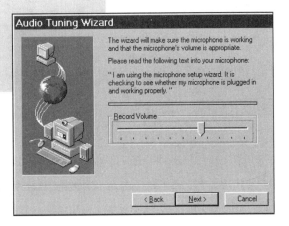

**Figure 17.13**
Speak from the position you will be using for NetMeeting.

9. Click on <u>N</u>ext and then click on Finish. NetMeeting launches, and you're ready to use it.

The opening NetMeeting window has several components in addition to the standard Windows menu and toolbars. Figure 17.14 shows some of the basic elements you might see in a NetMeeting window.

Several icons in the list area enable you to change the view in the NetMeeting window. The directory list shows a current list of users in a particular ULS. To switch to a different directory, click on the down arrow next to the server display and choose a different server.

To initiate a NetMeeting call, click on the name of the person you want to contact and then click on the Call button on the NetMeeting toolbar. When the call is connected, the directory closes and the Current Call screen shows the names of all participants (see Figure 17.15).

Talk away but do take turns. If you need to adjust your volume, you can adjust the volume control slide bar towards the top of the screen. Slide the bar to the right for increased volume or to the left to decrease it.

**Figure 17.14**
The contents of the toolbar change to reflect the different stages of NetMeeting.

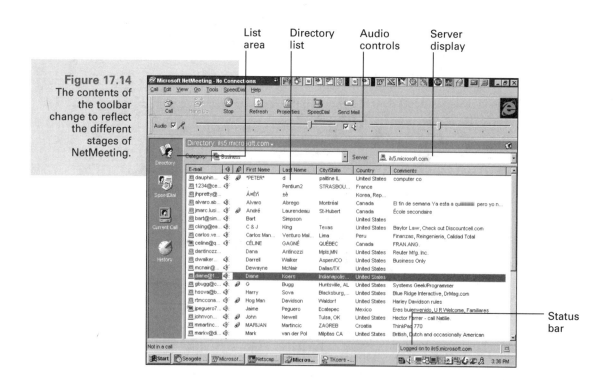

**Figure 17.15**
A speaker next to a participant's name means the person's computer has audio capabilities; a video camera means the person's computer has video capabilities.

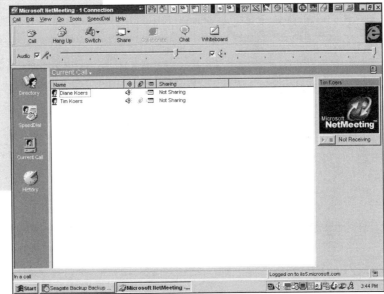

# Using the Whiteboard

If you need to illustrate an example, use the NetMeeting Whiteboard feature.

1. Click on Tools, Whiteboard, or press Ctrl+W to display the whiteboard. Each participant will see the same whiteboard.

*Tip*

You can also access the whiteboard by clicking on the Whiteboard button on the Current Call toolbar.

The NetMeeting Whiteboard feature looks and acts very similar to the Windows Paint program. The tools are on the left of the screen, and the colors are on the bottom.

See "Getting Creative with Paint" in Chapter 10.

2. If you want to call attention to a detail on the whiteboard, click on the Remote Pointer tool. It's the one that looks like a hand with a finger pointing out. Your mouse now becomes a hand, and you can direct the meeting to something on the whiteboard.

3. When you are finished with the Whiteboard feature, each participant has the option of saving the contents to a file.

4. If you want to save the contents of the Whiteboard, choose Yes. Enter a file name in the Save dialog box that appears, and then press the Enter key.

# Chatting in NetMeeting

The NetMeeting Chat feature is a real-time Internal Relay Chat. You type something, and the other person responds by typing something back (see Figure 17.16).

1. Click on <u>T</u>ools, <u>C</u>hat, or press Ctrl+C to display the Chat window. Each member of the meeting will see the same Chat screen.

• • • • • • • • • • • • • • • • • • • • • • • • • • • • • • • • • • • • • • • • • • • • •

You could also access Chat by clicking on the Chat button on the Current Call toolbar.

• • • • • • • • • • • • • • • • • • • • • • • • • • • • • • • • • • • • • • • • • • • • • •

2. Type your comment and then press Enter.

By default, NetMeeting Chat will send the comment to everyone participating in the meeting. You can decide whether you want your comments to be seen by everyone or by one person in particular. Click in the Send To drop-down list box and select the person to whom you want to send a *private* message (see Figure 17.17).

**Figure 17.16**
Chatting is handy if you're having audio difficulties or if too many people are trying to talk at once.

**Figure 17.17**
Only the person you specified will see the message on the Chat screen.

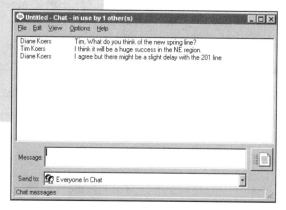

Send To box

Private message

# Sharing and Collaborating

Teamwork is essential for most projects. Whether you're planning a schedule or contributing to an outline, having all the players together is a real aid to productivity. But if the players are thousands of miles away, sending information back and forth can be time-consuming and tedious. NetMeeting closes the distance gap and enables each team member to make real-time contribution to a document. You make a change, the next person makes a changes, and so forth; everyone sees all the changes immediately.

The feature is called Sharing and Collaborating. Sharing an open application enables everyone in the meeting to see a common screen. Initially, only the person who shares the original application and or document can make any changes to it, but add the Collaboration feature and each member can then modify or change an open file.

## Sharing and Collaborating

Bob, Mary, and Ed are participating in a NetMeeting about an upcoming fundraising campaign they are heading for their company. One of the first steps is to establish a time frame for the project. Mary created an Excel spreadsheet with her initial plans, so Mary is going to *Share* both the Excel application and the spreadsheet itself. The application must be opened on Mary's machine.

Ed doesn't have Excel on his computer. Is this a problem? No, because he will be actually accessing Mary's Excel program. He doesn't need the application on his PC at all.

If Mary elects to *Share* the application, Bob and Ed can only see it. They cannot access any of the features of the application. To modify, or even to access the remote program or document, all three players must *Collaborate*. Each one, one at a time, will then have access to the document and Excel program to make any changes right in front of all participants. Only one person at a time can control the application. The initials of the person in control are displayed as his or her mouse pointer moves across the application screen. Another participant "takes control" by clicking the mouse in the application. No fighting—and please do take turns!

## Hands On: Sharing an Application

1. Open the application and optionally open the document to be shared.
2. Click on Tools, Share Application, or click on the Share button on the toolbar.
3. Choose from the available open applications.

   A message indicates that others can see the application, but not participate in it.
4. Click on OK.

   All participants will see a screen similar to the one in Figure 17.18.
5. Click on Tools, Start Collaborating, or click on the Collaborate button on the toolbar.

   A message will warn you not to leave your PC unattended while collaborating on a document.
6. Click on OK.

Alas, all good things must come to an end. When you are finished with your Net-Meeting, click on the Hang Up button. Other participants can continue, but each person must Hang Up when he or she leaves the meeting.

**Figure 17.18**
Participants can work on a program even if they don't have that application on their computer.

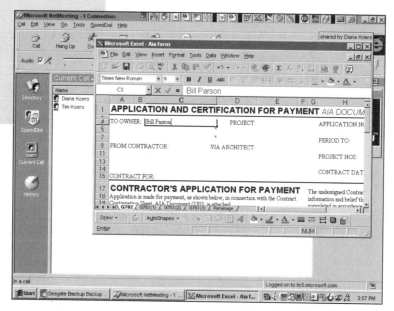

# Using NetShow Player

See Chapter 8 to learn how to add components.

NetShow is a video player that uses streaming multimedia. Streaming allows content to be delivered to your screen as a continuous flow of data with little wait time before playback begins. NetShow enables you instant play to experience events as they are happening and eliminates the frustration of waiting for content to download (see Figure 17.19).

NetShow is not installed by default. You'll need to add it. It's in the Multimedia section of Windows components.

To play a NetShow presentation, double-click on the indicator in the Web page (see Figure 17.20) or whatever you are using that indicates video is available. The video begins to play immediately.

Some NetShow presentations have built-in markers. *Markers* are stopping points on a presentation. With markers you can jump forward to the next marker or return to a previous marker. This system is great for longer presentations. When a file has markers, the markers appear at the bottom of the video picture. Figure 17.21 illustrates a NetShow presentation with markers.

The marker tools are:

- **Previous Marker**—Goes to the previous marker.
- **Back**—Goes backwards in the current marker range.

**Figure 17.19**
The multimedia clips can be played right on the Web page you are viewing.

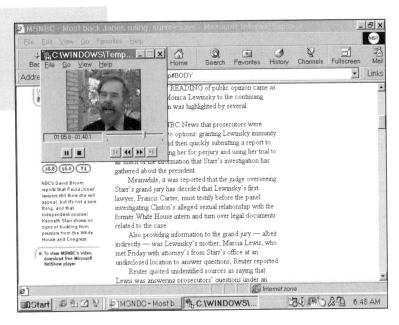

**Figure 17.20**
Using less than a 28.8 modem will make NetShow video hard to follow.

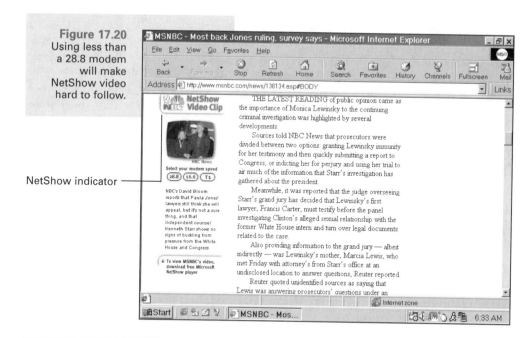

NetShow indicator

**Figure 17.21**
Marker tools enable you to move around quickly in a video.

Marker tools

- **Forward**—Goes forward in the current marker range.
- **Next Marker**—Goes to the next marker.
- **Slider**—Moves freely around the markers in the presentation.

# Chatting with Microsoft Chat

Chatting is one of those features people either love or hate. Microsoft Chat is an Internet Relay Chat program, which is a method of communicating in real-time mode. You type a question or statement and someone else responds. Actual conversations are being typed back and forth by a group of people with a common interest.

Most chat rooms are text based, but Microsoft Chat is text or graphics based. In graphic mode, instead of seeing text on the screen, you'll see comic strip-like characters with little talk balloons over their heads. The words you type appear in your character's talk balloons. You can even give your character some lifelike characteristics with emotions that you can specify.

Actually it's kind of fun. I found myself laughing out loud as I watched things transpire.

## Starting Microsoft Chat

When you're ready to chat, all you have to do to conduct real-time conversations is enter a Chat Room on an Internet server.

You'll have the opportunity to chat in Comic mode where your conversation displays inside a comic strip, or Text mode, which displays in text only.

### Hands On: Starting Microsoft Chat

1. Click on the Start button and choose <u>P</u>rograms.

2. Choose Internet Explorer, Microsoft Chat. A Chat Connection dialog box like the one in Figure 17.22 is displayed. Many chat servers are available, but by default, Microsoft Chat tries to connect you with the Microsoft chat server.

   If Chat is not listed, you may have to install it.

> **For information on installing Windows components, see "Adding and Removing Software" in Chapter 8.**

**Figure 17.22**
You'll need to connect to a chat server before you can chat.

| Chat Connection |
|---|
| Connect \| Personal Info \| Character \| Background |
| Welcome to Microsoft Chat. You can specify chat server connection information here, and optionally adjust your Personal Information from the next tab. |
| Users of comics mode can choose a character and background from two additional tabs. |
| <u>F</u>avorites: |
| <u>S</u>erver: chat.msn.com |
| ○ <u>G</u>o to chat room: #JesusBelievers |
| ⦿ Show all available chat rooms |
| OK   Cancel   Apply |

3. If you have a specific chat server that you want to connect to, enter the addresses in the Server box.

4. If you know the name of a chat room you want to join, enter it in the Go to Chat Room box; otherwise, click on Show All Available Chat Rooms and then click on OK.

5. If you're not already connected to the Internet, you'll be prompted to do so now. Click on Connect.

   As soon as you are connected, a Chat Room list dialog box like the one in Figure 17.23 appears on your screen and you can select the topic you are interested in. The number of chat rooms available will vary with different servers and the time of day.

   Before you begin chatting, you'll probably want to define your character.

**Figure 17.23**
In this figure, 113 different chat rooms are available with topics ranging from Pets to Religion to Wrestling.

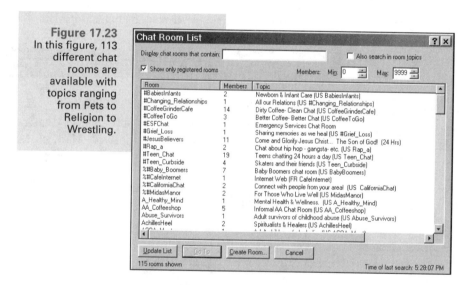

6. Click on Cancel to temporarily close the Chat Room list dialog box.

## Setting Up a Character

In Comic Mode, you and other chat participants are displayed as cartoon characters, with your conversation appearing as word balloons inside the frames of a comic strip. You pick the character you want, and even select the background you like for the comic strip.

You can choose things like the appearance and general emotions of your character, as well as a name for your character. The information you enter here will be accessible to other users.

## Hands On: Choosing a Character

1. Click on the <u>V</u>iew menu and choose <u>O</u>ptions.
2. On the Personal Info tab, enter the <u>R</u>eal Name, <u>N</u>ickname, and an <u>E</u>-mail address you want to use.

*Note*

**A word of advice here. Don't use your real name and real e-mail address. Instead, make something up. You'll notice that's what almost everyone does. Disclosing your real name and e-mail address can result in unwanted e-mail. If you want to divulge this information to someone in the chat room, you can "whisper" it to them.**

An emotion wheel in the bottom right corner of your chat window displays facial expressions. As you type your chat responses, you can click the expression you want your character to make.

3. Click on the Character tab and select a character you want to use as well as a starting emotion from the emotion wheel (see Figure 17.24).

*Tip*

Additional characters can be downloaded for free by visiting the Microsoft download web site: http://www.microsoft.com/msdownload/ieplatform/chat/char/04000.htm

**Figure 17.24**
Click on an emotion and watch your character change in the Preview window.

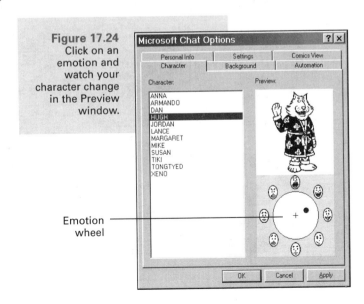

Emotion wheel

4. Click on the Background tab and choose from one of the three available backgrounds you would like to see in your comic strip.

*Tip*

If you are a parent and want to restrict the type of chat that is accessible, click on the Settings tab and enable Ratings from the Content Advisor. See "Using Parental Controls" earlier in this chapter.

5. Click on OK.

## Chatting with Others

Now you're ready to join in the chat. You can choose to jump into the conversations or you can just sit back and observe.

### Hands On: Chatting with Others

1. Click on Room, Room List to display the list of available chat rooms again.

2. Click on a room that sounds interesting to you and then click on Go To. Now you're in and ready to talk (see Figure 17.25).

**Figure 17.25**
The chat window has four panels. You may find others greeting you.

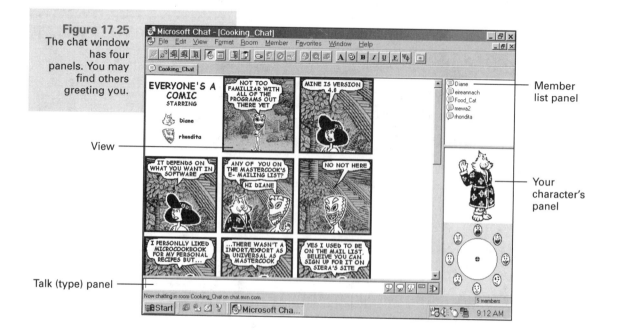

View

Talk (type) panel

Member list panel

Your character's panel

The chat window also has a toolbar at the bottom to give you one-click access to the features you use most often. Before you click any button, you can hold the cursor over the button to get its description.

- Say. After you type your message, you can click on the Say button or press Enter to post it.
- Whisper. Use to send secret messages that only you and your intended recipient(s) can see.
- Think. Lets you post a message that tells everyone what you're thinking. In Comic Mode, your words display in a "thought balloon."
- Action. Type in an action that tells your chat friends what you are currently doing, such as "thinks of a response." When you click on the Action button, it posts the message with your nickname automatically entered (e.g., "Diane thinks of a response.")

3. To talk to another character:

Click on the person you want to talk to from the Member list panel.

Select an emotion for your character by dragging the black dot around in the emotion wheel in your character's panel.

*Tip*

Add a sound effect to your message: Click on the Sound button, pick a sound file, and type a message. Both the message and sound will be inserted into your conversation. Click on the Test button to hear the sound before you attach it to your message. Note that only those chatters who have sound installed and the same sound file loaded on their computers will be able to hear the sound effect.

Type the text you want to say in the Talk panel box and then press Enter. Your text and character will appear in the comic strip View panel.

4. To leave a chat room, click on Room, Leave a Room. You will no longer be accessible in that chat room.

5. To return to a chat room, click on Room, Enter a Room.

6. To quit Microsoft Chat, click on File, Exit.

# Creating Web Pages with FrontPage Express

Until recently, creating a Web page for the Internet was a tedious process requiring specialists experienced in HTML coding.

FrontPage Express is a Windows 98 program that enables you to create an HTML page for the Internet or your local intranet. One of the nicest features of Front-Page Express is that you don't have to learn the cumbersome HTML language. FrontPage Express converts your commands to HTML for you.

OK, you ask, what is HTML? Well, HTML stands for Hypertext Markup Language. HTML uses *tags* to control the appearance of a page. You must add the tags in a very specific order for your document to turn out the way you expect it to. Figure 17.26 illustrates an HTML document in its raw form.

FrontPage Express is a scaled down version of FrontPage, one of the leading Web publishing programs on the market today. You should know, however, that Microsoft really didn't scale down the features that count! You'll be able to add backgrounds, graphics, video, tables, forms, hyperlinks, and many other features with FrontPage Express.

## Creating a Web Page

FrontPage Express includes a Wizard to assist you with creating a Web page. With the Personal Home Page Wizard you can create a Web page by simply following the commands on the screen. It's a good place to start. This exercise shows you how to create a personal Web page.

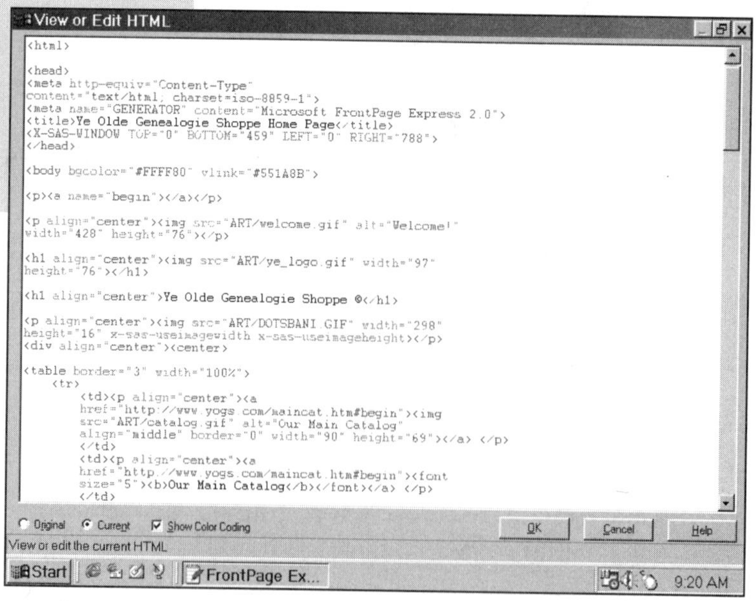

**Figure 17.26**
It can be very confusing to work on a document with all the HTML tags in the way.

## Hands On: Creating a Personal Home Page

1. Click on the Start menu and choose Programs.
2. Choose Internet Explorer and then FrontPage Express.

   FrontPage Express launches into a blank page like the one in Figure 17.27. You can now create your own text or let the Wizard do the work.
3. Click on File and choose New, or press Ctrl+N.
4. Choose the Personal Home Page Wizard and then click on OK.

Choose the Form Page Wizard to create a form that your readers can fill in and submit to you.

Figure 17.28 shows a list of topics you might want to publish on your home page, for example, your name, job titles, or hobbies.
5. Choose the topics you want to publish. Because the Web page is going to be personal, select Hot List, Biographical Information, Personal Interests, and Contact Information.

Forms    Standard    Formatting
toolbar    toolbar    toolbar

**Figure 17.27**
The toolbars make most Web publishing features only a mouse click away.

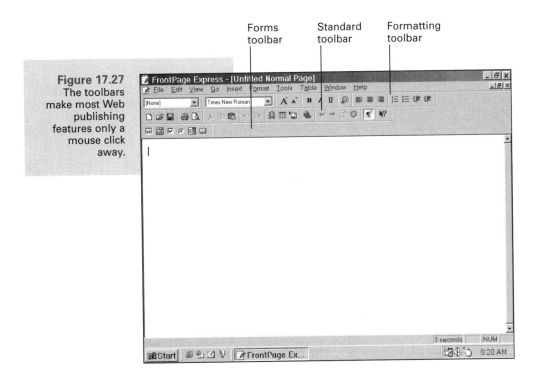

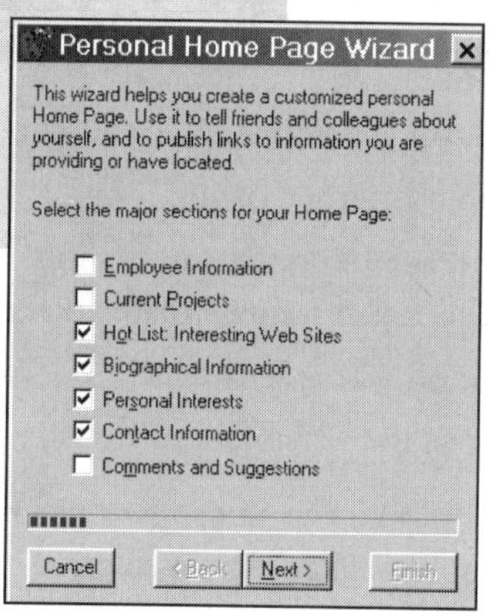

**Figure 17.28**
Choose the type
of information
you want
others to see.

> **Personal Home Page Wizard** ☒
>
> This wizard helps you create a customized personal Home Page. Use it to tell friends and colleagues about yourself, and to publish links to information you are providing or have located.
>
> Select the major sections for your Home Page:
>
> ☐ Employee Information
> ☐ Current Projects
> ☑ Hot List: Interesting Web Sites
> ☑ Biographical Information
> ☑ Personal Interests
> ☑ Contact Information
> ☐ Comments and Suggestions
>
> [ Cancel ] [ < Back ] [ Next > ] [ Finish ]

6. Click on Next.

   Now you need to specify a couple of titles for your home page. The first title, the Page URL, is the file name the computer and the Web will use to identify this Web page. The file extension should be htm.

   The Page Title is the title that your users will see when they open their Web browser. The Page Title appears in the title bar of the Web browser.

7. Enter the Page URL and the Page Title and then click on Next. For this example, the Page URL is myhome.htm, and the Page Title is Diane's Home Page (see Figure 17.29).

   The next screen depends on the selections you made in step 5. In this case, FrontPage prompts you for a style for a list of hyperlinks that you'll create later.

8. Choose a style and then click on Next.

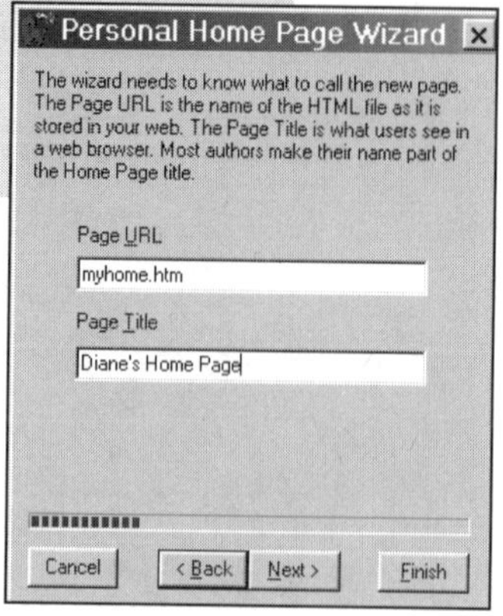

**Figure 17.29**
Be sure to type
the .htm after the
page URL.

> **Personal Home Page Wizard** ☒
>
> The wizard needs to know what to call the new page. The Page URL is the name of the HTML file as it is stored in your web. The Page Title is what users see in a web browser. Most authors make their name part of the Home Page title.
>
> Page URL
>
> [ myhome.htm ]
>
> Page Title
>
> [ Diane's Home Page ]
>
> [ Cancel ] [ < Back ] [ Next > ] [ Finish ]

FrontPage prompts you for a style for the Biography section. Notice that the dialog box is not asking you for the biographical information, only the style in which to display it.

9. Make a selection and then click on <u>N</u>ext.

10. In the displayed text box, enter some personal interests you want to publish on your Web page. Examples might include your hobbies, pets, or goals. You can change any of these later. You'll also need to decide on the type of list to use for these interests (see Figure 17.30).

11. Click on <u>N</u>ext.

12. Enter any contact information you want to disclose on your Web page.

13. Click on Next.

If you want to change the display order of the topics on your Web page, you can click on any topic and then click on the Up or Down button.

14. Make any desired changes and click on <u>N</u>ext. For this example, move the Hot List to the bottom of the sections.

15. Click on Finish. That's it!

Figure 17.31 shows the Web page you just created. A lot of the work has already been done for you, but it's not very attractive, and it needs additional information.

Editing an HTML document is almost identical to editing a standard word processing document. As you scroll down the page, you'll notice the sections for Biographical Information and Personal Interests. Type any additional text you want for these sections, deleting the prompts displayed on the screen.

You can also use the Windows Cut, Copy, and Paste commands to move information from one location to another.

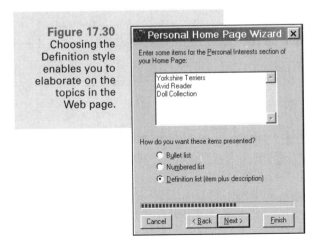

**Figure 17.30**
Choosing the Definition style enables you to elaborate on the topics in the Web page.

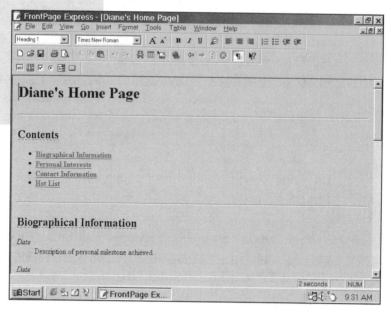

# Formatting a FrontPage Express Document

Add a background to give your page some color or add graphics for additional effects.

## Hands On: Formatting a FrontPage Express Document

1. Click on the Format menu and then choose Background to display the Background tab of the Page Properties dialog box (see Figure 17.32).

2. Click on the Background drop-down list box and choose a background color.

   Optionally, you could click on Background Image and/or Watermark and then click on the Browse box to select a GIF or JPG image for your Web page.

3. Click on the Text and Hyperlink drop-down boxes and choose colors for the Text and Hyperlinks on your Web page.

4. Click on OK.

   In Figure 17.33, I changed the background to dark blue, the text to white and hyperlinks to red. I also added a background image of stars.

**Figure 17.32**
Items changed
from the Page
Properties dialog
box affect the
entire Web page.

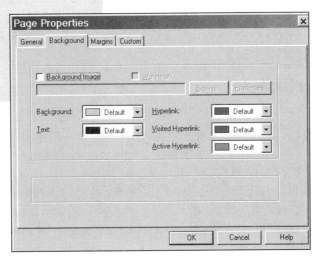

Although FrontPage Express doesn't come with graphic images, you can add GIF or JPG images that you've created or from other collections. You can even add AVI video or WAV sound files for your viewers to enjoy.

5. Click on Insert and then choose Image, Video or Background Sound. Locate the file to be included and then click on OK.

**Figure 17.33**
I didn't say it
would be pretty,
I just said you
could do this!

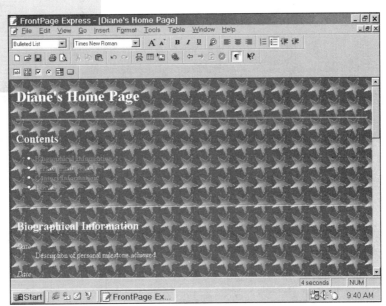

> *Tip*
>
> You can add more horizontal lines by choosing Insert, Horizontal Line.

## Adding Hyperlinks

If you want to add a hyperlink to other Web sites, you'll need to know the URL to the specified site.

1. Select the text that will point to the hyperlink and then click on Insert, Hyperlink (or press Ctrl+K.)

2. Choose a Hyperlink Type. Choices include http, mailto, or ftp.

   Choose "http" if you're creating a hyperlink to a specific Web page. Choose "ftp" if you want to create a hyperlink to a file transfer location or choose "mailto" if you're creating a hyperlink to an e-mail address.

3. Enter the URL in the URL box. The prefix is already typed in for you depending on the Hyperlink type you selected in step 2 (see Figure 17.34).

4. Click on OK.

> *Tip*
>
> To edit a hyperlink, click anywhere in the middle of the link text and press Ctrl+K.

**Figure 17.34**
Type the entire URL for the hyperlink.

Selected text for hyperlink

URL address

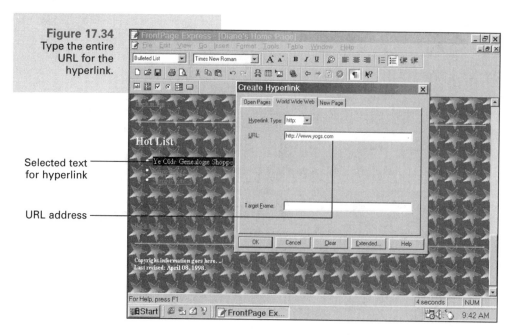

The file is now ready to be saved and uploaded to your ISP or to the server on which you are going to display your Web page.

# Personal Web Server

The usual purpose of creating a Web page is to put it onto the World Wide Web. To publish a document to the Web, you need to place the document on a server. Most ISPs will rent space on their servers, for a fee of course, or you can use your own machine as a server. The disadvantage of using your own computer is that a server must run 24 hours a day and have a permanent Internet connection. That can present a myriad of problems, including security risks.

Nevertheless, if you want to use your own computer as an Internet server, you can use a program included with Windows 98 called Personal Web Server (PWS).

Microsoft Personal Web Server also can be used to develop and test a Web site before hosting the site with an ISP.

If you look under the Start, Programs, Internet Explorer, you'll see Personal Web Server. However, before you can actually use the PWS you'll need to install it.

To install Personal Web Server:

1. Insert your Windows 98 CD-ROM in its drive.
2. Click Start and then click Run.
3. In the Run dialog box, type **x:\add-ons\pws\setup.exe** (where **x** is the letter of your CD drive) and then click OK.
4. Follow the directions in the Personal Web Server Setup Wizard (see Figure 17.35).

**Figure 17.35**
You can decide which components of the Personal Web Server you want to install.

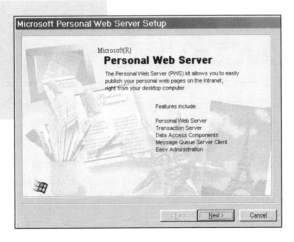

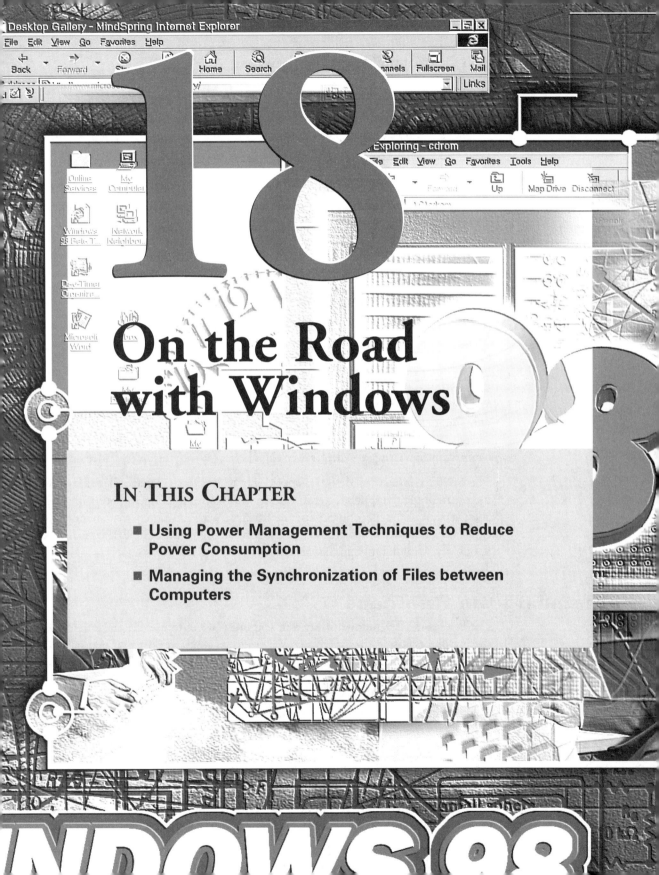

# 18

# On the Road with Windows

## IN THIS CHAPTER

- Using Power Management Techniques to Reduce Power Consumption
- Managing the Synchronization of Files between Computers

Many people use computers to work both at the office and away from the office. Often, the computer used away from the office is a notebook computer. In this chapter, I'll discuss how you can keep files "in sync" between the office computer and the other computer. Then, I'll describe power management techniques that you can apply to your notebook computer to help extend its battery life. And although the concept of power management seems to apply primarily to notebook computers, in Windows 98 you can apply the power management tools and techniques you'll learn about in this chapter to desktop computers as well.

# Using the Briefcase to Manage Updates between Computers

In this era, with the number of computers in use growing at an astronomical rate, people frequently take computer files home or on the road, make changes, and then return to the office with the files. Some files go back and forth several times, and you can forget which version of the file is "the latest." If you're working with only one file, the situation isn't that difficult to manage; if you're working with several files and several people are making changes simultaneously, it can become cumbersome. We suggest you let Windows help you—by using the Briefcase.

The Briefcase is a utility designed specifically to help you manage files that you use on multiple computers—and to keep both computers up-to-date with the latest version of the file. You can use the Briefcase with computers that are linked, either via a network or via a cable connection, or you can use the Briefcase and a floppy disk with computers that are not linked.

## Installing the Briefcase

The Briefcase is a Windows utility that you must install to use. To make the file-sharing process using the Briefcase easier to understand, assume that you have a main computer and a notebook computer on which you share files. If the two computers are not connected and you will use a floppy disk to share files between them, you should install the Briefcase on the main computer. If, however, the two computers are connected via LAN, dial-up, or direct cable connection, install the Briefcase on the notebook computer. Open the Control Panel (choose Start, Settings, Control Panel) and click on the Add/Remove Programs icon to display the Add/Remove Programs Properties box.

In the Add/Remove Programs Properties box, click on the Windows Setup tab. Highlight the Accessories component and click on the Details button to display the Accessories dialog box. Place a check next to the Briefcase component and choose OK. Choose OK in the Add/Remove Programs Properties box, and Windows will install the Briefcase.

If you had ever previously installed the Briefcase, you won't see it in the Accessories dialog box. But if you don't see the icon on your Desktop (because it was deleted), you can create a Briefcase.

## Hands On: Creating a New Briefcase

If you don't have a Briefcase icon and can't install the Briefcase because it doesn't appear on the Windows Setup tab of the Add/Remove Programs box, follow these steps to create a new Briefcase.

1. Open Windows Explorer (right-click on the Start button and choose Explore).

2. Select the folder in which you want to store the Briefcase.

• • • • • • • • • • • • • • • • • • • • • • • • • • • • • • • • • • • • • • • • • • • • • • • • • • • • •

If you want the Briefcase to appear on your Desktop, open the \Windows\Desktop folder.

• • • • • • • • • • • • • • • • • • • • • • • • • • • • • • • • • • • • • • • • • • • • • • • • • • • • •

3. Choose File, New, Briefcase (see Figure 18.1). Windows creates a Briefcase icon in the folder you selected.

**Figure 18.1**
Create a new Briefcase icon from Windows Explorer.

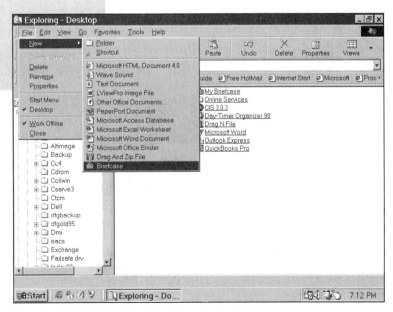

# Synchronizing Computer Files Using a Floppy Disk

Now that you have the Briefcase installed, use it to make sure that both computers have "the latest" version of the files that you use on both computers. You move files into the Briefcase to use them on another computer; if the two computers cannot be connected, use a floppy disk.

## Hands On: Using a Floppy Disk to Work in the Briefcase

If the two computers on which you want to share files are in separate geographic locations and you have no means to connect them, use the Briefcase and a floppy disk to move files between them.

1. Use Windows Explorer to copy by dragging the files you intend to use on both computers to the Briefcase on the main computer (see Figure 18.2).

2. Release the mouse button after dragging the files to the Briefcase. You'll see the dialog box that appears in Figure 18.3.

3. Insert a floppy disk into the disk drive.

**Figure 18.2**
Copying files to the Briefcase.

Figure 18.3
The first time
you copy files to
the Briefcase,
you'll see this
dialog box,
which is an
overview of the
Briefcase.

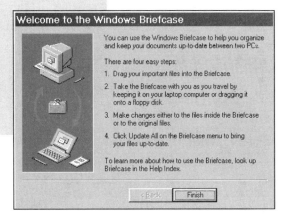

Figure 18.3
The first time
you copy files to
the Briefcase,
you'll see this
dialog box,
which is an
overview of the
Briefcase.

4. Move the Briefcase to a floppy disk by opening My Computer and opening the disk drive. Then right-drag (press and hold the *right* mouse button while dragging) the Briefcase into the disk drive window. When you release the mouse button, choose Move Here (see Figure 18.4). Windows copies the Briefcase to the floppy disk.

5. Take the floppy disk to the notebook computer and insert it in the disk drive.

Figure 18.4
Moving the
Briefcase to a
floppy disk.

**Figure 18.5**
Open files in the Briefcase the same way you open files stored in any folder on any drive.

6. Use your program's Open dialog box to open a file in the Briefcase (see Figure 18.5) or double-click on a file in the Briefcase to start its associated program.

*Note*

**It is important to move, not copy, the Briefcase.**

*Tip*

Although the Briefcase icon is different from the traditional icon used for a folder, the Briefcase is simply a folder with special properties. You can, to speed up your work, copy the files from the Briefcase to the hard disk of the notebook computer. When you finish, be sure to copy the files back to the Briefcase.

7. Work on the file and save it to the Briefcase on the floppy disk.

Eventually, you'll be ready to move the files back to the main computer.

### Hands On: Moving Files from the Floppy Disk Briefcase to the Main Computer

When you're ready to work on the main computer again, use the Briefcase to move modified files.

1. Take the floppy disk to the main computer and insert it in the main computer's disk drive.
2. Open My Computer and your floppy drive so that you can see the Briefcase on the floppy disk.
3. Open the Briefcase on the floppy disk (see Figure 18.6).
4. Choose Update All on the toolbar. Or select a file and choose Update Selection. Windows displays the Update My Briefcase dialog box (see Figure 18.7), which shows the actions Windows will take if you choose Update.

You can change these actions by right-clicking on the file in the Update My Briefcase dialog box.

**Figure 18.6**
Viewing the contents of the Briefcase on floppy disk.

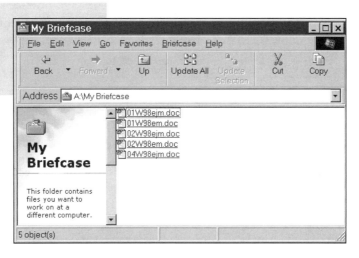

**Figure 18.7**
Use this dialog
box to
synchronize files
between the
Briefcase and the
main computer.

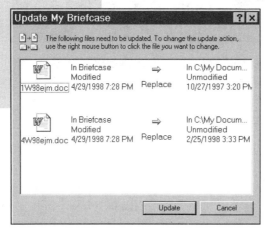

5. Choose Update. Windows replaces the older version on the main computer with the newer version on the floppy disk. Unchanged files don't appear in the Update My Briefcase dialog box.

*Note*

If someone in your office changes one of the files you placed in your Briefcase, Windows will let you choose whether you want to update the copy in your Briefcase. If you changed the Briefcase copy and someone in your office changed the original copy of the same file, Windows warns you so that you can check both copies of the file to determine which version you want to keep.

# Synchronizing Computer Files between Connected Computers

You can use the Briefcase with computers that are connected using a LAN connection, dial-up connection, or a direct cable connection.

See Chapter 16 for information on connecting computers using a direct cable or dial-up networking connection. See Chapter 14 for information on connecting computers using a LAN connection.

## Hands On: Copying Files to the Briefcase When Computers Are Connected

If a LAN, a dial-up, or a direct cable connection connects the two computers on which you want to share files, you can copy files to the Briefcase using that connection.

1. Open Windows Explorer by right-clicking on the Start button and choosing Explore.

2. Copy the files you intend to use on both computers from the main computer to the Briefcase on the notebook computer (see Figure 18.8). Highlight the files you want to copy, right-click, and choose Copy. Then open the Briefcase on the notebook computer (Drive E in the figure), right-click, and choose Paste.

3. Move to the notebook computer.

4. Use your program's Open dialog box to open a file in the Briefcase or click on a file in the Briefcase to start its associated program.

*Tip*

• • • • • • • • • • • • • • • • • • • • • • • • • • • • • • • • • • • • • • • • • • • • • • • • • • •

Remember, the Briefcase icon is different from the traditional icon used for a folder, but the Briefcase is simply a folder with special properties. You can open the Briefcase by clicking on it.

• • • • • • • • • • • • • • • • • • • • • • • • • • • • • • • • • • • • • • • • • • • • • • • • • • •

**Figure 18.8**
Copying files to
the Briefcase.

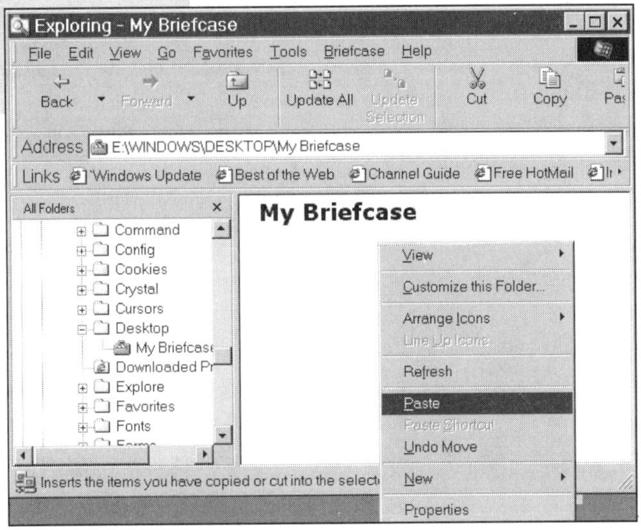

5. Work on the file and save it to the Briefcase on the notebook computer. Eventually, you'll be ready to move the files back to the main computer.

## Hands On: Moving Files from the Briefcase on the Notebook to the Main Computer

When you're ready to work on the main computer again, connect the computers and use the modified files in the Briefcase to update the main computer.

1. Connect the two computers using a LAN, a dial-up, or a direct cable connection.

2. Use Windows Explorer on the main computer to open the Briefcase on the notebook. In Figure 18.9, the notebook is Drive E and the Briefcase resides on the Desktop of the notebook.

3. Choose Update All. Or select a file and choose Update Selection. Windows displays the Update My Briefcase dialog box (see Figure 18.10).

4. Click on Update. Windows replaces the older version on the main computer with the newer version in the Briefcase on the notebook computer. Unchanged files don't appear in the Update My Briefcase dialog box.

**Figure 18.9**
Viewing the contents of the Briefcase on the notebook computer from the main computer.

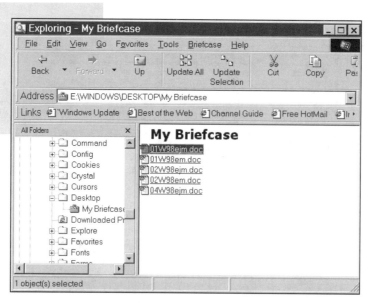

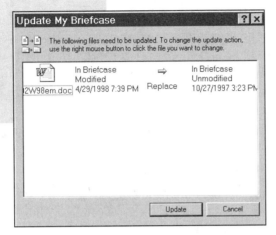

**Figure 18.10**
Synchronizing files between the Briefcase on the notebook computer and the main computer.

*Note*

**If someone in your office changes one of the files you placed in your Briefcase, Windows will let you choose whether you want to update the copy in your Briefcase. If you changed the Briefcase copy and someone in your office changed the original copy of the same file, Windows warns you so that you can check both copies of the file to determine which version you want to keep.**

# Managing Your Computer's Power

BIOS stands for Basic Input Output System. The BIOS is a piece of software that, at its most elemental level, is responsible for performing all the tasks that occur when your computer starts. For example, the BIOS performs a power-on self-test to check for standard hardware devices such as a floppy disk drive and a hard disk drive. The BIOS also looks for, and passes control to, an operating system on either a floppy disk or a hard disk. And, in the past, the computer's power consumption was managed by the computer's BIOS.

Advanced Configuration and Power Interface (ACPI) is a new power management specification that intends to save power by placing full control of the computer's power management in the operating system. As we explained in Chapter 1, ACPI contains the OnNow feature, which is similar to a notebook computer's resume

*Note*

You may have added, at some point, components to your computer and discovered they wouldn't work unless you "updated your BIOS." Because the BIOS is responsible for recognizing hardware, you need a recent version of the BIOS to recognize newer hardware.

feature. ACPI monitors the devices on your computer and shuts down any device not being used—including drives, monitors, and even the power supply's fan—to minimize power consumption and extend battery life.

If your computer supports ACPI and OnNow and uses Windows 98 as the operating system, you won't need to power off your machine. The OnNow feature, in conjunction with power schemes, will make your computer "go to sleep"—and allow you to immediately resume your original work without rebooting your computer. In the near future, turning on your computer will seem more like turning on a TV, radio, and or stereo. And computers that seem to be off can do work like download files, receive faxes and mail, back up, or tune up the operating system.

*Note*

You can use power management tools on any computer that supports power management—not just notebook computers. Depending on the age of your computer, you may be able to use some of the power management tools discussed in this chapter. Generally, the various power management tools available on your computer appear in the Power Management Properties box. If you think your computer is capable of power management and you don't see the options discussed in this chapter, contact the manufacturer of your computer.

If components of your computer support power management, you can control the behavior of these components. You can use a power scheme to reduce the power consumption of any of your computer components or of your entire system. A *power scheme* is a collection of settings that manages your computer's power usage. You can use Windows 98 default power schemes, modify the defaults, or create your own power scheme. If your system supports standby and hibernation, you also can control the way the computer uses these power management tools. Open the Control Panel (choose Start, Settings, Control Panel) and click on the Power Management icon. The Power Management Properties dialog box appears (see Figure 18.11).

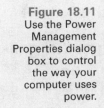

**Figure 18.11**
Use the Power Management Properties dialog box to control the way your computer uses power.

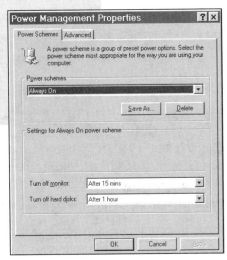

On the Power Schemes tab, open the Power Schemes list box and choose a power scheme. To modify the scheme, use the list boxes to change the time frame associated with the event. To save the power scheme, click on the Save As button and supply a name. From the Advanced tab, choose the behavior patterns you want to enable.

**Figure 18.12**
You can place an icon that opens the Power Management Properties box in your System Tray.

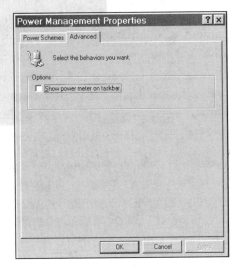

If your computer supports standby or hibernation, you'll see additional options specifically for these power management tools on the tabs of this dialog box.

## Standby Mode and Hibernation

Standby and hibernation are two methods you can use to conserve power. In both methods, your computer "rests" and uses less power, but can also perform activities such as send and receive faxes, make backups, and download files.

If you plan to be away from your computer for a while, you can place your computer in standby mode. Standby is particularly useful for conserving battery power in portable computers. While on standby, your computer seems to shut down, but, in fact, it is still running; it just uses less power.

While a computer is in standby mode, information in the computer's memory is vulnerable to loss from power interruptions. (Information on the hard disk has already been saved and is therefore not vulnerable.) You should save your work before putting your computer on standby so that no information will be lost if a power outage occurs or you need to change a notebook computer's battery.

Some computers support hibernation as a form of power management. Like Standby mode, hibernation appears to shut down your computer. Hibernation has two behavioral characters you won't find with Standby mode:

- Windows saves everything in memory to your hard disk when you place the computer in hibernation.

- Bringing a computer out of hibernation takes longer than bringing a computer out of standby mode.

You would put your computer in hibernation when you expect to be away from the computer for an extended time, such as overnight. When you restart the computer, typically by pressing the computer's power switch, your Desktop looks exactly the same as when you left it.

# A
# Upgrading to Windows 98

## IN THIS APPENDIX

- **Windows 98 System Requirements**
- **Installing Windows 98**
- **Uninstalling Windows 98**
- **Registering Online**

If you go out today and buy a new computer, it will most likely have Windows 98 preinstalled on it. But if you're upgrading from an earlier version of Microsoft Windows, you'll be pleasantly surprised with the ease of installing Windows 98.

Setup is a very simple process with Windows 98 and requires very little interaction between you and the computer. During the Setup process, Windows 98 recognizes your current configuration on the PC and retains those settings.

Windows 98 easily detects your hardware and existing software and it has a built-in setup recovery system. If the setup process should fail in the middle, Windows 98 remembers where it left off and begins at that step. This feature saves time because you won't have to redo the successful installation steps.

Windows 98 can be installed on or over a network. Windows 98 offers the same networking capabilities as Windows 95 but also has added provisions for better support of networks.

# System Requirements

To run Windows 98, your PC must be at least a 486-based machine with a minimum of 16MB of RAM memory. This requirement is, indeed, a minimum. If you only have the minimum requirements, expect Windows 98 to run very slowly. If you can add memory to your "minimum" PC, you'll see a marked improvement in performance. Disk space requirements vary with the options you install and with the FAT file system you are using, but you can expect to use anywhere from 120MB to 350MB of hard disk space.

# Installing the Windows 98 Upgrade

Installation of the Windows 98 upgrade requires six basic steps, all of which are run almost automatically by the Setup program. Step 1 checks your existing system information. Step 2 asks for your agreement to Microsoft licensing terms and prepares you for uninstallation if necessary. Step 3 creates a Startup disk, step 4 copies the files from the installation disk to your computer, step 5 detects the hardware on your machine, and step 6 detects your current configuration and matches it with Windows 98.

# Step 1

Insert the Windows 98 CD-ROM. If you are installing Windows 98 over Windows 95, when you insert the Windows 98 CD-ROM a dialog box immediately appears. Windows detects that the version of software on the CD-ROM is newer than the existing operating system. The Windows 98 Setup program asks if you want to upgrade now. Click on Yes to continue.

*Note*

**If you are upgrading from Windows 3.*x*, the Windows 98 CD-ROM may not pop up automatically. If it doesn't, click on File and then click on Run. From the Run box, type E:SETUP. If E is not the drive letter for your CD-ROM drive, then use the appropriate letter.**

Windows first checks out your existing system; you can track the process with the progress bar. On the left side of your screen, a display lists the steps to be done during the upgrade and the estimated time remaining to accomplish it. The current step is displayed in yellow.

The exact time depends on the speed and configuration of your machine. It can range from about 30 minutes to an hour or more. I did one installation on a Pentium 100 megahertz machine with 64MB of RAM memory that took approximately 45 minutes.

# Step 2

The Windows 98 Setup Wizard begins and displays the Microsoft licensing agreement. Read through the agreement. You can press the Page Down key to see more of it. When you have completed reading the agreement, you must tell Windows that you agree with its terms. Click on "I Accept This Agreement" and then click on Next.

The Setup Wizard begins collecting information about your computer, including the components that are already installed in your existing operating system. Next, it checks for available disk space. If you don't have enough, a dialog box advises you that Setup cannot continue.

The Setup Wizard asks you about saving the existing system files so you can uninstall Windows 98 if necessary. This step requires an additional 50MB of disk space. If you want to save the existing files, click on Yes, which is the Microsoft recommendation, or click on No if you don't want those files saved. You will not be able to uninstall Windows 98 if you choose No. Click on Next to continue to the next screen.

The CD key code that Setup asks for pertains to your license to use Windows 98. This code could be located in one of two places. First, look on the CD-ROM case. Second, look on the certificate of authenticity that came with your Windows 98 upgrade. Enter the CD code in the available box and then click on Next to continue.

Now the Setup Wizard asks about which Internet Channels you want to use. Internet Channels enable you to get region-specific news and other information through Channels, which are Web sites designed to deliver content from the Internet to your computer. Choose your country from the selections available and click on Next to continue to the next screen.

## Step 3

The Setup Wizard creates a Startup disk for you to use if you later have trouble starting Windows 98. Creating a Startup disk isn't mandatory, but I highly recommend it. You know—better safe than sorry. Click on Next to continue to the next screen.

Insert a floppy disk into the floppy disk drive. If the floppy disk has existing files on it, those files will be erased. Click on OK to continue.

• • • • • • • • • • • • • • • • • • • • • • • • • • • • • • • • • • • • • • • • • • • • • • • •

If you do not want to create a Startup disk, click on Cancel.

• • • • • • • • • • • • • • • • • • • • • • • • • • • • • • • • • • • • • • • • • • • • • • • •

Setup transfers the files that are necessary to start your computer using a floppy disk. A message box appears when the startup disk is complete. Remove the disk from the disk drive and label the disk "Emergency Windows 98 Startup Disk." Store this disk in a safe, convenient place; then click on OK to continue the setup process.

## Step 4

Now you're ready to get down to the nitty gritty. The Setup Wizard has enough information about your systems and is ready to start copying Windows 98 files to your hard drive. Click on Next to continue.

This part may take a little while. The Welcome to Windows 98 screen is displayed with some pretty fluffy clouds and information about Windows 98's new features and enhancements. These screens change periodically, and they are kind of interesting to read. On the left side of the screen, a progress indicator keeps you up-to-date on the status of the upgrade.

At several different points, the Setup Wizard will restart your machine. It does so automatically, so you don't have to do anything. As your machine is restarting, you'll see a message—Please Wait While Setup Updates Your Configuration Files. This May Take a Few Minutes. The Windows opening screen appears with a message that it is getting ready to run Windows for the first time.

The Setup program then jumps back to the black screen that appears when you first turn on your computer and advises you that it has completed updating files and is continuing to load Windows 98.

## Step 5

The Windows 98 Setup Wizard reappears and begins looking for hardware attached to your machine.

*Note*

**If the computer stops responding for a long time, turn it off and then back on.**

Again, Setup will restart your computer, and you will see the same type of updating messages that were displayed the last time Windows 98 restarted.

Windows may ask you to please insert the Windows 98 CD-ROM. It's probably still in the CD drive. If not, put it back in and click on OK. The hardware detection process continues.

## Step 6

Almost there! Setup now sets up Control Panel, Start menu items, Help, DOS programs settings, system configuration, and other settings. It is also looking for the various software programs you have installed on your machine and configures them to work with Windows 98. A small box announces that Windows 98 is updating system settings, and Windows restarts one more time!

When Windows restarts this time, it finishes building a driver database and sets up personalized settings for other Windows components, such as Internet Explorer 4, Multimedia, Channels, and Accessories. The dialog box displayed as Windows sets up each component appears several times.

Finally! You're finished! Windows 98 has been installed, and you're ready to use it!

# Uninstalling Windows 98

Microsoft hopes you'll like Windows 98 so much you won't want to remove it, but you can if you want to, provided that you allowed Windows to back up your system files on the hard disk when you were installing Windows 98.

Microsoft gives you two ways to uninstall Windows 98. The first is to insert the Windows 98 CD-ROM into the drive and click on Add/Remove Software when the opening screen appears. The other method is to select Add/Remove Programs from the Windows Control Panel.

Either way, when the Add/Remove Programs Properties box appears, choose Windows from the Install/Uninstall tab, and then click on the Add/Remove button. The uninstall process will begin.

# Online Registration Wizard

You should register your software. Microsoft can then notify you of updates or other information concerning Windows 98. Usually, when you buy software, you fill out a registration card and mail it to the manufacturer. Microsoft has made it a little more convenient to get that task completed and over with quickly and easily. You can now register via your computer's modem. It's more convenient for you and for Microsoft to handle registration using this method.

One of the first items to be displayed after you install Windows 98 is the Welcome to Windows 98 screen, as shown in Figure A.1. If you have speakers and a sound card on your machine, you also hear about 10 seconds of music associated with this screen.

This screen greets you and gives you a quick tour of the new features of Windows 98. It also has a spot for you to register your software.

Click on Register Now to start the Registration Wizard. Follow the screens and enter your personal information such as name, address, company, and phone (see Figure A.2).

The next screen asks where you purchased your copy of Microsoft Windows 98. Notice in Figure A.3 that this screen also asks whether you want to receive offers of non-Microsoft products and services. If you like getting this type of information, click on Yes, then click on Next.

Another registration option asks whether you want to send a system inventory to Microsoft, which consists of a list of your hardware, memory, disk space, and so on. This information assists Microsoft in the development of software that meets the needs of its users. Figure A.4 shows a sample system information screen.

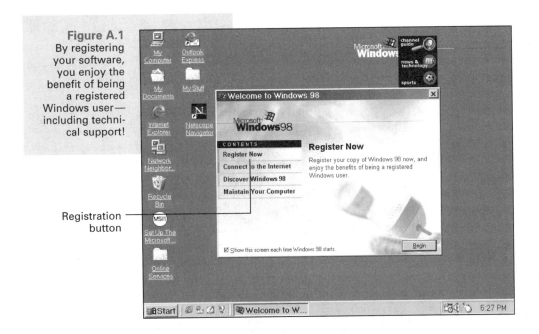

**Figure A.1**
By registering your software, you enjoy the benefit of being a registered Windows user—including technical support!

Registration button

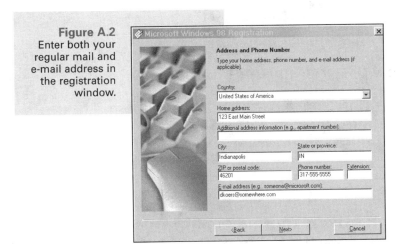

**Figure A.2**
Enter both your regular mail and e-mail address in the registration window.

If you decide not to send this information to Microsoft, rest assured that it **will not** be sent. The Registration Wizard doesn't send any information you don't authorize.

Click on Next to continue to the final registration screen. When you click on Register, the Registration Wizard connects to Microsoft and sends the information. The process takes only a few minutes, and you're registered!

**Figure A.3**
Click on No if
you don't want
to receive extra
advertisements.

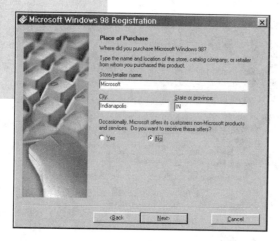

**Figure A.4**
Sending the
system inventory
is optional.

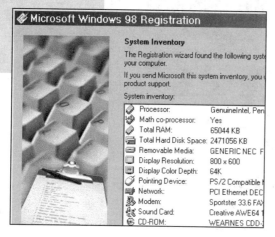

*Note*

**If you need to update your registration, click on the Start menu, choose Run, and then type REGWIZ /R. The Registration Wizard starts, and you can update the information you sent to Microsoft.**

# Windows 98 and TV

## IN THIS APPENDIX

- **Hardware Requirements**
- **Installing the TV Viewer**
- **Using the TV Viewer**

As you learned in Chapter 1, Windows 98 supports TV viewing from your computer. To actually take advantage of Windows 98's support for TV, you need some special hardware in your computer; if you install that hardware, then you also need to install the Web TV for Windows applet.

If you don't own the hardware to actually view TV on your computer—and the hardware is very new at this stage—you can still use the Web TV for Windows applet to download the television programming available in your area from the Internet. After you download the Program Guide, you can ask Windows to remind you when programs that you want to watch are coming up—so that you don't miss them.

# Hardware Requirements for a Broadcast-Enabled Computer

A TV tuner card, typically a video card that supports broadcast viewing—such as the ATI All-in-Wonder or ATI All-in-Wonder Pro—is only one piece of hardware that you need if you want to watch TV on your PC. Microsoft supplies the minimum and recommended hardware in a Knowledge Base article found at the following Web site:

http://support.microsoft.com/support/kb/articles/q182/7/53.asp

The minimum hardware configuration and the recommended hardware configuration you'll find at that Web site appear below.

## Minimum Hardware Configuration

- Intel Pentium 120 MHz processor or compatible
- High-speed bus with adequate slots to accommodate high-speed broadcast network and video card
- 16MB RAM
- 1GB hard disk
- 27" SVGA display capable of 640x480 resolution with 60 Hz noninterlaced refresh rate
- 3.5" 1.44MB floppy disk drive
- Quad-speed CD-ROM drive
- 14,400 bps internal or external modem (TAPI compatible)
- Standard computer keyboard
- Pointing device with two buttons

## Recommended Hardware Configuration

- Intel Pentium 150 MHz processor
- PCI bus with at least four slots available
- Consumer-electronics-style case with low-noise fan or noiseless cooling system (OnNow capable)
- Support for Simply Interactive PC (SIPC) initiatives such as OnNow, Device Bay, IEEE 1394, and USB to provide a more consumer-friendly appearance
- 16MB RAM or more
- 2GB or larger hard disk with fast data transfer rate
- 3.5" 1.44MB floppy drive
- 6x-speed CD-ROM drive or DVD-ROM
- 31" display capable of 800x600 resolution with 60 Hz noninterlaced refresh rate
- 28,800 bps or higher internal fax modem (AT command set compatible)
- Wireless (RF or IR), battery-operated keyboard with built-in pointing device
- Wireless TV-style remote control
- Battery-operated, combination remote control/wireless mouse with power/sleep button, TV buttons (channel up/down, volume up/down, mute, TV)
- Sound system expansion card with digital audio (wave) support, a MIDI port, a MIDI-controlled wave table synthesizer, multiple analog and digital audio inputs, software-controllable low-noise audio mixer/preamplifier, and multiple audio outputs
- A built-in microphone or a front-mounted microphone jack suitable for teleconferencing, education, karaoke, and other applications requiring sound input
- AC-3 audio decoding for DVD compatibility
- IR blaster capable of controlling consumer electronic devices

# Installing Web TV for Windows

By default, the Web TV for Windows applet is not installed when you install Windows 98. You install the applet from the Control Panel.

## Hands On: Installing the TV Viewer Applet

1. Choose Start, Settings, Control Panel to open the Control Panel window.

2. Click the Add/Remove Programs icon to display the Add/Remove Programs Properties box and then click the Windows Setup tab.

3. Scroll down the Components list (see Figure B.1) until you see Web TV for Windows.

**Figure B.1**
Use the Windows Setup tab to install the Web TV applet.

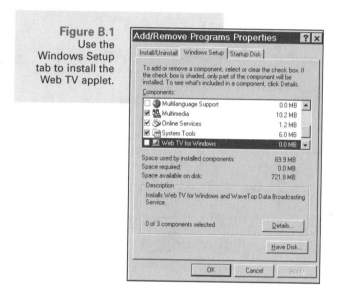

4. Place a check in the Web TV check box and click on OK. You will be prompted to insert your Windows 98 CD-ROM, and Windows will install the applet. You'll also need to restart your computer when the installation completes.

After you restart your computer, Windows will want to connect you to the Internet if that doesn't happen automatically; in addition, you'll see two new icons on the Desktop: one on the Quick Launch toolbar and one in the System Tray (see Figure B.2).

The Launch Web TV for Windows icon helps you launch the Web TV applet so that you can download a list of TV programs available in your area—if you also have a broadcast-enabled PC, you use the TV Viewer to watch TV on your PC.

The Web TV for Windows Video and Data Services icon works with the Web TV applet to bring you program information.

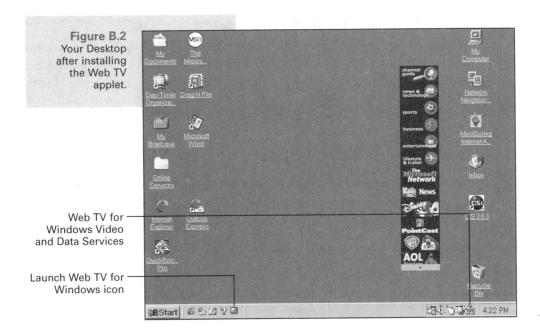

**Figure B.2**
Your Desktop after installing the Web TV applet.

Web TV for Windows Video and Data Services

Launch Web TV for Windows icon

*Note*

**You may notice, after shutting down your computer, that the Web TV for Windows Video and Data Services icon appears in the System Tray only if you launch the Web TV for Windows applet.**

# Using Web TV

If your PC is broadcast enabled and you want to watch TV on your computer, you must use the Web TV for Windows applet to download program listings scheduled for broadcast in your area. By downloading program listings, you set up your local TV channels.

*Tip*

Even if your PC does not contain the hardware necessary to become broadcast enabled, you can use the Web TV applet to download a program guide and schedule reminders.

# Downloading TV Program Listings

Program listings are similar to the information typically listed in your newspaper's TV section. When you click on the Launch Web TV for Windows icon for the first time, Microsoft Web TV for Windows program opens and starts a wizard. The wizard supplies information using both audio and video, and guides you through the process of setting up your computer to use Web TV.

*Note*

**Because the Microsoft Web TV is graphics intensive, be patient. When the wizard is running, you won't see a title bar for a window or the Taskbar. If you need to navigate back to Windows, use the Windows key on your keyboard to display the Start menu and the Taskbar.**

After you click on Next a few times, you'll see a screen that contains a web link that you can use to search for program listings (see Figure B.3).

The G-Guide web link launches your browser and asks you for your zip code so that you can look for program listings in your area (see Figure B4).

On the next screen (see Figure B.5), click on the Get Listings button, and you'll see bytes being transferred. After the download, the Loader, which loads program listings into the Web TV applet, runs. The Loader measures its progress in sec-

**Figure B.3**
Click on G-Guide
to look for
download free
TV program
listings.

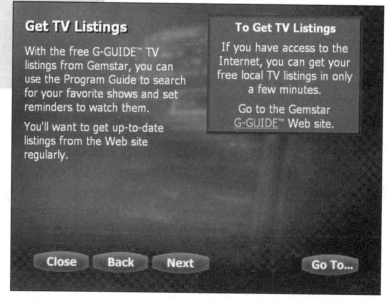

**Get TV Listings**

With the free G-GUIDE™ TV listings from Gemstar, you can use the Program Guide to search for your favorite shows and set reminders to watch them.

You'll want to get up-to-date listings from the Web site regularly.

**To Get TV Listings**

If you have access to the Internet, you can get your free local TV listings in only a few minutes.

Go to the Gemstar G-GUIDE™ Web site.

Close     Back     Next                    Go To...

Figure B.4
Select the correct broadcast area or cable system for your region and click on Save.

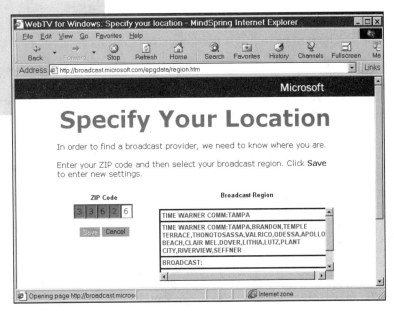

Figure B.5
Download Program Listings

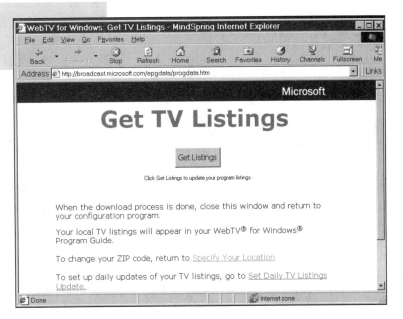

onds—and should take about 90 seconds to complete using a 28.8 modem. The process should take no longer than 10 minutes. You'll know that the download process has completed because you'll see a message just below the Get Listings button telling you the Loader has completed.

Once the download process ends, you can close your browser (if you connect through an ISP, you can also close the connection) and return to the Web TV applet. The wizard continues to teach you how to use the Web TV applet. When you complete the wizard by clicking on Finish, you'll see a screen similar to the one in Figure B.6.

To view the listings, use the scroll bars at the side and the bottom of the window. To view listings for yesterday or tomorrow, open the list box showing the date at the top of the window and choose either yesterday or tomorrow. To get more information about any listing in the Program Guide, connect to the Internet, highlight that listing, and click the web link that appears on the right side of the screen. To revise listings, connect to the Internet, if necessary, and then use the Web TV for Windows wizard, also known as the Configuration channel. To display the wizard once again, double-click the TV Configuration channel that appears in the Program Guide. Then, click the Go To button (see Figure B.7).

From the menu, choose Get TV Listings. You'll see the G-Guide link once again. Click it to launch your browser and download listings as you did earlier. When you return to the wizard, redisplay the Program Guide by clicking Close.

## Setting Up a Reminder

You can have the Web TV applet remind you about an upcoming program that you want to watch. To set up a reminder for a program, click the program—

**Figure B.6**
A sample Program Guide listing.

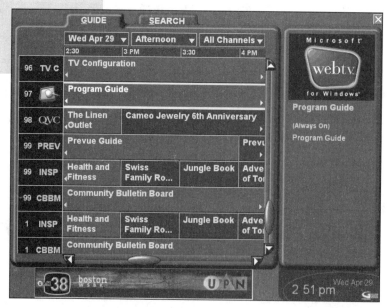

**Figure B.7**
Click the Go To button to open a menu of choices.

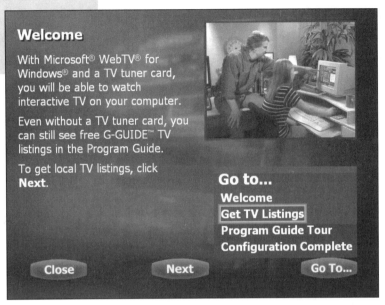

the viewing time must be in the future. Then click on the Remind button (see Figure B.8).

The dialog box in Figure B.9 will appear, allowing you to set up a single reminder or a repeated reminder. Further, you can set the amount of notice you want (up

**Figure B.8**
Click on the Remind button to set up a reminder.

Remind button

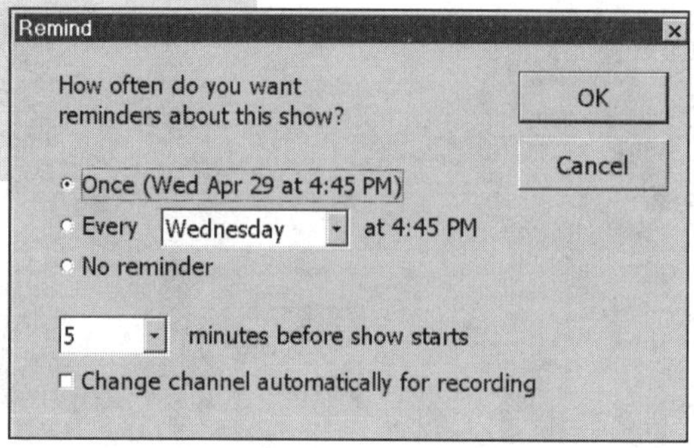

**Figure B.9**
Set up a
reminder in this
dialog box.

> **Remind**         ☒
>
> How often do you want         [ OK ]
> reminders about this show?
>
>                                   [ Cancel ]
>
> ⦿ Once (Wed Apr 29 at 4:45 PM)
> ○ Every [ Wednesday ▾ ] at 4:45 PM
> ○ No reminder
>
> [ 5 ▾ ] minutes before show starts
> ☐ Change channel automatically for recording

to 30 minutes) before the program begins. If your PC is broadcast enabled and you want to record the program using a VCR that you have attached to your TV tuner card, you can enable that option as well.

To close the Web TV for Windows applet, click on the X in the upper-right corner.

When appropriate, if your system is on and not asleep, a reminder like the one in Figure B.10 appears on-screen—regardless of what you're doing at the time. That is, you don't need to be watching TV to see a reminder.

*Note*

**If your system is asleep, only a reminder to record will wake it up; any other type of reminder will be ignored.**

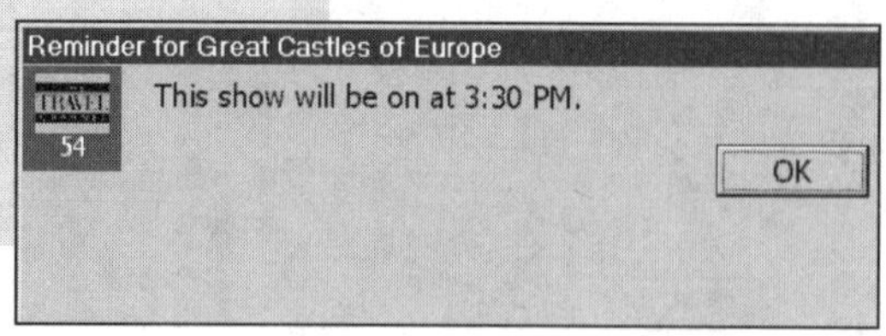

**Figure B.10**
A typical
reminder from
the TV Viewer.

> **Reminder for Great Castles of Europe**
>
> This show will be on at 3:30 PM.
>
> TRAVEL
> 54                              [ OK ]

# Glossary

**Accelerated Graphics Port**. A PC connection for high-end video boards to use main memory for 3-D acceleration.

**Access Number**. The telephone number used to dial into an online service such as Microsoft Network, America Online, or CompuServe.

**Active Desktop**. A feature to customize the Windows Desktop to display information that you can update from the Internet. A term that is synonymous with viewing the Desktop as a Web page.

**Active Movie**. Digital video technology developed for online and desktop multimedia.

**Active Window**. The last window you worked on. The active windows is designated by a different color toolbar than other open windows.

**Alignment**. The arrangement of text to the margins of a document or the edges of a table cell. Also called *justification*.

**AOL**. (America Online) A widely used online information service offering access service to the Internet.

**Applet**. A small piece of code that can be transported over the Internet and executed on the recipient's machine. The term is especially used to refer to such programs as they are embedded in line as objects in HTML documents on the World Wide Web.

**Application**. Computer programs designed to enable users to perform specific job functions. Word processing, accounting, and engineering programs are examples of application programs.

**AT&T WorldNet**. A widely used Internet access service.

**Attributes**. Items that determine the appearance of text such as bolding, underlining, italics, or point size.

**Back Up**. To make additional copies of your computer files so that you don't lose your data to an unexpected disaster.

**Bar Chart**. A type of chart that uses bars to represent values. Normally used to compare items.

**Baud**. The conventional unit of measurement used to describe data transmission speed. One baud is 1 bit per second.

**Baud Rate**. The speed at which data is transmitted from one digital device to another, such as over a modem or between a computer and printer. The devices must be configured at the same baud rate for information to transfer between them correctly.

**BIOS**. Basic Input/Output System. The set of essential software routines that test hardware at startup, start the operating system, and support the transfer of data among hardware devices. The BIOS is stored in read-only memory (ROM) so that it can be executed when the computer is turned on. The BIOS is usually invisible to computer users.

**Bitmap**. A graphics file format made up of small dots.

**Block**. To highlight text that will be affected by the next action.

**Bold**. A font attribute that makes text thicker and brighter.

**Border**. A line surrounding paragraphs, pages, or objects.

**Briefcase**. A special folder on the Windows Desktop used to keep documents up-to-date when they are shared between computers.

**Browser**. A software program especially designed for viewing Web pages on the Internet.

**Bullet**. A symbol, such as a filled circle, that may precede each item in a list.

**Button**. A graphics representation of an option or a command that activates the option.

**Byte**. The amount of space needed to store a single character, such as a number or a letter. 1,024 bytes equal 1 kilobyte (KB).

**Cache**. A special section of random access memory (RAM) in a computer that is continually updated to contain recently accessed contents of main storage. Cache memory provides faster access to data by serving as a temporary storage area between the main storage area, which can be slower, and the CPU.

**Card**. A removable circuit board that is plugged into an expansion slot inside the computer (such as a graphics card, sound card, or fax card).

**Cascading Menu**. An additional list of menu items opening from a single menu item.

**CD-ROM**. (Compact disc[nd]read-only memory) Means of data storage using optical storage technology. A single CD-ROM can hold more than 650 megabytes of information, or half a billion characters of text.

**Cell**. The intersection of a row and column in a table or spreadsheet.

**Channels**. A link to Web sites used to transfer information from the Internet to your computer.

**Chart**. A graphics representation of data. Also called a *graph*.

**Check Box**. A small box next to an option in a dialog box. Clicking an empty check box selects the option; clicking a marked check box deselects the option.

**Check Mark**. A mark placed next to a menu item that is turned on or next to items in list boxes that are active. When the item is turned off or when it is not active, the check mark is removed.

**Choose**. To use a mouse or the keyboard to pick a menu item or dialog box option that initiates an immediate action. Compare with *select*.

**Clear**. To remove the X from a check box or to remove a check mark from a menu item. If the box is clear or the menu item has no check mark, that option is turned off.

**Click**. To push and release the mouse button.

**Clip Art**. A piece of artwork to be inserted into a document.

**Clipboard**. An area of computer memory where text or graphics can be temporarily stored. It is a holding place for items that have been cut or copied. The item remains on the Clipboard until you cut or copy an additional item or until you turn off the computer.

**Close Button**. The small X in the upper right corner of a window. Used to shut down or exit a dialog box, window, or application.

**Command**. An instruction given to a computer to carry out a particular action.

**Command Button**. A button in a dialog box that carries out a command such as Open, Close, Exit, OK, or Cancel. The selected command button is indicated by a different appearance, such as a dotted rectangle or another color.

**Comment**. Used to add annotations to a document. Comments do not print with the document.

**CompuServe**. A widely used online information service offering access service to the Internet.

**Connect Charge**. The fee that a user must pay for the privilege of having access to an online information service or Internet access. Generally, a connect charge is based on a monthly rate.

**Control Panel**. A group of utilities that control aspects of the operating system or hardware, such as system time and date, keyboard characteristics, and networking parameters.

**Conversion**. A process by which files created in one application are changed to a format that can be used in another application.

**Copy**. To take a selection from the document and duplicate it to another location.

**CPU**. (Central processing unit) The basic component of a computer, where commands are executed.

**Cursor**. A symbol (usually a blinking horizontal or vertical bar) that designates the position on the screen where text or codes will be inserted or deleted. Compare with *mouse pointer*.

**Cut**. To remove a selection from the document and place it in another location.

**Data**. The information to be entered into a spreadsheet.

**Default**. A setting or action predetermined by the program unless changed by the user.

**Delimiter**. Most commonly refers to a character or code that marks the beginning or end of an item, such as a sentence, paragraph, page, record, field, or word. *Dynamic delimiter* refers to a character that expands to enclose part of an equation.

**Deselect**. To remove the check mark from a check box or to remove a check mark from a menu item.

**Desktop**. The screen background and main area of Windows where you can open and manage files and programs.

**Destination disk**. A disk to which files are written. Traditionally used when making a copy of a disk.

**Device Manager**. A software utility that allows viewing and changing hardware configuration settings, such as interrupts, base addresses, and serial communication parameters.

**Dialog Box**. A box that appears on-screen that contains or requests information.

**Dimmed**. The faded appearance of an icon, a command, or a button that cannot be chosen or selected.

**Directory**. A guide to the files that are contained in storage.

**DirectX**. Software that give applications access to computer sound and graphics hardware.

**Document**. A letter, memo, proposal, or other file that is created in a software application.

**Double-Click**. Pushing and releasing the left mouse button twice in rapid succession.

**Drag and Drop**. To move text or an object by positioning the mouse pointer on the item you want to move, pressing and holding the mouse button, moving the mouse, and then releasing the mouse button to drop it into its new location.

**Driver**. A computer software program to run a certain device. For example, a printer needs a driver to communicate with the computer.

**Drop-down List**. Selections that drop from an area of a dialog box.

**DVD.** (Digital video disk) Optical disk storage technology that stores video, audio, and data onto a compact disk. DVD disks can hold from 4.7GB to 17GB of data per disk.

**Ellipsis.** A punctuation mark consisting of three successive periods (...). Choosing a menu item or command button with an ellipsis opens a dialog box.

**E-mail.** The exchange of text messages or computer files over a local area network or the Internet.

**Endnote.** Reference information that prints at the end of a document.

**Exit.** To leave a program.

**FAT.** File allocation table. A table, or list, within the operating system that keeps track of a user's files and their locations. The system uses this table as users create and modify files.

**Fax Modem.** An internal modem that enables documents to be sent directly from the computer to either another fax modem or to a standard facsimile machine.

**File.** Information stored on a disk under a single name.

**File Format.** The arrangement and organization of information in a file. File format is determined by the application that created the file.

**File name.** The name given to a text or graphics file, which a user uses to identify the contents of the file or a program uses to open and save a file.

**File Name Extension.** A set of characters added to a file name that serves to extend or clarify its meaning or to identify a file as a member of a category.

**Fill.** The background color or pattern of an object such as a cell of a table or a paragraph.

**Folder.** A container for programs and files symbolized by an icon of a file folder. A folder is a means of organizing programs and documents on a disk and can hold both files and additional folders.

**Font.** A group of letters, numbers, and symbols with a common typeface.

**Footer.** Text entered in an area of the document that will be displayed at the bottom of each page of the document.

**Format.** The arrangement of data. For example, word processing programs offer commands for modifying the appearance of text with fonts, alignment, page numbers, and so on. An alternative use of format relates to the preparation of a disk with sectors so that it can be used for storing data.

**Function Keys.** A set of keys, usually labeled Fl, F2, F3, and so forth, used alone or with Shift, Ctrl, and Alt keys to provide quick access to certain features in an application.

**Gigabyte.** (GB) Approximately one billion bytes.

**Go To.** A feature that enables you to jump to a specific page or location of your document quickly.

**Group.** A set of related options in a dialog box, often with its own subtitle.

**Handle.** Small black squares that appear when you select an object that enable you to resize the object.

**Header.** Text entered in an area of the document that will be displayed at the top of each page of the document.

**Help.** A feature that gives you instructions and additional information on using the program.

**Help Topic.** An explanation of a specific feature, dialog box, or task. Help topics usually contain instructions on how to use a feature, pop-up terms with glossary definitions, and related topics. You can access Help topics by choosing any command from the Help menu.

**Hidden File**. A file that, in order to protect it from deletion or modification, is not shown in the normal listing of the files contained in a directory. These files are often used to store information critical to the operating system.

**High color (16-bit)**. A display that can produce 65,536 distinct colors.

**Highlight**. The change to a reverse-video appearance when a menu item is selected or area of text is blocked.

**HTML**. Hypertext Markup Language. The type of computer language used to write Web pages for the Internet.

**Hypertext Link**. Provides a connection from the current document to another document or to a document on the World Wide Web.

**Icon**. A small graphics image that represents an application, command, or tool. An action is performed when an icon is clicked or double-clicked.

**Imaging**. The operations in the capture, storage, display, and printing of graphics images.

**Inactive Window**. A window that is not currently being used. Its title bar changes appearance, and keystrokes and mouse actions do not affect its contents. An inactive window can be activated by clicking in it.

**Incrementing Button**. A button in a dialog box that enables you to specify program-selected amounts by clicking the mouse instead of typing numbers.

**Indent**. Used to move a complete paragraph one tab stop to the right.

**Input**. The process of entering data into a computer from a keyboard or other device.

**Internet**. An international network connecting businesses, government agencies, universities, and other organizations for the purposes of sharing information.

**Internet Explorer**. A browser made by Microsoft for viewing documents on the World Wide Web.

**Internet Service Provider (ISP)**. A business that supplies Internet connectivity services to individuals, businesses, and other organizations. Also called access provider or service provider.

**Intranet**. An network designed to distribute information, documents, files, and databases within an organization.

**Justification**. See *Alignment*.

**Kilobyte**. (KB) 1,024 bytes of information or storage space.

**Landscape**. Orientation of a page in which the long edge of the paper runs horizontally.

**Line Spacing**. The amount of space between lines of text.

**Link**. A connection between two objects that allows data to be passed between them. Used with OLE as well as with the Internet.

**List Box**. A box that displays a list of choices. When the complete list is too long to fit into its box, it will have a scroll bar so that you can view additional items.

**Local Area Network (LAN)**. A group of computers and other devices connected by a communications link that enables any device to interact with any other on the network. LANs commonly include computers and shared resources such as laser printers and large hard disks.

**Log In or Log On**. The process that a user goes through to begin using a computer system. Usually involves entering some type of identification, followed by a password.

**Log Out or Log Off**. The process that a user goes through to end a session on the computer.

**Macro**. A series of commands and keystrokes stored in a file that can be replayed by a few keystrokes or a mouse click.

**Mail Merge.** A feature that uses data from a data file and combines it with a document called a form file to produce personalized letters.

**Mailbox.** An area of memory or disk that is assigned to store electronic mail messages sent by other users.

**Margin.** The width of blank space from the edge of the page to the edge of the text. All four sides of a paper have a margin.

**Maximize.** The step of making a window take up the entire screen.

**Megabyte.** (MB) Approximately one million bytes. 1,024 kilobytes (1,048,576 bytes) of information or storage space.

**Memory.** A generic term for storage areas in the computer. The area in a computer where information is being stored (temporarily)_while it is being worked on.

**Menu.** A list of options displayed on-screen from which you can select a particular function or command.

**Menu Bar.** The area at the top of a window containing headings for pull-down menu items.

**Message Box.** A type of dialog box that appears with information, a warning, an error message, or a request for confirmation to carry out a command.

**Microsoft Network.** A widely used online information service offering access service to the Internet.

**MIDI.** (Musical Instrument Digital Interface) A format that allows communication of musical data between devices such as computers and synthesizers.

**Minimize.** To hide a window without shutting down the program responsible for the window. A button is placed on the Taskbar. When the user clicks on the button, the window is restored to its previous size.

**Mnemonics.** Underlined, bolded, or colored letters on menu commands or dialog box options that indicate keystroke access for that item or option.

**Modem.** A device used to connect a personal computer with a telephone line so that the computer can be used for accessing online information or communicating with other computers.

**Mouse Pointer.** A symbol that indicates a position on screen as you move the mouse around on your desk.

**Movement Keys.** Keys on the keyboard that control cursor movement within a document. They include the arrow keys, Page Up, Page Down, Home, and End.

**Multimedia.** A generic term for computer applications that combine standard computer capabilities with other media such as video and sound.

**Multitasking.** The capability of a computer to perform multiple operations at the same time.

**Netiquette.** Short for network etiquette. Internet rules of courtesy for sending e-mail and participating in newsgroups.

**NetMeeting.** A feature for digital conversations that enable teams to work together by drawing on an electronic shared white board, sending text messages, and transferring files.

**Netscape Navigator.** A popular browser made by Netscape to view documents on the World Wide Web.

**NetShow.** A feature to provide multimedia across the Internet and corporate intranets for training, communication, advertising, and entertainment.

**Network.** An information system based on two or more computers connected through hardware and software for the purpose of sharing files and resources.

**Network Neighborhood.** An icon on the Windows 98 desktop that references any accessible network computer.

**Newsgroup.** An Internet discussion forum. It consists of articles and follow-up messages related to a specific subject.

**NIC.** (Network Interface Card) A circuit board inserted into a computer and used to connect it to a network.

**Object.** A picture, map, or other graphics element that you can place in a document.

**OLE.** (Object Linking and Embedding) A technology for transferring and sharing information among applications.

**Open.** To start an application, to insert a document into a new document window, or to access a dialog box.

**Operating System.** Software that controls how a computer does basic operations and interfaces between the hardware and software.

**Option.** A choice inside a dialog box.

**Option button.** See *radio button*.

**Orientation.** A setting that designates whether a document will print with text running along the long or short side of a piece of paper.

**Output.** Data generated by a computer, including whatever appears on the screen or is printed or sent across a telecommunications line.

**Partition a Disk.** The process of dividing a disk drive into several sections called partitions. No physical division occurs, only a logical division. For example, a 6GB hard drive C could be partitioned into three 2GB sections, labeled C, D, and E.

**Password.** A secret code that restricts access to a file. Without the password, the file cannot be opened.

**Paste.** The process of retrieving the information stored on the Clipboard and inserting a copy into a document.

**Path.** A series of folder names used to designate the location of a file.

**Peripheral Devices.** Additional pieces of hardware attached to a computer. Examples are printers, scanners, or speakers.

**Pixel.** Short for "picture element." A pixel is the smallest dot that can be represented on a screen or in a paint (bitmap) graphic.

**Plug and Play.** A set of hardware standards that computer manufacturers are following to improve compatibility with software. Also known as *PnP*.

**Point.** To move the mouse until the tip of the mouse pointer rests on an item.

**Point Size.** A unit of measurement used to indicate font size. One point is 1/72" in height.

**Pop-up List.** A list of options that appears when a pop-up button is selected. Most pop-up buttons are marked by double arrows or triangles and display mutually exclusive options. The button itself shows the selected option. Other pop-up lists, marked by single arrows or triangles, show the feature name rather than the selected option.

**Pop-up Term.** A box that appears when you click an underlined word in a Help topic. Pop-ups contain additional information or glossary definitions.

**Port.** A connection device between a computer and another component, such as a printer or modem. For example, a printer cable is plugged into the printer port on the computer so information can be sent to the computer.

**Portrait.** The orientation of the page in which the long edge of the page runs vertically.

**Print Preview.** A feature that enables you to see how your printed document will look on screen before you print it.

**Print Queue.** The list of print jobs waiting to be sent to a particular printer.

**Print Spooling.** The process of sending documents off to a storage area on a disk, called a buffer, where they will remain until the printer is ready for each one in turn.

**Printer Driver.** The software that enables a program to communicate with the printer so that the program's information can be printed.

**Prodigy.** A widely used online information service offering access service to the Internet.

**Program.** A set of instructions for a computer to execute. Software designed for a certain use, such as word processing, electronic mail, or spreadsheet entries. Sometimes called an *application.*

**Property.** A characteristic of an object or device. Properties of a file, for example, include type, size, and creation date.

**Protocol.** A set of rules or standards designed to enable computers to connect with one another and to exchange information with as little error as possible.

**Queue.** A waiting or holding location usually for printing.

**Quick Launch Toolbar.** A toolbar on the Taskbar that provides shortcuts to frequently used Windows features: the Desktop, the Web browser, Outlook Express, and channels.

**Radio Button.** One of a set of buttons found before options in a dialog box. Only one radio button in a set can be selected at a time. Sometimes called *option buttons.*

**RAM.** (Random access memory) The main memory that holds the application program(s) and data that are in use.

**Recycle Bin.** An icon on the Desktop that represents a temporary holding place for files that are deleted.

**Redo.** Used to reverse the last Undo action.

**Registry.** A central file in which Windows 98 stores information about the hardware, software, and preferences on a specific computer.

**Resolution.** The fineness of detail attained by a printer or a monitor in producing an image.

**Resource.** A printer or other hardware device that can be shared among users in a network.

**Restore.** To copy files from a backup storage device to their normal location.

**Right aligned.** Text that is lined up with the right side of a tab setting or document margin, as with a row of numbers in a column.

**Right-Click.** The practice of using the right mouse button to access a shortcut menu.

**ROM.** (Read-only memory) The part of a computer's main memory that contains the basic programs that run the computer when it is turned on. ROM cannot be erased.

**Ruler.** Used to change page format elements such as tabs and margins.

**Save As.** To save a previously saved worksheet with a new name or properties.

**Save.** The process of taking a document residing in the memory of the computer and creating a file to be stored on a disk.

**Script.** A series of commands and keystrokes stored in a file that can be replayed by a few keystrokes or a mouse click. Sometimes called a *macro.*

**Scroll Bars.** The bars on the right side and bottom of a window that enable you to move vertically and horizontally through a document.

**Select**. To highlight a command or option (from menus or dialogs) to be applied to an object or block of text. Compare with *choose*.

**Selection Cursor**. The highlighted text, dotted rectangle, or cursor that shows you where the next keystroke or mouse action will apply in a dialog box or window.

**Serial Port**. A port on a computer through which data are sent and received 1 bit at a time.

**Server**. On a local area network (LAN), a computer running administrative software that controls access to the network and its resources, such as printers and disk drives, and provides resources to computers functioning as workstations on the network.

**Shortcut**. An icon that represents a quick way to start a program or open a file or folder.

**Shortcut Key**. A keystroke or keystroke combination that gives you quick access to a feature.

**Shortcut Menu**. A menu of common choices accessed by clicking the right-mouse button.

**Shut Down**. The process of saving all settings before a computer is physically turned off. Accessed from the Start menu.

**Size**. To change the size of a selected object by dragging the comer and sizing handles that surround it.

**Sizing Handle**. The small solid squares that appear on the borders of a graphics box or a graphics line that has been selected. You can drag these handles to size the box and its contents.

**Software**. The instructions created from computer programs that direct the computer in performing various operations. Software can also include data.

**Sort**. To arrange data in alphabetical order.

**Source disk**. A disk containing data. Traditionally used when making a copy of a disk.

**Spell Check**. A feature that checks the spelling of words in your document against a dictionary and flags possible errors for correction.

**Start Button**. The button in the lower-left corner of the Taskbar that is used to access programs.

**Status Bar**. The line at the bottom of a window that shows information such as the path, page information, or location of the insertion point.

**Style**. A way to format similar types of text, such as headings and lists.

**Submenu**. An additional list of menu items opening from a single menu item.

**Subscribe**. Enables you to receive updated information from a channel on a regular basis.

**Symbol**. Used to access characters that are not on your keyboard, such as iconic symbols, phonetic characters, and characters in other alphabets.

**System Tray**. The icons displayed in the lower-right corner of the screen that represent programs running in the background.

**Tab**. Settings in your document to determine where the insertion point moves.

**Table**. A table consists of rows and columns of cells that you fill with text, numbers, or graphics.

**Taskbar**. The bar (usually at the bottom of the screen) that lists all open folders and active applications.

**Telephony**. A general term for the technology of the telephone, including the conversion of sound into signals that are transmitted to other locations and then converted back into sound. A modem uses telephony.

**Template**. A document file with customized format, content, and features. Frequently used to create faxes, memos and proposals.

**Temporary File**. A file that a program creates when it is running. Temporary files are deleted when the program is exited properly.

**Text File.** A file saved in ASCII file format. It contains text, spaces, and returns, but no formatting codes.

**Tile.** A display format for open windows. Tiled windows are displayed side by side, with no window overlapping any other window. Compare with *cascade*.

**Toggle.** Refers to something (like a feature) that turns on and off with the same switch (like a keystroke).

**Toolbars.** Appears at the top of the application window and are used to access the features available in an application.

**Trackball.** A pointing device consisting of a small platform with a ball resting on it, similar in size to a mouse. The platform remains stationary while the user manipulates the ball with his or her hand to move the cursor or arrow on the screen.

**True color (24-bit).** A display that can support over 16 million different colors.

**Undo.** To reverse the last editing action.

**Upgrade.** To install a new release of a software program so that the latest features are available for use.

**Uppercase.** A capital letter.

**Views.** Ways of displaying documents to see different perspectives of the information in that document.

**Virus.** A computer program that infects computer files by inserting into those files copies of itself. Although not all virus programs are damaging, some can destroy a computer's hard disk.

**Wallpaper.** A photograph, drawing, or pattern displayed on the background of the Windows 98 Desktop.

**Web page.** A document on the World Wide Web. A Web page consists of an HTML file, with associated files for graphics and may contains hyperlinks to other Web pages.

**Wildcard.** Character used to replace one character (?) or any number of characters (*) in a search string. These two characters are conventions in most applications.

**Window.** A method of displaying a document so that many of its elements appear graphically and many features are immediately available as on-screen choices. You type your documents in a "document window."

**Windows Explorer.** A utility in Windows 98 that enables the user to locate, open and manage files and folders. The user can select folders from a list displayed on the left side of the screen and access.

**Wizards.** The interactive programs supplied with Windows 98 that help you with a project or problem by asking a series of questions.

**Word Wrap.** A word processing feature that determines where the right margin is located and drops the current text to the next line when the margin is reached.

**World Wide Web.** A series of specially designed documents—all linked together—to be viewed over the Internet.

**WYSIWYG.** (What You See Is What You Get) Refers to a computer screen display that approximates the printed page, showing fonts and graphics in correct proportions.

**Zoom.** Used to enlarge or reduce the way the text is displayed on the screen. Zoom does not change the appearance of the printed document.

# Index

# MICROSOFT HELP ON THE WEB

Because Windows 98 is very tightly integrated with the Internet, here is a sample of some of the additional assistance you can receive from Microsoft via the World Wide Web.

Because the Web is constantly changing, some of the screens you see here may be different from the actual screen.

## Online Search

- Search the Microsoft Knowledge Base for answers
- Type a question and view multiple possible responses

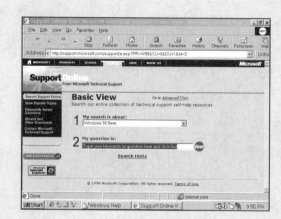

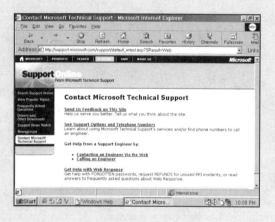

## Technical Support

- Learn Technical Support options
- Get Microsoft Support telephone numbers
- Submit questions to Microsoft Support Engineers

## Frequently Asked Questions

- Find answers to common questions with FAQ support
- Discover hidden tips and tricks to using Microsoft Windows 98

# Troubleshooting

- Choose from many different Troubleshooting Wizards to step through difficult problems
- Use interactive responses to solve various issues

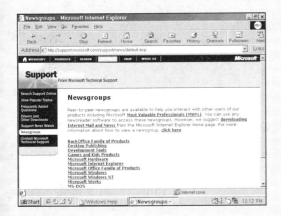

# Newsgroups

- Interact with other users
- Download drivers and other support files

# Product Updates

- Keep your system up to date with the latest patches and drivers

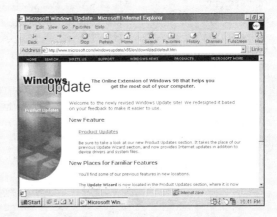

# OTHER BOOKS FROM PRIMA PUBLISHING
## Computers & Technology

| ISBN | Title | Price |
|------|-------|-------|
| 0-7615-1363-9 | Access 97 Fast & Easy | $16.99 |
| 0-7615-1175-x | ACT! 3.0 Fast & Easy | $16.99 |
| 0-7615-1412-0 | ACT! 4.0 Fast & Easy | $16.99 |
| 0-7615-1348-5 | Create FrontPage 98 Web Pages In a Weekend | $24.99 |
| 0-7615-1294-2 | Create PowerPoint Presentations In a Weekend | $19.99 |
| 0-7615-1388-4 | Create Your First Web Page In a Weekend, Revised Edition | $24.99 |
| 0-7615-0428-1 | The Essential Excel 97 Book | $27.99 |
| 0-7615-0733-7 | The Essential Netscape Communicator Book | $24.99 |
| 0-7615-0969-0 | The Essential Office 97 Book | $27.99 |
| 0-7615-0695-0 | The Essential Photoshop Book | $35.00 |
| 0-7615-1182-2 | The Essential PowerPoint 97 Book | $24.99 |
| 0-7615-1136-9 | The Essential Publisher 97 Book | $24.99 |
| 0-7615-0967-4 | The Essential Windows 98 Book | $24.99 |
| 0-7615-0752-3 | The Essential Windows NT 4 Book | $27.99 |
| 0-7615-0427-3 | The Essential Word 97 Book | $27.99 |
| 0-7615-0425-7 | The Essential WordPerfect 8 Book | $24.99 |
| 0-7615-1008-7 | Excel 97 Fast & Easy | $16.99 |
| 0-7615-1534-8 | FrontPage 98 Fast & Easy | $16.99 |
| 0-7615-1194-6 | Increase Your Web Traffic In a Weekend | $19.99 |
| 0-7615-1191-1 | Internet Explorer 4.0 Fast & Easy | $19.99 |
| 0-7615-1137-7 | Jazz Up Your Web Site In a Weekend | $24.99 |
| 0-7615-1379-5 | Learn Access 97 In a Weekend | $19.99 |
| 0-7615-1293-4 | Learn HTML In a Weekend | $24.99 |
| 0-7615-1295-0 | Learn the Internet In a Weekend | $19.99 |
| 0-7615-1217-9 | Learn Publisher 97 In a Weekend | $19.99 |
| 0-7615-1251-9 | Learn Word 97 In a Weekend | $19.99 |
| 0-7615-1296-9 | Learn Windows 98 In a Weekend | $19.99 |
| 0-7615-1193-8 | Lotus 1-2-3 97 Fast & Easy | $16.99 |
| 0-7615-1420-1 | Managing with Microsoft Project 98 | $29.99 |
| 0-7615-1382-5 | Netscape Navigator 4.0 Fast & Easy | $16.99 |
| 0-7615-1162-8 | Office 97 Fast & Easy | $16.99 |
| 0-7615-1186-5 | Organize Your Finances with Quicken Deluxe 98 In a Weekend | $19.99 |
| 0-7615-1405-8 | Outlook 98 Fast & Easy | $16.99 |
| 0-7615-1513-5 | Publisher 98 Fast & Easy | $19.99 |
| 0-7615-1192-X | SmartSuite 97 Fast & Easy | $16.99 |
| 0-7615-1138-5 | Upgrade Your PC In a Weekend | $19.99 |
| 1-55958-738-5 | Windows 95 Fast & Easy | $19.95 |
| 0-7615-1007-9 | Word 97 Fast & Easy | $16.99 |
| 0-7615-1316-7 | Word 97 for Law Firms | $29.99 |
| 0-7615-1083-4 | WordPerfect 8 Fast & Easy | $16.99 |
| 0-7615-1188-1 | WordPerfect Suite 8 Fast & Easy | $16.99 |

# Send Us
# YOUR COMMENTS

### Dear Reader:

Thank you for buying this book. In order to offer you more quality books on the topics *you* would like to see, we need your input. At Prima Publishing, we pride ourselves on timely responsiveness to our readers needs. If you'll complete and return this brief questionnaire, *we will listen!*

Name: (first) _____ (M.I.) _____ (last) _____

Company: _____ Type of business: _____

Address: _____ City: _____ State: _____ Zip: _____

Phone: _____ Fax: _____ E-mail address: _____

May we contact you for research purposes? ❏ Yes ❏ No

(If you participate in a research project, we will supply you with your choice of a book from Prima CPD)

---

**❶ How would you rate this book, overall?**

❏ Excellent    ❏ Fair
❏ Very Good    ❏ Below Average
❏ Good    ❏ Poor

**❷ Why did you buy this book?**

❏ Price of book    ❏ Content
❏ Author's reputation    ❏ Prima's reputation
❏ CD-ROM/disk included with book
❏ Information highlighted on cover
❏ Other (Please specify): _____

**❸ How did you discover this book?**

❏ Found it on bookstore shelf
❏ Saw it in Prima Publishing catalog
❏ Recommended by store personnel
❏ Recommended by friend or colleague
❏ Saw an advertisement in: _____
❏ Read book review in: _____
❏ Saw it on Web site: _____
❏ Other (Please specify): _____

**❹ Where did you buy this book?**

❏ Bookstore (name) _____
❏ Computer Store (name) _____
❏ Electronics Store (name) _____
❏ Wholesale Club (name) _____
❏ Mail Order (name) _____
❏ Direct from Prima Publishing
❏ Other (please specify): _____

**❺ Which computer periodicals do you read regularly?** _____

_____

_____

_____

**❻ Would you like to see your name in print?**

May we use your name and quote you in future Prima Publishing books or promotional materials?

❏ Yes      ❏ No

---

**❼ Comments & Suggestions:** _____

_____

_____

**PRIMA PUBLISHING**

Computers & Technology
3875 Atherton Road
Rocklin, CA 95765

PLEASE
PLACE
STAMP
HERE

---

**⑧ Where do you use your computer?**

| | | | | |
|---|---|---|---|---|
| Work | ❏ 100% | ❏ 75% | ❏ 50% | ❏ 25% |
| Home | ❏ 100% | ❏ 75% | ❏ 50% | ❏ 25% |
| School | ❏ 100% | ❏ 75% | ❏ 50% | ❏ 25% |

Other _____

**⑨ How do you rate your level of computer skills?**

❏ Beginner
❏ Advanced
❏ Intermediate

**⑩ What is your age?**

❏ Under 18
❏ 18-24          ❏ 40-49
❏ 25-29          ❏ 50-59
❏ 30-39          ❏ 60-over

**⑪ I would be interested in computer books on these topics**

❏ Word Processing     ❏ Database:
❏ Networking          ❏ Spreadsheets
❏ Desktop Publishing  ❏ Web site design

Other_____

## SAVE A STAMP

Visit our Web Site at **www.primapublishing.com**
and simply fill in one of our online Response Forms

## TO ORDER BOOKS

Please send me the following items:

| Quantity | Title | Unit Price | Total |
|---|---|---|---|
| _____ | _____ | $_____ | $_____ |
| _____ | _____ | $_____ | $_____ |
| _____ | _____ | $_____ | $_____ |
| _____ | _____ | $_____ | $_____ |
| _____ | _____ | $_____ | $_____ |
| | Subtotal | | $_____ |
| | **Deduct 10% when ordering 3–5 books** | | $_____ |
| | 7.25% Sales Tax (CA only) | | $_____ |
| | 8.25% Sales Tax (TN only) | | $_____ |
| | 5.0% Sales Tax (MD and IN only) | | $_____ |
| | Shipping and Handling* | | $_____ |
| | TOTAL ORDER | | $_____ |

Shipping and Handling depend on Subtotal.

| Subtotal | Shipping/Handling |
|---|---|
| $0.00–$14.99 | $3.00 |
| $15.00–29.99 | $4.00 |
| $30.00–49.99 | $6.00 |
| $50.00–99.99 | $10.00 |
| $100.00–199.99 | $13.00 |
| $200.00+ | call for quote |

Foreign and all Priority Request orders:
Call Order Entry department for price quote at 1-916-632-4400

This chart represents the total retail price of books only (before applicable discounts are taken).

**By telephone:** With Visa, Mastercard, or American Express, call 1-800-632-8676. Mon.–Fri. 8:30–4:00 PST.

**By Internet e-mail:** sales@primapub.com

**By mail:** Just fill out the information below and send with your remittance to:

### PRIMA PUBLISHING

P.O. Box 1260BK

Rocklin, CA 95677-1260

www.primapublishing.com

Name_____ Daytime Telephone_____

Address _____

City _____ State _____ Zip _____

Visa /MC# _____Exp. _____

Check/Money Order enclosed for $_____ Payable to Prima Publishing

Signature _____